Johannine Christology

Johannine Studies

Editor

Stanley E. Porter (*McMaster Divinity College*)

VOLUME 3

The titles published in this series are listed at *brill.com/jost*

Johannine Christology

Edited by

Stanley E. Porter
Andrew W. Pitts

BRILL

LEIDEN | BOSTON

Library of Congress Cataloging-in-Publication Data

Names: Porter, Stanley E., 1956- editor. | Pitts, Andrew W., editor.
Title: Johannine Christology / edited by Stanley E. Porter, Andrew W. Pitts.
Description: Leiden ; Boston : Brill, 2020. | Series: Johannine studies, 2214-2800 ; volume 3 | Includes index.
Identifiers: LCCN 2020022160 (print) | LCCN 2020022161 (ebook) | ISBN 9789004427365 (hardback) | ISBN 9789004435612 (ebook)
Subjects: LCSH: Bible. John—Criticism, interpretation, etc. | Jesus Christ—History of doctrines.
Classification: LCC BS2615.52 .J646 2020 (print) | LCC BS2615.52 (ebook) | DDC 226.5/06—dc23
LC record available at https://lccn.loc.gov/2020022160
LC ebook record available at https://lccn.loc.gov/2020022161

Typeface for the Latin, Greek, and Cyrillic scripts: "Brill". See and download: brill.com/brill-typeface.

ISSN 2214-2800
ISBN 978-90-04-42736-5 (hardback)
ISBN 978-90-04-43561-2 (e-book)

Copyright 2020 by Koninklijke Brill NV, The Netherlands.
Koninklijke Brill NV incorporates the imprints Brill, Brill Hes & De Graaf, Brill Nijhoff, Brill Rodopi, Brill Sense, Hotei Publishing, mentis Verlag, Verlag Ferdinand Schöningh and Wilhelm Fink Verlag.
All rights reserved. No part of this publication may be reproduced, translated, stored in a retrieval system, or transmitted in any form or by any means, electronic, mechanical, photocopying, recording or otherwise, without prior written permission from the publisher.
Authorization to photocopy items for internal or personal use is granted by Koninklijke Brill NV provided that the appropriate fees are paid directly to The Copyright Clearance Center, 222 Rosewood Drive, Suite 910, Danvers, MA 01923, USA. Fees are subject to change.

This book is printed on acid-free paper and produced in a sustainable manner.

Contents

Series Preface   IX
Abbreviations   XI
Contributors   XIV

Johannine Christology: an Introduction   1
  Stanley E. Porter

PART 1
The Formation of Johannine Christology

1   Johannine and Pauline Christology   11
      Stanley E. Porter

2   The Quest for the Messiah: an Inquiry Concerning the Formation of the Johannine Christology   31
      John Painter

3   Jesus the *Messiah/Christos* and John's Christology   55
      Panayotis Coutsoumpos

PART 2
Johannine Christology in Hellenistic and Jewish Contexts

4   Creational Light as Christological Theodicy in the Fourth Gospel   75
      Andrew W. Pitts

5   The Christological Appropriation of Zeal in John's Use of Psalm 69   90
      Jonathan Numada

6   Jesus, Moses, and the Johannine Community after the Jewish Revolt   111
      Travis D. Trost

7   The King on the Cross: Johannine Christology in the Roman Imperial Context   127
      Arthur M. Wright, Jr.

PART 3
Christology and the Literary Character of the Johannine Writings

8 The Narrative Structure and Flow of the Prologue to John's Gospel 155
   Derek Morton Hamilton Tovey

9 John's Portrayal of Jesus as the Divine-Adamic Priest and What It Means for the Temple Cleansing in John 2:13–25 169
   Chris S. Stevens

10 Jesus, the λόγος, and Recognition: a Study of Concealed and Revealed Identity in John's Gospel 186
   Adam Z. Wright

11 The Effusion of Blood and Water for Purity and Sanctity: Jesus's Body, the Passover Lamb, and the Red Heifer in Johannine Temple Christology 203
   Tat Yu Lam

12 The Person of Christ in John's Revelation and Gospel 223
   Stephen S. Smalley

PART 4
The Application of Christology for the Johannine Audience and Beyond

13 Jesus in Word and Deed through the Ritual Activity of Tabernacles in John 7:1–10:21 239
   Sherri Brown

14 Elevated Christology and Elusive Ethics: Unity and Identity in the Gospel according to John 260
   Lindsey Trozzo

15 Jesus and the Demonic Powers in the Johannine Tradition 307
   Jin Ki Hwang

16 Brief Concluding Observations on This Volume on Johannine
    Christology   322
        Stanley E. Porter

    Modern Authors Index   327
    Ancient Sources Index   333

Series Preface

This is the third of a series of volumes in the Johannine Studies series being published by Brill Publishers of Leiden. This volume is on the topic of Johannine Christology. Narrow parameters have not been set on this topic, as is reflected in the varied nature of the individual contributions. These contributions have been divided into four sections to reflect the range of studies included. The first volume in the series was Stanley E. Porter and Andrew K. Gabriel, *Johannine Writings and Apocalyptic: An Annotated Bibliography*, JOST 1 (Leiden: Brill, 2013), and the second was Stanley E. Porter and Hughson T. Ong, eds., *The Origins of John's Gospel*, JOST 2 (Leiden: Brill, 2016). It is encouraging to see the strong and positive response to these first two volumes as we continue the series through the completion of the first five volumes. Subsequent volumes currently scheduled to appear are as follows:

> Volume 4: The Johannine Prologue and its Resonances
> Volume 5: John's Gospel and its Sources

Johannine studies has seen a resurgence of interest in the last several years, with many of the assured results of previous Johannine scholarship being re-examined. These include theories regarding the origins of John's Gospel, its relationship to the Synoptic Gospels, its theology, its historiography, and many other topics. This volume is part of a concerted effort to address the need for avenues of dedicated publication of Johannine studies. Study of the Johannine writings, including the Gospel, three Johannine letters, and Revelation, has been hampered by a lack of such dedicated publication. There are many such opportunities, including specific series and journals, for study of the Synoptic Gospels, and an equivalent number for the Pauline writings. Therefore, it is appropriate and necessary to publish a series devoted to the Johannine writings and their many attendant research questions. This Johannine Studies series concentrates upon topics of special relevance for Johannine research, especially where recent work is re-conceptualizing old topics or introducing new ones. The number of scholars devoting their efforts to such areas continues to grow, as is evidenced by the numbers of sessions dedicated to Johannine studies at recent major conferences, as well as the variety of Johannine publications finding their ways into various journals and other works.

I would like to invite any scholars interested in making contributions to one or more of these scheduled volumes to be in contact with me regarding their proposed work, including submitting their paper (please submit in Word file and pdf, following SBL guidelines). Contact information is provided below. The topics of the volumes are being defined and interpreted broadly, so that papers that deal, for example, with clearly related subjects (and especially those that encompass the breadth of the Johannine corpus), we hope will be able to find a home in these collections of papers. Plans for the fourth and fifth volumes are already underway, so those interested in publishing in these volumes should not hesitate to make contact immediately. As with similar series, the anticipated and ideal rate of publication is one volume per year, although our timing has not lived up to this expectation. We are also contemplating extending the series according to interest in these initial five volumes. I would request that submissions be made by 31 January of a given year for publication later in that calendar year. This means that papers for the fourth volume, *The Johannine Prologue and its Resonances*, should be submitted (due to publication delays with this volume) by 31 January 2021, so as to allow time for review and then editing. I will be in contact with all authors of submissions regarding the status of their essays.

I would like to thank my Graduate Assistant, Zachary Dawson, for his editorial acumen in helping to see this volume through to publication when there had been a number of delays that hindered it. I would also like to thank those who have encouraged the development of this project at Brill, especially Louise Schouten, Laura Morris, and Tessa Schild, who have continued to be an encouragement as this project took shape and is now finally coming to its full fruition.

Stanley E. Porter
McMaster Divinity College, Hamilton, Ontario, Canada
princpl@mcmaster.ca

Abbreviations

AB	Anchor Bible
ABR	*Australian Biblical Review*
AbrN	*Abr-Nahrain*
ABRL	Anchor Bible Reference Library
AGJU	Arbeiten zur Geschichte des antiken Judentums und des Urchristentums
AnBib	Analecta Biblica
ANF	*Ante-Nicene Fathers*
ANTC	Abingdon New Testament Commentary
BBR	*Bulletin for Biblical Research*
BDAG	Danker, Frederick W., Walter Bauer, William F. Arndt, and F. Wilbur Gingrich. *Greek-English Lexicon of the New Testament and Other Early Christian Literature*. 3rd ed. Chicago: University of Chicago Press, 2000
BDF	Blass, Friedrich, Albert Debrunner, and Robert W. Funk. *A Greek Grammar of the New Testament and Other Early Christian Literature*. Chicago: University of Chicago Press, 1961
BECNT	Baker Exegetical Commentary on the New Testament
BETL	Bibliotheca Ephemeridum Theologicarum Lovaniensium
Bib	*Biblica*
BibInt	Biblical Interpretation Series
Bijdr	*Bijdragen: Tijdschrift voor filosofie en theologie*
BINS	Biblical Interpretation Series
BKAT	Biblischer Kommentar, Altes Testament
BNTC	Black's New Testament Commentaries
BR	*Biblical Research*
BRev	*Bible Review*
BTB	*Biblical Theology Bulletin*
BZNW	Beihefte zur Zeitschrift für die neutestamentliche Wissenschaft
CBET	Contributions to Biblical Exegesis and Theology
CBQ	*Catholic Biblical Quarterly*
CEV	Contemporary English Version
CTR	*Criswell Theological Review*
CurBS	*Currents in Biblical Research*
CV	*Communio Viatorum*
DJG	*Dictionary of Jesus and the Gospels*
DNTB	*Dictionary of New Testament Background*

DSD	*Dead Sea Discoveries*
ESV	English Standard Version
EvT	*Evangelische Theologie*
ExpTim	*Expository Times*
FRLANT	Forschungen zur Religion und Literatur des Alten und Neuen Testaments
HBT	*Horizons in Biblical Theology*
HNT	Handbuch zum Neuen Testament
HNTC	Harper's New Testament Commentaries
HThKNTSup	Herders theologischer Kommentar zum Neuen Testament Supplementband
HTR	*Harvard Theological Review*
HTS	Harvard Theological Studies
HvTSt	*Hervormde teologiese studies*
ICC	International Critical Commentary
IEJ	*Israel Exploration Journal*
JB	Jerusalem Bible
JBL	*Journal of Biblical Literature*
JETS	*Journal of the Evangelical Theological Society*
JGRChJ	*Journal of Greco-Roman Christianity and Judaism*
JSJ	*Journal for the Study of Judaism in the Persian, Hellenistic, and Roman Periods*
JSJSup	Supplements to the Journal for the Study of Judaism
JSOTSup	Journal for the Study of the Old Testament Supplement Series
JSNT	*Journal for the Study of the New Testament*
JSNTSup	Journal for the Study of the New Testament Supplement Series
LBS	Linguistic Biblical Studies
LCL	Loeb Classical Library
LNTS	The Library of New Testament Studies
LSTS	The Library of Second Temple Studies
LXX	Septuagint
MNTS	McMaster New Testament Series
MT	Masoretic Text
NETS	New English Translation of the Septuagint
NICNT	New International Commentary on the New Testament
NIGTC	New International Greek Testament Commentary
NIV	New International Version
NLH	*New Literary History*
NLT	New Living Translation
NovT	*Novum Testamentum*

NovTSup	Supplements to Novum Testamentum
NRSV	New Revised Standard Version
NT	New Testament
NTD	Das Neue Testament Deutsch
NTL	New Testament Library
NTM	New Testament Monographs
NTS	*New Testament Studies*
NTT	New Testament Theology
NTTS	New Testament Tools and Studies
OT	Old Testament
RB	*Revue biblique*
RSV	Revised Standard Version
SBG	Studies in Biblical Greek
SBLDS	Society of Biblical Literature Dissertation Series
SJT	*Scottish Journal of Theology*
SJOT	*Scandinavian Journal of the Old Testament*
SNTSMS	Society for New Testament Studies Monograph Series
SP	Sacra Pagina
ST	*Studia Theologica*
TEV	Today's English Version
THKNT	Theologischer Handkommentar zum Neuen Testament
TJ	*Trinity Journal*
TRu	*Theologische Rundschau*
TynBul	*Tyndale Bulletin*
VT	*Vetus Testamentum*
VTSup	Supplements to Vetus Testamentum
WBC	Word Biblical Commentary
WTJ	*Westminster Theological Journal*
WUNT	Wissenschaftliche Untersuchungen zum Neuen Testament
ZNT	*Zeitschrift für Neues Testament*
ZNW	*Zeitschrift für die neutestamentliche Wissenschaft und die Kunde der alteren Kirche*
ZEE	*Zeitschrift für evangelische Ethik*

Contributors

Sherri Brown
Creighton University, Omaha, Nebraska, USA

Panayotis Coutsoumpos
University of Montemorelos, Nuevo León, Mexico

Jin Ki Hwang
Georgia Central University, Atlanta, Georgia, USA

Tat Yu Lam
McMaster Divinity College, Hamilton, Ontario, Canada

Jonathan Numada
Northwest Seminary and College, Langley, British Columbia, Canada

John Painter
Charles Sturt University, New South Wales, Australia

Andrew W. Pitts
McMaster Divinity College, Hamilton, Ontario, Canada

Stanley E. Porter
McMaster Divinity College, Hamilton, Ontario, Canada

Stephen S. Smalley
Gloucester, United Kingdom

Chris S. Stevens
McMaster Divinity College, Hamilton, Ontario, Canada

Derek Morton Hamilton Tovey
College of St John the Evangelist, and University of Auckland, New Zealand

Travis D. Trost
Independent Scholar, British Columbia, Canada

Lindsey Trozzo
Princeton Theological Seminary, Princeton, New Jersey, USA

Adam Z. Wright
College of Emmanuel & St. Chad, Saskatoon, Saskatchewan, Canada

Arthur M. Wright, Jr.
Baptist Theological Seminary at Richmond, Virginia, USA

Johannine Christology: an Introduction

Stanley E. Porter

Christology is an immense topic within New Testament studies, to the point where those who undertake to write Christologies must tread carefully as they explore the topic. What is true of the entire New Testament is certainly no less true of many of the individual corpora within the New Testament, and the Johannine corpus in particular. The topic of Johannine Christology, the focus of this volume, is itself an expansive topic to attempt to treat in a single volume such as this. As a result, this volume does not attempt to cover all of the possible topics that fall within the scope of Johannine Christology, nor does it attempt to describe the state of play regarding this subject. Instead, this volume provides a snapshot of various investigations of the topic by a range of scholars writing in the field, organized into four major parts. The evidence from the variety of papers within this volume, however, attests to the broad scope and, even more importantly, major significance of the field of Johannine Christology.

Although somewhat similar statements could be made about other corpora within the New Testament, the Johannine literature, and in particular the Johannine Gospel, seems particularly bedeviled by a variety of textual, literary, historical, source, and related issues that make attempts to describe its Christology problematic. When we speak of the Christology of the Johannine literature, are we talking of the Christology of the final text, of the receiving community, of earlier or originating communities, of the earliest Christian communities, or even of those who are depicted within the texts? By Christology, do we mean to examine christological conceptions as they have been developed within Christian theology or do we mean notions as they first emerged from and within the Johannine literature as it was formed and transmitted? Related to this is the question of what is meant or understood by the purportedly high Christology of the Johannine literature, and how does this relate to the thought of other New Testament writers? What is the historical relationship between christological topics depicted within the Johannine literature and the historical events of early Christianity, including the life of Jesus or the mission of his earliest—and in this case Johannine—followers? How do the Johannine writings, including their Christology, relate to other religious thought within the Mediterranean context? These and a variety of other issues are always at the forefront of the discussion of the Johannine literature and are at least as relevant to discussion of Johannine Christology. Nevertheless, even though such discussion is notoriously problematic—as are recent discussions in other areas of Johannine studies, some of them reflected in volumes in this series—this does not mean that discussion of the topic is not possible or is hindered to such an extent as being unworthwhile. To the contrary, as the essays in this volume attest, many are determined and intent upon undertaking to explore various dimensions of Johannine Christology.

To help guide the reader through the various sub-areas within, this volume has been divided into four major parts, each one dealing with a major area of research related to Johannine Christology. The four parts follow a logical progression from the earliest stages of Johannine Christology to the settings and then the literature and finally the application of Johannine Christology to its audience and beyond. This is not the only way that these essays could be organized, but this arrangement allows for a number of major commonalities and diversities to be noted.

The first of these major sections contains three papers that address the topic of the formation of Johannine Christology. The second volume in the Johannine Studies series was addressed to the topic of the origins of John's Gospel.[1] It is noteworthy that within that volume there was minimal discussion of the origin of John's Gospel and its Christology, with only a single essay devoted to the "Son of Man" sayings.[2] There are many possible reasons for this, one possibility being the implicit assumption of the high Christology within the Johannine Gospel, that is, that it depicts a Jesus whose divine character is seen from the outset, including his pre-existence as the logos and his incarnation, his being one with the Father, and his divine pronouncements. The essays within this volume, however, add new dimensions to these conceptions by addressing christological questions from some new and different angles, some with significant possible implications.

In the first chapter, Stanley E. Porter engages the developmental hypothesis of Christian theology established long ago by David Friedrich Strauss and Ferdinand Christian Baur, which still maintains a prominent place in New Testament studies and provides one of the major reasons for assigning a late date to John's Gospel with its high (i.e. developed) Christology. Challenging this view, Porter compares the Christology of John's Gospel with the Christology of the Pauline letters—some of the earliest writings of the New Testament—based on a grid of three comparative factors: equative, positional,

---

[1] Stanley E. Porter and Hughson T. Ong, eds., *The Origins of John's Gospel*, JOST 2 (Leiden: Brill, 2016).

[2] See Panayotis Coutsoumpos, "The Origin of the Johannine 'Son of Man' Sayings," in *Origins of John's Gospel*, 285–300.

and proto-Trinitarian statements. He concludes that apart from different ways of representing their Christologies, John and Paul share much of their christological views in common, which presumably indicates, at least on theological grounds, that John could have been written as early as Paul's letters. This carries with it the implication that the whole developmental hypothesis of Christian theology might need to be rethought.

In the second paper, John Painter deals with how the Fourth Gospel transforms the notion of Messiahship into Christology by demonstrating how the Gospel narrates a "quest for the Messiah." The witness of John the Baptist (John 1:15) plays an integral role in connecting the prologue of the Gospel with the rest of the narrative, which ties the Gospel's "quest for the Messiah" with the revealing, creative, and life-giving presence of God that the prologue so heartily articulates. As the Gospel progresses, Painter sees the definition of Messiahship being further cast as Christology by means of the father–son relationship of God and Jesus and through the giving of the Son who reveals the Father and brings new life to his creation by doing his work and making him known.

In the last paper of this section, Panayotis Coutsoumpos offers a study on the distinctive character of Johannine Christology and how Jesus imbued the term "Messiah" with new meaning. He argues that John's Christology is unique due to the manner in which he emphasizes Jesus's ministry—namely, through his method of performing signs followed by his teaching about himself. This contributes to the evangelist's means of affirming that Jesus's messiahship transcends all other messianic expectations of his day and that the term "Messiah" became newly defined by Jesus's mission to refer not to a military ruler as expected by Jews but rather to the spiritual king of Israel.

The second part of the volume offers a number of papers that deal with Johannine Christology in relation to its Hellenistic and Jewish contexts. In some ways, it is unfortunate to still be characterizing the context of the Johannine writings in terms of such an opposition, as we have come to recognize more and more that Judaism within Hellenism is probably a more appropriate means of describing the bold contours of these various factors. Nevertheless, much of the discussion of the Johannine context considers the tension between Jewish and non-Jewish factors as they are evidenced within the Johannine writings, along with other competing contextual considerations, such as diversity within Judaism itself whether it be Qumranic Judaism or Hellenistic Judaism. Several essays in this volume address various contours of this discussion.

Andrew W. Pitts opens this section with a paper on the light motif in John's Gospel. Pitts challenges the current predominant view championed by

Raymond Brown and Richard Bauckham that the light motif in John's Gospel adapts or is most comparable to the Qumran community's conception of light and darkness. Pitts points out a number of significant problems with this view, including the fact that Qumran's use of dualisms differs significantly from those found in John's Gospel, especially regarding light and darkness; that the Qumran texts espouse a sectarian ideology quite at odds with the openly public character of John's Gospel; and that John's Gospel is composed in Greek rather than in Hebrew and Aramaic like the texts at Qumran. Pitts then offers an alternative view that understands the light motif in relation to the more appropriate parallel of the Hellenistic Jewish reception of Gen 1–9, especially as exemplified in the works of Philo, which display a special interest in convincing pagans of the existence of the one God on the basis of Yahweh's creation of light. Since Jesus is the light of the world (John 8:12) and since John's Gospel is highly mission oriented, the apologetic texts of Hellenistic Judaism appear to be a much more appropriate match, and this clarifies how the light motif corresponds culturally with Johannine Christology.

In the next chapter, Jonathan Numada addresses the question of how the characterization of Jesus in John's Gospel engages with the broader Jewish culture. To bring more clarity to an issue lacking in scholarly consideration, he explores how the Fourth Gospel responds to prevalent zeal traditions within the ideological environment of early Judaism. By making use of Michael Riffaterre's model of intertextuality, Numada demonstrates how John uses the words of Psalm 69 in John 2:17—"zeal for your house will consume me"—to portray Jesus as fulfilling Scripture in unexpected ways due to the Davidic, Maccabean, and eschatological overtones the psalm would have carried within Jewish cultural memory.

In the third paper of this section, Travis D. Trost deals with the question of how the Gospel of John was meant to communicate to a wide audience that extended beyond the Johannine community. Assuming a date of composition after the Jewish revolt of between 70 CE and 85 CE, Trost contends that the Johannine community was living in an aggressive political climate, and this directly influenced the language of John's Gospel. As seen first in the prologue, John's Gospel makes use of language that was at home in a non-Jewish world to introduce Moses as the representative of Jewish law alongside Jesus, who is later identified as the Good Shepherd of a peaceful kingdom. Such choices of language demonstrate how the Johannine community attempted to effectively communicate its message about Jesus and Jewish law to the wide audience that encompassed both Jews and Gentiles.

For the final paper of this section, Arthur M. Wright, Jr. reviews the significance of the symbol of crucifixion within the Roman empire and addresses how such a brutal means of demonstrating dominance problematized the early church's Christology. Answering the question of how the Gospel of John, with its elevated Christology, dealt with this apparent problem, Wright contends that the Fourth Gospel's Christology reaches its height at the crucifixion by means of an irony. This is accomplished by ascribing a second meaning to Jesus's crucifixion in addition to its meaning of shame and death—that is, a meaning of triumph and glorification, since it effectively serves as the agent by which God enthrones Jesus as King. The cross therefore becomes the symbol not of Rome's dominance of the world, but of the King on the cross.

In the third part of the volume, the authors offer a number of essays that approach Christology through the lens of the literary character of the Johannine writings, including discussions of narrative structure, genre, literary motifs, thematic imagery, and the like. One typically thinks of Christology as consisting primarily of a theological configuration, but the essays in this section remind us that Christology comes in a variety of forms and expressions, and that various literary characteristics are used to create and convey John's Christology. These characteristics include some features that are not always taken into consideration in traditional or usual treatments of Christology. Several of the essays in this section touch upon an important area of recent Johannine scholarship, the study of character, especially in relation to features of narrative conveyance. How the account is told becomes essential to the meaning of the narrative.

Providing the first paper for this section, Derek Morton Hamilton Tovey addresses the questions of how the prologue to John's Gospel fits in and functions with the rest of the book. He argues that the implied author uses several techniques that both establish the prologue as the beginning of the narrative—as opposed to having been added on later—and show that the prologue functions as a highly structured introduction that gradually reveals the human identity of Jesus, which is cloaked initially under the metaphors of λόγος and φῶς that attribute to him a number of supra-human characteristics. Tovey claims that the pattern of unfolding information in the prologue connects the metaphors with the character of Jesus, which brings about a view of Jesus both "from above" and "from below." In this way, the prologue introduces the character of Jesus who then becomes the subject of the rest of the Gospel.

In the next chapter, Chris S. Stevens argues the thesis that the first two chapters of John's Gospel identify Jesus as the Divine-Adamic priest. Stevens explores the literary dimensions of John 1–2 by means of two analytical tools from modern linguistics: linguistic frames or scenarios and transitivity structure as conceived by systemic-functional linguistics. Demonstrating that John interweaves various parallels from Gen 1–3 into his Gospel, particularly in

John 1:14–2:25, Stevens finds that this section of text creates the scenario, structured according to the creation week in Genesis, that presents Jesus as the new Adam, and his action in the Temple cleansing contrasts and distinguishes Jesus from the Adam of Genesis because he zealously defends the purity of the place where God dwells with his people.

For the third essay in this section, Adam Z. Wright explores the various ways that the conception of recognition functions in the Gospel of John and argues that John's Gospel belongs to the genre of ancient tragedy. Making use of a methodology developed by A.J. Greimas and J. Courtes on the functions of concealment and recognition in narrative discourse, Wright investigates the "I am" statements to demonstrate how Jesus reveals his nature as the λόγος. This nature is explicitly stated for the reader in the prologue, but the fact that the characters in the story fail to recognize Jesus as the λόγος creates dramatic irony for the reader. This irony ultimately resolves with Thomas's recognition of the resurrected Jesus. Wright finds significant parallels between the Jesus of John's Gospel and Dionysus in the *Bacchae* who introduces himself to the reader as a god but conceals himself as a beggar in the story and thus goes unrecognized for his true identity. Due to this literary similarity and the fact that Jesus dies because people fail to recognize him for who he is, Wright concludes that John's Gospel is best understood as a tragic drama.

Next, in her essay, Tat Yu Lam investigates the relationship between the blood and water motifs that recur throughout John's Gospel and their theological significance as they converge at Jesus's crucifixion (John 19:34–35). To narrow the focus of the many passages that mention water or blood in John's Gospel, Lam chooses to analyze select passages that relate to some aspect of "Johannine Temple Christology." These include: John 2:21, where Jesus's body, the source of the blood and water, is identified as the new Temple; John 19:36–37, where Jesus fulfills Old Testament scripture as the "Passover Lamb" and the "pierced one"; and the literary relationship between John 2:1–25 and 19:23–37, where the narrator connects the first and last of Jesus's signs—the turning of water into wine and the ultimate "sign" of Jesus's crucifixion. When taken together, Lam argues, these passages reveal that John depicts Jesus as the new Temple who purifies and sanctifies people through blood and water.

In the last paper of this section, Stephen S. Smalley begins by sketching his broad proposals about John's Gospel and the book of Revelation, including his views on their genre, date of composition, purpose, and theology. This provides the avenue by which Smalley examines the nature of Jesus as presented by John in both books. He finds in them a central feature of Christology unique to John—namely, the idea of God "invading" humanity. Through the person of

Jesus, God dwelt among his people, which John captures and explains through the metaphorical language of "voice," "tent," and "word," and each of these images carries with it theological implications related to the nature of God's invasion of humanity.

The fourth part of the volume contains three essays that address various ways Johannine Christology was either interpreted or actually applied by its audiences, including its first readers, but extending this to the early church fathers and beyond. Such notions as audience response, tradition, and ethical implications are all part of a broad conception of how the Johannine literature played a role in early Christian reception, whether that was an immediate or more extended reception. The essays in this final section show that Johannine Christology had implications that extended beyond the text to those who read and used the Johannine literature.

In the first essay of this section, Sherri Brown in her chapter examines the ministry and deeds of Jesus in John's so-called Book of Signs for their intended effect on the young Jewish Christian community. Brown observes that the signs Jesus performs are regularly narrated within the context of important feasts on the Jewish calendar. The purpose for this, she contends, is to address the situation among the Johannine Christians who had been in some way marginalized from participating in Jewish ritual feasts and festivals, and so may have thought they were losing contact with God. To reshape the community's experience of God, the evangelist uses Jesus's signs to teach that God sent Jesus to complete and embody these rituals himself as the Christ. Focusing in on John 7:1–10:21, which takes place during the Festival of Tabernacles, the most popular of the three Jewish pilgrim feasts, Brown argues the more narrow thesis that Jesus is presented as the embodiment of the ritual activity of Tabernacles and thereby christologically redefines life in the presence of God.

In the next chapter, Lindsey Trozzo addresses the problematic topic of Johannine ethics. Many have found it difficult to lay hold of Johannine ethics for the reasons that John's Gospel does not contain the forms of moral instructions characteristic of the Synoptics and that Jesus is christologically elevated to the point of being co-equal with God so that any replicable pattern for moral formation is hopelessly futile. Trozzo finds a way forward by considering three topics. First, Trozzo examines the rhetorical topics for encomium that are employed in John's Gospel to show how Jesus is presented as surpassing the expectations of even the most honorable hero in the ancient world. Second, Trozzo gives due attention to the perceived reasons this characterization creates for ethical imitation. Then, in the last topic, Trozzo explains how the encomiastic topics attributed to Jesus are extended also to Jesus's followers through the Gospel's theme of unity. This unity with Jesus, argues Trozzo, becomes the matrix through which followers of Jesus derive their ethics; they are to behave like Jesus because they are one with him.

In the final essay of this section and concluding the volume, Jin Ki Hwang addresses a topic of Johannine Christology that occupied the attention of the early church fathers. Despite the fact that John's Gospel does not share the same kind of emphasis on Jesus's healing ministry, including exorcisms, with that of the Synoptic Gospels, Hwang makes the case that John's Gospel, as well as the Johannine Epistles, displays great interest in demonic powers that articulate a theological message of Jesus's victory over demonic powers. It was believed, since demonic powers were agents of Satan, the father of lies, that deception was the root of demonic powers. Isolating this belief, Hwang then traces the influence of the Johannine tradition of Jesus and demon powers through the early Christian writings of Polycarp, Ignatius, and Irenaeus, where John's Gospel and 1 John are used to combat the prominent heretics of their time, whose beliefs, being viewed as deceptive, are portrayed as under the influence of demonic powers.

As is evident from this brief introduction, this volume puts forward a substantial number of creative ideas about Johannine Christology as well as fresh ways of addressing many of the critical problems that have generated much of the scholarship on the Johannine writings over the years. While not exhaustive in its scope, this volume contains a number of substantial essays that not only partially reflect the state of current scholarship on a variety of topics, but push such discussion forward in new ways that are bound to arouse further interest. The area of Johannine Christology, while vast in its scope, is also one that lends itself to a variety of individual and discrete discussions such as are found in this volume, and thereby further enhance our understanding.

PART 1

The Formation of Johannine Christology

CHAPTER 1

Johannine and Pauline Christology

Stanley E. Porter

1   Introduction

The scholarly consensus maintains, almost without doubt, that John's Gospel displays a "high" Christology. Even though what is meant by a "high" Christology is not always defined, the usual implication is that, even if there are some contra-indications within John's Gospel itself, Jesus is depicted in the Gospel as being a preexistent divine being, of similar or equal status to God. So much has generally been conceded from the time of the Church Fathers to the present, and has resulted in John's Gospel being seen as the "spiritual gospel" (Clement of Alexandria, according to Eusebius, *Hist. eccl.* 6.14.7) or the most theological (and, by usual implication, least historical) Gospel in the New Testament. The result of such widespread agreement regarding Christology is that the Christology of John's Gospel has served an important role within modern reconstructions of early Christianity. The role that such a high Christology has played has usually been to mark a terminal or near terminal point in the supposed theological development of the New Testament documents. This function of the Johannine Christology is evidenced in regard to the relationship of John's Gospel to the other Gospels, and even of John's Gospel to most of the rest of the New Testament. Thus, the Synoptic Gospels, with their supposedly very human and not as christologically high Jesus,[1] are often posited as being written earlier than John's Gospel with its high Christology and other-worldly Jesus.

This theological assessment is no doubt one of the important, even if not always clearly articulated, reasons that John's Gospel has been assigned a date in the closing decades of the first century. Before there was papyrological and other evidence to exclude a date into the second century, the leading figures who argued for a second-century date of John's Gospel, such as David Friedrich Strauss and Ferdinand Christian Baur, placed John's Gospel firmly in the middle of the second century, because it encapsulated many of the major streams

---

[1] See the differing positions in J.R. Daniel Kirk (*A Man Attested by God: The Human Jesus of the Synoptic Gospels* [Grand Rapids: Eerdmans, 2016]) and Simon J. Gathercole (*The Pre-Existent Son: Recovering the Christologies of Matthew, Mark, and Luke* [Grand Rapids: Eerdmans, 2006]).

of development within New Testament thought.[2] These streams included the synthesis of Jewish or Petrine and Greek or Pauline thought, but also the high Christology that represented the culmination of the deification of Jesus that took place within the early church, beginning with earlier books and finding its highest point in John's Gospel. This developmental model has been firmly in place within New Testament studies for much of the post-Enlightenment period, and usually goes unchallenged when discussing the formation of the New Testament, at least from a theological perspective. The implication of this perspective is that John's Gospel not only was written late in the formation process, certainly later than any other Gospel, but is remarkably unparalleled—or at least not explicitly seen to be paralleled—in any other of the significantly earlier books within the New Testament, such as the authentic Pauline letters.[3]

This reconstruction not just of the position of John's Gospel within contemporary scholarship but of the thought processes that surround the usual discussion is found in most treatments of the New Testament. Throughout the history of recent discussion of the date of composition of John's Gospel, there have nevertheless been a few proponents of an early date, by which is meant a date of composition before the fall of the temple in AD 70. A number of arguments have been marshalled in defense of such a position, but one of the traditional stumbling blocks has been the supposed high and unparalleled Christology of the Gospel. If the developmental hypothesis summarized above is correct, even though there are not sufficient historical reasons to exclude an earlier date, there is still the apparent problem of the high Christology. Such a Christology is thought to be much better reflected in the later theological development of the early church than it is in the New Testament documents themselves. So, rather than looking to the other New Testament books, many discussions of Johannine Christology turn to the fathers instead. One of the few exceptions is John A.T. Robinson, who in rejecting the developmental model does not see the theological argument as at all decisive in determining

---

2   See Stanley E. Porter, *John, His Gospel, and Jesus: In Pursuit of the Johannine Voice* (Grand Rapids: Eerdmans, 2015), 13–36; and Porter, "Dating the Composition of New Testament Books and Their Influence upon Reconstructing the Origins of Christianity," in *In Mari Via Tua: Philological Studies in Honour of Antonio Piñero*, ed. Israel M. Gallarte and Jesús Peláez (Córdoba: Ediciones El Almendro, 2016), 553–74.

3   One way to avoid some of the implications of the Pauline letters for such reconstructions is to dispute some of the letters. See Stanley E. Porter, *The Apostle Paul: His Life, Thought, and Letters* (Grand Rapids: Eerdmans, 2016), esp. 157–79, but throughout, for discussion of authorship of the Pauline letters. I believe that all of the letters attributed to Paul in the New Testament are authentic, and defend such a position in the above book.

the dating of John's Gospel.[4] He claims that the high Christology of John's prologue to his Gospel—which virtually every scholar recognizes—is not significantly different from the high Christology of Paul the Apostle, especially as evidenced in Phil 2:6–11 and Col 1:15–20.[5] Robinson believed the prologue was added to the body of the Gospel later, but this does not affect his analysis significantly, as he believes it was written by the same author and that the entire Gospel with prologue and epilogue was published by the late 60s (before the destruction of the temple). There have been few who have pursued Robinson's argument and even fewer who have accepted it as the basis of their reconstructions of early Christianity. However, the implications of such a position—if Robinson were correct—are so numerous as to call for a complete revision of not only our findings, but of our approach to the New Testament context. The most fundamental implication is that such a position would undermine the developmental model of New Testament origins. No longer would one be able to categorize and arrange individual books of the New Testament on the basis of their Christology. If a high Christology can be found in Paul's letters—with Paul by virtually all accounts one of the earliest writers of the New Testament—then it can be found everywhere and is not a reliable guide to the linear development of the New Testament. A second implication is that the conflict model of Baur and others since might need to be rethought, in which high Christology is seen as in some ways evidence of the protracted synthesis of competing parties within the early church. A high Christology, if found at the virtual outset of the early Christian movement, would not warrant these dialectical-synthetic models.

As mentioned above, however, very few scholars have followed Robinson in his positing an early date for John's Gospel, in part because of its indications of high Christology that is paralleled in Paul's letters. One of the reasons may be that in some contemporary theological discussions the high Christology of Paul has come into question, even if the high Christology of John's Gospel is affirmed;[6] another reason may be that for some it is simply unconscionable

---

4 See John A.T. Robinson, *Redating the New Testament* (Philadelphia: Westminster, 1975), 283; cf. Robinson, *The Priority of John*, ed. J.F. Coakley (London: SCM Press, 1985), 379–94, with some tempering in his understanding of Phil 2:6–11 and Col 1:15–20. For a critical analysis of Robinson, see Stanley E. Porter, "John A.T. Robinson: Provocateur and Profound New Testament Scholar," in *The Gospel of John in Modern Interpretation*, ed. Stanley E. Porter and Ron C. Fay, Milestones in New Testament Scholarship (Grand Rapids: Kregel, 2018), 141–71.

5 Even if Colossians is pseudepigraphal, the similarity to Philippians would indicate that the Colossian pseudepigrapher was reflecting Pauline Christology.

6 The most well-known of these is perhaps James D.G. Dunn, *Christology in the Making: A New Testament Inquiry into the Origins of the Doctrine of the Incarnation* (Philadelphia:

that John's Gospel could be written earlier, no matter what its Christology. In this chapter, I wish to explore Johannine Christology in relationship to Pauline Christology in two major ways. The first is to define what we mean by "high" Christology, so that we are able to recognize not just the vague notion of what constitutes a high Christology but the specific formulations of the Christology and how it is represented in the Pauline letters and John's Gospel. The second way is to make some comparisons and contrasts between Pauline and Johannine Christology, with the goal of providing a more informed view of New Testament Christology, and in particular Johannine Christology and its implications.

2   Defining High Christology in Paul

To make a comparison with John's Christology, it is appropriate to begin with a discussion of how to define Paul's "high" Christology.[7] There are a number of passages that are often cited as representing Paul's most expressive christological statements. If one examines these and some other passages, one is able to identify (at least) three major types of christological statements in Paul's writings: equative, positional, and proto-Trinitarian. There may be other types, but this is not meant to be a paper in Pauline Christology, only one that identifies the nature of Pauline Christology as a means to examine the Christology of John's Gospel.[8]

Equative christological statements are those in which there is an equation between entities, where one entity has a fixed or known value and the other is equated with it, presumably with the idea that they are then to be seen as equal to each other so far as their status or being is concerned. The most common example within the Pauline literature is when Paul equates Jesus Christ (by one

---

Westminster, 1980), who sees the first emergence of a "high" Christology as defined here in the prologue of John's Gospel, but not in Paul. This proposal has met with much opposition.

7   In what follows, I draw upon the materials presented in Stanley E. Porter, *Sacred Tradition in the New Testament: Tracing Old Testament Themes in the Gospels and Epistles* (Grand Rapids: Baker, 2016), 227–45, although I clearly conceptually organize the data in a different way that gives more precise labels to the kind of christological statements found in the Pauline material.

8   I am not attempting to define all of Paul's Christology, but some features that would best represent his so-called "high" Christology, to provide points of comparison with John's. I especially do not focus upon christological titles, primarily because, apart possibly from "son of God," these only indicate high Christology in context. "Son of God," however, is treated where appropriate, although it too is highly contextual. See Porter, *Sacred Tradition*, 107–15, for placement within the Greco-Roman and Jewish worlds of understanding.

of his names) with an already known divine being or at least indicates a similar identity as the divine being. The clearest example of an equative christological statement in Paul is his statement "Jesus is Lord" (in particular Rom 10:9; 1 Cor 12:3).[9] In such a statement, the use of "Lord" reflects the first to second century BC translational tendency to render the divine name, YHWH, by means of "Lord."[10] Lord, therefore, is seen to represent the Jewish divine figure YHWH. In such equative statements, in which Paul states (that early Christians confessed) that "Jesus is Lord," Paul is saying that there is a known Lord, the God of the Old Testament, and Jesus is said to be equal to him. In other words, Jesus is the Lord God. There is no necessary further elaboration of what this equation entails, but it seems to represent an important kind of identity, so that they can be equated with each other. In some ways, these explicit equative statements are the most basic christological statements to be found within Paul's letters. This is not just because they seem to reflect early Christian creedal statements but because the statements are linguistically uncomplex and do not require the elaboration found in the other types of statements.

Such equative Pauline christological statements, however, can also be seen in less explicit forms. These include passages where Paul cites an Old Testament passage that, in its original context, referred to YHWH, but Paul equates the reference with Jesus Christ. For example, in 1 Cor 2:16, Paul cites Isa 40:13, with the statement "For who has known the mind of the Lord so as to instruct him?" He then states that "we have the mind of Christ," thus equating the Lord (God) with Jesus Christ. This implicit equation occurs in both direct quotations and allusions within Paul's letters. A second example is the highly contentious Rom 9:5. This passage is perplexed by whether it affirms that Christ is God over all or not, based upon syntax and punctuation. I have argued elsewhere that theological presuppositions have often clouded judgment of this passage. The statement is probably best interpreted as referring to Christ, "who is God over all, blessed into the ages" (rather than Christ "who is over all. God be blessed ..."). The reasons for this interpretation are the non-doxological but attributive use of "blessed," the likelihood of the articular attributive participle modifying "Christ," the need to understand "above all" as syntactically part of the participial phrase, and the unlikelihood of "God" being anarthrous. If this is the case, then Paul is making a statement that Christ is

---

[9] See Stanley E. Porter, "Saints and Sinners: The Church in Paul's Letters," in *The Church: Then and Now*, ed. Stanley E. Porter and Cynthia Long Westfall, MNTS (Eugene, OR: Wipf & Stock, 2012), 41–67, esp. 43–45.

[10] For a summary of the evidence, see Stanley E. Porter, *When Paul Met Jesus: How an Idea Got Lost in History* (Cambridge: Cambridge University Press, 2016), 85; cf. Porter, *Sacred Tradition*, 235.

God.[11] Similar interpretive difficulties attend Titus 2:13 (besides questions of authorship), but the more likely interpretation is that Paul is referring to the hope and revelation "of the glory of our great God and savior, Jesus Christ."[12] He is implicitly equating Jesus Christ with God.

The second type of christological statement is positional. Positional christological statements do not rely upon explicit equation of an entity with a divine being to be operative. Positional christological statements place one entity in a position that is to be equated with the position of another. This positional placement is very similar to and often entails functional similarity. There are two major examples often cited within the Pauline literature that reflect positional Christology: Philippians 2:6–11 and Col 1:15–20. These examples are similar in their positional christological representation, but different in the ways that this position, and hence function, is represented. Philippians 2:6–11 utilizes a three-stage movement to represent three different positional stances.[13] Christ is positioned first as being in divine form even though he is said not to cling to such status. The second position is one of becoming humanized (the traditional term is incarnation) and going through the various representations of humanity, including servant, human being, humiliation, and death. The third position also involves an instance of equative Christology, when Paul states that Jesus was placed in a position (Paul uses the term "hyperexalt") of being worshipped. Worship is only appropriate for God to receive, with the worshippers bowing and declaring not something about God but that "Jesus Christ is Lord," and this with God's approval as it is to his glory. The second example, Colossians 1:15–20, is also a positional christological statement, but one that only utilizes a single positional depiction, along with an equative description. Jesus Christ, even though he is not mentioned by name due to the hymnic structure, is said to be the image of the unseen God, an initial equative christological depiction. The unseen God is imaged in Jesus Christ, a visual representation for an unseen one. There are two major movements in this Colossian passage. Jesus Christ is first said to have been involved in divine creation of the cosmos. God created (although Paul uses the passive voice form in two instances of the same verb), but this creation was "in" or "by" Jesus Christ, "through" Jesus Christ, and "for" Jesus Christ. This is not a limited creation, but one that encompasses everything, both seen and unseen and at

---

11   See Porter, *Sacred Tradition*, 242, relying upon Murray J. Harris, *Jesus as God: The New Testament Use of Theos in Reference to Jesus* (Grand Rapids: Baker, 1992), 143–72.
12   Harris, *Jesus as God*, 173–85.
13   The two-stage Adamic Christology of James Dunn (*Christology in the Making*, 114–19) is only two-thirds correct, at most.

all ranks of existence. The second movement is the result that Jesus Christ occupies a position of authority and preeminence over the church and all humanity, on the basis that the fullness of (implied divine) being dwelled within him, so that he had the divine function of reconciliation of humanity to God. In both movements, Jesus Christ is positioned to function in God's role—as creator and as reconciler so as both to bring into being humanity and its world, but also as the firstborn from the dead to reconcile this sinful humanity, and its world, to God through the cross. The examples within this category can no doubt be expanded. What is important to note here is that the positional representation also includes, at least in these two examples, textual movements that clarify the description and depiction.

Proto-Trinitarian christological statements are the third category of christological representation that I wish to identify in this short prelude regarding Pauline theology.[14] I also implicitly include binitarian statements (besides those noted above, see Rom 8:9, 11; 1 Cor 8:6, among many others), but Paul goes well beyond such statements and I focus upon those here. Proto-Trinitarian statements represent in their description what later theologians came to identify as the Trinity, the three persons that constitute God's being.[15] Even though the terminology of Trinity was a later development, increasing numbers of scholars have recognized that some of the biblical authors, and Paul in particular, had a conception of the Trinity and its members, God the Father, the son Jesus Christ, and the Holy Spirit, and depicted them in relationship. These relationships are not couched in the terminology of later Christian creedal theology but depict the members of the Trinity in what might be called active differentiated yet sympathetic relationships. There are a number of Pauline proto-Trinitarian passages. These include, among others, Rom 1:1–4. Romans 1:1–4 is part of the opening of the letter, in which Paul identifies himself in relationship to the good news of God. God is said to be the one who proclaimed through the prophets in the Scriptures concerning his son, who was human (from the seed of David and fleshly) but nevertheless designated "son of God" in power on the basis of the Spirit of Holiness who raised him from the dead, the person known as Jesus Christ our Lord.[16]

---

14   See Stanley E. Porter, *Linguistic Analysis of the Greek New Testament: Studies in Tools, Methods, and Practice* (Grand Rapids: Baker Academic, 2015), 377–84 on the Trinity.
15   See Gordon D. Fee, *Pauline Christology: An Exegetical-Theological Study* (Peabody: Hendrickson, 2007), 63.
16   In this passage, Paul seems to make "son of God" language as part of his proto-Trinitarian language. For other son of God passages, see 2 Cor 1:19; Gal 2:20; Eph 4:13; cf. also Rom 1:9; 5:10; 8:3, 29, 32; 1 Cor 1:9; 15:28; Gal 1:1; 4:4, 6; Col 1:13; 1 Thess 1:10. The language elsewhere

The final honorific is not formally equative in its formulation, but relies upon such an equation that Jesus Christ is Lord. More important for this particular proto-Trinitarian christological category, however, is that God is seen as the one who instigates these actions in regard to his son who is also called "son of God," and these actions are said to be enacted by the Spirit of Holiness, all three working together as part of a complex proto-Trinitarian tableaux. Other passages to consider proto-Trinitarian are Rom 5:1–8; 8:9–11; 1 Cor 12:4–6; 2 Cor 13:14; Eph 5:19; Col 3:16; and 2 Thess 2:13–14.[17]

These three types of christological statements go well beyond the kinds of categories used by Robinson in his identification of similar christological interests in Paul and John. However, I think that identifying such patterns is necessary in order to examine more closely the nature of the Christology found within John's Gospel.

3 Defining Johannine Christology

I have derived a basic formulation of the types of christological statements found within Paul as a means of comparison with John's Gospel. The reason that it is appropriate to begin with Paul is that, as noted in the introduction, most statements regarding John's Gospel begin with the assumption that the high Christology of the Gospel is the result of its being later in time of composition than most other works within the New Testament, hence giving time for the author to further develop early Christian Christology. If we were to begin with Johannine Christology we may well be able to find some similar patterns in other writings, posited as early foreshadowings of what the author of John's Gospel draws upon in the development of his thought. I believe that it is better to begin with Paul's Christology as a means of formulating a number of meaningful categories, and then using these as points of specific comparison with the material in John's Gospel. In other words, rather than using John's Gospel as a lens by which to peer back into Christian theological incipience in an attempt to discover points of possible connection, I begin with Paul's Christology and use the developed categories of his thought as a mirror to see if John's theology is a reflection of the same type of theological stance. I will therefore

---

shows the close association in Paul's mind between Jesus Christ and God, so much so that Jesus can be called God's son. The term is not necessarily indicating the kind of relationship that we see in Rom 1:1–4, but is compatible with it in context.

17 See Gordon D. Fee, *God's Empowering Presence: The Holy Spirit in the Letters of Paul* (Peabody: Hendrickson, 1994), 48 n. 39, for further possible examples.

use the Pauline christological categories to provide the points of comparison so that equivalent categories can be compared.[18]

4 Equative Christology

Equative Christology was the first category identified above. The question for this chapter is whether equative christological statements are used within John's Gospel. They do, indeed, seem to be used.

The most obvious equative christological statements are arguably found in John 1:1, 18 and 20:28. In John 1:1, John states that "the word was God." We must admit that this is not an explicit statement regarding Jesus Christ, but about the *logos* that yet awaits incarnation later in the prologue. Nevertheless, an implication of the phrasing is that the *logos*, in its condition before incarnation, is to be equated with God. Despite various discussions of the syntax (e.g. regarding the use of the article), there are clear indications on the basis of patterns of usage of concrete nouns and syntax that the equation is between the word and God.[19] In John 1:18, a verse with a major textual variant whether "God" or "son" is to be read ("God" is definitely the better attested reading), John states that "the only begotten God who is in the bosom of the father, that one has made known" (implied God). There are actually two christological statements in this passage, one an arguably implicit equation of Jesus Christ with God, by means of calling God the only-begotten one, and the other the positional one of this only-begotten God being located in the bosom of the father (the latter also mentioned below). In John 20:28, Thomas upon seeing Jesus and being invited to touch his wounds declares "My Lord and my God." This also is an implicit equative christological statement, with Thomas declaring (using the nominative of address)[20] that the person who is standing before him, Jesus, is Lord and God. There is a definite indication that these equative statements form an inclusio for John's Gospel, with the account opening and then closing with strong christological statements.[21]

---

18 See Paul A. Rainbow, *Johannine Theology: The Gospel, the Epistles and the Apocalypse* (Downers Grove, IL: InterVarsity, 2014), esp. 146–72, who provides a handy compendium of recent discussion.

19 See Harris, *Jesus as God*, 51–72; cf. Stanley E. Porter, *Idioms of the Greek New Testament*, 2nd ed. (Sheffield: Sheffield Academic, 1994), 109–10.

20 This is not a vocative form, even if it is used "vocatively," that is, as a form of address. Contra Rainbow, *Johannine Theology*, 148.

21 This may form at least part of an argument against Robinson's seeing the prologue as added later, since the Christology is high from start to (near) finish. There is also no reason simply to treat the prologue and not the rest of the Gospel.

There are two further implicit equative statements in John's Gospel to note. The first is in John 5:18, where the Jews are reportedly seeking to kill Jesus, because he was not only disobeying the Sabbath but "he was saying that God was his own father, making himself equal with God." This is a report by John of what others were saying and thinking, and the language is framed in an indirect way to signal the equation involved. The notion of making oneself equal with God (an implicit equative statement) follows on from the identification of Jesus with God as his own father. The second implicit equative statement is in John 12:41. John says that the Jews did not believe in Jesus even though they had seen signs, so that the words of Isaiah were fulfilled regarding such unbelief. Then John says that Isaiah said these things because he had seen "his glory" and had spoken "concerning him." As Rainbow points out, the "only passage in which the prophet claims to have seen the divine glory is Isaiah 6:1."[22] In other words, John understands that when Isaiah sees God's glory he is seeing Christ's glory, and that the two can be seen as one substituting for or being equal to the other.

There are also a number of more explicit equative statements in John's Gospel. The most obvious ones are in John 10:30–36. In Jerusalem, Jesus is confronted, and he engages in a discussion with his opponents regarding their lack of acceptance of him, even though he does the work of the father. He finally says that "I and the father are one," using a copulative verb and the neuter pronoun for "one" to indicate their oneness in being. At this point, the Jews take up stones so that they might stone him. Jesus enquires regarding the reasons for this, and the Jews reply that it is because "you, being a human being, have made yourself God." The equative construction is interpreted by Jesus's disputants, according to John, as him understanding himself to have indicated that he is God. Later in the dispute, Jesus questions the Jews again about the charge of blasphemy, because he said, "I am son of God." In most instances in John's Gospel the notion of Jesus being the "son" indicates subordination.[23] In this instance of an equative construction, more is implied as it is linked directly to blasphemy. In Judaism, blasphemy was the charge against those who made the claim to be equal to or in fact to be God.[24] They continued to try to stone him.

Another important equative statement is John 8:58, with its well-known "I am" construction, but we cannot consider v. 58 without also considering

---

22 Rainbow, *Johannine Theology*, 157.
23 Rainbow, *Johannine Theology*, 105.
24 See Porter, *Sacred Tradition*, 71–76.

vv. 24 and 28 along with it.[25] In the midst of Jesus's discussion with a crowd that included his disciples, but also other Jews, Jesus treats a number of subjects. These include the fact that they cannot go where he is going at least at this time. In fact, there are a number of "I am" constructions within this chapter of John's Gospel, including also John 8:12 and 28 with predicate usage ("I am the light of the world" and "I am the one who bears witness concerning myself") and John 8:23 with two instances of locative usage ("I am from above" and "I am not from the world"; see below). I will return to these other kinds of "I am" constructions below after first considering John 8:58, and then John 8:24 and 28, three instances of absolute usage. After Jesus contrasts himself with his auditors and discusses their sin and begins to discuss his identity, Jesus then discusses the nature of truth with his disciples, and engages in discussion with other Jews who clearly do not believe in him but who look to Abraham as their father. In John 8:58, Jesus says that "truly truly I say to you, before Abraham came into being, I am." There has been great debate over exactly what is being said and indicated by this passage, but there are several reasons for thinking that it is an equative christological statement that makes an affirmation of divine being. There are several contextual factors that indicate this christological usage. These factors include, first, the changed reaction of the crowd from earlier in the chapter. Whereas earlier Jesus's words are addressed to those who believe (John 8:31), once the discussion turns to Abraham in John 8:39 the atmosphere sours, such that Jesus recognizes that they are intending to kill him (8:40). Further, the reaction of his auditors when Jesus makes the statement of John 8:58 is the most potentially violent in the Gospel to this point: they take up stones to hurl at him, implicating a suitable cause that warrants this strong reaction. Jesus appears to be making a multi-faceted claim, one chronological and the other concerning status. Jesus in this scene makes the claim that he has previous existence, superior knowledge, and superior status to Abraham, his auditors' religious forefather. The absolute construction differs from the predicate or locative structures in which an equation or situation is indicated by not offering any kind of qualification. What sounds strange in English translation—"before Abraham came into being, I am"—apparently also sounded odd to the first-century hearers of this statement. The absolute "I am" construction in John 8:58 is made more emphatic by the use of the initial "amen, amen" or "truly, truly" used to introduce it. This is the first time in John's Gospel that this emphatic marker is linked with an "I am" construction. The use of the absolute "I am" construction reflects Old Testament language,

---

25   See Porter, *John, His Gospel, and Jesus*, 137–40; and Rainbow, *Johannine Theology*, 152.

especially of Exod 3:14, with the statement by God to Moses that "I am who I am," as well as possibly Deut 32:34 and various passages in Isa 40–55 (e.g. 41:4; 43:10, 13, 25; 46:4; 48:12; 51:12; 52:6).[26] This usage, as shocking as it may have been to Jesus's auditors, resonates with the prologue of the Gospel. Even though Abraham was the chronological and positional head of the Jewish people, Jesus's usage here puts Jesus in a position chronologically and positionally superior to Abraham, and in John's Gospel that position of chronological and positional authority is reflected in the prologue, in which the *logos* that becomes incarnate is depicted as eternally existing before such an action. In other words, the statement of John 8:58, which forms a turning point in the Gospel, serves as a culminative indication of a pattern that was first instigated in the prologue of the Gospel and continued to this point.

This interpretation of the "I am" construction of John 8:58 has clear implications for a number of other passages in John's Gospel that probably should be interpreted as equative christological statements as well. The first set of passages is John 8:24 and 28, the earlier usage of the absolute construction mentioned above. In John 8:24, Jesus discusses his hearers' lack of belief, and notes that unless they believe that "I am," they will die in their sins. The reaction is twofold. First, the hearers ask who Jesus is. Second, Jesus asks them in return, "with respect to the beginning what indeed did I say to you?" (John 8:25). I note that Jesus's statement in John 8:24 begs for a predicate, but not just any predicate. Jesus's hearers ask who he is, a legitimate question in light of the formulation. Even the formulation of their question merits attention, as they ask using an emphatic initial personal pronoun: "You, who are you?" (John 8:25). The hearers sense that Jesus is more than a simple predicate. This is allusively confirmed in his reciprocal question, which is also formulated to emphasize its object, the "beginning." Jesus is quoted as using a phrase with the same word as appears in the prologue of the Gospel, placed syntactically first (although not in a prepositional phrase). Even if the ostensive or surface indication is that Jesus is referring to the beginning of his ministry, the reference to the "beginning" may well here refer to the prologue with its "in beginning." In John 8:28, Jesus brings the son of man into conjunction with an absolute "I am" construction. He says that when they see the son of man, then they can expect to know that "I am," and that he is doing nothing from himself but that he is speaking to them what "the father" taught him. Jesus says also that the one who sent him is with him and does not leave him alone because he is doing things pleasing to him. The Johannine son of man, similar to the Synoptic son of man, invokes the son of man of Daniel 7, a messianic apocalyptic figure with incarnational

---

26   See Rainbow, *Johannine Theology*, 156.

overtones.[27] The response to these words is that many believed in Jesus. The passage equates the son of man as an apocalyptic figure who accomplishes God's purposes with Jesus as the one who is acting on behalf of the father who sent him and to whom he is pleasing. The language of "pleasing" (John 8:29), although it is reminiscent of the Synoptic baptism when God affirms his beloved son (an affirmation not explicitly found in John's Gospel), is also reminiscent of the Johannine episode with John the Baptist's testimony, which involves not only language of ascent and descent but culminates in the testimony of John that he has seen and bears witness that Jesus is the son of God (John 1:34). These statements in John 8:24 and 28, although they are not explicit equative christological formulations, certainly draw in the kind of imagery and language that culminates in the more explicit statement of John 8:58.

A similar case can be made for the three instances of absolute usage in John 18:4, 6, and 8. When Jesus is being arrested, those who approach him ask if he is Jesus the Nazarene, to which he replies "I am." When he says "I am," the crowd falls back and to the ground. Jesus then turns the tables on his captors and asks them whom they seek, and when they answer "Jesus the Nazarene," Jesus answers again, "I tell you that I am." These three instances have typically been interpreted as idiomatic use of "I am." However, as I have elsewhere argued, in light of the development of John's Gospel, there are good reasons to see that the usage here has christological overtones.[28] These factors include the narrative buildup that has taken place throughout the Gospel and then within this episode, leading to this revelation of Jesus's identity. A second consideration is that, even though the captors are aggressively approaching Jesus and seeking him out, once Jesus gives his answer, they fall back and to the ground in response. Their repulsion is unusual and indicates that Jesus is depicted as more than simply using an idiomatic "it's me." The saying seems to carry the full impact of the weight that it has accumulated throughout the Gospel, particularly in John 8 culminating in the statement regarding his relationship to Abraham. Furthermore, despite the reaction of his captors, Jesus still allows himself to be arrested. Jesus first requests that his followers be released, satisfying what he said earlier (John 17:12, 24). Only when their safety is ensured does he allow himself to be arrested and taken into custody.[29]

---

[27] See Francis J. Moloney, *The Johannine Son of Man* (Rome: LAS, 1976), 208–20; cf. Porter, *Sacred Tradition*, 51–78, on the Synoptic usage.

[28] See Porter, *John, His Gospel, and Jesus*, 143–45.

[29] Other absolute uses earlier in John's Gospel may well carry similar theological weight. Those instances worth considering are John 4:26, when in a discussion of the coming Messiah, Jesus says that "I am"; and John 6:20, when Jesus walks on the water to his

The locative "I am" construction will be treated in the section to follow, as it involves language of above and below, which is better discussed as positional Christology. However, the fact that instances of absolute and locative "I am" constructions are part of christological formulations raises the question of whether such implications are to be found in the use of the third type, the predicate construction.[30] The predicate "I am" construction is found in a number of suggestive contexts. Jesus is said to be the bread of life in John 6:35, 41, 48, 51; the light of the world in John 8:12; the one who bears witness in John 8:18; the door of the sheep in John 10:7, 9; the good shepherd in John 10:11, 14; the resurrection and the life in John 11:25; the way, the truth, and the life in John 14:6; and the vine in John 15:1, 5. This is not the place to treat all of these examples in detail, but the use of predicates with the "I am" construction is at least christologically highly suggestive.

There are a range of equative statements in John's Gospel regarding Jesus. A number of them are clearly christological in origin, but a number of them are not as explicitly so, even if they intimate that there is more to Jesus and his metaphorical equivalent than the literalistic understanding that one might at first be inclined to see.

5 Positional Christology

There are a number of different positional christological statements in John's Gospel. I will focus upon two of them here, with the second being one of the most prominent christological metaphors used in the Gospel.

The first example is the position of Jesus being in the father and/or the father being in Jesus. This language occurs at several places within John's Gospel. The major passage is the one already mentioned above, John 1:18 regarding Jesus being in the bosom of the father. As John 1:18 states, Jesus (stated here to be the only-begotten God) is "in the bosom of the father." The force of the positional metaphor here is made stronger by characterizing Jesus as the "only-begotten God," in which case it makes logical and conceptual sense for Jesus being God to be positioned in a place of intimacy with the father, of whom he is presumably the only-begotten. Several other passages also offer positional christological depictions of intertwined relationship between Jesus and God. For example, in John 10:38, Jesus says that "the father is in me and I am in the

---

disciples and greets them with "I am" and "don't be afraid," at which point he enters the boat and it was at the shore.

30 See Porter, *John, His Gospel, and Jesus*, 133–37; Rainbow, *Johannine Theology*, 153–54.

father," with the copulative verb implied. Immediately after this statement (and on the basis of previous ones as well; see above), Jesus's opponents seek to kill him. In John 14:10, 11, and 20, similar positional christological constructions are found. In dialogue, Jesus asks whether his hearers don't believe that "I am in the father and the father is in me." More than that, "the father remains in me" (John 14:10). Jesus then repeats his previous statement, when he says that his hearers believe that "I am in the father and the father is in me," again with the copulative verb implied. Jesus prepares his hearers for his departure and the coming of the paraclete when he states that "I am in my father and you are in me and I am in you," what might well be argued is a subtle incipient proto-Trinitarian passage (see below) (John 14:20). Finally, in John 17:21, at the conclusion of his prayer to God, Jesus wishes unity upon his followers, "as you, father, are in me and I am in you." This reciprocal relationship between Jesus and the father might well be seen as binitarian in nature.

The second positional statements concern a variety of spatial metaphors regarding Jesus's descending and ascending, coming and going, and especially coming from God or heaven and the like.[31] This language is spread throughout John's Gospel. For example, language of Jesus's ascending is found in John 3:13; 6:62; 20:17, and his descending is found in John 3:13; 6:33, 38, 41, 42, 50, 51, 58.[32] John 3:13 contains both images. In this passage, Jesus is reportedly speaking to Nicodemus (although where Jesus leaves off and the Gospel author begins is not entirely clear), when he states that "no one ascends into heaven except one who descends from heaven, the son of man." In this passage, Jesus's ascent to heaven is seen as established on the basis of his being one who is descended from heaven as the son of man.[33] "Son of man" is Jesus's favorite self-referential statement in the Synoptic Gospels, but has a slightly different sense in Johannine usage, one that includes both appeal to the son of man figure of Dan 7:13 and a spiritual sense linked to the pre-existent logos incarnated in Jesus.[34] Here the son of man is linked to an ascending-descending figure,

---

[31] See Godfrey C. Nicholson, *Death as Departure: The Johannine Descent-Ascent Schema*, SBLDS 63 (Chico, CA: Scholars Press, 1963), for a more expansive treatment that moves well beyond Christology. Cf. Wayne A. Meeks, "The Man from Heaven in Johannine Sectarianism," *JBL* 91 (1972): 44–72; repr. John Ashton, ed., *The Interpretation of John*, 2nd ed. (Edinburgh: T&T Clark, 1997), 169–206, who interprets the language sociologically; and Adesola Joan Akala, *The Son-Father Relationship and Christological Symbolism in the Gospel of John*, LNTS 505 (London: Bloomsbury, 2014), esp. 111–14.

[32] See Rainbow, *Johannine Theology*, 171, for references.

[33] There is a textual variant that extends the designation of the son of man as "the one who is in heaven." This is found in later manuscripts, not in the earlier majuscules, and so is to be rejected as an attempt to clarify where the son of man is located.

[34] See Moloney, *Johannine Son of Man*, 208–20.

and in that regard becomes a christological statement about Jesus's identity in John's Gospel.[35] There are further images of coming and going that are worth noting even if they are not always or even primarily as explicitly christological (note the use of the two together in John 8:14 twice and 13:3).[36] Related to the coming and going and the ascent and descent is language, as noted above, of coming from heaven or the father, and related phrases (including not being of the world).[37] The structure of the Gospel has an ascent–descent structure to it, reinforced continuously by reference to Jesus's ascent and descent and his not being of this world but from above. The prologue to John's Gospel, even if it begins with the *logos* preexistent with God, sees the *logos* become incarnate and living among other humans so that it can be seen by others. However, there is no direct depiction of the ascent of Jesus. Some scholars have thought that the Johannine ascent takes place between Jesus appearing to Mary in the garden, when she, confusing him with the gardner, attempts to cling onto Jesus, and he tells her not to, and Jesus's appearance later to Thomas, when he is allowed to touch Jesus.[38] As I have argued elsewhere, I believe that this conjecture is based upon a misunderstanding of how to interpret the command by Jesus not to touch him, not evidence of the ascension occurring.[39] The Gospel of John does not end with a final ascent.

---

35 There has been much scholarly debate over two major issues regarding this passage. One is its source and the other is its purported time of occurrence. These are not germane here. See Craig S. Keener, *The Gospel of John: A Commentary*, 2 vols. (Peabody: Hendrickson, 2003), 1:561–63.

36 Coming: John 1:9, 11; 3:2, 19, 31; 5:43; 7:28; 8:14, 42; 9:39; 10:10; 11:27; 12:13, 27, 46, 47; 13:3; 15:22; 16:27, 28, 30; 17:8; 18:37. Going: John 7:33, 34, 35, 36; 8:21, 22; 13:1, 33–34, 36; 14:2, 3, 4, 5, 12, 18, 27, 28; 16:5, 7, 10, 17, 28; cf. 17:11. These references are mostly from Rainbow, *Johannine Theology*, 171.

37 One finds such phrases as being "from God" (John 3:2; 8:42, 47; 13:3; 16:30); "from heaven" (John 3:3, 31; 6:31–33, 38, 41–42, 50–51, 58); "from the father" (John 16:28); "from above" (John 8:23); and even "alongside God" (John 6:46; 16:27); "alongside the father" (John 1:14; 16:28; 17:8); "alongside the one who sent me" (John 7:27); and "from above" (John 3:31). The Greek formulations differ and are amalgamated above. References to entering into the world or exiting out of it or not being of it are found in John 1:9; 3:17, 19; 6:14; 8:23, 26; 10:36; 11:27; 12:46; 13:1; 16:28; 17:14, 16, 18; 18:37. Some of this language is also linked with the locative "I am" constructions (e.g. John 17:14, 16). These references are mostly from Rainbow, *Johannine Theology*, 171.

38 E.g., Lee Martin McDonald, *The Story of Jesus in History and Faith: An Introduction* (Grand Rapids: Baker Academic, 2013), 310–18.

39 See Stanley E. Porter, *Verbal Aspect in the Greek of the New Testament, with Reference to Tense and Mood*, SBG 1 (New York: Peter Lang, 1989), 356; and Porter, "Ascent in the New Testament," in *Patristic Spirituality: Classical Perspectives on Ascent in the Journey to God*, ed. Don W. Springer and Kevin M. Clarke (Leiden: Brill, in press).

There are many references to Jesus being descended from heaven and not being of the world and ascending to heaven, sometimes with the two images used together but often with reference to one or the other. Positional christological statements are clearly frequent within John's Gospel.

6   Proto-Trinitarian Christology

There are many of what might be called binitarian christological statements in John's Gospel, including many noted above when a relationship of divine similarity is established between God and Jesus. There are also some proto-Trinitarian statements as well that are worth examining.[40]

The Johannine proto-Trinitarian christological statements are found especially in the episodes when Jesus speaks of sending the Paraclete.[41] There are three passages in particular to note in this regard. In John 14:16, Jesus says that he is asking the father and he is going to give another paraclete to his hearers to be with them forever, and this paraclete is defined (apposition) as the spirit of truth (v. 17; cf. John 16:13). In John 15:26, in a somewhat similar statement, Jesus speaks of the paraclete coming, whom he has sent from the father, defined as the spirit of truth that comes from the father to bear witness concerning Jesus. In these two passages, there are three recognizable participants, God or the father and Jesus and a third participant, the paraclete. We already have some idea of how John views God and Jesus in their relationship based upon the previous discussion. However, we see in these two passages that Jesus is in communication with the father, that the father is the one who gives the paraclete, that the paraclete is with the father, that the paraclete bears witness concerning Jesus, and that the paraclete is defined as the spirit of truth, thereby implying that the paraclete has a role to play as a spiritual being in attesting truthfully to Jesus's identity. In John 14:26, Jesus speaks of the paraclete, whom he appositionally defines as the holy spirit that the father sends in

---

40   For a much more expansive and systematic theological treatment, see Andreas J. Köstenberger and Scott R. Swain, *Father, Son and Spirit: The Trinity and John's Gospel* (Downers Grove, IL: InterVarsity, 2008), although they are more concerned with the individual entities of the Trinity, as seen within the theological doctrine, than they are proto-Trinitarian passages (although they emphasize the same passages that I discuss).

41   See Rainbow, *Johannine Theology*, 235–50, who sees what he calls a "nascent trinitarianism" in these passages; cf. Porter, *John, His Gospel, and Jesus*, 185–88; and, for a full treatment, Tricia Gates Brown, *Spirit in the Writings of John: Johannine Pneumatology in Social-Scientific Perspective* (London: T&T Clark International, 2003), although one need not adopt her social-scientific patronage model to appreciate John's use of the paraclete.

Jesus's name to teach and bring to mind what Jesus had told his hearers. In this passage, which falls between the other two, the paraclete is defined not just as the spirit of truth, but as the holy spirit, with the function of continuing to attest or bear witness to Jesus. There has been much further discussion of the paraclete, to the point of defining the paraclete in specific theological terms. However, if we simply draw upon the information in these three passages in which all three participants are mentioned, we can see that there is at least the hint, and perhaps something slightly stronger, of a proto-Trinitarian theology. That is, there is an indication of a relationship of God, Jesus, and the holy spirit (I intentionally do not capitalize here) in some type of identification of God and Jesus, who have already been identified with each other in John's Gospel, with a third being that is identified as the Holy Spirit (with capital letters), and that will come to be recognized as the full third member of the Trinity in later theological reflection.

7 Implications of Pauline and Johannine Christology

There are a number of implications of my comparison of the Christologies of Paul and John. I concentrated upon elements that are usually discussed in relation to establishing and defining a high Christology. If we examine the three categories, we see that both Paul's letters and John's Gospel have explicit equative christological statements, as well as some implicit equative statements. John's Gospel implicitly develops some of his imagery in conjunction with "I am" constructions in suggestive ways that are not necessarily found in Paul's writings. In positional christological statements, again both Paul and John have such statements. The difference here seems to be that Paul has two well-developed and extended statements, while John relies upon a large number of continuous references throughout his Gospel. On the one hand, one might argue that Paul has the more overt and developed positional Christology that he is able to develop into a full picture of Christ's relationship to God. On the other hand, one might equally well argue that John's Gospel is permeated throughout with statements that indicate that the assumption of the entire perspective of the book is that Jesus is one with the father because he has descended from the father and will ascend to him. In the proto-Trinitarian theological statements, both Paul and John have a number of statements. However, this time the tables are turned. Paul has a number of different statements in several of his letters, while John seems to concentrate upon one section, when he introduces the paraclete.

The results of the analysis can be interpreted in a number of different ways. The usual formulation of the question is to begin with the assumption of John's high Christology and examine how it relates to other New Testament authors, usually seeing it as a culminative high level of development. However, if we change our perspective and compare Paul's letters and John's Gospel, one might well conclude that, whereas John's Gospel has a number of passages subject to interpretation in support of a high Christology, Paul's letters also have several major statements that lay out such a Christology, perhaps even more explicit ones. In that regard, one might well argue that Paul has a higher Christology than does John's Gospel—or at least that they both reveal high Christologies, so much so that it would be difficult to judge between them because, although they have a number of elements in common, they also express their Christologies in differing ways. Paul tends to use more explicit equations, several graphic locative depictions, and numerous proto-Trinitarian passages, while John uses many more implicit equations filled with a variety of imagery despite several explicit ones, more suggestive metaphorical representations of location, and a limited number of proto-Trinitarian passages. Perhaps the best conclusion is to recognize that both have a surprisingly high Christology, but each goes about presenting this Christology in different ways.[42]

Through the years, scholarship has raised the question of what level of interaction might have occurred between Paul and John.[43] If we are to believe that John's Gospel was written from Ephesus[44]—whether it was written pre-AD 70 or AD 80–90 would make a major difference in how one formulates this—one of the Pauline church cities, then there is some reason to believe that John's Gospel might well reflect the influence of Pauline thought or at least reflect similarities. There are no doubt christological similarities between the two authors that suggest they might have had some theological contact. However, the differences far exceed the similarities and make a notion of dependence seem unlikely. If the date of composition of John's Gospel is late in the first century, then this is perhaps an understandable conclusion, because there would be sufficient time for the Pauline church in Ephesus to undergo a

---

42   Cf. G.B. Stevens, "The Theology of Paul and John Compared," *The Biblical World* 3/3 (1894): 166–75.
43   See Wilbert Francis Howard, rev. C.K. Barrett, *The Fourth Gospel in Recent Criticism and Interpretation* (London: Epworth, 1955), passim, for representative studies. Such interaction is already assumed in C.F. Burney, *The Aramaic Origin of the Fourth Gospel* (Oxford: Clarendon, 1922), esp. 132–33, 145–46, who argues for a common rabbinic background.
44   See Sjef van Tilborg, *Reading John in Ephesus* (Leiden: Brill, 1996), who shows how context is important for interpretation.

variety of changes, including some theological ones, before John took up residence to write (however one conceives of the writing process). If the date of composition of John's Gospel is pre-AD 70 and in Ephesus, then the situation becomes even more complex. On the basis of the evidence marshalled above on the comparative Christologies, there is no reason on the basis of this analysis to see John's Christology as appreciably different—and certainly not any higher—than the Christology of Paul's letters. This reason—although admittedly there may be others—is not substantial enough to warrant a separation in their dates of composition. But if they were written from the same general milieu, whether that was Ephesus or some other similar location within the northern Mediterranean, then it would appear that their points of contact and connection—at least so far as Christology is concerned—are minimal.

8 Conclusion

In this study, I have attempted to sketch the Christology of Paul and John as points of comparison regarding the question of how their similar or differing Christologies might reflect upon their relationship and how this might affect reconstructions of early Christianity. On the basis of what I have presented here, despite some differences in language and expression, both John's Gospel and Paul's letters reflect Christologies that have many fundamental similarities. To some extent this conclusion is expected, because when these writers have been considered on their own in the past, numerous scholars have recognized their so-called "high" Christologies. I have attempted to define what these high Christologies might look like by using a grid of three different comparative factors—equative, positional, and proto-Trinitarian statements—as a means of examining how John and Paul represent their Christologies. On the one hand, the findings are that they have relatively equal but differently represented high Christologies, that is, Christologies that represent a high view of Jesus's divinity though in different terms and formulations. On the other hand, while this conclusion would tend to eliminate efforts to distance John's Gospel from the other New Testament writings as representing a high Christology, if John's Gospel and Paul's letters are seen to reflect similar theological development, presumably then John's Gospel could have been written as early as Paul's letters. This conclusion, however, especially in light of thought regarding John's Gospel reflecting a Pauline connection or Pauline school, now encounters its own difficulties in attempting to place John within a pre-AD 70 context.

CHAPTER 2

The Quest for the Messiah: an Inquiry Concerning the Formation of the Johannine Christology

John Painter

Because of the nature and paucity of the relevant evidence and the need to build on conclusions for which there is no consensus, the task of scholarly interpretation may seem futile. In the last 100 years any apparent scholarly consensus has soon disappeared. No doubt one reason for this is that scholars are driven to find original insights, but the main reason is that the early evidence is fragmentary and often ambiguous, leaving plenty of room for speculative hypotheses. The problem of fragmentary evidence is exacerbated by the culture of the time in which it was common *to make use of* the works of others without acknowledgement or concern for accuracy, leading to uncertainty of identification. As far as the Fourth Gospel is concerned, it is near the end of the second century before we have testimony to the authorship of that Gospel, of its relationship to the Epistle(s), Revelation, and to the other Gospels.[1]

1 The Johannine Writings

Methodologically it is appropriate to say something about the complexity of the relationship of the Fourth Gospel to other Johannine writings and the bearing this has on the interpretation of the Christology of the Gospel, an aspect of which is the subject of this chapter and is captured by the title. Possibly four other writings were attributed to the author of the Gospel by the end of the second century, though Revelation and 2 and 3 John remained disputed when Eusebius wrote c. 324 (*Hist. eccl.* 3.24.17–25.7). Only *Revelation* penetrates the veil of

---

[1] See John Painter, *The Quest for the Messiah: The History, Literature and Theology of the Johannine Community* (Edinburgh & Nashville: T&T Clark & Abingdon, 1991; 2nd ed., 1993; 3rd ed., 2002), esp. 1–135; Painter, "The Point of John's Christology: Christology, Community and Conflict in John," in *Christology, Controversy & Community: New Testament Essays in Honour of David R. Catchpole*, ed. David G. Horrell and Christopher M. Tuckett, NovTSup 99 (Leiden: Brill, 2000), 231–52; and Painter, "The Death of Jesus in John: A Discussion of the Tradition, History, and Theology of John," in *The Death of Jesus in the Fourth Gospel*, ed. G. Van Belle (Leuven: Leuven University Press, 2007), 327–61.

anonymity revealing the *name* John as its author (Rev 1:1, 4, 9; 22:8). Though Irenaeus argued that the Gospel, at least one Epistle, and Revelation were the work of the Beloved Disciple, whom he identified as John the son of Zebedee, the authorship of Revelation was questioned quite early. Irenaeus appealed to his relationship to Papias as a hearer of John (*Adv. haer.* 5.33.4) and to Polycarp (*Adv. haer.* 3.39.1) as the basis of his view.

1.1 The Fourth Gospel

One of the best-attested early views, and one that has been commonly held since then, is that *John* is the Fourth Gospel. Eusebius outlines the work of the apostle John in Asia (*Hist. eccl.* 3.23) before referring to his Gospel, "for it was reasonable for the ancients to mention it in the fourth place after the other three ..." (*Hist. eccl.* 3.24.2). Later he appeals to the witness of two of these ancients. First, Irenaeus (c. 180) placed John as the last of the four Gospels setting out what became the canonical order as well as the chronological order (*Adv. haer.* 3.1.1–2 and see Eusebius, *Hist. eccl.* 5.8.2–4). Eusebius adopts the same order in his summary found in *Hist. eccl.* 3.24.6–7. He also refers to Clement of Alexandria's now lost *Outlines* (*Hypotyposes*), where he placed John last of the four Gospels (*Hist. eccl.* 6.14.4b–7). While the Synoptic order varies in these testimonies, the place of John as fourth/last does not.

That John is the Fourth Gospel is reflected in the nature of its composition. It is manifestly the fruit of long and deep reflection in which the interpretative language and style of the evangelist have shaped and illuminated both the narrative and discourse material. Consequently, the narrator and Jesus both speak the Johannine language. More surprisingly, so does the man sent from God whose name was John.

Thus, it is likely that the author knew the other Gospels, though it is clear he did not use them as sources *in the way* that Mathew or Luke seem to have used Mark. Rather, the fourth evangelist has reflected on the life and teaching of Jesus so long and deeply, that narrative and discourse are now expressed in terms of his own thought. Following C.H. Dodd, who found evidence of an independent stream of tradition in the Fourth Gospel and found it to be Synoptic-like, I take the distinctively Johannine characteristics to be the work of the author.[2] I leave open the extent to which the author may have drawn on Synoptic tradition as distinct from Synoptic-like tradition, though the Gospel

---

2 See C.H. Dodd, *Historical Tradition in the Fourth Gospel* (Cambridge: Cambridge University Press, 1963).

seems to reveal connections with Mark at least.[3] All of this has implications for the Christology of the Fourth Gospel (FG).

1.2 *The Gospel and Revelation*

Eusebius notes that the Gospel and 1 John were received as authentic, but 2 and 3 John and Revelation remained disputed (*Hist. eccl.* 3.24.17–25.7). He set out to discredit the basis of the testimony of Irenaeus concerning the apostolic authorship of Revelation. To do this he appeals to Papias's Preface to his five books (*The Sayings of the Lord Explained*) to show that Papias was not a hearer of John the apostle but of his follower John the Elder (*Hist. eccl.* 3.39.1–7). What drove Eusebius to identify the Elder with Revelation was the strong conviction that Revelation, whose author reveals himself as John, was not written by the same author as the Gospel. Thus, he argues that Irenaeus was mistaken in attributing Revelation to the apostle.[4] Indeed, differences between the Gospel and Revelation make the view of common authorship precarious. Dionysius of Alexandria (d. 264/5) challenged the view of common authorship by the apostle on stylistic grounds long before Eusebius produced his argument based on a dubious reading of the Papias Preface.[5] Thus the challenge to the common authorship of the Gospel and Revelation is not just a modern view, nor was it an innovation by Eusebius.

Eusebius identified John the Elder as the author of Revelation and the apostle as the author of the Gospel and 1 John. Given that the author of 2 and 3 John identifies himself as "the Elder" we might wonder why John the Elder was not identified with this author. Paradoxically, some modern scholars have identified the Elder as the author of the Gospel, linking the apostle with Revelation. Though the differences are overwhelming, some significant Johannine features are found in Revelation, leading C.K. Barrett to conclude that the authors of the

---

3 On this see the second edition of C.K. Barrett's *The Gospel according to St John* (London: SPCK, 1978), 42–54. See also John Painter, "The Fourth Gospel and the Founder of Christianity," in *Engaging with C.H. Dodd on the Gospel of John*, ed. Tom Thatcher and Catrin H. Williams (Cambridge: Cambridge University Press, 2013), 257–80, esp. 267–75.

4 Because Papias's work has not survived independently, we are dependent on Eusebius for the preservation of the Preface. Even as reported by him it is open to Irenaeus's reading. See Craig S. Keener, *The Gospel of John: A Commentary*, 2 vols. (Peabody: Hendrickson, 2003), 2:95–98.

5 See Barrett, *St John*, 105–9, 132–34; and R.H. Charles, *Revelation*, 2 vols., ICC (Edinburgh: T&T Clark, 1920), 1:xxxvii. Charles considered that he completed the work of Dionysius of Alexandria (d. 264–265) in providing evidence for rejecting common authorship of Revelation and the Gospel because the two works are very different in their use of language, symbolism, point of view, and expression of theology.

Gospel and Revelation each belonged to the Johannine School.[6] Nevertheless, Revelation is of marginal interest for the Christology of the Gospel.

1.3   The Gospel and Epistles

The case is different with the Johannine Epistles, in terms of both their relation to the Gospel, and their potential to influence the interpretation of its Christology. Eusebius recognized the Gospel and 1 John as authentic works of the apostle John. They are closely associated, whether or not by a common author, and 2 and 3 John are closely associated with each other, as are 1 and 2 John.[7] Some scholars distinguish the author of 1 John from the Elder of 2 and 3 John, but the absence of this address from 1 John is better explained by the recognition that it is not a popular Hellenistic letter as they are. The overlap in content between 1 and 2 John supports common authorship, as does the early evidence of their use together by Polycarp (*Phil.* 6.3; 7.1–2) and Irenaeus (*Adv. haer.* 1.16.3; 3.16.5, 8).[8] The shared Hellenistic letterform unites 2 and 3 John. The more formal tract or homily *genre* of 1 John, with its wide-ranging content, accounts for its differences from these brief Hellenistic letters.

Common authorship of the Gospel and first Epistle was traditional from the time of Irenaeus. However, because of differences between them, many scholars conclude that they are the works of different authors. I once sought to explain the differences on the basis of their very different circumstance of writing.[9] I remain convinced that the Gospel was fashioned by a Jewish author in the context of Jewish life and community, while 1 John (and 2 and 3 John) reflects community life somewhere in the Roman Empire where Jewish life and culture are not evident or important. The Gospel is redolent with scriptural allusion and quotation, which are absent from the Epistles.[10] The author of the Gospel was Jewish and writing for Jewish readers and has colored his description of Jesus's conflict with Jewish authorities in a way that reflects the later conflicts of Jewish believers. The best-known example is in John 9, where action is taken against the once blind man, while Jesus walks authoritatively free. Unlike any other story in the Gospel, John 9 is the story of the once blind

---

6   See Barrett, *St John*, 132–34.
7   See John Painter, *1, 2, and 3 John*, SP 18 (Collegeville: Liturgical Press, 2002), 51–57.
8   See Painter, *1, 2, and 3 John*, 41–42.
9   John Painter, *John Witness and Theologian* (London: SPCK, 1975) and subsequent editions, 103–8.
10 The reference to Cain in 1 John 3:12 seems to be an exception, but is dependent on John 8:39–44, not on Gen 4:1–16. Like the Gospel, 1 John 3:12 goes beyond Genesis, attributing murder to the Evil One. Neither the Gospel nor 1 John mentions Abel by name. See Painter, *1, 2, and 3 John*, 232–34.

man rather than of Jesus. Jesus is absent from 9:8–34, appearing only at the beginning (9:1–7) and the end (9:35–38). Indeed, it is the man who is cast out, not Jesus, who continues to act with authority until the end (9:35–41). I prefer to describe this as the sporadic reflection of the story of the believers in the telling of the story of Jesus than as two levels of story.[11] The conclusion of the chapter (9:39–41) becomes an opportunity for Jesus to speak, ostensibly to the Pharisees, but especially to the reader, about the purpose of his coming into the world (cf. 3:19–21). In this respect, Jesus's voice functions like that of the narrator, speaking directly to the reader.

The Gospel itself implies a process of growth over a long period of time, probably being shaped in the reflection, teaching, and preaching of the author. It involves "watersheds" caused by crises in the lives of Jewish believers in Jesus in the region of the author.[12] John 9 is the fruit of one of these watersheds, which has shaped the tradition that became the Gospel so that the telling of the story of Jesus reflects and is colored by comparable events in the lives of the author and the Jewish believers around him. Here I am thinking about the shaping in the mind of the author, the evangelist. It is likely that a small school gathered around him and members of it were unevenly but more closely influenced than a wider group. Much of the influence and shaping probably took place in the context of the broader Jewish community without social separation. But the Gospel contains tradition that reflects growing tensions and conflicts with the broader Jewish community.[13]

The transition from the Gospel to the Epistles is marked by a move from a Jewish world to the Roman world in which Jewish presence is not apparent. In some places there were strong concentrations of Jewish population while in others, even in the same city, there was no marked Jewish presence. The Gospel belongs to the one and the Epistles to the other. The difference is also temporal. The Gospel came first and the Epistles came later and 1 John is dependent on the Gospel. Similarities between the Gospel and the Epistle are explicable in terms of the Johannine School so that the author of the Epistles was probably Jewish, but is writing to readers who did not share his Jewish roots.[14] Because none of the Epistles addresses life in a Jewish community,

---

11   J.L. Martyn, *History and Theology in the Fourth Gospel*, 3rd ed. (Louisville: WJK, 2003 [orig. 1968]) was right to focus on John 9 for evidence of the way the conflict of believers with Jewish authorities shaped the way the Gospel describes Jesus's conflict with them. His book changed the direction of John studies. See Painter, *1, 2, and 3 John*, 10–12.

12   See Painter, "The Death of Jesus in John," 327–61, esp. 332–41.

13   For the relevance to John's Christology, see Painter, "The Point of John's Christology," 231–52.

14   See C.K. Barrett, *The Gospel of John and Judaism* (London: SPCK, 1975), Chapter 2.

I conclude that they come from a time later than the situation within which the Gospel was shaped. While working on the Epistles I became convinced by H.J. Holtzmann that, *if the same author wrote* the Gospel and 1 John, then the Epistle must have been significantly earlier than the Gospel to allow opportunity for the significant literary and theological development evidenced in the Gospel. Because I am convinced that the Epistles follow the Gospel and depend on it, like Holtzmann I conclude that the Gospel and Epistles have different authors and that the author of the Epistles was thoroughly familiar with the Gospel, if not fully in command of the profundity of its message in form and content.[15]

1.4   The Epistles and the Christology of John

In treating the Christology of the Gospel, Udo Schnelle asserts the temporal priority of the Epistles. Building on the work of his mentor and colleague Georg Strecker, he argues that the Epistles came first and were followed by the Gospel, and that the Gospel, like 1 and 2 John, opposes Docetism with an anti-docetic Christology.[16] He argues that the Epistles and Gospel are the work of different members of the Johannine School. One author, referred to as John the Elder by Papias in the fragment preserved by Eusebius (*Hist. eccl.* 3.39.4), first wrote 2 John, then 3 John; a second member of the school wrote 1 John, and finally a third wrote the Gospel. John the Elder was the founder of the School and the docetic controversy underlies all writings. The sequence of Epistles before the Gospel provides an interpretative basis for an anti-docetic interpretation of the Gospel.[17]

Contrary to this I argue that the Gospel came first, the work of the founder of the Johannine School. 1 John is dependent on the Gospel and was used in the house church of the Elder, who then circulated it to related house churches with 2 John as the covering letter. 3 John followed to deal with an emerging crisis concerning hospitality.[18] My reading builds on the recognition of the Jewishness of the Gospel in contrast with the absence of any sign of Jewish presence in the Epistles. The Gospel, unlike 1 and 2 John, does not confront

---

15 See H.J. Holtzmann, "Der Problem des ersten Johanneischen Briefes in seinem verhältnis zum Evangelium," *Jahrbücher für protestantische Theologie*, Art. I in 7 (1881), 690–712; Art. II in 8 (1882), 128–52; Art. III in 8 (1882), 316–42; Art. IV in 8 (1882), 460–85; and in his commentaries *Evangelium, Briefe, und Offenbarung des Johannes,* Hand Kommentar zum Neuen Testament 4 (Freiburg: Mohr, 1890, 1910). See also Painter, *1, 2, and 3 John*, 3, 7, 26, 64, 68, 111.

16 See esp. Georg Strecker, *The Johannine Letters* (Minneapolis: Fortress, 1996); and Udo Schnelle, *Antidocetic Christology in the Gospel of John*, trans. Linda M. Maloney (Minneapolis: Fortress, 1992 [German org. 1987]).

17 See Schnelle, *Antidocetic Christology*, 47–54, 71–73.

18 See Painter, *1, 2, and 3 John*, 51–77.

those who have a docetic view of Jesus but those who reject the revelation of God in Jesus, in his words and actions. See John 1:14–18; 3:34–35; 5:17–23; 8:58–59; 10:28–33, especially 10:33. The Christology of the Gospel should be read in its own terms, in the literary context of the Gospel, and the Jewish social context that it reveals. No one questions the humanity of Jesus in the Gospel, rather there is violent reaction to his claim that God is present, acting and speaking in him (3:31–34; 5:17, 19–20, 30, 36; 8:26–29, 38, 40, 47; 15:15).

2 The Quest for the Messiah

The title chosen for this contribution gives expression to a literary theme in the Fourth Gospel and also to the quest the text of the Gospel evokes for the reader. Both of these quests find expression in the opening chapter of the Gospel in the person named John, both in the prologue and the body of the Gospel.

The subtitle refers to *an inquiry concerning the formation of the Johannine Christology* and this relates *more* to the literary function of the Gospel for the reader than to the factors shaping the views of the author. The quest for the Messiah leads to Christology and Christology leads to theology. In this context the quest for the Messiah is the symbol for the quest for God and participates in the reality of what is symbolized.

2.1 *The Prologue and Its Transforming Perspectives*

The prologue initiates the reader, in a consistently Jewish way, into the quest for the Messiah. In so doing it transforms messianic views and deepens the vision of God by means of the motif of the Father/Son relationship, initiated in the prologue.

2.1.1 God, Creation and Christology

The opening words of the prologue, "In the beginning ..." resonate with the opening words of the creation story of Gen 1:1, where God *calls* the creation into being, "And God *said* ..." (1:3, 6, 9, 11, 14, 20, 24, 26). The Psalmist interprets "said" imaginatively and creatively as "By the *Word* of the Lord were the heavens made, and all their host by the *breath* of his mouth" (Ps 33:6). The prologue also deals with creation, but not before revealing the λόγος in relation to God. For this the interpretative move in Ps 33:6 is helpful, as is the Wisdom Literature where the overlapping motifs of Wisdom, Word, and Spirit are used creatively to develop the themes of creation, providence and revelation. The newly introduced metaphors of Wisdom and *breath*, given its alternative expression of *spirit*, are joined with λόγος. See Wis 7:7; 9:17; Sir 24:3; Gen 1:2–3; Ps 33:6. "In the beginning" echoes Gen 1:1, but the first fourteen verses of the prologue seem to have been creatively and imaginatively woven together from Prov 3; 8; Wis 7–8; Sir 24 and *1 En.* 42.[19] The narrative of the revelation of the Word made flesh, culminating in the believing witness, "and we beheld his glory …" was the evangelist's creative achievement, by means of a synthesis of elements that were already converging in the Wisdom Literature.[20]

The *narrator* reveals the presence and status of the λόγος in relation to the Father/God (cf. 1:1 and 1:18), culminating in the role of the λόγος as God's agent in the creation of all things (1:1–3). The consequent shining of the light of the life of the λόγος in the darkness follows (1:4–5).

2.1.2 The Role of the Witness of John

John is then identified as a witness to the coming of the true light into the world (1:6–9). The *narrator reveals* that the purpose of John's mission was to bear witness to the true light, the life-giving light of the λόγος that was coming into the world (1:7, 9). No words of John are given here. His introduction at this point prepares the way for the transformation of the words of the historical John (from 1:27) by introducing them in the prologue at 1:15. They are *narrated* when Jesus appears on the scene in the context of John's baptizing mission (1:19–28) and are thrown forward into the prologue in the second phase of John's witness (1:15). There, John's words are shaped by the initial introduction of John in 1:6–8 and their new literary context in the communal confession of faith in response to the revelation of glory in the incarnation and exaltation of Jesus in his *return* to the bosom of the Father (1:14, 16–18). In the midst of the reported anonymous witness, "*we* beheld his glory …," only the witness of John is identified in 1:15. The corporate witness ("we") in 1:14 continues in 1:16–18, having been interrupted by John's witness in 1:15. The response of faith is not only to the incarnation, but also to the *return* of the Son to the bosom of the Father (1:18; cf. 1:1).

---

[19] See J. Rendel Harris, *The Origin of the Prologue of St John's Gospel* (Cambridge: Cambridge University Press, 1917), esp. 4–5; C.H. Dodd, *The Interpretation of the Fourth Gospel* (Cambridge: Cambridge University Press, 1953), esp. 274–75; Painter, *Quest for the Messiah*, esp. 146–47.

[20] See John Painter, "The Prologue of John: Bridge into a New World," in *Bible, Borders, and Belonging(s): Engaging Readings from Oceania*, ed. Jione Havea, David J. Neville, and Elaine M. Wainwright (Atlanta: SBL, 2014), 73–92; John Painter, "The Prologue as an Hermeneutical Key to Reading the Fourth Gospel," in *Studies in the Gospel of John and its Christology*, ed. Joseph Verheyden, Geert Van Oyen, Michael Labahn, and Reimund Bieringer (Leuven: Peeters, 2014), 37–60; and John Painter, "Sacrifice and Atonement in the Gospel of John," in *Israel und seine Heilstraditionen im Johannesevangelium*, ed. Michael Labahn, Klaus Scholtissek, and Angelika Strotmann (Paderborn: Ferdinand Schöningh, 2004), 287–313, esp. 294–96.

2.1.3   Incarnation Viewed from the Perspective of Exaltation

The prologue is written from the perspective of the return of the Son (λόγος/ μονογενὴς θεός) to the bosom of the Father. It speaks of the beginning and creation *from* that perspective. Thus 1:18 provides an illuminating *inclusio* with 1:1b, ὁ λόγος ἦν πρὸς τὸν θεόν. The perspective of the prologue is a vision constituted by the completed story and the belief it evoked.[21] The advantage of this view is open to the reader. The only narrative person to appear in the prologue, apart from the λόγος made flesh, is the witness named John.[22]

John is the identified voice of witness amongst the otherwise anonymous witnesses to the completed work of the incarnate λόγος (1:14, 16–18). Only he, and the incarnate λόγος, bridge the prologue and the body of the Gospel. In a literary sense, the narrator, who is responsible for 1:1–13, is also a bridge. There are places where the narrator explicitly provides the reader with an "end" perspective not available to the participants at the time (2:21–22; 12:16). The reader has the benefits of these "asides," as well as the prologue, which provides a second level reading of the story as a whole, along with John 17. In addition, there are occasions when a speaker seems to lose his dialogue partner, so that what is said seems to be directed to the reader alone. This is true in Jesus's dialogue with Nicodemus in 3:1–21. Somewhere along the way, Nicodemus, who came to Jesus out of the night, apparently vanishes into the night again, probably after 3:12. In what follows (3:13–21), Jesus functions as narrator, whose words provide a second level understanding, and are addressed directly to the reader. This is true also of the dialogue of John with his disciples in 3:22–36. At 3:31 his disciples seem to have disappeared and, although there is no indication of change of voice, what follows is a monologue, which, like 3:13–21, is relevant to the reader as a second level narrator's discourse. We could say that the narrator and John speak with the voice of the Johannine Jesus.

2.1.4   Reader Perspective and Narrative Perspective in the Gospel

Although, for the reader, the Gospel as a whole is *written* from the perspective of the end, in the Jesus tradition embodied in the Gospel, the disciples and others lack this view, which is shared only by Jesus, the narrator, and John. The end perspective is explicit in the prologue, and John 17. The prologue is implicitly addressed to the reader, as are the notes of 2:22 and 12:16, which relate a second

---

21   It is, however, the beginning that constitutes the "worldview" of the Gospel (see 1:4–5; 3:19–21; 8:12; 9:5, 39–41; 12:35–36, 46), from which flow much of the literary development of the Gospel.

22   Significantly, the λόγος made flesh is identified as "Jesus Christ" only in 1:17 and 17:3, in a prayer addressed to God ("Father"), written from the perspective of Jesus's completed mission, and overheard only by the reader.

level understanding for the reader along the way, while the "prayer" (or discourse on mission) of John 17 is overheard by the reader. It is explicitly directed to the Father, without any suggestion that it was overheard by the disciples. In it, Jesus speaks as one who is no longer in the world, 17:11. The prayer is for the disciples and those who believe through them, who remain to complete God's work for the world. The commission of the disciples to continue God's mission in the world is reported in the prayer (17:18), although it is not narrated until John 20:21. This signals the end perspective of John 17.

Of course, the other Gospels were also written after the resurrection, but it is generally agreed, they keep closer touch with historical tradition, which has not been as thoroughly transformed by resurrection faith as the Fourth Gospel, though the birth stories of Matthew and Luke move in that direction. Even these fall short of John 1:14, and its Christological implications in the Gospel as a whole.

2.1.5 Conclusion Concerning the Role of the Prologue

If the prologue begins "In the beginning … the λόγος was *with* God," it concludes with the incarnate and exalted λόγος in the bosom of the Father, forming an *inclusio* between 1:1 and 1:18. Indeed, 1:18 elucidates the πρὸς τὸν θεόν of 1:1. In this context, John also speaks from the perspective of the completed life of Jesus and his exaltation. The post exaltation perspective is especially clear in 1:18, which refers to the "only begotten God who is in the bosom of the Father, he has made God known" (ἐκεῖνος ἐξηγήσατο) (whom no one has seen). If John has been drawn forward into the prologue, his witness has also been adapted to the opening theme of the prologue making the reader aware of *the beginning* and the priority of the incarnate λόγος (1:1–5). Thus, the traditional words of John in 1:27 are recalled and transformed by the recognition of the absolute priority of the one who comes after him, ὅτι πρῶτός μου ἦν (in 1:15 and 1:30). Did the "follower" emerge as one who took absolute priority as the incarnate λόγος emerged with the completed mission of Jesus (1:18). The traditional saying of 1:27 is radically transformed in 1:15 by the impact of the prologue's dual perspectives of the absolute beginning seen from the completion of the mission of the incarnate λόγος. When the historical traditional saying of 1:27 is repeated the next day in 1:30, it is in the transformed wording of 1:15, it is with part of the traditional saying not used in 1:27. See 1:33.

2.2 *The Narrative Quest for the Messiah*

While the witness of John uncovers an underlying quest for the Messiah as the context of his mission, he reveals that his mission has another source, that underlying the human quest is the divine quest, mission, 1:6, 33–34. This double quest forms the basic structure of this chapter: the narrative human quest for the Messiah; and the divine quest or mission to bring life to the world. "Jesus is himself portrayed as a quester. These stories mesh into the distinctive presentation of Jesus and his mission, as one sent from above, sent by the Father."[23] Both the prologue and the initial scenes of John's witness reveal the quest for the Messiah and begin to unveil this mission, being an essential part of it.

2.2.1 Transition

The opening narrative (1:19ff.) begins, "Now this is the witness of John ..." referring back to 1:15, "John bore witness saying ..." The overlap of the saying in 1:15 with the saying in 1:27, and its repetition in 1:30, make the connection clear, though the agreement between 1:15 and 1:30 against the traditional form of 1:27 is suggestive. In this narrative context John's witness initiates the historical mission of Jesus.

The narrative beginning of 1:19–51 introduces a carefully constructed sequence of four scenes over the course of four days. The first three scenes of 1:19–42 involve John: First, John and the inquiry through the delegation from Jerusalem, which reveals the quest for the Messiah, 1:19–28; Second, John and Jesus, where John announces Jesus as the "lamb of God," "the coming one," to no internal audience but to the reader and in a way that reflects the perspective of the prologue, 1:29–34; Third, John bears witness to two of his disciples in the presence of Jesus, 1:35–42. In these three scenes the focus is shifting from John to Jesus; Fourth scene, John has disappeared and the focus is on Jesus and his disciples, 1:43–51.

2.2.2 An Inquiry Reveals a Quest 1:19–28

The first scene, day one (1:19–28) is an *inquiry story* that introduces the messianic question and leads to John's response in a way that strongly suggests connections with the Synoptic tradition (see John 1:23, 26–27, 30–33; Mark 1:3, 7–8; Matt 3:3, 11–12; Luke 3:4, 15–17; Acts 13:25).[24] First, there is reason to note the distinctive setting of 1:19–28, and sequence it initiates. The inquiry story of 1:19–28 uncovers John's quest for the Messiah. The narrative describes the sending of a delegation of priests and Levites (identified as Pharisees in 1:24) by the Jews of Jerusalem to question John, asking "Who are you?" Although this appears to be an open question, his preaching and baptizing activity raised

---

23 See Painter, *Quest for the Messiah* [2002], 8–9, 22. The quotation is p. 22.
24 See Painter, *Quest for the Messiah*, 5–31, 163–88 and esp. 166–77 concerning Inquiry stories. See also the earlier John Painter, "Quest Stories in John and the Synoptics," in *John and the Synoptics*, ed. Adelbert Denaux (Leuven: Leuven University Press, 1992), 498–506.

the Messianic question. John's answer, "I am not the *Christ*" (cf. 1:41), implies recognition of the underlying question, "Are you (or do you claim to be) the Messiah?" This assumption is confirmed by the follow up questions, "If you are not the Christ, are you Elijah? Are you the Prophet?" To each of these questions John answered "No." At this point the delegation shows some frustration, as if to say, denying that you are any of these does not answer our opening question, "Then who are you? [Tell us] that we may give an answer to those who sent us." To this John famously replied,

> I am the voice of one crying in the wilderness,
> Make straight the *way* of the Lord,
> Just as Isaiah the prophet said.
> 1:23, quoting ISA 40:3. Cf. MARK 1:3; MATT 3:3; LUKE 3:4

John, like the sect at Qumran, interpreted his presence in the wilderness of Judaea in the light of this text from Isaiah (cf. 1QS 8.13). The complexity of messianic figures inquired about by the delegation is also reflected in their writings (1QS 9.9–11 and 4Q 175). Thus, although not the common-view today, the opening narrative of the Fourth Gospel suggests a widespread messianic expectation in the Palestine of Jesus's day.[25] In the Fourth Gospel, messianic language is not used until John's answer in 1:20 unveils the hidden question of 1:19.

John's answer to renewed questions sets out his relation to the coming one in terms of Isa 40:3. This provoked the delegation to ask a new question. If he was not the Messiah, Elijah, or the Prophet, *why did he baptize?* (1:25). John's response in 1:26–27 does not answer this question. Rather, he contrasts himself

---

25   Absence of evidence of this in the early Rabbinic writings is not surprising following two disastrous revolts (in 66 and 132 CE), the second of which certainly had messianic overtones. Emerging Rabbinic Judaism adopted a mode of community building in which the role of the Messiah had no prominent or important place. See Jacob Neusner, *Messiah in Context: Israel's History and Destiny in Formative Judaism* (Philadelphia: Fortress, 1984). See the review by John Painter in *AbrN* 28 (1990): 139–42. Though Josephus took part in the first revolt, he had no reason to look kindly on those he *later blamed* for the disastrous outcome. By the time he wrote his earlier work dealing with the *Jewish War*, the Roman conquerors had become his patrons, and he blamed a rabble he names as Zealots for the revolt. In his later work, *Antiquities of the Jews*, he acknowledges the role of the Jewish ruling class, of which he was a part. Josephus had reason to play down the place and importance of messianic expectations in the history he recorded. In spite of this, he records the role of a number of "signs prophets" in the first half of the first century. Though he brands them as imposters, it is likely that they were widely regarded as messianic figures at the time. See Painter, *Quest for the Messiah*, 259–66, for details and discussion.

and his baptism with the greater one who was coming after him, the straps of whose sandals he was not worthy to loose. Reference to the purpose of his baptism and the superior baptism of the coming one is deferred to the next scene 1:30–33. The narrator concludes this scene (1:19–28) with reference to the location, in Bethany beyond the Jordan, where John was baptizing (1:28, cf. 10:41–42). The delegation disappears without further ado, and without an answer, but the reader has been awakened to the messianic question. The question of John's place among messianic figures receives an answer in the next scene, too late for the delegation, but not for the reader.

The character of 1:19–28 as an inquiry story is borne out by the focus on the question and answer, and the disappearance of the delegation once their question had been asked and given a detailed, if unsatisfactory, answer. The questions concerned the Messiah and revealed the complexity of John's role. Failure to answer the question of why John baptizes makes this scene a transition to the next.

Overlap with the Synoptic tradition includes John's reference to himself as the voice crying in the wilderness (of Isa 40:3), his contrast of his baptism with that of the one coming after him, and John's words in 1:27, "The one coming after me, I am not worthy to loose the strap of his sandals." But the reference to the contrasting baptism by the coming one is moved to the events of the following day, placing it with John's explanation of the purpose of his baptizing activity (1:31–34), and following the transformed saying in 1:30, which recalls 1:27 more or less in its transformed 1:15 form.

2.2.3 John and Jesus 1:29–34

On the second day (τῇ ἐπαύριον) a new scene is introduced. Unlike the previous scene and the one that follows, no audience within the text is mentioned in this scene, which gives the fullest account of the nature and purpose of John's activity, and of the one he came to reveal. The narrator tells that when John saw Jesus approaching he announces, "Behold the lamb of God who bears away the sin of the world." This is not addressed to Jesus or to any other person in the narrative, but directly to the reader, for whom alone this scene is written.[26] The saying is repeated in abbreviated form on the next (third) day, this time with an audience (1:35–36), but without the reformed saying of 1:30, or the fuller version of John's statement about the purpose of his baptism, distinguishing it from the baptism of the coming one, which is the appropriate answer to the question of the delegation in 1:25. If John is none of those

---

26 When characters within the narrative address only the reader they provide internal commentary and take on the role of the narrator.

eschatological figures, "Why do you baptize?" Here, with no audience but the reader, John says plainly that he did so in order to reveal the coming one to Israel, 1:31–32.

This intermediate scene distances John's reference to the baptism of the coming one from the Synoptic form of the Baptist's saying in 1:27, placing it after the transformed saying of 1:15, now repeated in 1:30. John again speaks in the presence of Jesus, "This *is* he concerning whom I said, 'after me comes *a man* who has become before me ὅτι πρῶτός μου ἦν.'" The introduction of ἀνὴρ may be responsible for the minor grammatical changes. Otherwise the saying agrees with 1:15 against 1:27.[27]

Though this saying *recalls* the saying from the previous day, it no longer concerns the unworthiness of the witness. Rather, with slight grammatical variations, it follows 1:15, to affirm the absolute priority of the one who comes after John. Only after this saying is the contrasting baptism of the coming one identified by John. But first John reveals that he was sent to baptize in order to identify and reveal the coming one to Israel, 1:31–33. Though the baptism of Jesus by John is not mentioned in this Gospel, it seems to be presupposed. Here it is said that it was John who saw the Spirit descending and abiding on Jesus, fulfilling the designated sign to identify the coming one, who baptizes with the Holy Spirit. John concludes this scene with his witness (1:34), "And I have seen and borne witness that this person is the Son of God." In the Markan account, it is possibly Jesus who sees the Spirit descending on him (Mark 1:10), and the voice from heaven addresses Jesus, "You are my beloved son …" (1:11). But the Fourth Gospel has taken John to be the one who saw and bore witness, "This is the Son of God." In so doing, John becomes the first witness to explicitly express the Son of God Christology, but only to the reader (cf. 3:29–34; 10:40–41).

2.2.4 John, Jesus, and Two Disciples 1:35–42

On the third day (τῇ ἐπαύριον) John initiates the quest of two of his disciples (1:35–42) with its consequences (1:43–51). The Baptist's quest culminates when his witness initiates the quest of two of his disciples in 1:35–37 and they follow Jesus. When Jesus observes them *following*, he speaks for the first time in this Gospel. The first words of the incarnate Word are significant, "What are you *seeking*?" (τί ζητεῖτε;) (1:38).[28] Jesus acknowledges their initiative in what

---

27   That Jesus is a man is an unstressed and uncontested observation. The paradoxical recognition of his priority is the point of the text. See 5:18; 8:52–59; 10:30–33.

28   This question occurs in a sequence of scenes initiated by the delegation from the Jews of Jerusalem asking John if he is the Messiah. In response, John turns attention to the one he was commissioned to reveal to Israel, which he does in this scene. As a result, two of his disciples follow Jesus. This is the context of his first words, spoken to them.

becomes a significant pattern in this Gospel of disciples *seeking* Jesus rather than Jesus calling them. They answer, "Where do you *dwell* [*abide*]?" (ποῦ μένεις;), using an expression that is given a depth of meaning in the discourses of Jesus. Jesus answered, "Come and *you will see*" (ἔρχεσθε καὶ ὄψεσθε). This appears to be a command with a promise to those who obey. "So they came and they saw where he *abides* ..." (1:39). Given the depth of meaning of this word in the discourses of Jesus (especially John 15), it is likely that seeing where Jesus was to *stay* that night did not exhaust the meaning.[29] The narrative reveals the marks of a successful quest-story sequence. Andrew, one of the two disciples who followed Jesus, first found his brother Simon and says to him, "We have *found* the *Messiah* [which is translated *Christos*] and he led him to Jesus" (1:40–41). Jesus's considered response was to rename Simon as "*Cephas* (which is translated *Petros*)." In each case an Aramaic word/name is given its Greek equivalent by the narrator. Both the affirmation of Andrew and the response of Jesus confirm a successful quest for the *Messiah*. That Semitic term is transliterated only here (1:41) and in 4:25 in the New Testament, and in each case the narrator supplies the Greek translation.

2.2.5   Jesus Moves to Galilee and the Quest Continues 1:43–51

On the fourth day (τῇ ἐπαύριον) Jesus chose to go to Galilee, where he *found* Philip, who, like Andrew and *Peter*, was from Bethsaida. That the narrator chose to tell us of the association of these three suggests that Andrew and Peter had something to do with the decision.[30] When Jesus called Philip to follow him, Philip went and found Nathanael, initiating another successful sequence ending with a confession, "Rabbi, you are the son of God, you are the king of Israel," a messianic confession open to a deeper meaning that is reinforced by Jesus's response, which implies the need to take this confession to another level, "You will see the heaven opened and the angels of God ascending and descending on the Son of Man" (1:49–51).

Significant words, just two in Greek, the second being a frequent word in this Gospel (34 times and only 39 times in the Synoptics). This context, which portrays inquiry/quest for the Messiah is reinforced by Jesus's question, τί ζητεῖτε.

29   It is possible that the fulfillment is alluded to by Jesus in the promise to Nathanael in 1:51. On such a reading, "*you will see* the heavens opened" (1:51) suggests vision into the presence of God, where the only begotten is in the bosom of the Father, 1:18.

30   The ambiguity arises because 1:41 says that Andrew *first* finds his brother Simon, implying *second*. Then 1:43 is not explicit about who wished to go into Galilee. Further, it is explicitly noted that Philip was from the town of Andrew and Peter.

3 Transition from Messiah to Christology

This transition is signaled in three places in the first chapter: at the beginning and end of the prologue (1:1 and 17–18); in John's last words in the opening scenes of 1:19ff. (1:34); and in Jesus's dialogue with Nathanael (1:49–51).

First, the prologue deals with the relationship of the λόγος to God in 1:1, then the incarnate, crucified, and exalted λόγος is spoken of "as an *only-begotten* from the Father" (1:14), and "the *only-begotten* God in the bosom of *the Father*" in 1:18. The parallel uses of μονογενής in 3:16, 18 raise interesting questions. God is spoken of as Father in 1:14 and 18, and Jesus is spoken of as *God's only-begotten Son* in 3:16, 18. In neither case does the expected pairing of Father and Son occur, though in each case the one implies the other, and the Father Son relationship is the key category for the Johannine Christology.

Second, accepting that to be the case, the final words of John in 1:34, "This is the Son of God," take on greater weight. Two elements in the narrative confirm this. First, the transformed saying in 1:30 asserts the absolute priority of the one who comes after John, giving John's final words added depth, "And I have seen and borne witness that this is the Son of God" (1:34). Second, John indicates the purpose of his water baptism was to reveal the coming one and "he will baptize with the Holy Spirit" (1:31–33). John, who begins as the forerunner of the Messiah, becomes the one who unveils the Son of God.[31] The linking of John's baptizing activity with the sign revealing Jesus as the coming one seems to presuppose the Synoptic tradition (John 1:31–33; Matt 3:16–17; Mark 1:10–11; Luke 3:21–22) where the voice from heaven declares "You are (This is) my beloved Son" (Matt 3:17; Mark 1:11; Luke 3:22) at the baptism of Jesus. In the Fourth Gospel the witness John performs the role of the heavenly voice, "This is the Son of God."

Third, the messianic confessions of Andrew (1:41) and Nathanael (1:49) are challenged by the promised vision of greater things, the heavenly vision of angels converging on the Son of Man (1:51).[32]

3.1 *The Father/Son Relationship*

While the relationship of the λόγος to God is illuminated implicitly by the Wisdom tradition, the inclusion of 1:1 with 1:18 implicitly introduces the Father/Son relationship. The agency of the λόγος (1:3, cf. 1:10) and of the Son (see 3:35;

---

[31] Certainly 1:31–34 presuppose the tradition that the Messiah would remain hidden until the moment he was revealed, and this is the point of 1:34. See also 7:3–13, 25–31 and Painter, *Quest for the Messiah*, 171–74, 290–93. The one greater than the Messiah is here.

[32] See John Painter, "The Church and Israel in the Gospel of John: A Response," *NTS* 25 (1978): 103–12, esp. 109–10; and Painter, *Quest for the Messiah*, 187–88.

5:17, 19–20) are also mutually illuminating. Thus, the λόγος made flesh reveals the glory of God as δόξαν ὡς μονογενοῦς παρὰ πατρός, making the unseen Father known (1:14, 18). Though the λόγος made flesh is from the Father and has returned to the bosom of the Father having made the unseen God known, the Father/Son relationship remains allusive and elusive in the prologue, where there is no explicit reference to "the Son." But the Son in the body of the Gospel, like the λόγος in the prologue, is the agent of God's revelation and action, even creation. The Son makes the Father known by performing the works of the Father (cf. 5:17, 19–30). This view is supported by the first and second explicit uses of the Father/Son relationship. They assert that the Father loves (ἀγαπᾷ and φιλεῖ) the Son and that this love is expressed in the bestowal (δέδωκεν) of all things (πάντα) by his hand (3:35), which seems to be another way of saying that God created all things (πάντα) through/by him (1:3).

3.1.1   The Father/Son Relationship in 3:31–36

The *first* explicit reference to the Father/Son relationship occurs in 3:31–36, in what appears to be the continuing witness of John (3:22–30). Though 3:31–36 continues with no explicit change of speaker, it moves to a new level of witness, suggesting that it is commentary by the narrator. Only the lofty claims made by the narrator concerning the witness of John in the prologue (1:6–8) warn us against hastily distinguishing this from the continuing witness of John. He is "a man *sent* from God to bear witness to the light that all may believe through him." However, 3:31–36 does not fit the context of his witness in 3:22–30 and lacks any response from his disciples. Rather, 3:31–36 is addressed directly to the reader. Nevertheless, the transformation of the witness of John in the prologue (especially 1:7b), and the opening scenes of 1:19–42, where he becomes the one who reveals "the coming one" to Israel (1:31), makes it appropriate for him to move the focus from his own witness to the witness of the one who is from above, who is sent from God, speaks the words of God, and who gives the Spirit, not by measure (3:31–34 and note 1:15, 30–34). Either way, 3:31–36 are addressed directly to the reader and the Father Son relationship is foundational because:

> The Father loves (ἀγαπᾷ) the Son
> and *has given* (δέδωκεν) all things (πάντα, cf. 1:3) by his hand (3:35).

This second reference in John to God's *love* is surprisingly second.[33] Unlike the first, which uses the aorist tense, the verb here is in the continuous present

---

33   The first use of *love* in John refers to God's *act of love* (οὕτως γὰρ ἠγάπησεν ὁ θεὸς τὸν κόσμον) in 3:16, to be discussed below. That act of love is expressed in God's generous gift, God

tense to express the Father/Son *relationship*. That the Father *loves* the Son is the foundation for the Son's role as the agent of the Father's action. The language is suggestive of the notion of the Father as the fount of Godhead. As an expression of the love of the Father for the Son, the Father "*has given* all things by his hand." This assertion is comparable to God's relation to and action by the λόγος in 1:1–3. "*All things* became *through* him." Together, 3:35 and 1:1–3 make the Son/λόγος the agent of the Father's/God's creative works. Distinctively 3:35 makes the Father's love for the Son the source of God's creative work through the agency of the Son. The *Father's* love is not circular, but through the Son leads to creation. The continuous present tense (ἀγαπᾷ) suggests more, implying that God's action is not yet finished, is continuous.

3.1.2 The Father/Son Relationship in 5:20

The *second* explicit Father/Son saying in 5:20 echoes the Father/Son statement of 3:35, but is based on the text of 5:17, "My Father is working until now and I am working." Though this is not a Father/Son saying, Jesus's "*My* Father" implies "Son." In this context, 5:17 is the text upon which the discourse of 5:19–30 is based and defends, and says all that 3:35 says and more.[34]

The context for 5:19–20 is Jesus's provocative defense of a Sabbath healing. Rather than entering a legal debate to justify his action on the Sabbath, Jesus identified his work with God's work, God's work with his work, "My Father is *working* until now and I also am *working*" (Ὁ πατήρ μου ἕως ἄρτι ἐργάζεται, κἀγὼ ἐργάζομαι). This defense increased the anger of "the Jews" and led to their renewed attempt to kill Jesus, now not only because he broke the Sabbath, but more seriously, because they recognize that he was identifying himself with God and God's action/work, which they wrongly took as a rival claim, ἴσον ἑαυτὸν ποιῶν τῷ θεῷ (5:17–18).[35]

Jesus then elaborates his argument in a two-part Father/Son saying. He speaks first from the perspective of the Son and then of the Father. In so doing he rules out any sense of rival action, affirming the Father's action in the Son:

> Truly, truly I tell you,
> the Son is not able to *do* anything from himself,
> only whatever *he sees* the Father *doing*;

---

gave. The second use of love (3:19) asserts that humans corruptly loved (ἠγάπησαν) the darkness rather than the light, exposing the world's need of God's transforming saving love.

34 John Painter, "Text and Context in John 5," *ABR* 35 (1987): 28–34; Painter, *Quest for the Messiah*, 216–49, esp. 224–35.

35 See Michael H. Burer, *Divine Sabbath Work* (Winona Lake, IN: Eisenbrauns, 2012).

for whatever he *does* (ἃ γὰρ ἂν ἐκεῖνος ποιῇ),
these things also the Son likewise *does* (ταῦτα καὶ ὁ υἱὸς ὁμμοίως ποιεῖ).
For *the Father loves* (φιλεῖ) *the Son*
and shows him *all things* (πάντα) that he *does*,
and greater works than these he will show him
in order that you may marvel (5:19–20).

Like the first explicit Father/Son saying, this one expresses the Father's love for the Son using the present, indicative active. Though 5:20 echoes 3:35, 3:35 uses ἀγαπᾷ whereas 5:20 uses φιλεῖ. Clearly ἀγαπᾷ and φιλεῖ are used without difference of meaning.[36] In each instance, the love of the Father for the Son is the ground or source of the Son's activity, and in each instance the present tense expresses a continuing mode of operation.

In the text (5:17), Jesus asserts that whatever God does he does. In the exposition of this text in 5:19–20 the identity of action in Father and Son is grounded in the Father's love for the Son. The exposition affirms that the Son does only what he sees the Father doing (5:19), and because the Father loves (φιλεῖ) the Son he shows him all that he does. There is an identity of action because the Son does only what the Father does and all that the Father does. All of the Father's actions are mediated by the Son. This is the divine mode of being and action according to John.

The mutually illuminating power of these two texts is signaled by the way:

1. Each saying commences with the affirmation that "the Father loves the Son" (3:35; 5:20).
2. In each case "all things" (πάντα) are involved as they are also in the relationship between the λόγος and God in 1:1–3, leading to the creation of all things (πάντα) in 1:3, where God created through the agency of the λόγος (δι' αὐτοῦ).

    But 5:17, 19–20 affirms more clearly the continuing work of God (ὁ πατήρ μου ἕως ἄρτι ἐργάζεται, κἀγὼ ἐργάζομαι), which implies the unfinished creation.[37]
3. On these two points, 3:35 and 5:20 with the first three and last five verses of the prologue are mutually illuminating. Indeed, 1:1–3 and 1:14,

---

36 The character of the Father's love for the Son is not conveyed by a particular word but is exemplified by the action of love described. This is true also of the first expression of God's love in 3:16 where the character of the love is signaled by οὕτως and the exemplified action is described in what follows. See also the interchangeable use of ἀγαπᾶν and φιλεῖν in 21:15–17.

37 See John Painter, "Earth Made Whole: John's Reading of Genesis," in *Word, Theology, and Community in John*, ed. John Painter et al. (St. Louis: Chalice Press, 2002), 65–84.

18 are mutually illuminating. Together they suggest that the Johannine Christology is an exercise in theology, expounding the mode of God's action.

3.1.3 Characteristic Father/Son Formulae

The formulation ὁ πέμψας με πατήρ is used with minor variations twenty-four times by Jesus to refer to God (John 4:34; 5:23, 24, 30, 37; 6:38, 39, 44; 7:16 (18), 28, 33; 8:16, 18, 26 29; 9:4; 12:44, 45, 49; 13:20; 14:24, 26; 15:21; 16:5). In this formulation the focus/emphasis is on the Father, the sender, though that Jesus is the one sent is implied. But the focus/emphasis is on the one sent in the seventeen uses of some form of ἀποστέλλω, usually ἀπέστειλεν or ἀπέσταλκεν John 3:17, 34; 5:36, 38; 6:29, 57; 7:29; 8:42; 10:36; 11:42; 17:3, 8, 18, 21, 23, 25; 20:21.[38]

These two groups of texts bring a sharp focus on the *mission* of the Son so prominently expressed by Jesus in his references to "the Father who sent me" and to himself as the one sent. It is extraordinary that the first appearance of this *motif* fails to use the characteristic sending formulae. This is almost as surprising as the first mention of *love*, indeed the divine *love*, which is not a reference to the Father's love for the Son, but of God's love for the world.

3:16:
For God loved the world in this way (οὕτως),
he *gave* (ἔδωκεν) the only begotten Son (τὸν υἱὸν τὸν μονογενῆ)
in order that everyone who believes in him may not perish but have eternal life.

3:17:
For God did not send (ἀπέστειλεν) the Son into the world to condemn the world
but to save the world through him (δι' αὐτοῦ).

It continues to be a common view of scholars that the Fourth Gospel has a narrow view of God's love and the love command expressed in the new commandment (13:34–35). It is argued that *the message of 3:16* is overwhelmed by the inner-group love for one-another. Yet the evangelist's first use of *love* in the Gospel is in the grand statement of God's love for the world in 3:16. At the same time, *this love* underlies the *mission* of the Son in the world, for the world,

---

[38] See Painter, *Quest for the Messiah*, 224–35 (231 n. 67), 244–49. It is worth noting the first reference to God *sending* is in 1:6–7 where the *man* John is sent by God to bear witness to the light so that all may believe through him.

which is the story this Gospel tells. Although the Father and the Son are involved in this saying, it is not a *Father/Son* saying, it is a *God/world* saying that involves God's act of love (ἠγάπησεν) for the world and has the sense of the generous giving of grace in God's act of love, the act of *giving* (ἔδωκεν) God's Son for the life of the world. The sending motif is appropriate to express the love of the Father for the Son, authorizing and empowering the Son in the fulfillment of the mission of God in the world. But in 3:16 the love of God *for the world* is described in terms of gracious, generous *giving*, directed towards the wellbeing of the life of the world.

The context changes in 3:17, which is focused on the Son, defining his mission negatively and positively. Because the predicament of the world is in view, the text refers to God, not the Father. But the relationship between God and the Son is described in terms of sender and sent. So, it is that God *sent* (ἀπέστειλεν) the Son, not to condemn but to save the world, and this terminology of sender and sent dominates the Gospel. It appears again in 3:34–35:

> For the one whom God sent (ἀπέστειλεν) speaks the words of God
> For he does not give the Spirit by measure (ἐκ μέτρου)(3:34).
> The Father loves (ἀγαπᾷ) the Son
> and *has given* (δέδωκεν) all things (πάντα, cf. 1:3) by his hand (3:35).

God is present in Jesus, speaking, acting, and working, a point reinforced by 5:17, 19–20. While 3:35 is rightly interpreted as acting in the creation of all things in the beginning, 5:17, 19–20 appeal to working in the present, "My Father *is working until now and I am working*." Further, both 3:35 and 5:20 assert the continuing love of the Father for the Son as the basis of the identity of action of Father and Son performing creative and saving acts and speaking the words of God (3:34). Thus, not even 3:35 is restricted to action "in the beginning."

4 John 17: Christocentric Is Theocentric in God's Mission[39]

The Father/Son relationship, expressed in the Father's love for the Son, issues in the creation of all things by the Father through the Son, and in the mission of the Son from the sending Father to and for the world. That mission was to

---

[39] See Painter, *John Witness and Theologian*, 59–61; Painter, *Quest for the Messiah*, 432–34. The prayer is a "mission statement" from the perspective of the completed mission of Jesus. It does not speak to the situation of crisis to be faced by the disciples, but to the mission beyond the mission of Jesus.

make God's ways known upon earth (17:3), and to bring to the world the fullness of life, completing creation. *God's mission* is the focus of the great prayer of John 17, in which Jesus addresses God as "Father" six times (17:1, 5, 11, 21, 24, 25).[40] The Prayer has a focus on the three parts of that mission: the *mission* of Jesus (1–5); the *mission* of his disciples (6–19); the *mission* of those who believe through their word (20–26).

4.1   John 17:1–5

Jesus's initial focus, at the end of his mission, is bounded by two petitions (17:1 and 5) addressed to God as "Father." Jesus asks the Father for glorification at the completion of his work on earth to glorify God. In one sense, this part of the prayer deals with what is settled and sure. Jesus requests, "Glorify your Son that the Son may glorify you … that they may know you the only true God and Jesus Christ whom you sent (ὃν ἀπέστειλας)" (17:1–3). This part of the prayer ends with the second address "Father" (forming an inclusion with 17:1), and a repeated and amplified request for glorification, a return to his former glory (17:5).

4.2   John 17:6–19

John 17:6–19 forms the main body of the prayer and deals with what is precarious and fragile, but upon which all else depends. Jesus prays for his faithful disciples to whom he revealed God's *Name* and who have kept God's *Word*, given to them by Jesus. They know that he has come from God and believe God sent him. They constitute the living connection with the departing Jesus. Jesus prays for them, aware that their situation is precarious, not so much because of persecution, but because of the corrupting power of the world. Paradoxically, the future well-being of the world hangs by the thread of continuity between the departing Jesus and those he leaves in the world, kept only by the *name* Jesus revealed to them and the *Word* he gave them (17:6, 8, 14, 17). Thus, Jesus prays, "*Holy* Father, *keep* them in your *name* which you gave to me, *that they may be one as we are*" (17:11, and see the recurring petition in 17:21–23).[41] Thus preserving their integrity from corruption is crucial to the fulfillment of their mission, Jesus's mission, the Father's mission, God's mission. "In the same way as and because (καθώς) you [Father] sent me into the world I also have sent

---

40   Four of the six use the name "Father" without addition (17:1, 5, 21, 24); but the third and sixth (middle and final) identify vital attributes of God as "Holy Father" (17:11) and "Righteous Father" (17:25). These epithets are vitally relevant to the situations of the disciples (17:6–19) and those who believed through their word (17:20–26).

41   Interestingly, in *Gospel of Truth* 38.7, in a section that may be based on John 17:11, we read, "The name of the Father is the Son."

them into the world (17:18)."[42] Oneness with the Father through the Son is the only ground for the mission of God in the world. Faithfulness to the revelation of God in the mission of Jesus is the foundation of the continuing mission. So, Jesus addresses God as "*Holy Father*" in the petition to keep the disciples from the corrupting power of the world and true to their mission *for the sake of the world*.

4.3   John 17:20–26

John 17:20–26 begins with a renewed and expanding petition for future generations who believe without having seen and known Jesus, upon whom Jesus speaks a special blessing in 20:29. Maintaining the living presence of the Father and the Son is vital for the world, but is an added challenge for those who have not seen and heard. The mission remains the same (17:18), and success depends on remaining one with the Father and the Son in God's mission for the world. Whatever the merits of the ecumenical movement are, 17:21–23 are not about Christian unity. Their orientation is outward to the world not inward to the church. The foundation of unity is the Father revealed in the Son. The function of the Christology of the Gospel is to reveal and make present God who wills life for the world and that life is the goal of the living presence of the Name and the Word in the believing Community (17:6, 17–18, 21–23). Not surprisingly, the final address to God as Father is "*Righteous Father*, the world does not know you, but I know you, and these know that you sent me; and I have made known your *name* to them and I will make it known, so that the love with which you love me may be in them and I in them" (17:24–25). So, Jesus addresses God as "*Righteous* Father" in the petition to keep the believers *faithful* in the mission.[43]

4.4   John 17

It is extraordinary, following the teaching about the Spirit of Truth, Paraclete in John 14–16 that, in John 17, there is no mention of the Spirit. Instead, Jesus prays to the Father for them, leaving a pastoral and theological map for their life of faith and mission in the world. There are two other rocks upon which to build. There is the *Name* that Jesus has revealed and the *Word* that he has

---

42   On the double sense of καθώς, see Painter, *1, 2, and 3 John*, 124 and references under *kathōs*, 406. See also R. Bultmann, *Theology of the New Testament*, vol. 2 (London: SCM, 1955 [German org. 1951]), 81. The actual commission occurs only in 20:21, confirming the retrospective status of John 17, brought forward into Jesus's "farewell" scenes.

43   Righteousness and faithfulness are overlapping terms in Hebrew and Johannine Greek.

given. Both are tied up with the crucial recognition-belief that *Jesus is the Son sent by the Father, whose mission is to bring life to the world.*

5   Concluding Remarks

In the beginning of the Gospel, the witness of John reveals and initiates the quest for the Messiah. His witness also uncovers the *priority* of the *coming one* and culminates in his witness in 1:34, "This is the Son of God." The witness of John bridges the prologue and the narrative of the Gospel, making the reader aware that the prologue plays a *key* role in reading the Gospel. In this way it becomes clear that the quest for the Messiah is symbolic of the quest for the presence of God in revealing, creative, and life-giving power. In the prologue and in the body of the Gospel this is spoken of in terms of the Father-Son relationship and of the Father sending the Son into the world for the sake of the world, to speak the words of the Father and to perform the life-giving deeds of the Father for the sake of the world. Thus, the Son is the revelation of the hidden Father, making the Father known, doing the Father's works to make creation whole. Messiahship is transformed into Christology, which speaks of God in terms of revealing, creative, and life-giving power.

CHAPTER 3

Jesus the *Messiah/Christos* and John's Christology

Panayotis Coutsoumpos

Contemporary research in Johannine Christology has focused its attention on the numerous titles given to Jesus in the New Testament; many interpreters are unwilling to admit that Jesus himself used any of these titles to explain his own person and functions. The issue whether Jesus had a "messianic self-consciousness" is one of the major dilemmas involved in understanding his life, ministry, and teaching.[1] The Christology of the fourth evangelist is one of the most frequently discussed topics in Johannine scholarly circles and studies. The Gospel of John stands separate from the first three (Synoptic) Gospels in that it describes a set of events and teachings in many ways distinct from what the first three evangelists recount. The several uses, however, of the Messiah title may have opened the door for Jesus to give the title a new meaning.[2] Some of the situations or events are the same, while others are of a fundamentally similar character.

All four Gospels focus on the earthly life and ministry of Jesus and are thus fundamentally a christological and theological interpretation of the importance of Jesus's life. This fact raises significant and difficult questions regarding the relationship of the Jesus described by John to the picture we receive from the other Gospels.[3] At the outset, it must be admitted that men of faith who belonged to the believing Christian community wrote each of the Gospels—what they held to be good news of what God has done in Jesus.[4]

---

1 Oscar Cullmann, *The Christology of the New Testament*, rev. ed. (Philadelphia: Westminster, 1963), 117; John Painter, *The Quest for the Messiah: The History, Literature and Theology of the Johannine Community* (Edinburgh: T&T Clark, 1991), 22. See also I. Howard Marshall, *The Origins of New Testament Christology* (Downers Grove: InterVarsity, 1976), 43: "Such an attitude may spring from a rationalistic attitude to Jesus which refuses to allow that he could have identified himself with any of the 'Messianic' figures of Jewish thought."
2 Ben Witherington, *The Many Faces of the Christ: The Christologies of the New Testament and Beyond* (New York: Crossroad, 1998), 58.
3 Andreas J. Köstenberger, *A Theology of John's Gospel and Letters: Biblical Theology of the New Testament*. (Grand Rapids: Zondervan, 2009), 105; Köstenberger, *John*, BECNT (Grand Rapids: Baker Academic, 2004), 69. See also T.E. Pollard, *Johannine Christology and the Early Church*, SNTSMS 13 (Cambridge: Cambridge University Press, 1970), 3.
4 George E. Ladd, *The New Testament and Criticism* (Grand Rapids: Eerdmans, 1967), 153.

The question is: Do the known facts of history sustain the belief that the Gospel writers were committed and believing men? The problem is the modern understanding of the nature of history and faith. History, it is claimed, is entirely the study of humanity and its existence.[5] The Gospels, on the other hand, are witnesses to faith in God and what this faith held that God had done in Jesus. Further, many studies regarding Jesus place faith and history in antithetical categories. Whatever in the Gospels corresponds to Christian faith cannot, from this perspective, be historically reliable. This, however, is an untenable presupposition.

For John, however, the christological titles about Jesus are very important. J. Ashton asserts that, "as soon as we turn to a close study of the Christology of the Fourth Gospel, we come face to face with one of its greatest puzzles."[6] John's Christology is very clear throughout the whole gospel. That Jesus and his disciples redefined messiahship is hardly surprising, given the flexibility of Jewish eschatological anticipation in general and messianic anticipation, in particular.[7]

In fact, all major New Testament writers affirm Jesus as the Messiah and go over the concept in light of his exclusive ministry. Interestingly, while the one to come as the Messiah was to be king of Israel and heir of the Davidic line, the fact remains that John—in contrast to Matthew, Luke, and even Paul—makes nothing of Jesus's Davidic sonship, not even calling him son of David.[8] The serious questions some have raised about the Messiah concept in John are based not on arguments regarding criteria, but on the usefulness of this concept in coming to terms with this elusive and insistent Gospel.[9] It is interesting to note that John selects some signs performed by Jesus to prove that Jesus is in fact the Messiah.[10] To some extent, however, Otto Betz gives a different estimate of Jesus's role. He has called attention to the manner in which a number of traits in Jesus's ministry are "Messianic" in the strict sense. There is enough evidence

---

5   George E. Ladd, *A Theology of the New Testament*, rev. ed. (Grand Rapids: Eerdmans, 1998), 172: "History always tries to understand the meaning of the events it reports; and the fact that a person has a viewpoint does not mean that person is a poor historian and distorts facts to support his or her interpretation."
6   John Ashton, *Understanding the Fourth Gospel*, 2nd ed. (Oxford: Oxford University Press, 2008), 141.
7   Craig S. Keener, *The Gospel of John: A Commentary*, 2 vols. (Peabody: Hendrickson, 2003), 1:289.
8   D. Moody Smith, *The Theology of the Gospel of John*, NTT (Cambridge: Cambridge University Press, 1998), 124.
9   Andreas J. Köstenberger, *Encountering John: The Gospel in Historical, Literary, and Theological Perspective* (Grand Rapids: Baker Academic, 1999), 32.
10   Ashton, *Understanding the Fourth Gospel*, 143.

here to demonstrate that at least some aspects of Jesus's ministry cannot be explained as other than Messianic.[11]

It is not that John no longer subscribes to the traditional belief that "Jesus is Messiah" (a christological title), but that John additionally is attached to the special relationship between the twin titles of "Messiah" and "Son of God." Furthermore, according to John Painter, "John is certainly not an anti-Semitic work. It is clearly stated in John's Gospel that Jesus was himself a Jew, and it is accepted in the present study that the Johannine Christians were Jewish."[12] Most interpreters, in fact, acknowledge that Christology is fundamental to the Gospel of John.[13]

Given that he has represented Jesus in Johannine idiom and for his characteristic purpose, does John exactly reflect and interpret some previous tradition here, or does John just make new material? The Messianic titles, which appear in the Gospels, are (particularly in the Gospel of John)[14] to be reassessed in the light of the fact that Jesus knew himself to be the Messiah. Karl Wengst's assertion that Jesus implicitly saw himself and his mission in this term seems to be justified.[15] Above all, he understands Jesus in John's Gospel to be the "messiah coming out of Israel" (John 4:42). Once one accepts the implied self-understanding of Jesus's role in terms of the eschatological perspective, the complete ministry as recounted in this Gospel moves along a pattern of related and clear prophetic mission.[16]

What, then, is the nature of this unique position that Jesus was aware of occupying? Was Jesus really aware of his messianic mission? Did the disciples expect Jesus's messianic role and authority to be fulfilled in their own time? We will argue that the importance of all this is that it points not only to some authority on the part of Jesus, but also to a position of uniqueness as the prophetic Messiah expected for Israel.[17] The point to be remembered here is that even the application of radical methods of research to the Gospel of John leads to this unavoidable messianic characteristic so far as the ministry of Jesus is concerned. Wengst, however, considers the Christology of John to be strictly God-centered messianology—more exactly, a Christology that places

---

11 Otto Betz, "Die Frage nach dem messianischen Bewusstsein Jesu," *NovT* 6 (1963): 20–48.
12 Painter, *Quest for the Messiah*, 23.
13 John Ashton, *Studying John: Approaches to the Fourth Gospel* (Oxford: Oxford University Press, 1998), 107.
14 Marshall, *Origins of New Testament Christology*, 50.
15 Karl Wengst, *Das Johannesevangelium*, 2 vols., THKNT (Stuttgart: Kohlammer, 2001), 149.
16 Marshall, *Origins of New Testament Christology*, 52.
17 Marshall, *Origins of New Testament Christology*, 47.

emphasis on the Son as the one who was sent.[18] John's Christology is unique because of the focus he brings to Jesus and his ministry. In the following section we will deal with the Messiah term and its Old Testament context, the use of the term in Second Temple Judaism, and the messianic concept in the Gospel of John.

1   Messiah and the Old Testament Context

The title Messiah has a special place among the various christological titles. The concept of Messiah originates in the OT, which makes mention of anointed priests, kings, and prophets.[19] The Hebrew title *mashiach* (*Christos* in Greek) simply means, "Anointed one." In this sense it refers specifically to the *king of Israel*.[20] The Greek term Χριστός is a verbal adjective that comes from χρίω meaning, "to rub, anoint."[21] It is found, however, just twice prior to the LXX, both times used as a subst. with the meaning "ointment."[22] In OT times, however, the king was called "the Lord's Anointed," or "the Anointed of the God of Israel," or simply "the Anointed" (1 Sam 2:10; 24: 6; 26:16; 2 Sam 1:14, 16; 23:2).[23]

On the one hand, it is significant to note that since the New Testament was written in the Greek language, in secular Greek *Christos* was by no means a technical term for a religious person. On the other hand, *Christos* in Biblical Greek appears as a new usage, or at least with a different meaning from the common secular usage of the Greco-Roman world.[24] John's Gospel gives us the impression that Palestinian Jews understood the title "Messiah" and expected his coming.[25] Some scholars have also observed that the OT says few things about the coming of a future anointed one. In other words, the progress of the messianic expectations in the OT cannot be easily found in detail.[26] Do they, then, totally misread the Old Testament?[27]

---

18   Wengst, *Das Johannesevangelium*, 34.
19   C.A. Evans, "Messianism," in *Dictionary of New Testament Background*, ed. C.A. Evans and S.E. Porter (Downers Grove: InterVarsity, 2000), 699.
20   Cullmann, *Christology*, 113.
21   Moisés Silva, *New International Dictionary of New Testament Theology and Exegesis*, 5 vols. (Grand Rapids: Zondervan, 2014), 4:688.
22   Aeschylus, *Prom.* 480; Euripides, *Hipp.* 516.
23   Köstenberger, *Theology of John's Gospel*, 313.
24   Witherington, *Many Faces of Christ*, 59.
25   Keener, *Gospel of John*, 284.
26   Silva, *New International Dictionary*, 690.
27   Thomas R. Schreiner, *New Testament Theology: Magnifying God in Christ* (Grand Rapids: Baker Academic, 2008), 198.

In contrast, W. Horbury has argued that the canonical shaping in the OT itself points toward a messianic hope.[28] For instance, the OT messianic expectation is connected to King David and his heirs. Jewish expectations of God's redemption were not consistent; the Messiah—literally, the anointed one—appears to have been the expected king of Davidic ancestry who was to "restore the kingdom to Israel" (Acts 1:6).[29] According to the Scriptures, however, David was anointed as a future king by the prophet Samuel (2 Sam 7:11–29; 1 Chron 17:10–27).

God's pact with David is presumed to be unchangeable; hence God will never remove his pact from David's successors.[30] Certainly, the expectation of a Davidic Messiah denotes just one type of messianism in the time between the exile and Bar Kokhba's uprising in the early second century after Christ. It should also be noted that "the decisive feature of the NT against the background of contemporary messianic expectation is the conscious and categorical identification of a contemporary historical figure, Jesus of Nazareth, as the Messiah."[31] This is an important fact for judging rightly what is represented in the NT as messianism. For the entirety of the NT, therefore, messianism no longer stands under the sign of expectation, but under its fulfillment.[32] The issue here is not means or manner of birth, but lineage and family connection.

A Jewish text dated to the first century BCE, *Psalms of Solomon,* testifies to the expected fulfillment of God's promise in 2 Sam 7. Its author anticipates the Messiah/king who will destroy unrighteous rulers and purge Jerusalem from Gentiles. That is, *Psalms of Solomon* waits for the coming Messiah to found his kingdom by driving out non-Jews from Jerusalem.[33] Thus the term Messiah refers to Israel's king, as mentioned by one of the most known Old Testament passages that created messianic expectations for the Christ and/or Son of God in 2 Sam 7.

These expectations were still alive and well in the time of Jesus, as the promised land was part of—and under the rule of—the Roman Empire. For John, readers must understand exactly what kind of Christ Jesus is, because he was not the kind that Jews like the writer of *Psalms of Solomon* expected. In fact, Jesus's lineage comes from that of David. It is interesting to note that according to 2 Sam 7:2, God promised David that his kinship would last forever. The Jews

---

28 William Horbury, *Jewish Messianism and the Cult of Christ* (London: SCM Press, 1998), 13–25.
29 Smith, *Theology of the Gospel of John,* 86.
30 Schreiner, *New Testament Theology,* 199.
31 Silva, *New International Dictionary,* 690–91.
32 Marshall, *Origins of New Testament Christology,* 55.
33 *Ps. Sol.* 17.22.

took it for granted that an earthly kingship would be necessary in order to introduce future salvation.[34] Psalm 89 echoes an understanding of the Davidic covenant after David's death. The Scripture says that God's promise to David is bases on the former's continued love for David (Ps 89:2–4).

And Psalm 132 also reaffirms God's promise to place one of David's sons on the throne (Ps 132:11).[35] Psalm 132:12 maintains that the promise depends upon the obedience of David's heir. It should also be noted that all the Gospels, as well as the rest of the New Testament, take Jesus to be the Messiah—the Christ of biblical and Jewish expectation. John, however, recognized most obviously that the crucifixion of Jesus suggested the end of the traditional messianic expectation.[36] Was any expectation of the Messiah found among the members of the Qumran community? Or Is John's view of the Messiah found in Second Temple Judaism?

2   Messiah in Second Temple Judaism

Interpreters agree that the concept of the Messiah—or rather, numerous concepts of the Messiah—existed in Second Temple Judaism during the first century AD.[37] The Qumran scrolls, in fact, attest to the presence of the messianic hope in the Second Temple period, mentioning a "messiah of Aaron and Israel" (4Q266; 1QSa=1Q28 2:12: "the messiah").[38] From this viewpoint the Qumran text gives us our most significant proof regarding John's belief world.[39] Some understood the Messiah as a title of the Davidic king, while others anticipated a Prophet like Moses or some comparable figure.

It is most likely that this term (Messiah), like others, originally denoted a temporal savior rather than a divine one.[40] In the Dead Sea Scrolls, however, there are around thirty texts that mention the anointed Messiah. Half of these

---

34 Cullmann, *Christology*, 114.
35 Schreiner, *New Testament Theology*, 199–200.
36 Smith, *Theology of the Gospel of John*, 86.
37 James H. Charlesworth, ed., *The Messiah: Developments in Earliest Judaism and Christianity* (Minneapolis: Fortress, 1992), 24: "The other body of early Jewish literature that contains explicit references to 'Messiah' or 'Christ' is the Dead Sea Scrolls. The discussions of this aspect in the Scrolls is so well published and known that some refer to a consensus."
38 Köstenberger, *Theology of John*, 314.
39 Painter, *The Quest for the Messiah*, 29: "The Text reveals the influence of Hellenization on Judaism. Hellenization was a complex process. Through the overarching influence of Alexander's political and cultural conquest Greek language and thought reached every part of the empire."
40 Ashton, *Understanding the Fourth Gospel*, 164.

make reference to what seems to be a royal, strictly human Messiah, while most of the other texts speak of such one in terms of an anticipated prophet. A few mention such a one in a priestly role, and one is a reference to Moses.[41] Qumran's messianic expectation seems to involve two major eschatological figures—a Davidic Messiah and a high priest (1QSa 2.11–17; 4Q174 3.11–12).[42]

Like kings, prophets and priests were anointed in Jewish society, so when the discussion concerns "an anointed one," or even "*the* anointed one," a king need not be in reference.[43] There was the expectation of a prophet such as Moses, based on Deut 18:15ff. and found in the Qumran scrolls (1QS 9:11; 4QTest 1–8). In addition to the Messiah from Judah, there is also found in the *Damascus Document* and in the *Qumran passages* the "Messiah from Aaron" (Levi), who clearly has the features of a priest.[44] It is interesting to note that in this context two Messiahs are expected—the priestly and the political—the former being superior to the latter. It seems that the priestly Messiah takes precedence over the kingly (1QSa II, 12–21; 4QpIsa III, 23–25; 4QSM 5; 4QFlor I, 11). However, when we read the Dead Sea Scrolls, it can be noted that the messianic hope is not tied only to the Davidic heritage.[45] But the "branch of David" is anticipated as destroying the ungodly and conquering the nations (1QSb V, 20–29).

Several other Jewish manuscripts from Second Temple Judaism, like *4 Ezra*, *2 Baruch*, and the *Testament of the Twelve Patriarchs*, address the Messiah and frequently link him with the final judgment.[46] According to Schreiner, in *4 Ezra*, however, the Messiah is chosen as the Son of God, but his reign is limited to four hundred years, and after those years have finished, he will die (*4 Ezra* 7.28–29).[47]

This notion is completely different from the notion of John and his Gospel, where the Messiah will die and subsequently reign. For instance, priestly prestige is emphasized in the *Testament of Judah*. Judah deals with earthly matters, and Levi with heavenly ones.[48] Messianic themes, however, predominate in *T.Jud.* 24, where Num 24:17 is mentioned, so that the same OT passage is

---

41   Evans, "Messianism," in *Dictionary*, 701.
42   Keener, *Gospel of John*, 286–87. "It was natural for a community with Qumran's history and priestly orientation to anticipate an eschatological purification of the priesthood (cf. Mal. 3:3) as well as the promised Davidic Messiah; priest as well as kings were to be anointed for office."
43   Witherington, *Many Faces of Christ*, 59.
44   Cullmann, *Christology*, 116.
45   Schreiner, *New Testament Theology*, 202.
46   Keener, *Gospel of John*, 285.
47   Schreiner, *New Testament Theology*, 204.
48   *T. Jud.* 21.1–6.

applied to the tribes of both Levi and Judah. Thus, Jewish sources are not silent with regard to the Messiah.[49] According to Schreiner, "when we take the entirety of *Testament of the Twelve Patriarchs* into account, it appears that the priestly Messiah takes precedence over the kingly one."[50] Josephus's narrative of the several national deliverers fit a similar idea, though it should be noted that not all these persons necessarily thought they were the Messiah.[51]

This prophet was expected to perform messianic functions, particularly miraculous signs.[52] In other words, people expected the Messiah to perform an abundance of supernatural deeds. The miracles of healing are the work of the Messiah in his capacity as Savior. It is interesting to note that both the Essenes and the early Church were animated by an intense expectation of the Messiah's imminent return.[53] Messianic hope flourished in both groups, but with some notable differences. In mainstream Judaism and the New Testament, these several figures merged into a single person. Is this Messiah the one portrayed in the Gospel of John? Is it realistic to hold that even at the outset the Johannine community's faith in Jesus included a confirmation of his messiahship?[54]

3 Jesus the Messiah/*Christos* in John's Gospel

The term *Messiah/Christos*, with very limited exceptions, emerges in all four Gospel as a title and not as a proper name. In three places (Matt 1:1; Mark 1:1; John 1:1), the term is in fact used as a proper name. But numerous researches of the Jewish messianic expectation ignore one of the most significant sources: the Gospels themselves.[55] Is the New Testament expectation for Messiah, then, not properly understood? Since the early dates of Christianity, Christians were accustomed to link the designation "Christ" with the name Jesus. Jesus-Christ means Jesus-Messiah.[56] It seems clear that John 6:14–15 declares that

---

49 J. Louis Martyn, *History and Theology in the Fourth Gospel*, NTL (Louisville: Westminster John Knox, 2003), 94–97. "He is almost always expected to be the Son of David, since at its heart the messianic hope is patterned on the glorious period of Israel's history under David."
50 Schreiner, *New Testament Theology*, 204.
51 Josephus, *Ant.* 17.271–285.
52 Marshall, *Origins of New Testament Christology*, 52.
53 Geza Vermes, *Jesus in His Jewish Context* (Minneapolis: Fortress Press, 2003), 122.
54 Ashton, *Understanding the Fourth Gospel*, 150.
55 Ladd, *Theology of the New Testament*, 136: "When one reads them to find the hope entertained by the Jewish people, he finds a hope similar to that reflected in the Psalms of Solomon."
56 Cullmann, *Christology*, 112.

the people in Israel wrongly viewed the coming Messiah as a political figure restoring Israel to its temporal glory, for the purpose of overthrowing the Roman rulers.[57]

This expectation was fundamental for many Jews, who of course were oppressed by the Romans in Palestine during Jesus's time. In fact, the land of Israel lay under Roman control and the province of Judea was ruled directly by the prefect of Rome; the hope of restoration must have been very much alive in Jesus's day. The fact that Jesus himself was from Davidic lineage (Rom 1:3; Matt 1:6–17; Luke 1:27) would in all likelihood have inspired them.[58] For instance, in Mark 9:41, *Christos* appear on Jesus's lips as a proper name; on the other hand, there is the possibility of the text being corrupted in transmission.[59] Throughout John's Gospel the issue of Jesus's identity (as the Messiah) is recounted—occasionally in the form of an acclamation, elsewhere in the form of an assumption about where Jesus came from, at other times in the form of a question or even a declarative statement.[60]

It should be noted that John's opponents within the Christian community challenged its Christology, as John makes that Christology the center of his message to the community. R. Brown concludes that some of the disciples of Jesus may have thought him the Messiah, but sometimes he was more concerned about his mission rather than his messiah expectation.[61] For Jesus, however, being the Messiah was the principal mission of his life, teaching, and ministry. Clearly, John would nowhere critique or imply any inadequacies in Jesus as the Messiah. It has been frequently observed, however, that the Christology of John is a late development of some of the Hellenist Christians' view.[62] Even though not everyone agrees with this view, several interpreters see this as a Jewish term rather than a Greek term.[63] But some scholars appear to have doubts about Jesus's role as Messiah.

In fact, all major writers in the New Testament affirm Jesus as the Messiah and revise the popular messianic concept in light of his ministry.[64] For John, all these witnesses support the view that Jesus is in fact the Messiah and the Son of God. But what kind of Messiah was Jesus? Was Jesus the *Messiah/Christos*

---

57 Köstenberger, *Encountering John*, 110.
58 Smith, *Theology of the Gospel of John*, 87.
59 Ladd, *Theology of the New Testament*, 139.
60 Witherington, *Many Faces of Christ*, 172.
61 Raymond E. Brown, *The Gospel of John 1–12*, AB (Garden City, NY: Doubleday, 1966), 249–50.
62 Keener, *Gospel of John*, 298.
63 Cullmann, *Christology*, 114–15.
64 Smith, *Theology of the Gospel of John*, 125.

(John 1:19–20, 24)?[65] John's account portrays Jesus as Messiah by selecting seven representative signs (John 1:19–12: 50; 20:30–31).[66] Did John use another sign source? If so, what theological importance was connected to these miracles in the source? On the one hand, the signs in the Gospel of John play a positive theological role in attesting to Jesus's origin, power, and purpose. On the other hand, Jesus's signs are in this sense an opening revelation; they have need of elucidation and understanding, which are given and made possible by Jesus's miracle deeds and words.[67]

Further, the signs are introductory in another sense, for their proper and full explanation waits upon Jesus's death and exaltation. Thus, Jesus's signs are rich with a symbolic meaning, which John must have intended. Clearly, this miracle draws attention to his person, and indeed at times Jesus acts in order to draw attention to his activity and ministry.[68] In John, the teaching of Jesus about his own role follows upon and develops out of his messianic signs and deeds.[69]

Certainly, the issue of Jesus's messiahship controls discussions, as Jesus demonstrates to proclaim publicly who he is.[70] For John without a doubt, and for the early Christians also, Jesus was the Messiah. As mentioned above, however, the expected Messiah was to be the king of Israel from David's lineage. That there is no need to look outside Jewish circles for the origin of the term is made clear in the study made by M. Hengel, who observes that this Aramaic text was not completely unknown to Palestinian Judaism.[71] Maybe John sees the church as the true Israel (those accepting Jesus as the Messiah) and the Christian movement as replacing Israel's spiritual fallen. At the bottom line, no other Gospel makes the element of fulfillment (the messianic expectation) more explicit than the Gospel of John.[72]

The evangelist's main concern, in fact, is the affirmation of Jesus as Messiah in a way that transcends all earlier expectations.[73] John is a theologian who places the faith of his community in Jesus and on the lips of Jesus. In fact,

---

65   C. Marvin Pate, *The Writings of John: A Survey of the Gospel, Epistles and Apocalypse* (Grand Rapids: Zondervan, 2011), 56: "In other words, was John the anointed Son of David predicted in the Old Testament who would defeat Israel's enemies and establish God's kingdom (see e.g. 2 Sam. 7:11b–16; Hos. 3:5)."
66   Köstenberger, *Encountering John*, 33.
67   Smith, *Theology of the Gospel of John*, 108: "Perhaps the source represented a simple miracle of faith, which John has seriously modified, if he did not oppose it."
68   Christopher Tuckett, *Christology and the New Testament: Jesus and his Earliest Followers* (Louisville: Westminster John Knox, 2001), 152.
69   Schreiner, *New Testament Theology*, 204.
70   D. Moody Smith, *John*, ANTC (Nashville: Abingdon, 1999), 31.
71   Martin Hengel, *The Son of God* (Philadelphia: Fortress, 1976), 45.
72   Smith, *Theology of the Gospel of John*, 86.
73   Gerard S. Sloyan, *What Are They Saying About John?*, rev. ed. (New York: Paulist, 2006), 27.

similar to the Synoptic Gospels, John identifies Jesus as the Messiah in keeping with Jewish expectations.[74] But the synoptic Jesus mentions very little regarding himself, his preaching about the kingdom of God, and the nature of God's demands.[75] However, John's Jesus is far clearer about himself, so that his teaching concentrates on his own person far more directly. The Jesus from the Gospel of John is the object of faith far more explicitly than in the Synoptic Gospels.

On the one hand, John's ethical teaching is not large in amount, nor prominent in substance. On the other hand, John's true purpose was not to teach ethics, but to show people Jesus as the Messiah.[76] According to Keener, "Some doubt that Jesus's earliest followers considered him messiah, but this position rejects all explicit testimony that remains in favor of a hypothesis argued virtually from silence. Others suspect that Jesus drew on 2 Sam 7 and others passages that lent themselves to a messianic interpretation."[77]

For our present question, it is of equal significance to point out what is not said about the Messiah's works. The apparent neglecting factor and doubts, however, may arise from the wrong feeling that Jesus's messianic claims are not, after all, very significant to the evangelist. If this is right, how far is such a feeling justified?[78] The evangelist presents Jesus in more explicit and far more exalted terms than anything we find in the Synoptic Gospels.

Characteristically, Jesus says who he is and debates with opponents his own status and role. He makes direct christological assertions and defends them against attack. In fact, this is John's way of anchoring Christology in Jesus's ministry and affirming that this human being really was the Messiah, the Son of God.[79] And it seems John acknowledged most clearly of all that the crucifixion of Jesus denoted the end of any traditional messianic conception. Further, it has become more common to see John's Christology about the Messiah in a clearer way than what is found in the Synoptics.[80] On the one hand, John may show an earlier christological tradition also among the Synoptics (especially Mark and Luke). For instance, it seems there is a parallel in the form the Gospels of Matthew and Mark report the answer of Jesus when placed under

---

74 Köstenberger, *Theology of John*, 315.
75 Tuckett, *Christology and the New Testament*, 151.
76 Leon Morris, *The Gospel According to John*, rev. ed., NICNT (Grand Rapids: Eerdmans, 1995), 121.
77 Keener, *Gospel of John*, 289.
78 Ashton, *Understanding the Fourth Gospel*, 148.
79 Smith, *Theology of the Gospel of John*, 110.
80 Tuckett, *Christology and the New Testament*, 152.

oath by the Jewish high priest—that in fact he was the Messiah. On the other hand, according to the Greek text of Mark, Jesus answered with ἐγώ εἰμί. In fact, it means "yes," but the parallel texts of the Gospel of Matthew and Luke's Gospel read in a different way.[81]

Evidence from the earliest aspects of the Jesus tradition, however, shows that Jesus taught that his disciples would have a role in the messianic kingdom. In contrast, another reason Jesus appears to be reluctant to use the title may have been because in early Judaism it was sometimes thought that no one could claim to be the Messiah until he had completed the tasks of the Messiah.[82] Jewish people expected that God was the ultimate physical healer, and thus sought his help through prayer. In addition, Jewish healers became common in the Diaspora, particularly through their supposed access to the secret name of God.[83]

As mentioned above, the Messiah is expected to do miracles. And there is also the evidence of the *sign prophet* mentioned in the writing of Josephus.[84] Indeed, Jesus's deeds include the signs he worked during his whole life and ministry. It should be noted that the connection between the signs accounts and the discourses material in John's Gospel is complex; much more complex than is sometimes thought.[85] It is not right that all accounts have become inextricably bound up with discourses. Generally speaking, the relation between accounts and discourses is more intricate than is supposed.

Some narrative can be given of the development of the Johannine tradition in the context of the history of the Johannine followers.[86] For this reason the technical inquiry of Jesus's messiahship is decisively held together through the right interpretation of his signs.[87] Some interpreters, however, pointing to the parallels between early Christian and other ancient miracle narrative, have suggested that both are fabricated.[88] Such a hypothesis cannot, however, be maintained in such a simple form without qualification.

In contrast, Vielhauer asserts that in first-century Judaism the Messiah was not believed to be a miracle worker (Da im zeitgenössischen Judentum der

---

81   Cullmann, *Christology*, 118.
82   Witherington, *Many Faces of Christ*, 172.
83   Keener, *Gospel of John*, 255–56.
84   Josephus, *Ant.* 19.162; 20.167–172, 188.
85   Painter, *Quest for the Messiah*, 90.
86   Painter, *Quest for the Messiah*, 91.
87   Martyn, *History and Theology*, 94.
88   Keener, *Gospel of John*, 258.

Messias nicht als Wundertäter galt).[89] It is not surprising that several others scholars have reached similar conclusions. But not all scholars agree. Although some form of messianic expectation was normal, there was no consensus about the exact figure whose coming was expected or the circumstances surrounding his arrival, and first-century Judaism displayed a diversity of messianic expectations.[90] We need to ask, therefore, whether or not the working of miracles is an activity expected of the Messiah. However, the proclamation of Jesus as the Christ (anointed one) is established with the least ambiguity in the witness of John,[91] which comes relatively late in the NT. Granting that the essential concept of *the Messiah* was formed by scriptural texts that mentioned a descendant of David, other texts were also connected with the messianic descendant of David, though not automatically so.

We find this particularly in John 1:41 and 4:25, where Μεσσίας and χριστός are exactly connected. In both texts, however, we see how the main concept comes from the NT. The context of it is the Hellenistic church, which originated from the Palestinian Jewish community.[92] On the one hand, the messianic expectation that was already part of the Jewish belief was neither spiritualized nor reinterpreted. On the other hand, to a certain extent, it was taken up and set out on a large scale. Furthermore, Josephus also mentions that even the Pharisees and Sadducees had concrete messianic hopes; they both looked for the coming Davidic messianic kingdom. The Messiah according to them would overthrow the Gentiles (in particular the Roman power) and restore the fortunes of Israel with Jerusalem as capital.[93]

The most astonishing characteristic in this connection is the part played by Jesus's messiahship in the Fourth Gospel. At the same time, however, the Gospel of John may show an earlier christological tradition, for which we have some—though limited—proof.[94] Nevertheless, all four Gospels take for granted that the phrase "Anointed One" was in general use as a designation of the man whom God was expected to make king of his people at the end of time.[95] It should be noted also, however, that the Messiah first appears as the ideal

---

89   P. Vielhauer, "Erwägungen zur Christologie des Markusevangeliums," in *Zeit und Geschichte*, ed. E. Dinkler (Munich: Kaiser, 1964), 69.
90   Köstenberger, *Theology of John*, 314.
91   Silva, *New International Dictionary*, 691.
92   Ashton, *Understanding the Fourth Gospel*, 314.
93   Josephus, *Ant.* 13.5.9, 171.
94   Keener, *Gospel of John*, 283.
95   N.A. Dahl, "Messianic Ideas and the Crucifixion of Jesus," in *The Messiah: Developments in Earliest Judaism and Christianity*, ed. James H. Charlesworth (Minneapolis: Fortress, 1992), 384.

successor to King David, and, normally, whenever "Messiah" is used without qualification in the New Testament, it is either as a proper name or with the allusion to the coming kingly personage.[96]

Further, John may reflect a complex expansion of the tradition history as shown in the way he uses the term *Messiah/Christos*. In fact, the way John uses the title seems to be undeveloped, at least when contrasted with some other writers in the New Testament.[97] If so, then it seems obvious to demonstrate that various views of "messiahship" had already undergone an important change and development. However, the question of whether Jesus acted or claimed to be the Messiah reaches a critical point with his trial and death, as John makes particularly obvious.[98] In any case, at most one can argue that Jesus suggested something about his own messianic identity and in particular his ministry and mission.

Furthermore, in the earthly phase of his mission, Jesus is the Suffering Servant who is to give his life a ransom for many, pouring out his blood in a sacrificial, atoning death.[99] It appears then that according to G. Theissen and A. Merz "there is no evidence prior to the New Testament for the notion of a suffering Messiah; moreover, there is no evidence of anyone becoming the Messiah through resurrection."[100] Theissen and Merz's viewpoint is a simple conjecture, because there is clear evidence of a pre-Christian notion of the suffering Messiah in the Old Testament and in the Essenes of the Qumran community (Isaiah 53 is interpreted in terms of the suffering Messiah in the Targum of the Prophets). The evidence known to this point is adequate to corroborate this notion. In contrast, however, the notion of a crucified Messiah was absurd to the Greco-Roman culture. Would not any position on it inevitably have created misunderstanding? For the Jews, the crucified Messiah was ideologically understood because they were expecting a Messiah as a liberator from the Romans power. It should be noted that on the second day of John the Baptist's special week he publicly pointed out Jesus as the Messiah of whom he had preaching.[101]

---

96   Ashton, *Understanding the Fourth Gospel*, 158.
97   Tuckett, *Christology and the New Testament*, 156.
98   Smith, *Theology of the Gospel of John*, 89.
99   Ladd, *Theology of the New Testament*, 171.
100 Gerd Theissen and Annnette Merz, *The Historical Jesus: A Comprehensive Guide* (Minneapolis: Fortress, 1998), 540.
101 Morris, *Gospel according to John*, 126.

For instance, Peter identifies Jesus as Messiah/Christ in his famous confession of Jesus in Mark 8:29: "You are the Messiah."[102] However, in fact, Jesus neither affirms nor denies the confession made by Peter.[103] For some interpreters what Peter meant by his confession of Jesus's messiahship is debated.[104] Clearly, Peter answered that Jesus is the Christ (Messiah). The Johannine parallel, however, also mixes Peter's confession with a saying about Satan (John 6:67–71).[105]

Without a doubt, Jesus could have responded to the confession that he was the Messiah. Certainly, Peter seems to have had in mind the contemporary Jewish hope of a divinely anointed Messiah from David's lineage who would destroy the contemporary Roman social and political power structures and gather Israel into God's kingdom. However, this was a wrong notion held not just by the disciples (Peter and the others), but by almost the whole of the Jewish nation. Most importantly, however, Jesus did not intend to fulfill the messianic promise in the way expected by most Jews; namely, to destroy Roman power and control.[106] Nevertheless, all this stands in contradiction to the fact that the Romans crucified Jesus as a political Messiah.[107] But this notion was completely different from the one mentioned in the Gospel of John.

Tom Thatcher asserts that John appears to be apolitical, on the ground that the interests of the passage are basically theological. On the other hand, Jewish nationalism and hatred against the Roman Empire was a common issue in the time of Jesus.[108] For early Christianity, in fact, the clear notion was that Christ is, in every manner, greater than Caesar of the Rome Empire. It is interesting to note that from the time of Julius Caesar (d. 44 BCE), Jews had been exempt from emperor worship, and as long as Jewish Christians were perceived as Jews who worshiped in synagogues, they too would be thus exempt.[109]

Some have doubts that Jesus's followers thought of him as a Messiah, but this viewpoint rejects all clear testimony that remains in favor of a supposition

---

102　In fact, in Matthew's account of Peter's confession, he confesses Jesus as Christ and Son of God (Matt 16:16).

103　Chris Keith, "Jesus outside and inside in the New Testament," in *Jesus Among Friends and Enemies: A Historical and Literary Introduction to Jesus in the Gospels*, ed. C. Keith and L. Hurtado (Grand Rapids: Baker Academic, 2011), 20.

104　Ladd, *Theology of the New Testament*, 139–40.

105　Theissen and Merz, *Historical Jesus*, 539.

106　Schreiner, *New Testament Theology*, 206.

107　Cullmann, *Christology*, 126.

108　Tom Thatcher, "The Death of Jesus and the End of Empire in the Gospel of John," in *Empire in the New Testament*, ed. S.E. Porter and C.L. Westfall (Eugene, OR: Pickwick Publications, 2011), 141: "At first glance, any discussion of the Fourth Gospel's response to empire seems futile, simply because John does not appear to be particularly interested in Rome."

109　Pate, *Writings of John*, 31.

argued virtually from silence.[110] In any case, the Gospels portray a man who was conscious that in him dwelt transcendence. The essential issue is that of transcendence. Jesus is shown as a transcendent being entirely conscious of this dimension. Jesus was the Messiah in whom God's kingly reign had come to humanity; but he wasn't seen as the nationalistic, political Messiah expected by some Jews.[111] Whereas some first-century Jews just desired peace, others sought revolt against the Roman rulers. As seen above, Jesus did not encourage violent revolution or any kind of bad sentiments against the Romans rulers. John's language regarding Jesus and about Jesus as Messiah has a number of different characteristics associated with it.[112] The language of "sending" on its own is thus possibly in prophetic traditions showing us a true Messiah prophet figure. Certainly, too, John implies this notion of Jesus as the one who reveals God to others as the Messiah of Israel.

On the contrary, Jesus preaches and proclaims that his kingdom was not from this earth. It was not an earthly kingdom (like the Roman Empire), but a spiritual one. More than any other Gospel writer, John recognizes and makes explicit the role of the Messiah as spiritual king of Israel.[113] Furthermore, Jesus not only claims to be the Messiah, he also reflects a consciousness of enjoying a unique relationship with God. It is important that this crucified Messiah is clearly said to be the king of Israel (John 1:49). How can the Messiah/Christ come from Galilee? In all probability, people expected the Messiah to be born in Bethlehem—from David's line—and from the town where David lived (John 7:41–42). Jesus the Messiah was in fact born in Bethlehem. One important aspect of Jesus as Messiah is his mission; the objective is the preparation of men and women for the future Kingdom of God. John mentions that Jesus constantly looked forward to the coming of the eschatological kingdom of the Messiah and the final judgment. People come across the powers of the future eschatological kingdom in the person of the messianic king.[114] While no other Gospel makes the element of fulfillment more explicit than John, in no Gospel is this expectation more completely transcended and transformed.[115] John appears to know more about the traditional expectation of the Messiah

---

110 Marshall, *Origins of New Testament Christology*, 54–56. "We have reached the conclusion that indirect Christology makes the existence of a direct Christology in the teaching of Jesus highly probable."
111 Ladd, *Theology of the New Testament*, 171.
112 Tuckett, *Christology and the New Testament*, 161.
113 Smith, *Theology of the Gospel of John*, 89.
114 Ladd, *Theology of the New Testament*, 181.
115 Ashton, *Understanding the Fourth Gospel*, 147.

than the other Gospel writers.[116] In fact, such a discussion (that of the crucified Messiah) is unique to the Fourth Gospel. Thus, in John's complete presentation it is obvious that the description of Jesus as *Messiah/Christos* is intended to say far more than this as well.

4 Conclusion

The Gospel of John appears purposely to use the term Messiah so as to emphasize how Jesus fulfills Jewish messianic expectation. In fact, for John's Gospel, Jesus was the Messiah. It seems clear, however, that all the Gospels—as well as the rest of the New Testament—take Jesus to be the Messiah, the Christ of biblical and Jewish expectation. Yet at the same time Jesus is the expected one (*the Anointed One*), the Messiah of Israel, the Christ, and the fulfillment of deep human need. The fact that John may well reflect a complex development of tradition history is in all probability made known in his use of the title Messiah/Christos. As seen above, the Synoptic Jesus says little about his role as Messiah, but the Johannine Jesus is far clearer about himself and his role as the expected Messiah. John thus presents Jesus in far more exalted terms than anything we find in the Synoptic Gospels. John is the most clearly christological of the Gospels. As a matter of fact, for John, Jesus was the true Messiah. John's message is that in Jesus, all the numerous scriptural messianic predictions and typology meet, not just in his life but most significantly in his death.

Thus, far from disqualifying Jesus from being the expected Messiah, John portrays his crucifixion as the place where Jesus most reveals that he is. As mentioned above, however, all the Gospels, as well as the rest of the New Testament, take Jesus to be the Messiah, the Christ of biblical and Jewish expectation. Accordingly, John saw himself as one whose ministry was to prepare the way for God's chosen one (the Messiah) to come and effect the true restoration of Israel, namely, to turn their hearts to God. In a very important sense, John's message is that Jesus was the Messiah and that salvation history finds its climatic fulfillment. Hence, no Gospel demonstrates a greater awareness of the nature of messiahship and whether Jesus could rightfully claim it, than the Gospel of John.

---

116   Smith, *Theology of the Gospel of John*, 87.

PART 2

Johannine Christology in Hellenistic and Jewish Contexts

∴

CHAPTER 4

Creational Light as Christological Theodicy in the Fourth Gospel

Andrew W. Pitts

Current scholarship on the Johannine light motif seems to largely agree with Raymond Brown and Richard Bauckham, that John adopts and christologically adapts something close to the Qumran conception of light/darkness.[1] The Gnostic (Bultmann) or Hermetic (Dodd) backgrounds for light and darkness in the Fourth Gospel are no longer taken seriously.[2] While certain similarities with the Qumran covenanters are undeniable, I will argue that John more closely reflects apologetic deployments of creational light in response to pagan/Greek objections to Jewish theism based on divine hiddenness and, correspondingly, the problem of evil. George Ladd and others have already noted significant differences between the Qumran dualism and the Johannine cluster of metaphors surrounding light and darkness, especially divergent theological emphases.[3] In addition, if we assume with Bauckham that John's Gospel was an "open" Gospel or with Porter a more "public" Gospel, then the sectarian Qumran documents probably do not provide the most suitable parallel materials. After all, they lack the missional emphasis on belief so important to the narrative infrastructure of the Fourth Gospel. John's Jesus speaks to the Greeks and the Samaritans and offers salvation to both. John's Gospel is also written in Greek, not Hebrew or Aramaic.

The creation of light in connection with Hellenistic Jewish reception of Genesis 1–9 (esp. Gen 1:1–3) seems on the surface more akin to John's apologetic aims than the highly exclusive aims of the sectarian texts discovered at

---

1 E.g., Raymond A. Brown, "The Qumran Scrolls and the Johannine Gospel and Epistles," in Raymond A. Brown, *New Testament Essays* (New York: Paulist, 1965), 102–31; Richard Bauckham, "Qumran and the Gospel of John: Is there a Connection?," in *The Scrolls and the Scriptures: Qumran Fifty Years After*, edited by Stanley E. Porter and Craig A. Evans, LSTS 26 (Sheffield: Sheffield Academic, 1997), 267–79; rep. (among other places) in Richard Bauckham, *The Testimony of the Beloved Disciple: Narrative, History, and Theology in the Gospel of John* (Grand Rapids: Baker Academic, 2008), 125–36.
2 E.g., George E. Ladd, *A Theology of the New Testament*, rev. ed. (Grand Rapids: Eerdmans, 1994), 253–58.
3 Ladd, *Theology*, 255–57.

Qumran. Philo, in particular, shows special interest in convincing the pagans of the existence of a singular creator-God, as described in the Genesis cosmogony on the basis of Yahweh's creation of light. In addition to being composed in Greek, John suggests a strong connection with Jesus as the light of the "world" (apparently, including pagans) and consistently emphasizes Jesus's ministry to non-Jews in Jerusalem. This chapter will argue, therefore, that certain apologetic deployments of creational light within Hellenistic Judaism seem to align more naturally with the Johannine light motif than the current Brown-Bauckham Qumran proposal.

1 Divine Hiddenness, Creational Light, and Theodicy in Hellenistic Judaism

A number of Hellenistic Jewish texts correlate divine revelation with light/goodness/day and darkness/evil/night with divine hiddenness. For certain Hellenistic Jews at least, the problem of evil is deeply linked to the hiddenness of God and the creation of light to revelation (i.e., an answer to the problems of evil and divine hiddenness). These themes find their development most clearly in the reception history of Genesis 1–9, and especially Genesis 1. Darkness seems to create a kind of tapestry in the original creation that forms the revelatory backdrop for the subsequent creation of light and its consequent overcoming of darkness. God's spirit/breath/presence was always amidst the darkness, overcoming it, but God was hidden in the darkness momentarily until light subsequently broke through the endarkned abyss as a sign God's sovereign activity within the cosmological waters of Gen 1:2–3.

3 Enoch, for example, paints an intriguing cosmological portrait that weaves together a variety of scriptural traditions involving the wind or breath of God as symbols of the divine presence amidst the darkness. Although only extant in Hebrew, *3 Enoch* was composed during the Hellenistic period and reflects many themes that emerge in later Greek Jewish texts of the same period. The רוּחַ אֱלֹהִים or πνεῦμα θεοῦ is interpreted almost universally in Hellenistic Jewish reception of Gen 1:2–3 not as the Spirit of God (implying some kind of binatarian conception of Yahweh) but as his wind, breath, or presence in the darkness that was upon the face of the waters, as it is in *3 En.* 23.1–2. R. Ishmael begins his revelatory exposition of Israel's story by indicating that he received this revelation from the angel Metatron, whom he calls the "Prince of the Divine Presence" (*3 En.* 23.1).

The angel reveals to R. Ishmael that God was driving the "dark sea" all night with a strong easterly wind. It was this easterly wind that brought the locusts of judgement upon Egypt in Exod 3:13. These waters not only embody cosmological but also eschatological power, as their trajectories flood through Israel's history as depicted by their Sacred Scriptures. How these events are connected is not explicated but it seems to be the intention of the author to indicate that God's power over evil forces has roots as far back as the original creation and likely in the mysterious time that preceded it. The wind of God is later equated with several divine attributes ranging from "a wind of wisdom and insight," "a wind of council and power," and "a wind of knowledge and fear of the Lord," reiterated twice over (*3 En.* 23.9).

According to R. Ishmael's revelation, the cosmological wind of Genesis 1 is equivalent to the presence of God, conceptualized in terms of his divine attributes. Furthermore, Meṭaṭron reveals that Satan was among these winds, enacting a storm of judgement (3 *En.* 23.15–17). The revelation renders God's presence behind the scenes, fighting against Satan within the deep, as a kind of eschatological power, setting into motion a range of future events connected with the struggle between good/God and evil/darkness. The cosmology of Gen 1:2 thus takes on eschatological functions for *3 Enoch*, impacting subsequent events in its retelling of Israel's story. For example, the winds of the storm that Noah endured are portrayed along the same lines as the wind of the presence of God in Gen 1:2–3. God's wrath and sorrow over sin are likewise depicted as winds (*3 En.* 23.13, 16). The author points to Ps 18:10 as an illustration of the existence of evil at the creation event with Satan described as a cherub and a presence (wind) in his own right, wrangling with God in the cosmological abyss of Gen 1:2. The revelator depicts both God's and Satan's presence as warring winds within the blackened waters. Similarly, the presence of God with Adam in the Garden of Eden is modeled by R. Ishmael as—again—divine wind. Chariots of wind then become chariots of fire, appearing with a dense cloud, apparently emblematic of the Lord's presence (3 *En.* 24.4).

R. Ishmael deciphers the events of Gen 1:2 with apocalyptic imagery, decrypting the Genesis cosmogony such that Yahweh's fight against darkness was something fundamental rather incidental to the original creation. The Genesis narrative forecasts future judgement, first with Noah and then at the end of time. When we return to the Mosaic creation account's opening lines, we discover that the creation of light—curiously absent from the portrait provided to R. Ishmael by Meṭaṭron—overcomes this darkness and would be called good, along with "day," until humanity eventually rebels, forcing God to judge Noah's generation through a stormy wind (i.e., presence). Ultimately, the Noah narrative points to a final judgement prior to the establishment of a new created order, where *3 Enoch* envisions the Lord on his throne at the climatic end of the chapter (*3 En.* 24.23; cf. Isa 7:1).

Given the previous invocation of the flood narrative in R. Ishmael's revelation, one cannot help but entertain the possibility that the cloud imagery in *3 En.* 24.3–4 continues motifs introduced from the flood narrative, with God's bow in the clouds functioning as the eschatological climax of the story (Gen 9:14–17). For *3 Enoch*, however, it is God himself rather than a bow of light that is found within the clouds. As R. Ishmael's revelation continues, we discover that God is not hidden from his creation. His presence is seen in a multitude of winds that apparently represent differing aspects of the divine presence, ranging from winds of divine knowledge and power to the winds of divine judgement. Knowledge of God's multifaceted presence through the forces of wind is only to be given to "a single one" who is wise (apparently at least Noah), i.e., the one who seeks God. The God-seeker is the one who presses against the apocalyptic winds of divine judgement, knowledge, wisdom, and power to see all aspects of God in the created order. The bow in the clouds from the Noah story further punctuates God's revelatory presence in the new creation, pointing to a time after the final judgement when God will ultimately be exalted and there will be no more darkness, only light (*3 En.* 24.23), as in the Noah narrative.

4 Ezra 6.38–40 refers to the events of Gen 1:2–3 in terms of revelation as well. At the hour of darkness, the presence of God hovered over the abyss when "silence embraced everything" and the voice of man had not yet spoken. God was amidst the darkness, though silent, but then "a ray of light" broke the divine silence "so that [his] works might then appear." The author contrasts divine silence and darkness, on the one hand, with divine light and appearance, on the other. What does the light reveal? It seems to reveal that God was always amidst the darkness, even if silent and undetected. Similarly, the *Testament of Adam* locates God's silent but active presence in the dark seas of Gen 1:2–3 as the protective force that hindered demonic oppression from injuring humanity. In the cosmological darkness, God opposed the forces of evil from succeeding in their opposition against humanity and in this way is yet again seen as an answer—even if a silent one—to the forces of evil that had been set in motion from the beginnings of creation (*T. Adam* 2.10). Similarly, in *Joseph and Aseneth*, the creation makes the invisible things visible, again with light serving a highly revelatory function (12.1–3) (on this point, see also *2 En.* 24.1–5).

According to Eusebius, Aristobulus emphasizes the importance of understanding divine revelation (i.e., the "divine voice") not as the spoken word but in the establishment of the cosmos. Aristobulus claims that the peripatetic philosophers (Pythagoras, Socrates, and Plato) imitate Moses here when they claim to "hear the voice of God" in the establishment of the cosmos. According to Aristobulus, the origin of light thus functions as a "metaphor" for divine wisdom. Here too some "belonging to the Peripatetic school" copy Moses in deploying wisdom as a lantern holder (cf. John 5:35) that, if followed, will result in peace for the philosopher's entire life (Eusebius, *Hist. eccl.* 13.12.9–16; Aristobulus Frag. 5.9–10).

As with R. Ishmael in the revelations recorded in *3 Enoch* 23–24, Pseudo-Philo suggests an eschatological relationship between the black abyss of Gen 1:2–3 and the flood narrative in Genesis 6–9. To begin with, the author correlates divine "silence" with "darkness" in Gen 1:2. The author says that "silence" then spoke a word and darkness became light. The author insists that God's hiddenness was only momentary since he eventually did reveal himself (i.e., "speak") in the creation of light (Pseudo-Philo 60.2). God's name in this way was "pronounced" (revelation) as the manifestation of light resulted in the division of the waters. The upper portion of the waters reveals impending divine justice (to be meted out through the flood "in due season"). The lower portion of the division, according to Pseudo-Philo, reveals divine goodness in that it produces food, life, and sustenance for all of God's creation. The upper parts anticipate the rebellion of humanity and would soon be used to judge the rebellious generation of Noah's days (Pseudo-Philo 60.2).

Philo, not Pseudo, provides one of the most detailed interpretations of the creation story, particularly Gen 1:1–3, from all of Jewish antiquity. In his essay *On Creation*, Philo provides a sustained treatment of Genesis 1, culminating in "five beautiful lessons" that take on a clearly apologetic function at the climactic end point of the exposition (*Opif.* 170–71). Philo locates the central worry of the non-theist, among other things, in their current existence in darkness (i.e., lack of revelation as a result of not seeking the Good/God), using Moses' creation account as a narrative axiom for addressing the problem of divine hiddenness and, by extension, the (pagan) problem of evil. For Philo, the problem of evil is tantamount to the problem of divine hiddenness. Therefore, revelation is seen specifically in the creation of light and its consequent overcoming of darkness in Genesis 1 as a crucial philosophical resource for addressing the primary pagan objections to theism (which he interprets in terms of belief in the existence of Yahweh, the sole creator of the cosmos), as configured specifically within the opening lines of the Jewish Scriptures.

Before turning to Philo's essay *On Creation*, his work *On the Giants* is worth briefly considering in our attempts to understand the role of the creation narrative in the formation of his theodicy. Philo interprets the πνεῦμα θεοῦ in Gen 1:2 as "the air of God flowing upon the earth," adding a third element in addition to the water, which was already present (*Gig.* 22). This "air" (ἀήρ), Philo says, is in its essence already light but in other respects this air also functions as divine "knowledge" (ἐπιστήμη), which every wise person takes part in (*Gig.* 22).

For Philo, then, to be filled with the πνεῦμα θεοῦ is to be filled with his "wisdom, understanding, and knowledge," as Bezaleel was (*Gig.* 23) (cf. Exod 31:1). Philo seems to think that the πνεῦμα θεοῦ equates to the presence of God (projected through air/light), defined in specifically revelatory terms (wisdom, understanding, and knowledge).

Philo begins his essay *On Creation* by representing Moses as the Greek philosopher *par excellence*. He begins the treatise with Moses' credentials. He then frames his account polemically against the pagans' disbelief in God, especially the God of Judaism. The entire essay assuages an assault on the Israelites' philosophical enemies against the revelatory backdrop of Israel's cosmogony in Genesis 1. The pagans' darkened (non-enlightened) prison inhibits their ability to see the manifestation of Yahweh in the created order and, therefore, leaves them without evidentiary excuse for denying Yahweh's existence (*Opif.* 7).

When Philo finally turns to the creation history that will ultimately drive his theodicy, he devotes detailed attention to the narrative's opening lines, especially Gen 1:2–3. In §§21–22, he positions "the Good" (i.e., God) as the originating source for the cosmos. Goodness prevails from the initiatory moments of creation, even though darkness has temporarily engulfed the good in apocalyptic waters that suspend its manifestation. For Philo, the problem is not lack of revelation or, in other words, divine hiddenness but the failure of the observer to pursue the Good. If anyone would "desire" and then take the time to "investigate" the enteral power and faculty that so clearly governs the cosmological order, Philo claims, they would quickly discover that the good underlying the arrangement of the universe is none other than the "Father and Creator" himself, defined as his consummate nature (i.e., inclusive of all of his enteral properties—goodness, justice, etc.) (*Opif.* 22).

After dispelling debates over the origins of a singular (i.e., theistic-type) God's beginning ("If God created all, who created God?" kinds of objections), as though the creator of space/time would require a space-time beginning (*Opif.* 26), Philo gets right to the epicentral issue—revelation. Philo appears to assume the existence of "visible" gods but since these require space/time, he dismisses them as the eternal good since the obfuscating force(s) behind the origins of the cosmos—whatever he/she/it may be—appears to have created space (i.e., motion or movement, κινήσεως) and time (*Opif.* 27–28). It must be kept in mind, Philo argues, that since the initial creative cause was immaterial, its environment would not need to be material. After all, Philo ponders, what use would a physical heavens and earth have been to an immaterial creator? Therefore, divine hiddenness in its first phases was simply a by-product of the non-material structure of divine existence and, by extension, his non-material environmental needs (*Opif.* 29).

Philo comes to conclude on the basis of this cosmological data that "air and light" should, therefore, be "considered worthy of the pre-eminence" (*Opif.* 30). Why? Because "the breath of God" (i.e., air/divine presence/revelation) gives life to all things (goodness) and because light is "surpassingly beautiful." And this is Philo's answer to the (esp. pagan) problem of evil: how can one deny the truth of a singular immaterial creator given the manifestation expressed in material goodness and beauty in the world. Philo seems to think, again, that material manifestations are based on immaterial models in the first phases of the heavens and the earth. The pagan is only perplexed because they focus only on material modes of existence without considering the purer immaterial models of goodness and beauty upon which they must be based (*Opif.* 30). Philo clearly draws here, with the pagans, heavily from Platonic thought, as he often does elsewhere, taking on Platonic assumptions as the philosophical foundation for advocating his specifically Jewish natural theology.

The divine reason (θείου λόγου, cf. John 1:1–4), Philo contends, is invisible and consequently, hidden (*Opif.* 31). Its revelatory effects, however, are not. This is because that which is only intelligible by the intellect (i.e., an observer's immaterial mind contemplating the immaterial divine mind) is "far more brilliant and splendid than that which is seen" (*Opif.* 31). Philo has in mind here a kind of contrast, comparing the phenomena of divine hiddenness and observation with binary physical realities that demonstrate underlying immaterial ones. The light/sun, he says, is more brilliant than the darkness, for even the moon depends upon light in the night, and so on (*Opif.* 31–32). Light, furthermore, is perceptible only to the intellect but the sun to the senses. What is better, Philo asks, the light or the sun? The light, he answers; because of course, it is immaterial, even if hidden from the senses. But what contrasts or reflects the model of darkness as the sun does for light? Nothing, Philo again answers, as darkness does not function as a model (for anything) in the way that light does for the sun and many further physical realities besides. Therefore, Philo says: the light (a substance), when it shines, devastates its adversary of darkness, a mere form which is also, incidentally, dependent upon light, according to Philo. And though Moses is correct when he says that darkness "was over" the face of the "abyss," he is also correct to indicate that the light (completely) overcame the darkness (*Opif.* 32–33) since darkness does not provide any foundational reality or substance—only light provides a model for the physical. Therefore, God did not destroy the darkness through his light/presence/revelation but only "divided" the light from the darkness. The light illumined the heavens, according to Philo's reading of Genesis 1, with darkness being relegated beneath it so that the darkness would continue to form yet another form or contrast to light. Therefore light, Philo argues, provides that fundamental reality or substance that functions as a model for many forms, even the darkness that once appeared to cover it in the abyss (*Opif.* 34–36) (see also *Opif.* 55–61).

I have already alluded to the important apologetic function of the closing to Philo's treatise *On Creation* (*Opif.* 168–72). Philo, again, understands the creation narrative as a kind of philosophical resource for addressing the related problems of evil and divine hiddenness. As with other Hellenistic Jews, Philo landscapes this sticky terrain not only through the Mosaic cosmogony but also on the basis of what he believes to be its climax in the flood narrative. He insists that the sun and moon "continually give light" since the time of original creation "for the sake of no other reason but because evil and disobedience are banished to a distance far from the boundaries of heaven." This, so that light manifests the "ever-flowing graces of God." Nevertheless, there came a time in the days of Noah at which point wickedness began to increase faster than virtue/goodness (*Opif.* 168).

God then revealed not only his goodness in supplying earth with its sustenance through light but also in causing the waters that once separated into darkness to become a force of his justice. These waters that covered the earth in the Genesis account represent for Philo then an initial triumph over evil/darkness. They become a prophetic pointer, in other words, to the eventual justice that God would execute on Noah's generation for their failure to enjoy the beauty of creation's goodness in the light of his revelation. The humanity that inhabited the original creation chose instead to walk in darkness, hiding from revelation as it were (a kind of self-inflected blindness, it seems to Philo), rather than pursuing the light/revelation. It was not God that was hidden. God had revealed himself from the moment that he created light and, concurrently, overcame darkness. Rather, humanity was hiding from the enlightening God in the darkness of disobedience (cf. the abyss of Gen 1:2) that would eventually become the mechanism (i.e., the separated waters) for their future judgement (*Opif.* 169–70).

After all, Philo urges, Noah's generation was clearly unworthy of the beauty of God's revelation, choosing the evil rather than the Good/God (*Opif.* 168–69). But the justice of God was paradoxically moderated by divine mercy toward corrupted humanity, permitting the human race to live on through Noah and his family. Philo thus frames the Mosaic creation—flood narrative (Gen 1–9) eschatologically as an answer to the pagan problem of evil by showing that God's allowance of evil (including divine hiddenness) was a necessary means for the greater good of eternal revelation. The existence of darkness and sin allowed the light of God's justice and mercy to shine forth in this way so that God's multi-faceted presence could be enjoyed by those who pursue the good/God. This, for Philo, represents a kind of greater good theodicy where light manifested as revelation functions to reveal the manifold eternal graces of

Yahweh in a way that seems impossible apart from his sovereign allowance of and fight against the forces of evil. This trajectory, for Philo, answers the many pagan objections to the existence of a singular creator-God, who provides the philosophical grounding for all that is good and worthy of observation in the world. Put another way, one cannot appreciate the light without the darkness (*Opif.* 168–72).

By way of summary, then: Philo (and other Hellenistic Jews to varying degrees) seems to raise, in strictly revelatory terms, a question that questions the pagan problems of evil, and the apparent hiddenness of God. According to Philo's conception of the original creation and the new creation that it anticipated (i.e., the flood narrative), temporal darkness/evil was necessary for the full manifestation of everlasting light/revelation. After all, Philo contemplates, without evil, how could God manifest the full spectrum of his everlasting kindness, especially his justice and mercy? How could Yahweh show himself to be a just creator if there were no evils to judge? And how could God fully reveal himself as a merciful God if there were no evils to be pardoned? Further, Philo and other Hellenistic Jews emphasize the temporality of evil in its subsequent judgement through several eschatological sequences that usher in a new creation, populated by Noah and his family. Evil—even in its most horrific forms—was temporary and ultimately judged so that it could provide a kind of everlasting backdrop or better, black-drop, for the eternal enjoyment of divine revelation among the new creation's new humanity.

2 Light Christology and Theodicy in the Gospel of John

It is well known to scholars that John rewrites the creation narrative found in the opening lines of the Greek Bible. As with Philo (cf. his use of θείου λόγου in *Opif.* 31), the Johannine Prologue emphasizes the unique role of the divine λόγος in the creation of the cosmos. John, however, prefers the nominative (ὁ λόγος) rather than the genitive, as in Philo. While both John and Philo understand the λόγος to be God, John remains distinct in also positioning the λόγος along "with" or perhaps better "to" (πρός) God as a kind of creative instrument/agent (cf. the role of wisdom in creation in Prov 8:21–36). A great deal of attention has been devoted to the relationship between LXX Gen 1:1–2 and John 1:1–3 but I think there is still more to say on John 1:4–9 in this connection, especially related the broader incorporation of light/darkness language in John 1–12.

John 1:4–9 plays a crucial role in the Johannine Prologue's re-writing of Genesis 1. As with several Hellenistic Jews that went before him, the author of the Gospel shows a special fascination with the origins of light (φῶς) and its subsequent relationship to darkness (σκοτία) (1:5) in the creation story as a kind of narrative-philosophical resource for addressing questions of belief (ἵνα πάντες πιστεύσωσιν) (1:7).

The use of κατέλαβεν with the negative particle in John 1:5 remains somewhat vague but still highly relevant, depending upon how we understand its relationship to the surrounding co-text of the Prologue. It may refer to the Light's (τὸ φῶς) power over darkness (e.g., the NRSV: "the darkness did not overcome" the Light) but κατέλαβεν may also admit of a less metaphorical (i.e., local) interpretation. Darkness could not "take the Light down," as it were, but instead darkness was divided downward and the light upward when the watery abyss was divided (esp. Gen 1:6–7). κατέλαβεν may likewise function with other revelatory language in the Prologue (e.g,. the KJV: the darkness did not "comprehend" the Light) so that it indicates a lack of belief, likely due to the non-believer's endarkened state. On this reading, the author could be accentuating the broader themes of divine hiddenness and evil (with its consequent lack of belief) that will occupy his attention throughout the Gospel. Regardless: whether we press the semantics of καταλαμβάνω in more metaphorical directions or restrict it to a more local sense (or even entertain a potential double entendre, taking on a local *and* metaphorical sense[s]), the language links up nicely not only with themes in Genesis 1 but with their distinctive (natural) theological reception among several Hellenistic Jewish authors.

As with other Hellenistic Jews, John clearly connects the λόγος and the Light to God's presence. The light becomes a source of sustenance or life in Gen 1:11–31 as does John's Jesus in the Johannine Prologue (e.g., John 1:4: ἡ ζωὴ ἦν τὸ φῶς τῶν ἀνθρώπων). The use of σκοτία in 1:5 (2×) refers most immediately to the darkness of the original creation, echoing Hellenistic Jewish reception of Gen 1:2–3 where the blackened abyss stands for the evil of humanity that will bring later judgement. This theme of judgement is most explicitly stated at light's next appearance in John's Gospel (John 3:19–21). John's outlook is less dim than other Hellenistic Jewish perspectives on judgement, however. Jesus (light) came into the world not to condemn the world but ultimately to save it (John 3:17). For John, as for (esp.) Philo, skepticism is a huge problem. Those who do not believe are condemned. But disbelief (in the pagan's mind) is justified by a deficiency of revelation within the cosmos. In response, John's Jesus declares that far from a scarcity of revelation, it will be the abundance of revelation that functions as the very mechanism that justifies impending judgement for disbelief. It is not divine hiddenness but the world's love for darkness that motivates them to turn away from God/Jesus (i.e., divine light/revelation).

It is not God that is hidden but humanity (κόσμος). Divine hiddenness results from humanity's desire to hide in the darkness, lest their deeds be exposed by the light (John 3:19) (ἵνα φανερωθῇ αὐτοῦ τὰ ἔργα). The divine judgement and apparent divine hiddenness are self-inflected and self-perpetuating in this way. The use of the versatile term κόσμος, therefore, is highly strategic for John. John's Jesus uses the surrounding co-text of John 3 to modulate between anthropological and cosmological nuances of κόσμος, punctuating the discourse with intertextual irony. For example, in John 3:16–17, terms for salvation and judgement indicate that Jesus uses κόσμος to refer to a universal humanity, apparently one inclusive of the Gentiles (i.e., pagans). But then in 3:19, κόσμος links back to the Johannine Prologue (and Genesis 1) where the author equates Jesus with the light that shined into the endarkened κόσμος (i.e., the created world), adopting a different (more frequent) term to refer to humanity (ἄνθρωπος) (see also John 9:5; 11:9–10 and 12:35–36 for similar ironic deployment of κόσμος). In fact, Jesus as the light of the created world is set in direct contrast to the ἄνθρωπος who love darkness instead of creational light (i.e., revelation). ἄνθρωπος anaphorically carries the prior reference to humanity introduced by κόσμος in John 3:16–17, in other words.

The Gospel of John then provides a stark but nonetheless relevant contrast to typical Hellenistic Jewish reconfigurations of the creation–flood narrative. God is no longer intent on destroying (most of) the world (through the flood) but instead exhibits now deep concern for its redemption (John 3:16–17). Unfortunately, love for darkness perpetuates blindness, justifies the world's disbelief, and yet at the same time (again, note the Johannine irony) provides the divine grounds for eternal justice/condemnation (John 3:18–21). But hope is not lost. For John, the solution to the problem of divine hiddenness is discipleship. Follow Jesus, become his disciple, walk in the light, and it will become clear (i.e., enlightenment [φωτίζω], John 1:9) that God is not hidden but it is in fact the non-believer that hides by living in darkness (John 8:12; 12:35–36, 46).

John entertains other questions current in the Hellenistic Jewish reception of Genesis 1–9 as well. The relation of divine hiddenness to the inability to "see" (ὁράω) God seems tied up with the problem of evil (darkness) in the Gospel of John. God has revealed himself in Jesus, as indicated by the many words for revelation within the prologue (e.g., 1:7: φαίνει, μαρτυρίαν; 1:8: μαρτυρήσῃ; 1:9: φωτίζει; 1:14: ἐσκήνωσεν; 1:18: ἑώρακεν). Similarly, while Philo understands the physical expression of God's invisible presence/light in terms of material elements that reflect the immaterial divine light that illuminates the cosmos, John recasts revelatory representation in terms of the eternal λόγος. Only the λόγος has seen God (1:17–18). Therefore, the λόγος is a suitable ἐσκήνωσεν of God (1:14), physically embodying his presence or glory (δόξα). Like Philo and other Hellenistic Jews, John emphasizes individual attributes of God as revealed by (christological) creational light (i.e., grace and truth). John's point to this effect is especially strong in 1:17, where christological revelation is compared directly to the law that was given (ἐδόθη) to Moses. God inscripturated himself in the law in the days of Moses and has now gone further, incarnating himself as grace and truth in the person of "Jesus Christ" (1:18).

As with several other Hellenistic Jewish texts, John's Gospel carries strong revelatory significance in its rendering of the divine light motif, especially prominent in John 5:30–47. But it is John the Baptizer rather than Jesus that the Fourth Gospel compares to light in John 5:35. Jesus indicates that John testified to him but that he is greater than John's light (i.e., John the Baptizer's testimony). Jesus retains the Fourth Gospel's connection between divine hiddenness and the light motif when he reminds his audience that no one has ever "heard [the Father's] voice or seen his form" (οὔτε φωνὴν αὐτοῦ πώποτε ἀκηκόατε οὔτε εἶδος αὐτοῦ ἑωράκατε) (5:37). Of course, the Jews searched the Scriptures for life, but these only point further to Jesus (note the revelatory overtones) as the light and life of the world (5:38–39). Jesus alone reveals the presence (δόξα) of the Father (5:41–44). In fact, according to Jesus, Moses' revelation (cf. Gen 1) provides yet another testimony to Jesus's authoritative revelation of the Father (5:45–47). John's development of the light motif in John 5:30–47 also seems charged with eschatological significance due to its distinctively apocalyptic co-text, occurring directly after Jesus's discourse on the future resurrection/judgement, where Jesus emphasizes his identity as the Son of Man (5:25–29).

Several scholars have promoted the purpose of the Gospel of John in connection with a more "public," "open," or at least non-Jewish audience. Whatever its rhetorical agenda, Jesus's audience for his discourse beginning in 12:20 included at least "some Greeks" ("Ελληνές τινες). This probably likewise entails that the discourse was given in Greek.[4] Otherwise, how would the Greeks among the audience have understood the message? As with other Hellenistic Jews, John's Jesus appears to deploy creational light motifs as a point of theodicy in his apologetic to the pagans for the (messianic) Jewish sect that he led. John apparently recruits christological light motifs for similar reasons. The author strategically locates his final two portrayals of Christ as the light of the world in Jesus's discourse toward the end of his Jerusalem tour, directly preceding the farewell discourse—again, including at least some Greeks.

The passage employs undeniably eschatological emphases. In John 12:35, Jesus indicates that "the light" is with you for only "a little longer" (ἔτι μικρὸν χρόνον). He then invokes again the discipleship motif as the answer to the problem of evil. If the hearer chooses to become Jesus's disciple by

---

[4] See, e.g., Stanley E. Porter, *The Criteria for Authenticity in Historical-Jesus Research: Previous Discussion and New Proposals*, JSNTSup 191 (Sheffield: Sheffield Academic, 2000), 151–52.

"walking" while they "have the light" (περιπατεῖτε ὡς τὸ φῶς ἔχετε) then darkness/evil will not "overtake" (καταλάβῃ) them, a clear reference back to the Johannine Prologue (cf. κατέλαβεν in John 1:5). However, if the non-believer continues in the darkness, God will continue to be hidden in that they will not "know" (οἶδεν) where they are going (12:35).

Jesus further emphasizes the temporality of revelation in John 12:36. Jesus's words in John 12:35 apparently assume the momentary nature of—or at least the ultimate victory over—evil in that the darkness will not overtake the child of light (disciple). But he also warns that revelation is temporary in certain respects. In 12:36a, Jesus urges his audience to believe in the light while they have the light.[5] The answer to the problem of evil and divine hiddenness for John's Jesus begins by walking in the light, then progresses to belief, and finally adoption into the family of light (i.e., children of light) or, in other words, a state of discipleship/revelation (ἵνα υἱοὶ φωτὸς γένησθε) (12:36a).

If the divine hiddenness motif in connection with the christological deployment of light in John's Gospel was subtle in John 12:35–36a, it becomes explicit in John 12:36b–46. In John 12:36b, the narrator's voice breaks the direct discourse by indicating that Jesus departed and "hid from them" (ἀπελθὼν ἐκρύβη ἀπ' αὐτῶν) because he had done many signs in their presence, but they still failed to believe. In another twist of Johannine irony, far from the audience's disbelief and Jesus's widespread rejection by the Pharisees falsifying Jesus's messiahship, it fulfills Isaiah's prophecy that God would blind the eyes of many to the Father's revelation of his presence (δόξα) in the person of Jesus (12:37–41). John is careful to note, however, that some of the current scribal elite did believe, including those among the Pharisees (12:42–43). Jesus then bursts back onto the scene with what seems to function as a kind of summarizing statement of his prior teaching, including a final climatic statement on christological light, prior to setting the stage in the upper room for the farewell discourse in John 13.

In 12:44–45, Jesus announces in no uncertain terms that he is the answer to the problem of divine hiddenness and, by extension, the problem of darkness/evil. He says: "whoever has seen me has seen the one who sent me" (12:45). He functions in this way as creational light did in Gen 1:2–3. After all, he has "come as light into the world," just as God had spoken light into the world to overcome the darkness that dominated the original creation. Therefore, the one who believes in Jesus will not remain in revelatory darkness. They will literally

---

5 The injunction seems to assume a basic principle: if Jesus's audience rejects the Father now, at the height of his revelation in Jesus, it seems unlikely that they will embrace him after the light has passed, i.e., at a point of lesser revelation.

see God (12:46). Note again the apologetic function of the light motif for John's Jesus. Jesus says that he has become creational light so that humanity might believe in him (ἵνα πᾶς ὁ πιστεύων εἰς ἐμέ) and thus overcome darkness (i.e., evil and lack of revelation) (John 12:46). And there are severe consequences for those who reject the light. Eschatologically, this light will judge the world (12:47). John's Jesus then introduces another christological metaphor from the Prologue, recast in light of final judgement—the divine λόγος. Not only does Jesus reflect the Father's presence as divine light, he also does so as his divine word, reason, or communication (i.e., Jesus as ὁ λόγος). Jesus's message is the message of the Father and those who have ears to hear the word and eyes to see the light (cf. the spiritual blindness and deftness in John 12:37–41) will have eternal life.

3 Conclusions

While the Brown and Bauckham Qumran proposal for the background of the Johannine light motif commends itself at many levels, John's clearly missional deployment of light/darkness metaphors seems to fit most naturally with Hellenistic Jewish reception of Genesis 1–9. John's emphases are more universal and his criteria for discipleship less exclusivist than those of the Qumran Sectarians.

The Fourth Gospel appears instead to adapt the Genesis cosmogony for apologetic purposes, reconfiguring the Genesis narrative with Christ as the light of the world and, therefore, the solution to the related problems of divine hiddenness and evil. By recasting the creation narrative in terms of light and darkness, John is able to project Jesus as a kind of living revelation (light) who perfectly manifests the character of God in physical form, as light did in Gen 1:1–3, for Philo and other Hellenistic Jews to varying degrees. The Johannine light motif is often set in contrast to evil/darkness in the context of divine condemnation. Darkness, therefore, provides a tapestry for the revelation of God's just character. But it also demonstrates the depth of his love in that God continues to love a world that loves darkness instead of him (John 3:16–20). John's Jesus, in fact, concludes his public ministry with a plea to his audience (including some Greeks) to accept the light while it remains, urging them to walk in the light (cf. Philo's conception of seeking "the good" as the gateway to revelation) so that they might become children of the light (i.e., disciples). As it did for Philo, darkness then functions as a black-drop for the display of God's manifold attributes in Jesus. Evil is allowed for the greater good of divine revelation. Therefore, the Father is not hidden at all. He has been fully revealed in the person of Jesus Christ, even more fully than when he created light itself at the beginning of time. God is not hidden. It is the unbeliever that hides—in the darkness that ironically forms the basis for their disbelief. But hope is not lost. The unbeliever only needs to begin to move toward the good (i.e., the light) to begin John's journey of enlightenment and thus a state of discipleship/revelation.

CHAPTER 5

The Christological Appropriation of Zeal in John's Use of Psalm 69

Jonathan Numada

1   Introduction[1]

The claim that Christology is at the heart of *John's* Gospel is commonplace. The truth of this can be seen in the theological nature of Jesus's dialogues with Jews in the book of signs, the Gospel's application of Old Testament metaphor to Jesus,[2] and the introduction of important christological themes in the Prologue.[3] A less-explored perspective on Johannine theology is the intersection of the characterization of Jesus with Johannine Christology. How does the

---

1   This essay is a revised form of a paper delivered to the Emerging Scholars section of the *Institute of Biblical Research* at the meeting for the *Society of Biblical Literature* in Baltimore, MA (November 21, 2013). I would like to thank Dr. Cynthia Long Westfall for her sponsorship of this paper at IBR, and Dr. Larry Perkins, whose question motivated the research that resulted in this paper.
2   Susan Hylen, *Allusion and Meaning in John 6*, BZNW 137 (Berlin: Walter de Gruyter, 2005); Beth M. Stovell, *Mapping Metaphorical Discourse in the Fourth Gospel*, LBS 5 (Leiden: Brill, 2012).
3   As a key to interpreting John, see Stanley E. Porter, *John, His Gospel, and Jesus* (Grand Rapids: Eerdmans, 2015), 113–19; Ernst Käsemann, *New Testament Questions of Today*, NTL (London: SCM Press, 1969), 138–39. C.K. Barrett argues that the Prologue is an integral part of the Gospel. See *The Prologue of St. John's Gospel* (London: Athlone Press, 1971), 15–16, 24–27. Building on the arguments of Barrett and others, many scholars argue that the Prologue mirrors the function of those found in Greek tragedy in terms of setting the stage for what follows. See Jo-Ann A. Brant, *Dialogue and Drama: Elements of Greek Tragedy in the Fourth Gospel* (Peabody: Hendrickson, 2004); Elizabeth Harris, *Prologue and Gospel: The Theology of the Fourth Evangelist*, JSNTSup 107 (Sheffield: Sheffield Academic, 1994), 12–25, 195; Peter M. Phillips, *The Prologue of the Fourth Gospel: A Sequential Reading*, LNTS 294 (London: T&T Clark, 2006), 39–55. For other elements that may reflect the influence of Greek literature, see Godfrey C. Nicholson, *Death as Departure: The Johannine Descent-Ascent Schema*, SBLDS 63 (Chico, CA: Scholars Press, 1983), 43; George L. Parsenios, *Departure and Consolation: The Farewell Discourses in the Light of Greco-Roman Literature*, NovTSup 117 (Leiden: Brill, 2005), 13–18 (see pp. 17–18 for bibliography).
   The Prologue is often seen as setting the stage for John by communicating a form of Wisdom Christology (e.g. Craig A. Evans, *Word and Glory: On the Exegetical and Theological Background of John's Prologue*, JSNTSup 89 [Sheffield: JSOT Press, 1993], 77–145; Marianne Meye Thompson, "Thinking about God: Wisdom and Theology in John 6," in *Critical Readings of John 6*, ed. R. Alan Culpepper, BibInt 22 [Leiden: Brill, 1997], 221–46, esp. 223–25. See also

characterization of Jesus speak to the theological claims made in the Gospel, and how should these claims be viewed as engaging broader Jewish culture?

Several scholars have proposed that the Fourth Gospel is in conversation with Judaism and Jewish culture following the destruction of the temple in 70 CE,[4] with so-called "temple Christology" becoming an accepted theme in Johannine theology. A neglected aspect is John's engagement with the circumstances that led to the temple's destruction: Jewish militarism. Jewish militarism was an important political and social dynamic in the first century and early second century, serving as the basis for the Great Revolt (66–73 CE), the Kitos War (115–117 CE), and the Bar-Kochba revolt (132–135 CE).[5] The warrant for Jewish militancy was often labelled as "zeal" for the Law of Moses or the ancestral traditions of Judaism. It has been the topic of much discussion in relation to the New Perspective on Paul,[6] and a monograph by Martin Hengel examines related Jewish ideologies in detail, particularly traditions grounded in the reception of the biblical figure Phinehas that emerged in the Hasmonean period.[7]

There has been relatively little discussion of this topic in Johannine studies. Francis J. Moloney suggests that the reference to zeal in John 2:17 is meant to evoke comparison of Jesus with Jewish heroes of the past. Moloney appears to assume the historical and cultural backgrounds described by Hengel and James D.G. Dunn but does not elaborate further, stating only that the psalm citation would evoke images of personages such as Phinehas, Elijah, or Mattathias and their careers.[8] Craig Keener offers a similar explanation in

---

Marianne Meye Thompson, *The God of the Gospel of John* [Grand Rapids: Eerdmans, 2001], 126–28, esp. 106).

4 These include James D.G. Dunn, "Let John be John: A Gospel for its Time," in *The Gospel in the Gospels*, ed. Peter Stuhlmacher (Grand Rapids: Eerdmans, 1991), 293–322; Stephen Motyer, *Your Father the Devil? A New Approach to John and "the Jews"* (Carlisle: Paternoster, 1997); Andreas J. Köstenberger, "The Destruction of the Second Temple and the Composition of the Fourth Gospel," *TrinJ* 26 (2005): 205–42; Paul M. Hoskins, *Jesus as the Fulfillment of the Temple in the Gospel of John* (Eugene, OR: Wipf & Stock, 2006); Alan R. Kerr, *The Temple of Jesus's Body*, JSNTSup 220 (Sheffield: Sheffield Academic, 2002).

5 Joseph M. Modrzejewski, *The Jews of Egypt* (Princeton, NJ: Princeton University Press, 1995), 228; Shaye J.D. Cohen, *From the Maccabees to the Mishnah* (Philadelphia, PA: Westminster Press, 1987), 30–34.

6 For example, see James D.G. Dunn, *The New Perspective on Paul: Collected Essays*, WUNT 185 (Tübingen: Mohr Siebeck, 2005; repr. Grand Rapids: Eerdmans, 2007).

7 Martin Hengel, *The Zealots*, trans. David Smith (Edinburgh: T&T Clark, 1989); on the zealots not being a singular militant force, see Morton Smith, "Zealots and Sicarii, Their Origins and Relation," *HTR* 64 (1971): 1–19.

8 Francis J. Moloney, *Belief in the Word: Reading John 1–4* (Minneapolis: Augsburg Fortress Press, 1993), 102.

his commentary.[9] In her monograph on the characterization of Jesus in John, Alicia D. Myers makes brief mention of this theme and cites Keener. She argues that the use of Psalm 68 (69) in John 2:17 establishes a *synkritic* relationship between Jesus and David, the ideal-type king in Israelite and Jewish cultural memory.[10]

The fullest exploration of a possible dialogue between a Jewish zealot *Zeitgeist* and John's Gospel is Jason Ripley's *JBL* article, "Killing as Piety? Exploring Ideological Contexts Shaping the Gospel of John."[11] Ripley places the Fourth Gospel in dialogue with the zeal traditions that formed part of the *Zeitgeist* of early Judaism. He concentrates his discussion on John's opposition to an opinion held in many Jewish circles that religiously-motivated violence was deemed acceptable.[12] The main passages he discusses are the possible reference to nationalism in John 8:33 and the prediction of martyrdom in John 16:2. Ripley argues that John 8:33 alludes to controversy over whether the Jewish nation should follow the strategies of the Hasmoneans in 1 Maccabees. John, meanwhile, presents an alternative vision of freedom grounded in obedience to Jesus through commitment to his self-sacrificial teachings. The corollary of this is that John denies much of the significance of Jewish ethnicity and nationhood.[13] Jesus's prediction of his disciples' martyrdom at the hands of Jews in John 16:2 describes the possible costs associated with obedience to Jesus in opposition to more militant philosophies found in Judaism at the time.[14]

---

[9] Keener writes, "Johannine Christians would remember that their Lord opposed not their Jewish heritage itself, but those he considered its illegal guardians. Throughout the Gospel, Jesus is zealous for his Father's will and ultimately dies in obedience to it (10:17–18; 14:31). This comports with the historical tradition, implied also in the Synoptics, that Jesus not merely predicted his death but deliberately provoked it; no one could act against the temple as Jesus did and not expect severe retaliation from the authorities" (Craig S. Keener, *The Gospel of John* [Peabody: Hendrickson, 2003], 1:528).

[10] Alicia D. Myers, *Characterizing Jesus: A Rhetorical Analysis on the Fourth Gospel's Use of Scripture in its Presentation of Jesus*, LNTS 458 (New York: T&T Clark, 2012), 141–47. See 147, "Thus, he reflects the prophets' critique of abuses of power in the temple, he embodies the zealousness of previous faithful, and he suffers for his righteousness like David."

[11] Jason J. Ripley, "Killing as Piety? Exploring Ideological Contexts Shaping the Gospel of John," *JBL* 134 (2015): 605–35.

[12] Ripley traces killings motivated by piety through the canon (e.g. Deut 13:1–5; 18:20; Exod 31:14–17; 35:2; enactment in Num 15:32–36; Exod 32:25–29), and particularly Phinehas's actions in Num 25:1–13 and those of Mattathias in 1 Macc 2. Ripley, "Killing as Piety," 609–21. Ripley argues that even Philo, a Jew who often viewed the Romans positively, viewed these parts of Jewish tradition positively (614–17).

[13] Ripley, "Killing as Piety," 621–33 (esp. 628).

[14] Ripley, "Killing as Piety," 605–609.

Another examination of zeal in John's Gospel is that of Steven M. Bryan. Bryan proposes that in the Gospel it is not Jesus's zeal, but that of his opponents, which results in his death.[15] For Bryan, Jesus's action symbolizes judgment on the temple for satisfying the criteria of an absence of traders found in Zech 14:21's eschatological temple, necessitating its replacement with Jesus.[16] Bryan presents a very strong argument, but he does not address the construction of John's quotation of Ps 69:9 where zeal is the grammatical subject, Jesus the grammatical object, and the verb is in the middle voice. Taken together with information in John 2:16, this seems to suggest Jesus is the zealous actor in 2:17, not his opponents. Bryan's argument also does not sufficiently account for passages such as John 10:15–18 where Jesus's death is purely by his own volition, or a possible expression of zeal in Jesus's claim to be totally obedient to the Father.[17] That said, Bryan is correct that Jesus's opponents would be zealous to protect Herod's temple.[18]

The point of divergence between Ripley and Bryan lies in the function of Ps 69:9 and precisely who it is who is zealous, a *lacuna* for which there has been relatively little discussion. We shall therefore focus our investigation on the narrator's use of Psalm 69 in John 2:17, where the disciples remembered the Scripture said "zeal for your house will consume me." Using Michael Riffaterre's model of intertextuality this paper will argue that the conflation of various stages in Jewish cultural memory led to this individual lament psalm being read with Davidic, Maccabean, and eschatological overtones. When John appropriates Psalm 68 (69), it adds another level of irony to the narrative because it is used to portray Jesus as fulfilling Scripture in unexpected ways.

2 Intertextuality

Intertextuality has developed into a fruitful area of research for biblical scholars in the examination of the use of earlier texts in later texts, either by direct

---

15   Steven M. Bryan, "Consumed by Zeal: John's Use of Psalm 69:9 and the Action in the Temple," *BBR* 21 (2011): 479–94.
16   Bryan, "Consumed by Zeal," 491–94.
17   E.g., "My food is to do the will of him who sent me" (John 4:34) or "for I have come down from heaven, not to do my own will, but the will of him who sent me" (6:38). All Septuagint translations are from the New English Translation of the Septuagint (NETS). All New Testament translations are from the NRSV.
18   Bryan, "Consumed by Zeal," 485–86.

quotation, indirect quotation, or allusion.[19] Riffaterre's approach to intertextuality attempts to account for both the activities of the author and the influence of the composition upon the reader. In his model a phrase is treated as similar to a symbol, with the new context influencing an intertext's meaning through the intersection of an intertext's present context with its previous context. Riffaterre describes this changed meaning as "conversion," which "transforms the constituents of the matrix sentence by modifying them all with the same factor."[20] In approaching an intertext as akin to a symbol, conversion can take the form of "displacing," "distorting," or "creating."[21] Displacing functions similar to metaphor or metonymy, where a word or phrase does not signify its literal meaning but represents something else, such as the "Big Cheese" referring to the boss, or "honey" referring to someone who is dear. The concept of "distorting" involves the alteration of meaning through use of ambiguity, contradiction, or apparent nonsense, while what Riffaterre terms "creating" entails "making signs out of linguistic items that may not be meaningful otherwise" through rhyme or other artistic use of language.[22] In each case mimesis compromises the literal representation of reality, requiring one to understand the new meaning in a figurative sense.

For Riffaterre, decoding a text occurs in two stages. The first stage is what Riffaterre terms a "heuristic reading," where an initial interpretation takes place and meaning in the text is perceived when the reader uses their linguistic and cultural background to understand what they are reading.[23] Riffaterre maintains this can be followed by a later "retroactive reading" which takes place at a "hermeneutical level" that decodes how meaning is converted in a literary context. The reader re-engages the text by applying background information to arrive at a more precise understanding of how meaning is created in the present literary context.[24]

In Riffaterre's model, heuristic and retroactive readings are especially important when dealing with poetry. He describes a poem as a symbolic description of reality that engages in figurative communication. A poem describes

---

19   Stanley E. Porter, "Further Comments on the Use of the Old Testament in the New Testament," in *The Intertextuality of the Epistles*, ed. Thomas L. Brodie, Dennis Ronald MacDonald, and Stanley E. Porter, NTM 16 (Sheffield: Sheffield Phoenix, 2006), 108–10.
20   Michael Riffaterre, *Semiotics of Poetry* (Bloomington, IN: Indiana University Press, 1978), 63. This is similar to Julia Kristeva's use of the terms "transposition" and "thetic breach" (*Revolution in Poetic Language* [New York: Columbia University Press, 1984], 60).
21   Riffaterre, *Semiotics of Poetry*, 2.
22   Riffaterre, *Semiotics of Poetry*, 2.
23   Riffaterre, *Semiotics of Poetry*, 5.
24   Riffaterre, *Semiotics of Poetry*, 5–6.

the effects of A on B in a heuristic reading, so that upon reflection in a retroactive reading the reader mentally pictures C. The relevance of this poetic approach to intertextuality is that one cannot understand A, B, or C without first understanding their place on the conceptual grid in the communicative system.[25] Riffaterre calls this previously-established grid of information a "sociolect," which is referred to in the text by markers he calls "hypograms," or "inter-texts."[26]

Graham Allen notes that Riffaterre is confident that a reader can arrive at a proper meaning for a text with just a general knowledge of background information. However, Allen is also correct in drawing attention to criticisms of Riffaterre for placing too much emphasis upon assumptions about the reader, as a lack of shared information could undermine the reading process as Riffaterre envisions it.[27] Yet, it is true that both the author and the reader would share at least some presupposed sociolect to allow readers to comprehend hypograms and their conversion. Delineating this may be difficult, but a possible solution may be found in the concept of cultural memory.

Cultural memory is a heuristic paradigm for examining the sociological construction of identity and the preservation and interpretation of knowledge. Theologically, this can take the form of a "symbolic universe" that provides order and a sense of cohesion for a group,[28] meaning that religion can form a core element in group identity,[29] especially for marginalized groups facing a more powerful opponent.[30] As an individual or group process, identity is negotiated in an open-ended social process.[31] As a social phenomenon cultural memory is a means by which a group recalls or reinterprets the past. Cultural memory can help a group resist assimilation by a dominant culture, even if the weaker culture is already integrated into the larger culture.[32]

---

25 Riffaterre, *Semiotics of Poetry*, 8–10.
26 Riffaterre, *Semiotics of Poetry*, 43; Riffaterre, "Intertextual Representation: On Mimesis as Interpretive Discourse," *Critical Inquiry* 11 (1984): 142–43.
27 Graham Allen, *Intertextuality* (London: Routledge, 2000), 124–32.
28 Peter L. Berger and Thomas Luckmann, *The Social Construction of Reality: A Treatise in the Sociology of Knowledge* (London: Allen Lane, 1971), 110–20; Peter L. Berger, *The Sacred Canopy: Elements of a Sociological Theory of Religion* (Garden City, NY: Doubleday, 1967), 3–28.
29 Jeanette Rodriguez and Ted Fortier, *Cultural Memory: Resistance, Faith, and Identity* (Austin, TX: University of Texas Press, 2007), 107.
30 Rodriguez and Fortier, *Cultural Memory*, ix, 107; Anh Hua, "Diaspora and Cultural Memory," in *Diaspora, Memory, and Identity: A Search for Home*, ed. Vijay Agnew (Toronto: University of Toronto Press, 2005), 200.
31 Richard Jenkins, *Social Identity* (New York: Routledge, 1996), 20–62.
32 Hua, "Diaspora and Cultural Memory," 193–95.

Cultural memory performs four major functions: to (1) provide a psychological form of "liberation" (an outlet for dealing with oppression), (2) serve as a medium for transmitting a social group's historical identity for cultural continuity, (3) form the emotional dispositions and values undergirding a culture's sense of identity, and (4) unite a group of people around a common cause. While individual memory is the foundation upon which cultural memory is constructed, the act of remembering cannot be isolated from social forces since personal memories are transmitted in collective settings to mold or reclaim an identity.[33] Much cultural memory may take the form of narratives:

> Narratives, then, are what constitute community. They explain a group to itself, legitimate its deeds and aspirations, and provide important benchmarks for non-members trying to understand the group's cultural identity.[34]

The mechanisms of cultural memory can be diagrammed as follows (see figure 5.1):

Traditio Transmission Process (remembering)		*Traditus* Content (what is remembered)
A	B	C
Who Remembers?	How is it Remembered?	What does it Evoke?
– people	– in memory	– feelings/biases
– society	– in celebration	– modes of action
– culture	– orally	– forms of language
	– in writings	– aspirations
		– interpersonal relations
		– images, ideas, ideals

FIGURE 5.1 Cultural Memory
Note: Adapted from Rodriguez and Fortier, *Cultural Memory*, 10.

Riffaterre's notion of sociolect, or knowledge shared between author and reader, is analogous to what Jeanette Rodriguez and Ted Fortier term the *Traditus* of cultural memory, referred to by the English "tradition" or "cultural tradition" in this essay. The historical depth of the reception histories of the Hebrew Bible and Greek NT as literary compositions is similar to a *Traditio*, or how

---

33 Rodriguez and Fortier, *Cultural Memory*, 6.
34 Lewis P. Hinchman and Sandra Hinchman, *Memory, Identity, Community: The Idea of Narrative in the Human Sciences* (Albany, NY: State University of New York Press, 1997), 235.

something is remembered. Accordingly, the development of collective memory is not necessarily a linear or progressively developmental process, and on occasion "there are historical memories that are so overwhelmingly significant that they define the essence of a people and become imperative for their survival."[35] Hengel has shown that in the NT period the Maccabean revolt was one such cultural tradition.[36]

According to Figure 1 above, the Maccabean revolt meets the requirements for a cultural memory pertinent to John as a first-century CE document. First, its *Traditio* is mentioned explicitly when the Feast of Dedication is referred to in John 10:22 (1 Macc 4:49), a feast which Jesus attends and whose observance meets the criteria in columns A and B. Additionally, Jesus's being zealous is mentioned in John 2:17, perhaps an allusion to 1 Macc 2:54, with perceived similarities between Jesus's and Phinehas's actions evoking the disciples to "remember" Ps 68:10 (69:9). Clearly, Jesus's somewhat violent response to the state of the temple evoked emotions that prompted the disciples to draw a parallel, meeting the criteria of column C.

As mentioned above, the cultural tradition of the Maccabean revolt likely inspired two, possibly three wars against Roman rule, again suggesting that in the Hellenistic period the zeal for Judaism tradition performed the four functions described above. It is likely that the Bar Kochba revolt was in part motivated by messianic and eschatological expectations, and although the propagandist of 1 Maccabees is careful to avoid making explicit claims, 1 Maccabees contains a number of veiled eschatological and royal allusions[37] that likely fed new messianic aspirations.[38]

The cultural memory of the Maccabean revolt is one of a divinely-assisted struggle against Gentile oppressors in the face of overwhelming odds.[39] A militant Jewish *Zeitgeist* in the Hellenistic period would meet the requirements of column C, especially in light of arguments that the Jewish War and destruction of the temple served as an occasion for the composition of John's Gospel.[40] It is thus safe to agree with Ripley that the cultural memory of religiously-motivated

---

35 Rodriguez and Fortier, *Cultural Memory*, 11.
36 Hengel, *Zealots*.
37 Jonathan A. Goldstein, "How the Authors of 1 and 2 Maccabees Treated the 'Messianic' Promises," in *Judaisms and their Messiahs at the Turn of the Christian Era*, ed. Jacob Neusner et al. (Cambridge: Cambridge University Press, 1987), 77.
38 William Horbury, *Messianism among Jews and Christians* (London: T&T Clark, 2003), 48–50.
39 Elias J. Bickerman, *The God of the Maccabees: Studies on the Meaning and Origin of the Maccabean Revolt*, trans. Horst R. Moehring (Leiden: Brill, 1979), 90.
40 Köstenberger, "Destruction of the Second Temple," 205–42.

violence could have formed part of the background "sociolect" in reading John's Gospel.

This study will employ Riffaterre's model of intertextuality while consulting Porter's taxonomy of formulaic quotation, direct quotation, paraphrase, allusion, and echo. It will use the concept of cultural memory to supply background information for heuristic and retroactive readings of the use of Psalm 68 (69). The data to be analyzed will be hypograms linking Psalm 68 (69), the Gospel of John, and 1 Maccabees in a three-way conversation. Key traditions from Jewish history with possible intertextual links to Psalm 68 (69) will serve as the shared "sociolect" against which the psalm is read to examine John's "conversion" of the psalm quotations and allusions.

3 Psalm 68 (69)

Psalm 69 (Psalm 68 in the LXX) appears numerous times in the New Testament and appears to have been received as a messianic psalm. How this came to be is uncertain, though possible reasons will be explored below.[41] Structurally the Psalm is composed of three parts that follow a lament-petition-praise formula (vv. 2b–14b, 14c–30, and 31–37 [English versification]).[42] The lament includes a description of danger from death and chaos (vv. 2–5), while vv. 6–14 state the troubles stem from members of the supplicant's community who mock their piety, with the primary threat being social isolation.[43] In the first part of the petition section the supplicant seeks deliverance from insults, ostracism, and despair (vv. 14–20). This is followed immediately by a probable reference to cultic matters in vv. 21–22,[44] a plea for justice and retribution in vv. 23–29, a thanksgiving/praise refrain in vv. 30–34, and a promise for the restoration of Zion, Judah, and the faithful in vv. 35–36.

Multiple stages of development have been proposed due to perceived inconsistencies. The Psalm begins with an individual perspective and ends

---

41 Court lists 8 explicit quotations of Psalm 68 (69). They are Ps 68:5 (69:4) in John 15:25; 68:10 (69:9) in John 2:17 and Rom 15:3; Ps 68:22 (69:21) in Matt 27:48, Mark 15:36, and John 19:28–29; Ps 68:23–24 (69:22–23) in Rom 11:9–11; Ps 68:26 (69:25) in Acts 1:20. See John M. Court, *Introduction to New Testament Writers and the Old Testament* (Eugene, OR: Wipf and Stock, 2002), 105. Citation of the Psalmic source text will refer to the LXX versification, with English versification given in parentheses.

42 Frank-Lothar Hossfeld and Erich Zenger, *Psalms*, trans. Linda M. Maloney (Minneapolis, MN: Fortress Press, 2005), 2:172.

43 Hossfeld and Zenger, *Psalms*, 2:173.

44 Hossfeld and Zenger, *Psalms*, 2:176.

with a national perspective, while cultic referents appear in 68:10 (69:9) and 68:21–22 (69:20–21). Verses 2 and 3 could refer to a terminal illness, but the Psalm switches to social pressures stemming from differing opinions of the cult, with the broad national (eschatological?) picture of vv. 35–36 seeming an addition to some.[45] This has led Norbert Tillmann to suggest a three stage development built around a core individual lament composed in the pre-exilic period, with elements of a Jeremianic critique of temple worship added during post-exilic debates over reconstruction.[46] Verses 35–36 would have been added at a later date,[47] with possible intertextual links to Zech 7:3 and Hag 1:4–8.[48]

The Psalm in its final form is about conflict over the significance and meaning of cultic worship (vv. 23–24),[49] reflecting either an early post-exilic setting as advocated by recent commentators, or possibly a Maccabean setting as suggested by D. Rudolf Kittel and W.O.E. Oesterly.[50] It is impossible to determine which proposal is correct, but the compositional discussion highlights important themes. These are (1) a conflict over proper cultic worship, (2) ostracism and persecution of an individual by the community because of their fidelity, (3) pleas for deliverance, and (4) restoration of the nation.

4 An Eschatological Psalm of David?

The reception history of Psalm 68 (69), as evidenced by its superscription, connects it to David. The LXX's superscription εἰς τὸ τέλος (concerning completion) hints at eschatological reception, though this translation was likely the

---

45 Hossfeld and Zenger, *Psalms*, 2:174–75.
46 Ps 68:5–13 (69:4–12), reflecting Jer 7:1–11; 12:6; 15:15; 26:1–19. See Norbert Tillmann, *Das Wasser bis zum Hals!: Gestalt, Geschichte und Theologie des 69. Psalms* (Altenberg: Oros Verlag, 1993), 118–35.
47 Hossfeld and Zenger, *Psalms*, 2:175–76.
48 Hans-Joachim Kraus, *Psalmen*, BKAT 15 (Neukirchen-Vluyn: Neukirchener Verlag, 1966), 2:62.
49 Hossfeld and Zenger, *Psalms*, 2:178–79.
50 The lack of firm contexts make this judgment very tentative. See W.O.E. Oesterly, *The Psalms* (London: Macmillan, 1939), 327; D. Rudolf Kittel, *Die Psalmen* (Leipzig: A. Deichertsche, 1922), 234–35; Alphonso Groenewald, "Post-Exilic Conflict as 'Possible' Historical Background to Psalm 69:19ab," *HvTSt* 61 (2005): 131–41; Arie van der Kooij, "The Septuagint of Psalms and the First Book of Maccabees," in *The Old Greek Psalter: Studies in Honour of Albert Pietersma*, ed. Robert J.V. Hiebert et al., JSOTSup 332 (Sheffield: Sheffield Academic, 2001), 229–47.

result of a misreading.[51] The tradition that David was a prophet who received the Holy Spirit would further encourage an eschatological reading (Matt 22:43; Mark 12:36; Luke 20:42; 2 Sam 23:1–7). In addition to the expected restoration of Judah (Ps 68:35–36 [69:34–35]), which could also be read with eschatological overtones, reference is made to the unrighteous being blotted out of the Book of the Living (1 En. 108.3; 47.3). While the Psalm in its final form probably had nothing to do with the life of David or eschatology, this is probably how the Psalms were received by some parties.[52]

Like the Psalmist, David is remembered as having suffered injustice for the sake of God. As God's anointed, David's continued fidelity to God despite persecution by Saul and his army is analogous to his bearing reproach for God's sake (1 Sam 20–26). The estrangement from one's kin could be read as reflecting an incident such as Absalom's rebellion (2 Sam 14:28–18:33), while mention of the table could depict Absalom or Saul feasting while David is in hiding, with the last stanza read as a prophetic prediction. Zeal for the house could be a nod to David's desire to build a temple (2 Sam 7:2–3) whom the Chronicler portrays as founder of the cult (1 Chron 23; 25:1–8). None of this can be substantiated from the Psalm itself, but these connections may have suggested themselves to later audiences.

5 Conflating Memory: Finding David in 1 Maccabees, and 1 Maccabees in Psalm 68(69)

Some scholars argue 1 Maccabees also creates parallels between the careers of David and the Maccabeans. Arie van der Kooij notes that lion imagery is applied to the sons of Mattathias, significant because Judah and the tribe of Judah are described as lions devouring their enemies (Gen 49:9; Mic 5:8). This

---

51 Albert Pietersma argues convincingly that the Psalmic superscriptions εἰς τὸ τέλος were a mistaken attempt at a literal rather than eschatological translation and later ascriptions of eschatological or prophetic status to the Psalms would be matters of reception history. See Albert Pietersma, "Septuagintal Exegesis and the Superscriptions of the Greek Psalter," in *The Book of Psalms: Composition and Reception*, ed. Peter W. Flint et al., VTSup 99 (Leiden: Brill, 2005), 468–71. For reading the Psalms as prophecy, see Susan E. Gillingham, *The Poems and Psalms of the Hebrew Bible* (Oxford: Oxford University Press, 1994), 256–70.

52 George J. Brooke, "The Psalms in Early Jewish Literature in Light of the Dead Sea Scrolls," in *The Psalms in the New Testament*, ed. Steve Moyise and Maarten J.J. Menken (London: T&T Clark, 2004), 5–24; Margaret Daly-Denton, *David in the Fourth Gospel: The Johannine Reception of the Psalms*, AGJU 47 (Leiden: Brill, 2000), 59–93; Margaret Daly-Denton, "The Psalms in John's Gospel," in *The Psalms in the New Testament*, ed. Steve Moyise and Maarten J.J. Menken (London: T&T Clark, 2004), 119–37.

imagery is then appropriated in an oblique allusion to David (1 Macc 3:4–5).[53] Like David, Mattathias escapes to the wilderness and gathers a band of warriors around him, which like David's flight is followed by a massacre of innocent people (1 Macc 2:27–38, 42–43; 1 Sam 22:1–2, 7–19; 23:14). Especially telling is the close parallelism between 1 Macc 2:38 and 1 Sam 22:19, where it is not simply allies of the protagonists who are murdered by the antagonists, but also innocent women, children, and animals.[54]

It has received some acceptance that the propagandist of 1 Maccabees seeks to present their achievements with a Davidic flavor.[55] The bands of both David and the Maccabees engage in war to deliver Israel (1 Macc 2:44–48; 1 Sam 23:1–5), with 1 Macc 4:30 appealing to Davidic precedent as a justification for a plea for divine assistance. Following a series of battles Judas "conquers" Jerusalem[56] and rededicates the temple in 1 Maccabees 4, while David conquers Jerusalem, erects the Tabernacle, and brings the Ark of the Covenant to Jerusalem (in 2 Sam 5:8–9 and 6:12–17; 1 Chron 13–15). While 1 Maccabees hesitates to explicitly present the Hasmoneans as inheritors of the Davidic promise, Davidic imagery is used to legitimate their rule.

1 Maccabees and Psalm 68 (69) share thematic similarities that could have served as hypograms linking these two compositions. The first is (1) the conflict over proper cultic worship. While the Maccabean rebels engage in their insurrection because of zeal for the Law, not zeal for the temple (1 Macc 2:26, 27, 50, 58), the temple and ceremonial purity still frequently appear as major concerns. Ἱερόν (temple) occurs in 1 Macc 6:2; 10:43, 84; 11:4; 13:52; 15:9; 16:20 while εἰδώλιον (idolatrous temple) occurs in 1:47 and 10:83. Meanwhile ναός (shrine) occurs in 1:22; 2:8; 4:49, 50, 57; and 7:36. Ἁγίασμα (holy precinct) occurs in 1:21, 36, 37 (twice), 39, 45, and 46. "Sacred Precinct" (τέμενος) is found in 1:47; 5:43 and 44, while τὰ ἅγια (translated by George T. Zervos as "holy things" and "holy

---

53 Arie van der Kooij, "The Claim of Maccabean Leadership and the Use of Scripture," in *Jewish Identity and Politics between the Maccabees and Bar Kokhba: Groups, Normativity, and Rituals*, ed. Benedikt Eckhardt, JSJSup 155 (Leiden: Brill, 2012), 29–49 (47).

54 Jonathan A. Goldstein, *1 Maccabees*, AB (Garden City, NY: Doubleday, 1976), 7. Goldstein perhaps stretches the allusion when he argues for additional parallelism in the fact that the priests of Nob were a rejected line of high priests, while the slaughtered Hasideans represented a rejected course of action (refusing to fight on the Sabbath [1 Macc 2:29–41]). Goldstein may be correct, but the conceptual parallelism is difficult to prove.

55 Horbury, *Messianism*, 49; John J. Collins, "Messianism in the Maccabean Period," in *Judaisms and their Messiahs at the Turn of the Christian Era*, ed. Jacob Neusner et al. (Cambridge: Cambridge University Press, 1987), 103–104.

56 The Seleucid garrison would not be removed until 1 Macc 13:49–53.

places") occurs 27 times.⁵⁷ In all, terms directly related to the temple occur 52 times in 1 Maccabees, and items related to the Law occur 34 times. While zealous for the Law, the Maccabean rebels demonstrate a clear interest in the temple, especially in its rededication that would inaugurate the observance of Hanukkah in 1 Maccabees 4.

The second thematic commonality is (2) ostracism and persecution due to religious fidelity. While Seleucid forces are presented as an opponent, the primary antagonists in 1 Maccabees are "lawless," "legally deviant," or "impious" Jews.⁵⁸ In cultural memory Jews would have identified with the suffering of protagonists.⁵⁹

The third thematic correspondence is (3) the theme of deliverance. Like the Psalm, deliverance is a theme that appears when 1 Maccabees gives credit to God for deliverance in the pivotal battles of chapter 4 (1 Macc 4:11, 30, 56). Deliverance also comes through divinely-enabled human actors who persevere in the face of opposition.⁶⁰

More prominent is (4) the restoration of the nation. The propagandist in 1 Maccabees is at pains to demonstrate that this came through the hands of the Hasmoneans when the temple is rededicated (1 Macc 4) and the Seleucid garrison in Jerusalem is expelled (1 Macc 13:49–53). National restoration to security, plenty, and fidelity in 1 Macc 14:4–15 could serve as hypogrammic links to Ps 68:36–37 (69:35–36).

As seen above, Psalm 68 (69) can be correlated to events in David's life with some difficulty. In terms of specific themes, Psalm 68 (69) contains clearer hypogrammic links to the cultural memory of the Maccabean revolt. Meanwhile, the Maccabean propagandist makes some effort to link the careers of the

---

57 Information on vocabulary pertaining to cultic matters is from George T. Zervos's foreword to his translation of 1 Maccabees in *The New English Translation of the Septuagint*, ed. Benjamin G. Wright and Albert Pietersma (Oxford: Oxford University Press, 2007), 479.

58 παράνομοι (1 Macc 1:11, 34; 10:61; 11:21), ἀσεβής (1 Macc 3:8, 15; 6:21; 7:5, 9; 9:25, 69, 73), ἄνομος (1 Macc 2:44; 3:5, 6, 20; 7:5; 9:23, 69; 11:25; 14:14).

59 1 Macc 1:43 states that many from Israel apostatized, while 1 Macc 1:48–53 states that there was legislated disobedience to the Law and the prevention of circumcision that was in part enforced by fellow Jews. In 1 Macc 2:23–26 Mattathias kills a Jew who is about to apostatize, while 1 Macc 3:8 implies that apostate Jews live alongside faithful ones. It is highly probable that at least some Jewish families would have been internally divided.

60 E.g., Judas in 1 Macc 3:6; 5:9–23; Jonathan in 9:43–49; most notably Eleazar's martyrdom in 2 Macc 6:30–31. In 4 Macc 17:20–22 the martyrs' deaths are described as purifying the homeland and serving as an ἱλαστηρίου (propitiation or atonement) for Israel. The precise dating of 4 Maccabees is uncertain and could possibly post-date the beginnings of the Christian era. For a discussion of the dating of 2 and 4 Maccabees, see Jarvis J. Williams, *Maccabean Martyr Traditions in Paul's Theology of Atonement* (Eugene, OR: Wipf & Stock, 2010), 28–36.

Maccabees and David. Davidic and eschatological reception of the Psalms, thematic parallels, and a conflation in cultural memory of David with the Maccabees may have occurred, creating a new hybrid "sociolect" that blurs the lines between all three. Jews would have understood the Hasmoneans and David were historically different individuals, but at the level of column C in figure 1, Maccabean and Davidic memories could easily be conflated in terms of emotions and aspirations for the nation, hardship due to fidelity, and cultic observance. The thematic correspondence of Psalm 68 (69)'s four major themes with 1 Maccabees would mean that cultural memory from this period would provide the framework against which these elements would be understood. It makes some sense that Psalm 68 (69) would be selected as an eschatological messianic psalm, since intertextually it corresponded with previous historical examples of Jewish-Israelite struggle and hope for God's deliverance.

6 Psalm 68(69) in the Gospel of John

The strongest allusion to 1 Maccabees in John is the reference to the Feast of Dedication (1 Macc 4:49//John 10:22). The reference to zeal in association with Jesus's act in John 2:17 is sufficient for demonstrating Johannine knowledge of the Maccabean period of Jewish cultural memory. Further, Margaret Daly-Denton has demonstrated that there are numerous intertextual ties between John, the Psalms, and David.[61] As discussed above, there are hypogrammic ties between John, 1 Enoch, David, the Maccabean revolt, and Psalm 68 (69).[62] We will see below that John refers to Maccabean motifs by "distorting" Psalm 68 (69) as a means of compounding Johannine irony.[63]

---

61   Daly-Denton, *David in the Fourth Gospel*. Also Dale A. Brueggemann, "The Evangelists and the Psalms," in *Interpreting the Psalms: Issues and Approaches*, ed. Philip S. Johnston and David G. Firth (Downers Grove: IVP Academic, 2005), 263–78.

62   According to Porter's taxonomy, some of these connections are best classified as echoes rather than allusions (Porter, "Further Comments," 108–10). Echoes are problematic in that they are difficult to establish. In one such example in Ps 68:9 (69:8), the supplicant complains of being estranged from family. A Johannine echo of this could be in John 7:2–10, where Jesus's non-believing brothers (sarcastically) urge Jesus to aggrandize himself.

63   R. Alan Culpepper, "Reading Johannine Irony," in *Exploring the Gospel of John: In Honor of D. Moody Smith*, ed. R. Alan Culpepper and C. Clifton Black (Louisville: Westminster John Knox Press, 1996), 194–98. John's use of irony is a key element in interpretation of the Fourth Gospel (as also is use of *double-entendre* and misunderstanding). See Paul D. Duke, *Irony in the Fourth Gospel* (Atlanta: John Knox Press, 1985), 139–40; Gail R. O'Day, *Revelation in the Fourth Gospel* (Philadelphia: Fortress Press, 1986), 30–31. This device is closely related to the Johannine motif of "misunderstanding," which often prompts

6.1 John 2:17

Psalm 68 (69) is directly quoted in John 2:17 when Jesus, using a whip of cords, overturns tables and expels the money-changers, vendors, and their animals (2:14–16). This apparent cleansing, at least in the Johannine context, evokes Jesus's disciples' remembrance of 68:10 (69:9): "Zeal for your house will consume me."[64] The Psalm quotation provides an explanation for Jesus's action in the temple that initiates the conflict between Jesus and the Judean leadership. John alters the verb to a third person singular future middle, versus LXX's third singular aorist active (κατέφαγεν). A Riffaterrean heuristic reading suggests that this alteration would suggest the Psalm is presented as a prophecy to prompt reflection on the part of the audience and foreshadow Jesus's destiny.

In a retroactive reading, the reader draws upon the shared cultural memory to decode the text. Mention of zeal serves as a hypogram that associates Jesus, however imperfectly, with the zeal of past Jewish heroes such as Phinehas. The most recent candidate would be the Maccabees who "cleansed" and rededicated the temple and established a period of political independence.[65] Such a retroactive reading may also characterize Jesus's opponents as similar to the antagonists of the Maccabean narrative who profaned the temple and led the people into disobedience. This characterization would be consistent with the use of irony in Johannine presentation of the Jews in that they are highly dedicated to Torah observance (e.g., John 5:10) but persecute Jesus as God's representative. The altered quotation of Ps 68:10 (69:9) evokes these thematic parallels with its original and received contexts, but the converted meaning implies distortion in the form of irony, as it is odd that someone who

---

exposition of the Gospel's theology (R. Alan Culpepper, *Anatomy of the Fourth Gospel: A Study in Literary Design* [Philadelphia: Fortress Press, 1983], 165–69).

64 It is uncertain whether Jesus's act should be seen as a protest, a cleansing, or a portent of destruction. See Bruce Chilton, *The Temple of Jesus: His Sacrificial Program within a Cultural History of Sacrifice* (University Park, PA: Pennsylvania State University Press, 1992), 119, 153–55; Jonathan Klawans, *Purity, Sacrifice, and the Temple: Symbolism and Supersessionism in the Study of Ancient Judaism* (Oxford: Oxford University Press, 2006), 79–89; C.H. Dodd, *The Interpretation of the Fourth Gospel* (Cambridge: Cambridge University Press, 1953), 300; Bruce G. Schuchard, *Scripture within Scripture: The Interrelationship of Form and Function in the Explicit Old Testament Citations in the Gospel of John*, SBLDS 133 (Atlanta: Scholars Press, 1992), 24; E.P. Sanders, *Jesus and Judaism* (Philadelphia: Fortress, 1985), 70–71.

65 Moloney, *Belief in the Word*, 97–98. Moloney prefers to keep the referent vague, suggesting that Jesus's actions would stir memories of heroes from Jewish history.

is zealous cleanses the temple because of those dedicated to observance of the Law.[66]

In a Riffaterrean heuristic reading, the Psalm citation explains Jesus's motivations, but a retroactive reading reveals John's distortion of the hypogram "zeal" presents a new meaning for this cultural tradition. Jesus's "sign" in promising to rebuild the temple in three days if destroyed functions as a metonymic displacement in reference to his bodily resurrection (John 2:19). This leads the audience to conclude Jesus did not fit conventional forms of zeal, while Jesus's opponents probably *would* meet the typical criteria of being zealous. John therefore appropriates and reinterprets this expression of Jesus's obedience to turn it on its head, with zeal resulting in his destruction at the hands of the Judean authorities, be it Jesus's zeal or that of the authorities.[67]

6.2   *John 15:23–25*

John 15:23 may contain an allusion to Ps 68:10 (69:9) in terms of parallels in content and logic.[68] In Ps 68:10b (69:9b) the supplicant is reproached because the enemies have contempt for the supplicant's fidelity to God, while in the Gospel Jesus is an object of hate because he is obedient to God's will (John 15:23). The Psalmist writes, "the reproaches (οἱ ὀνειδισμοί) of those who reproach you (τῶν ὀνειδιζόντων σε) have fallen on me." Explicitly describing Jesus as dishonored would run against the grain of Johannine Christology because it would undercut the cross being Jesus's glory, but a heuristic reading of John 15:18–27 alludes to a similar logic grounded in hatred, especially in 15:23: "Whoever hates me hates my Father also" (ὁ ἐμὲ μισῶν καὶ τὸν πατέρα μου μισεῖ). The hatred of Jesus by his enemies is then cited as fulfillment of Ps 68:5 (69:4) in John 15:25:

> ἀλλ᾽ ἵνα πληρωθῇ ὁ λόγος ὁ ἐν τῷ νόμῳ αὐτῶν γεγραμμένος ὅτι ἐμίσησάν με δωρεάν

> (It was to fulfill the word that is written in their law, 'They hated me without a cause').

---

66   Severino Pancaro argues John opposed interpretations of the Law that left no room for Johannine Christology, rather than the Law itself (*The Law in the Fourth Gospel: The Torah and the Gospel, Moses and Jesus, Judaism and Christianity according to St. John*, NovTSup 42 [Leiden: Brill, 1975], 496–533).

67   Bryan, "Consumed by Zeal," 479–94.

68   Daly-Denton, *David in the Fourth Gospel*, 206.

This Psalm citation contains the longest introductory formula of any quotation in John and its rhetorical effect is especially polemical.[69] John's allusion to Ps 68:10 (69:9) is reinforced by the direct quotation of Ps 68:5 (69:4), with the participle μισοῦντες (hate) changed to a finite verb (hated) to clarify it as an action that speaks to Jesus's rejection by the nation's leadership because of his fidelity to the Father. Notably, the passage is cited as a fulfillment of the Jewish Law rather than as a prophecy.[70]

While in John 15:23 the allusion involves close metonymy that corresponds to the mimetic use of the quotation of Ps 68:5 (69:4) in John 15:25, in a retroactive reading the reference to the Scriptures as "their Law" in the formulaic quotation clause serves as a displacement of meaning that attacks the Johannine Jesus's opponents. John uses this quotation to claim that it is in their Law for Jesus's enemies to hate him without cause, and because of their hatred for Jesus they will also persecute his followers in John 15:18–27. A heuristic reading leads to the understanding that Ps 68:10 (69:9) and 68:5 (69:4) is a literally fulfilled prophecy, but in a retroactive reading of the hypograms of ἐμίσησάν με δωρεάν and νόμος against cultural memory, Johannine irony emphasizes that those who would claim to live by the Law are now persecutors of the one foretold in Psalm 68 (69), one who was also presumably faithful to the Law but whose eschatological realization is in Jesus.

6.3 John 19:28–29

Several scholars see a reference to Ps 68:22 (69:21) in John 19:28–29.[71] Psalm 68:22 (69:21) also occurs in the Synoptics (Matt 27:34, 48; Luke 23:36; Mark 15:36), although these are allusions and not quotations. In the Synoptics, reference is made in terms of Psalm 68 (69) being a lament psalm, though without reference to its possible early post-exilic setting or its cultic connotations. In the Synoptics, some offer sour wine and gall to mock Jesus (bystanders in Matthew and Mark; soldiers in Luke). The connection between the literary contexts is the sour wine that is offered to an individual being shamed and

---

69 Daly-Denton, "Psalms," 131.

70 John is not alone in the NT in listing the Psalms as part of the Law (ὁ νόμος). See 1 Cor 14:21; Rom 3:19; John 12:34.

71 Schuchard does not include it in his treatment of explicit Johannine Scripture quotations but it is discussed elsewhere. See Schuchard, *Scripture within Scripture*; Court, *New Testament Writers and the Old Testament*, 118; Judith Lieu, "Narrative Analysis and Scripture in John," in *The Old Testament in the New Testament: Essays in Honor of J.L. North*, ed. Steve Moyise (Eugene, OR: Wipf & Stock, 2000), 150. Daly-Denton also cites Ps 21:19 (22:18) and Ps 62:1 as alternate possible source texts but suggests that Ps 68 (69) is the main referent text with the others functioning as "pre-texts" that add texture to the allusion. Daly-Denton, *David in the Fourth Gospel*, 219–23.

mocked.[72] The use of Ps 68:22 (69:21) in John 19:28–29[73] is different from that in the Synoptics and is portrayed more consistently with Psalm 68(69)'s apparent context of a cultic dispute, since matters of cultic observance[74] may be the referent in Pss 68:10 (69:9) and 68:22–23 (69:21–22), at least in terms of festal meals:[75]

> And they gave me gall as my food,
>   and for my thirst they gave me vinegar to drink.
> Let their table become a trap before them,
>   and a retribution and a stumbling block.

In the Psalm's narrative the supplicant cannot participate in worship because the opponents advocate practice that deviates from the festival legislation found in the Torah. In the Psalm, the zeal for the house of God in Psalm 68 (69) stems from a desire to see the temple rebuilt for the proper observance of festivals.[76] In 1 Macc 1:45, the defiled state of the temple serves "to profane Sabbaths and feasts" (βεβηλῶσαι σάββατα καὶ ἑορτάς), prompting Mattathias to leave Jerusalem for Modein and compose a psalm of lament (1 Macc 2:1–13). Mattathias's departure from Jerusalem is followed by forced apostasy from the Law and participation in pagan cultic practices at Modein (1 Macc 2:15–27).[77]

The Johannine claim that a hyssop branch was used at the crucifixion to lift the sponge to Jesus in John 19:29 establishes a three-way cultic connection between Jesus, Psalm 68 (69), and the Passover Lamb through a Riffaterrean act of "creating" a link with Exod 12:22.[78] While a more sturdy reed (κάλαμος) is used in the Synoptics, the flimsy hyssop branch, when taken together with the

---

[72] Robert L. Brawley notes: "There is no intrinsic relationship between the incident on the cross and the Johannine allusion to Psalm 68 [69].... the offer of vinegar is motivated by the malevolence of people who oppose God." The use of the Psalm and a possible cultic dispute may mean the connection is stronger than he suggests, though he is correct regarding motive. See Robert L. Brawley, "An Absent Complement and Intertextuality in John 19:28–29," *JBL* 112 (1993): 442.

[73] It is a paraphrase since the language is heavily altered (Porter, "Further Comments," 108–10). The changes were likely made to connect Ps 68:22 (69:21) to the crucifixion scene in John 19:28–29. This would be consistent with the findings of Schuchard, *Scripture within Scripture*, 151–52, who argues that the narrative context, the context of the citation, and synonyms are used in Johannine adaptations of the LXX.

[74] Hossfeld and Zenger, *Psalms*, 178–79.

[75] Hossfeld and Zenger, *Psalms*, 182.

[76] Hossfeld and Zenger, *Psalms*, 176.

[77] Bickerman, *God of the Maccabees*, 77–78.

[78] See especially Brawley, "Intertextuality in John 19:28–29," 433. Brawley notes that a hyssop branch could not support the weight of an object.

Passage	OT	Hypograms	Nature of Conversion	Effect
John 2:17 (19)	Ps 68:10 (69:9)	zeal, temple	distortion through displacement	irony
John 15:23, 25	68:10 (69:9); Ps 68:5 (69:4)	hate, law	mimesis (quotation), displacement through metonymy (Law, "reproach = hate")	irony
John 19:28–29	Ps 68:22 (69:21)	hyssop branch, sour wine	creating (hyssop), distortion through contradiction (sour wine)	irony

FIGURE 5.2 John's Use of Psalm 68 (69)

statement in John 19:28 that Jesus does this to fulfill the Scriptures,[79] suggests Jesus is deliberately drawing an analogy between himself as the Lamb of God (John 1:29, 36) and the Exodus Passover lamb whose blood is used as a protective covering. A Riffaterrean retroactive reading connects Jesus's intent to fulfill the Scriptures and his thirst (διψῶ) to obey his Father with the narrative of Psalm 68 (69) and Jewish cultural memory. This characterizes Jesus as zealous in offering the perfect cultic sacrifice of his body as the Lamb of God.

Like the Maccabees who were zealous for temple worship and the Law, Jesus was zealous for the will of his Father. This adds a level of irony to the Gospel narrative because Jesus's opponents are antagonistic towards him because they believe he disregards the Law, and they have him killed in a failed attempt to preserve the nation (11:48–50). The temple incident presents Jesus as the one who is truly zealous and, as Bryan observes, it is implied that zealots for the temple will have Jesus killed. In the allusion to Psalm 68:22 (69:21), the source text is distorted through Jesus's contradicting the text by asking for the hypogram of the sour wine and the Johannine addition of the symbolic hyssop hypogram. Irony is created when Jesus's enemies are unwitting participants in the perfect cultic sacrifice. The thematic parallels in Psalm 68 (69) are resolved in John's Gospel in a way no one would expect (see figure 5.2).

6.4 Summary

Riffaterre's semiotic approach to intertextuality is modelled on the poetic manipulation of language to indirectly communicate meaning. It argues

---

79 Daly-Denton, *David in the Fourth Gospel*, 135.

hypograms are used by an author to point audiences towards the "sociolect," or shared knowledge, with which to decode the text's symbols and perceive its intended meaning in retroactive readings. Present readers' historical removal from the context shared by the author of John's Gospel and its recipients requires drawing upon Jewish cultural memory to recreate a background against which John and Psalm 68 (69) can be interpreted, in this case cultural memories of heroic military resistance and religious perseverance.

An analysis using the Riffaterrean categories of mimesis, metonymy, distortion, creating, and displacement suggest John uses Psalm 68 (69) to engage in deprecation of certain competing ideological interpretations of the OT through portraying Jesus's ironic fulfillment of Scripture. While explicit links to the Maccabean literature cannot be established, by the criteria in Figure 1 there is sufficient evidence of a Maccabean *Zeitgeist* upon which readers and authors could draw in their communications.

If John is aware of Psalm 68 (69)'s possible historical, Davidic, and eschatological reception, the Gospel seems to read the psalm in a way that contradicts the expectations of some traditions in Jewish cultural memory. The Fourth Gospel portrays Jesus as zealous in his obedience to the Father, but a first-century reader familiar with late first-century Judaism would probably recognize resistance to Jesus in the Gospel as grounded in zeal for the Law. This results in a both-and conclusion: the observations of Ripley and Bryan should be understood as complementary elements in John's ironic appropriation of this Jewish cultural tradition. The converted meaning resulting from the dialogue of these perspectives in John's use of passages using Psalm 68 (69) would be ironic. Irony is perceived when it is recognized that both the Maccabees and those who would follow in their legacy sought to be faithful to God through fidelity to the Law, yet it is such as these who reject the truly righteous one. Further irony is conveyed when an audience understands that Jesus is condemned and hated by the religious authorities due to his attempts to be obedient to God. Irony is again emphasized at the crucifixion when the hated obedient one, in his zeal for proper cultic observance, sacrifices himself as the Lamb of God.

Christologically, Johannine appropriation of the zeal tradition would achieve three aims. The first is that it would justify apparently unlawful behavior and teachings through appeal to the source of the Law over the Law itself as the motivating factor in Jesus's ministry. Second, valorization of Jesus's actions and teachings, and opposition to these, place Jesus in the tradition of persecution due to fidelity found in Psalm 68 (69), and seen in characters such as David or the prophets. Such positioning would subvert protests that Jesus was a deviant or innovative "παράνομος" (lawless person), instead countering that, like an idealized picture of David or a prophet confronting Israel, Jesus was zealous in his obedience to the Father. Third, on a social level this would provide a rationale grounded in Jewish history for early Jewish Christians to persevere in the face of ostracism or rejection. Jesus was consumed in his zeal for God, setting the path for his followers.

CHAPTER 6

Jesus, Moses, and the Johannine Community after the Jewish Revolt

Travis D. Trost

1   Introduction

The opening eighteen verses of the Gospel of John are a well-constructed dogmatic expression of the theology of the Johannine community. The fact they are theology should not obscure their brilliance or their careful construction. Nor should the longstanding academic debate about how and why the Prologue relates to the remainder of the Gospel of John cloud the reality that the Johannine community wanted to use community-bridging language. The use of terms such as λόγος which is also seen in the Greek philosopher Heraclitus and the Stoics indicates that the Johannine community was not afraid of using language that originated outside of it. Since Philo as a Jewish thinker also used[1] this term, it suggests a possible bridge between non-Jewish and Jewish worlds. Equally as clear is that the language of John 1 echoes Genesis 1 which is unmistakably Jewish. It should also be noted that there would be readers of the Gospel of John that would be equally comfortable in both Jewish and non-Jewish contexts. Again Philo serves as a viable example. He was at ease with Hellenistic culture; any person of a Jewish background influenced by him or his writings would feel at home in both worlds. Equally Gentiles who were cognizant with Jewish culture and who later became part of the Johannine community would be conversant with both groups.

   Manifestly the Johannine community wanted to communicate its message to the widest possible audience. Yet the more difficult question for contemporary scholarship is to understand why this community would have had such a strong interest in speaking to both non-Jewish and Jewish worlds. That is a complex issue but at least part of that answer lies in understanding the historical context that the Johannine community faced.

   Just before the Prologue ends the contrast is made between Jesus and Moses. The penultimate verse of the Prologue, verse 17, is unabashed in expressing a

---

1   Donald A. Hagner, "The Vision of God in Philo and John: A Comparative Study," *JETS* 14 (1971): 81–93.

comparison between the two figures. Moses represents law and Jesus is grace. Now this contrast can be read as a hostile statement toward Moses. This interpretation certainly has had plenty of adherents in the history of Christianity. Yet it can also be read as a statement that needs to be understood in the context of its era. The Gospel of John was composed after the Jewish Revolt and after other Gospel accounts[2] of Jesus had been written. In the years between c. 70 CE and c. 85 CE the Roman empire was recovering from serious upheaval and the Johannine community was living with an aggressive political system. The long academic conversation on how the Prologue uses Semitic or Hellenistic influences should not distract from the historical situation facing the Johannine community. This community used a Hellenistic friendly hymn for the Prologue while still discussing Moses because it had a need to communicate to the broadest possible audience.

2   The Dead Sea Scrolls

No contemporary study of the Gospel of John would be complete without at least considering the impact of Rudolf Bultmann. Whether one is a supporter of his work, an opponent, or take a more nuanced view of his legacy, Bultmann definitively changed the study of the Gospel of John. His views on both the formation of the Gospel of John and the source material behind it are well-known. Ironically, Bultmann's interest in Gnostic dualism became influential while the Dead Sea Scrolls were still being discovered. His publications in the early 1940s like *Neues Testament und Mythologie* and *Das Evangelium des Johannes* were circulated[3] during the crisis of the Second World War. *Das Urchristentum im Rahmen der antiken Religionen* was published[4] after the Dead Sea Scrolls were discovered but still only in 1949. Significantly, caves 2 through 11 were only discovered in the early and mid-1950s. The dualism of light and dark in the Dead Sea Scrolls was not available to Bultmann until after he had published his seminal works in German. The fact that Bultmann wrote at least a decade too early to appreciate the impact of the Dead Sea Scrolls on the study of the Gospel

---

2   The consensus of contemporary scholarship is virtually unanimous in its position that the Gospel of John was written after the Synoptics. Since this fits with the patristic evidence, placing the Gospel of John after the Synoptics chronologically is an interesting instance in which critical and pre-critical opinion agree.
3   *Neues Testament und Mythologie: Das Problem der Entmythologisierung der neutestamentlichen Verkündigung* as an essay in 1941. *Das Evangelium des Johannes*, Kritisch-exegetischer Kommentar 2, 10. Aufl. (1. Aufl. dies. Bearbtg.) (Göttingen: Vandenhoeck & Ruprecht, 1941).
4   *Das Urchristentum im Rahmen der antiken Religionen* (Zürich: Artemis, 1949).

of John should serve as a reminder to all scholars that we are in many ways a prisoner of our sources.

If Bultmann was ultimately limited in his conclusions by his timing, his interest in the non-Jewish influences impacting the Johannine community were valid. One of the most overlooked aspects of messianic studies in early Christianity is the non-Jewish interest in a coming world ruler. The prospect of a prophetic sovereign from the east[5] in the first century CE is an expectation that went beyond Jewish anticipations of a Messiah. The non-Jewish interest in an eastern ruler is seen in authors like Tacitus (*Hist.* 5.13) and Suetonius (*Vesp.* 4.5) that were written to a Roman audience. This is a key point for understanding both the Jewish and non-Jewish cultural context that the Johannine community faced. Understanding the characteristics of Jesus's kingdom was of interest to non-Jews because the perspective of the Greco-Roman elite was influenced by an imperial ideology that was on the alert for rival claims of authority.[6]

The renewed contemporary interest in the Gospel of John as a significant source for historical Jesus studies marks a departure from previous trends in biblical scholarship in both the nineteenth and twentieth centuries. Part of the rationale for this revival of interest in using the Gospel of John as a principal historical source is connected with the discovery of the Dead Sea Scrolls. The discoveries at Qumran[7] have provided a new avenue for scholarship to deal with these issues; perhaps just as importantly the texts discovered at Qumran have now become an integral part of the contemporary academic debate surrounding Second Temple Judaism(s) and early Christianity. As is widely acknowledged the Qumran community had views that were both sectarian and non-sectarian. Yet the fact that the Qumran community had its own sectarian beliefs is not inherently a barrier to the use of the Dead Sea Scrolls for academic inquiry in relation to the Gospel of John. It is worth noting Collins's hypothesis that the Qumran settlement received the smaller libraries of other parts of its movement at the time of the Jewish Revolt.[8] Obviously there will be

---

5 Travis D. Trost, *Who Should Be King in Israel?* (New York: Peter Lang, 2010), 172.
6 Edward N. Luttwak, *The Grand Strategy of the Roman Empire* (Baltimore: Johns Hopkins University Press, 1976), 4. Luttwak views Josephus as a messenger for the Flavian dynasty's message of Roman prowess.
7 In this chapter the term "Qumran community" will refer to those who followed the teachings in the texts discovered in caves 1 through 11 regardless of where or when they lived. "Qumran settlement" will refer to the actual, physical site called Qumran destroyed by the Romans in 68 CE.
8 John J. Collins, *The Dead Sea Scrolls: A Biography* (Princeton: Princeton University Press, 2013), 29.

both support and disagreement with Collins's proposal but he has identified a crucial point. The Qumran community should not be viewed as a hermetically sealed group tied exclusively to the Qumran settlement; it had contact with other branches of Second Temple Judaism(s). By using these texts as a point of comparison with the Gospel of John a window of further historical investigation is now opened to contemporary scholarship.

2.1   *Moses and the Gospel of John*

The Gospel of John in its overview of the ministry of John the Baptist and then Jesus moves quickly to establish the purpose of Jesus's ministry within the framework of Jewish religious tradition. A parenthetical explanation in John 1:41 is given to explain Andrew's identification of Jesus as the Messiah which indicates the non-Jewish reader is not forgotten in this discussion. Nonetheless, it is obvious that having a strong familiarity with Torah and Jewish religious history is an asset in understanding the discussion in John 1.

In Deuteronomy 18 the expectation of "that prophet" is given as a future promise of hope to the Jewish people. In John 1:23 John the Baptist states emphatically that he is not That Prophet but the text further records him as stating that he is pointing toward the arrival of the future hope. From there the action moves to John 1:45 where Philip tells Nathanael that he has found the One whom Moses had predicted. Fast-forward to John 9:28–29 and the opponents of Jesus identify themselves with Moses. Between these discussions of Moses in John 1 and John 9, the references to Moses[9] are based on four groups of sayings identified with Jesus in the first half of the Gospel of John. Clearly the Moses motif is integral to the message of the Johannine community as well as its opponents and therefore deserves to be examined.

The opening to the Moses motif in John 3 shows signs of a careful thematic narrative strategy. This chapter is well-known for the discussion between Jesus and Nicodemus yet in discussing Moses it is worth remembering how the previous chapter ends. The Temple Cleansing and discussion of Jesus's body being a replacement for the Temple[10] comes at the end of John 2. Nicodemus is identified as a teacher of Torah in John 3 and the narrative strategy of the Gospel of John starts to reveal itself in discussing the role of Moses. For the first readers

---

9   The Byzantine text references Moses in John 8.
10 Whether the discussion in John 2:18–22 suggests a veiled reference to the destruction of the Temple is well beyond the scope of this chapter. What is clear is that the discussion around the role of the Temple serves as a theological primer to the conversation around the bronze serpent in the narrative strategy of the Gospel of John.

of the Gospel of John who read without chapter or verse divisions the progression from Temple and Torah to Jesus would be quickly apparent.

For in John 3:14 the discussion of the account of Moses using a bronze serpent in Num 21:9 is introduced. This incident comes perhaps at a disadvantageous time in the Torah narrative. The incident of the Golden Calf in Exodus served as a strong warning against the making of images. Exhortations against idolatry in passages like Num 33:51–53 where the Israelites are commanded to destroy Canaanite idols may cause observant readers to wonder why Moses used a bronze serpent. Indeed the bronze serpent issue was a matter that rankled large sections of ancient Judaism.[11] It would also appear that it occupied the interest of the Qumran community. Turnage identifies 1QH^a 10:13 as a reference to the bronze serpent due to the similarities with Num 21:8–9.[12] In Turnage's view the Teacher of Righteousness is identifying himself as a sign to the faithful by using this language.[13] Turnage makes the comparison to John 3[14] and if one accepts his line of reasoning on the *Hodayot* passage, the point of comparison seems fair. Given the challenge of identifying the Teacher of Righteousness and his impact on the Qumran community it is best to be careful in making too strong a judgment. Nevertheless Turnage definitely does have a strong point in seeing the bronze serpent issue as having at least some parallel between the *Hodayot* and Johannine passages.

2.2 *John 5:45 and 5:46*

When the Gospel of John records Jesus's appeal to the authority of Moses near the end of John 5, contemporary scholarship should not be surprised to see this type of appeal because of parallels found in the Dead Sea Scrolls. The discovery and publication of the text now known as 4QMMT demonstrates the value of the finds at Qumran for comparative research. Since 4QMMT has survived only in a fragmentary state, it is not surprising that there has been a great deal of discussion about what this text's genre is and the possible identification of the recipients of this text. This debate about 4QMMT has generated a whole cottage industry within Dead Sea Scrolls research and there is no need to retread previous debates here. What is critical to note is that the interest of contemporary scholarship in 4QMMT is well-founded. It is an important text because of the subject matter discussed within it and because it also appeals

---

11   Marc Turnage, "Is it the Serpent that Heals? An Ancient Jewish Theologoumenon and the Developing Faith in Jesus," in *Israel in the Wilderness*, ed. Kenneth E. Pomykala, Themes in Biblical Narrative 10 (Leiden: Brill 2008), 73.
12   Turnage, "Is it the Serpent that Heals?" 81.
13   Turnage, "Is it the Serpent that Heals?" 81.
14   Turnage, "Is it the Serpent that Heals?" 81.

to the authority of Moses to validate correct behavior. In 4QMMT the dispute about *halakh* provides evidence that there were clearly important issues to the debaters at stake[15] and to be on the right side of Moses was absolutely vital to winning that debate. Ritual purity was an important issue and different perspectives within Second Temple Judaism(s) believed in the rightness of their cause and that they had interpreted Moses correctly.

The parallel with the narrative in John 5:45 and 5:46 is manifest. In those verses the anti-Jesus opposition is informed they do not believe Moses. Clearly the Johannine community wanted to be perceived as being on the correct side of Moses as well. It is equally as clear that this type of vigorous debate about Moses is not unique to the Gospel of John. Biblical scholarship before the discovery of the Dead Sea Scrolls was handicapped in its examination of the Gospel of John because of the dearth of relevant Second Temple material for comparative purposes. Now with the advent of texts like 4QMMT it is clear that the debates about Moses seen in the Gospel of John fit the dynamics of the Second Temple era.

It appears obvious that no branch of Second Temple Judaism(s) wanted to appear to be disloyal to Moses. The more challenging question is discerning how different parts of the Second Temple Jewish world interpreted the role of Moses. The even more difficult question to ponder is what the implications of the fall of the Temple would mean in the immediate years after the Jewish Revolt. Over time rabbinic Judaism clearly replaced the Temple cultic system. Yet in the aftermath of the Jewish Revolt that transition would have had to endure the confusion of a challenging social and political milieu. What would loyalty to Moses mean in the Flavian era?

2.3 John 6:32

The Johannine community describes Jesus adopting the title of Bread of Life in John 6:32. Inherently an implicit critique is now made of the opponents of Jesus as not understanding the proper role of Moses. In Exodus 3 Moses has an encounter with the burning bush and he is commissioned to remonstrate with Pharaoh. Moses is the Divine messenger and not the message. The point is again repeated in John 8 when Abraham is the topic of discussion. Abraham is a messenger like Moses according to the Gospel of John. The Johannine community clearly wants the focus to be on Jesus.

This motif continues in christological expressions by describing Jesus as the light of the world in John 8:12, the resurrection and the life in John 11:25, the

---

15   James VanderKam and Peter Flint, *The Meaning of the Dead Sea Scrolls* (New York: HarperOne, 2004), 213.

way, the truth, and the life in John 14:6, and the true vine in John 15:1. Nestled within these "I am" (ἐγώ εἰμι) declarations is John 10:11 which identify Jesus as "the Good Shepherd." Now there is no doubt that asserting the title, "the Good Shepherd," has christological implications but the title of shepherd in the ancient world is one that virtually all cultural groups would certainly recognize as having royal implications. Many ancient rulers used the shepherd motif to describe their rule, the Hebrew Bible has repeated expressions of shepherd as ruler, and the Qumran connection can be found in 1Q34 and 4Q504.

Jesus's identification as the Good Shepherd also provides a sharp contrast between those who kill and destroy and Jesus who brings life. The peaceful, irenic nature of the Good Shepherd is on display. He protects and nurtures the sheep without resorting to violence. In John 10:16 Jesus states that other sheep need to be brought together with the existing sheep to bring about unity. This metaphor can be analyzed in different ways but what is quite clear is that the message being communicated here is one that seeks to bring the early Christian community together and not apart. Just as Jesus was open to speaking to the Samaritan woman in John 4, the message of Jesus is one that goes beyond ethnic or cultural divisions.[16]

Moses is acting as a shepherd in Exodus 3. To a careful reader of the Good Shepherd discourse Moses's occupational history as a shepherd would be evident. Likewise is the contrast between Jesus as the Good Shepherd/Gate versus the thieves and robbers. By definition, for the Johannine community, these thieves and robbers would also include non-Jewish religious saviors. The shepherd motif again highlights how the Johannine community communicated a message that crossed all cultural boundaries while still connecting with the issues within Second Temple Judaism(s).

2.4   *John 7:19–23*

The meaning of sabbath is integral to the question of the significance of observing Torah and respecting Moses in this passage. Earlier in John 5 the account of the cripple at the pool of Bethesda is couched in terms of whether healing on the sabbath is proper. The subject is again developed in John 7:19–23. The question of what is proper "work" activity for the sabbath was obviously a point of contention between the Johannine community and their opponents. It was also a question that needs to be examined for wider implications.

The Qumran community was as equally interested in the subject of the sabbath. A case in point is *The Songs of the Sabbath Sacrifice*. It was used as a liturgical work on the first thirteen sabbaths of the year to show the significance

---

16   Trost, *Who Should Be King in Israel?*, 152.

of this theme in matters of worship. The issue of the sabbath and what constitutes proper work further needs to be seen in the context of Jewish identity and nationalism in the late Second Temple era. In the Maccabean era there were some Jews who apparently refused to fight on the sabbath (1 Macc 2:32–41). Josephus notes that when Pompey advanced on Jerusalem during the Roman conquest of Jerusalem the Jewish defenders did not actively resist on the sabbath (*J.W.* 1.7.3). These are not the only examples in the Second Temple era of the observance of the sabbath coming before military action. The *War Scroll* planned for sabbatical years for the long eschatological war that was expected to come. The sabbath was a complex issue indeed for Jewish interpreters of that era.

The story of the Qumran community and settlement does not end in 68 CE with the Roman destruction of the Qumran settlement in their march on Jericho. The discovery at Masada of fragments from the *Songs of the Sabbath Sacrifice* is important to understanding the possibility of activity by possible survivors of the destruction of the Qumran settlement by the Romans. Magness notes in her reconstruction of the Qumran settlement for Period Ib that it was abandoned due to a manmade fire around 9/8 BCE and reoccupied during the time of Herod Archelaus.[17] She also raises the interesting possibility that the Qumran settlement's relatively brief abandonment may be associated with the turmoil surrounding the last days of Herod the Great.[18] The possible implications of Magness's comments suggest a conceivable but not certain historical context for the Qumran settlement and community. The demise of the Qumran settlement in 68 CE may not have been the first time that its residents had to flee a Roman backed enemy. Possibly they had made a comeback decades previously. Hypothetically were they then looking for a second comeback after the Roman attack on their settlement in 68 CE?

2.5　War?

If the *Copper Scroll* is the most enigmatic scroll in the corpus of the Dead Sea Scrolls, the *War Scroll* is an excellent candidate for being the second most ambiguous text. It could be viewed as a military instruction manual; conversely its literary genre may be something akin to apocalyptic fantasy. It even might be a combination of both literary varieties. Regardless of how it is interpreted, it is both an arduous and compelling text to engage.

---

[17] Jodi Magness, *The Archaeology of Qumran and the Dead Sea Scrolls* (Grand Rapids: Eerdmans, 2002), 67–68.

[18] Magness, *The Archaeology of Qumran*, 68.

To interpret the complexities of the *War Scroll* requires an appreciation of the nature of the habitation at Qumran. This is not the usual starting point in assessing the *War Scroll* but it is nonetheless a vital factor to consider. The settlement at Qumran was fortified centuries earlier[19] during the Iron Age. The protective possibilities of the topography around Qumran create a naturally defensible site. Now whether it was fortified during the first century BCE or CE is a more debatable question. Clearly if the settlement had been fortified it would suggest a much more aggressive context for the *War Scroll*.

Archeology alone will not settle this argument because of the complexities of this issue related to the history of the excavation at the Qumran site.[20] Therefore it is important to weigh the evidence from the works of Pliny the Elder (*Nat. His.* 5.73) and Josephus (*J.W.* 2.8.2–13 and *Ant.* 18.1.5). The substance from both on this issue would suggest that a fortified settlement at Qumran during the era from c. 150 BCE to 68 CE is not the most likely option. Pliny the Elder in his description of the Essenes emphasizes their otherworldliness. A fortified settlement in the wilderness near the Dead Sea truly does not fit with his description. Nor is there anything from Josephus that would suggest that the Qumran settlement should be viewed as a militant base. This is not simply an argument from silence. Both of these writers were cultural products of the ideology of the Roman empire. The political and military power of the empire depended on an impression of complete and inevitable power. That does not rule out the possibility that for some reason they could have glossed over possible Qumran militancy but it does provide a strong argument against it.

Equally as important to understanding the *War Scroll* is deciphering the history of its formation. The trend of scholarship in the last few decades has been to see the *War Scroll*, probable recensions from Cave 4, and related texts like 4Q285 and 11Q14 as being products of a long compositional history stretching back to the Seleucid empire. There has also been a focus on the *War Scroll* as having a primarily liturgical purpose.[21] This should be noted as not always having been the starring academic view. Yigael Yadin viewed the *War Scroll* as having an origin in the Roman era and the text as having less of a liturgical focus and more of a blatantly military message. He also would have seen a much greater unity in the composition of the text than most contemporary scholars envision. Presently the general academic consensus would suggest that the *War Scroll's* compositional history is a complex tangle that makes finding

---

19   Collins, *Dead Sea Scrolls*, 68–69.
20   Collins, *Dead Sea Scrolls*, 86.
21   Brian Schultz, *Conquering the World: The War Scroll (1QM) Reconsidered*, Studies on the Texts of the Desert of Judah 76 (Leiden: Brill, 2009), 324.

unity in its message problematic. Nevertheless, regardless of how one views the compositional history of the *War Scroll*, it is evident that this text has a strong eschatological and apocalyptic subject matter.

A long compositional history combined with a liturgical use for the *War Scroll* would suggest that the use of this text for the Qumran community was as an instrument of eschatological hope and not a call for immediate action. In this sense they could be compared to many groups ancient, medieval, and modern who had an eschatological expectation, discovered the apocalypse had not happened as expected, and then amended their understanding of their eschatology to await a now deferred expectation. Since the best evidence from both literary and non-literary sources at this point indicates that the pre-68 CE Qumran community and settlement were not actively hostile to Rome, this interpretation of the *War Scroll* is to be preferred.

This provides context for the Masada fragment of the *Songs of the Sabbath Sacrifice* discovered in a Yadin directed excavation of Masada in the 1960s. Yadin's interpretation of the significance of his important find at Masada went beyond the available evidence. His assumption of a direct[22] link with the Qumran settlement actively supporting the Masada resistance fails to account for the entire historical context of the Jewish Revolt. While it is dangerous to trust Josephus too much, his picture of the resistance to Rome in the Jewish Revolt suggests that it was equally a civil war between different Jewish communities as it was a war between Rome and the broader Jewish population in Judea and Galilee. Plausibly the Masada fragment of the *Songs of the Sabbath Sacrifice* could have been seized by an anti-Roman group. As the Qumran settlement survivors fled the violence surrounding them, this fragment could possibly have been captured and brought to Masada by force. Josephus indicates that intramural Jewish violence and pillaging by the Masada resistance at Ein Gedi (*J.W.* 4.7.2) was part of the Jewish Revolt. While this suggestion of a pillaged text cannot be regarded as conclusive proof as to how the Masada fragment of the *Songs of the Sabbath Sacrifice* came to Masada, it does have sound reasons to support it. It fits with the arguments from Qumran morphology and orthography as outlined by Tov to support a Qumran origin[23] for the *Songs of the Sabbath Sacrifice*. It also explains how this fragment came to be at Masada when the behavior of the Masada resistance showed key differences with the eschatology of the Qumran community.

---

22   Yigael Yadin and Carol Newsom, "The Masada Fragment of the Qumran Song of the Sabbath Sacrifice," *IEJ* 34 (1984): 77–88.
23   Emanuel Tov, "A Qumran Origin for the Masada Non-Biblical Texts?" *DSD* 7 (2000): 57–73.

Erho in his analysis of the *War Scroll* raises an important question concerning the tension within the *War Scroll* between the expectation of direct Divine supernatural intervention in the affairs of humankind and the need for the self-identified righteous to act as living instruments[24] of the Divine will. Part of this tension relates to the state of preservation of the *War Scroll*[25] and part relates to understanding whether the *War Scroll* is primarily a liturgical or a military instruction manual. What is clear nevertheless is that this tension still anticipated ultimate victory for the righteous no matter how great the crisis. The concept of contrived mass suicide/killing and abandonment of Divine intervention as Josephus describes the Masada resistance as foreign to the theology of the Qumran community. The expectation in the *War Scroll* was that the righteous would lead a reunited Israel and that there would be Divine intervention after significant setbacks. Further texts like 4QMMT demonstrated that allegiance to Moses demanded a full commitment to ritual purity. A direct link between the Masada fragment of the *Songs of the Sabbath Sacrifice* and the Masada resistance would force any survivors of the Qumran community to ironically abandon their prior theological commitments to purity and liturgically correct eschatological war. Given what is known of the nature and history of this community that reversal would seem unlikely.

The explanation offered in the preceding paragraphs is not the only option in assessing the Masada fragment of the *Songs of the Sabbath Sacrifice*. Schiffman has argued that this text could be viewed as a common, widespread Jewish text that is not[26] a sectarian creation of the Qumran community and so its discovery at Masada is simply a coincidence. Other plausible suggestions could be offered as well. Hopefully someday new discoveries will be made that provide greater clarity on this issue. Yet what is clear presently is that the Jewish Revolt was a dangerous time and that for the Johannine community the aftermath of that struggle would also be a challenging period. The war may be over but peace had not yet begun.

2.6   *A Peaceful Kingdom*

The Johannine community was clear about their understanding about how to deal with Rome and their Jewish opposition; the peaceful nature of Jesus's actions was to be stressed. Nathaniel proclaims Jesus the Son of God and King

---

24   Ted M. Erho, "The Motif of the Eschatological Battle in the War Scroll (1QM)," in *Celebrating the Dead Sea Scrolls: A Canadian Edition*, ed. Peter W. Flint, Jean Duhaime, and Kyung S. Baek (Atlanta: SBL, 2011), 370.
25   Erho, "The Motif of the Eschatological Battle," 370.
26   Lawrence H. Schiffman, *Reclaiming the Dead Sea Scrolls* (Philadelphia: Jewish Publication Society, 1994), 355.

of Israel in John 1 and starts the process of explaining Jesus's royal identity by highlighting the theological rather than political implications of that title. Jesus is Son of God. He is not another Hasmonean or Herodian pretender. He is preaching a transformation that is independent of both Roman and local Jewish power structures because its value system is fundamentally different. Further in the narrative of the Gospel of John Jesus resists a popular kingship in John 6:15. The contrast between other anti-Roman movements of that era like those of Judas of Galilee or Theudas is delimited as Jesus resisting rather than supporting a popular insurrection. For a Roman reader the irenic nature of Jesus's kingdom would be significant. All four Gospels indicate that Jesus preached the coming kingdom of God; however, the Synoptic tone in expressing this message is more vigorous than the Gospel of John. The Johannine community shows great carefulness in expressing Jesus as leading a kingdom that is not seeking war with Rome either eschatologically as expressed for example in the *War Scroll* or in tangible fact like the Jewish Revolt.

For it is in John 12 that the concept of Jesus as King of Israel is again reintroduced during the triumphal entry into Jerusalem. The timing of this declaration near the midway point of the narrative of the Gospel of John would appear deliberate. In John 11:48 Jesus's opposition is described as being concerned that the Romans would replace the Jewish elite with a more effective pro-Roman governing class. That statement in and of itself brilliantly summarizes the very cynical but nevertheless very effective Roman tactic of manipulating a local elite to rule over a conquered population. The juxtaposition of Jesus as the peaceful King being shadowed by the pro-Roman collaborators is clearly a part of the narrative strategy of the Gospel of John. The triumphal entry is non-violent and highlights both Jesus's popular support and the emphasis on Jesus's ministry being focused on people and not political advantage.

When the Gospel of John relates the final days of Jesus, it covers events published previously in the Synoptics. The Passion Narrative in the Gospel of John is definitely the most important portion of this Gospel that can be directly compared to the Synoptics. Comparisons between the various Gospel traditions are a relevant question for contemporary scholarship yet they also need to be appreciated from the perspective of the Johannine community. Unless one assumes that the Johannine community was sealed hermetically from the rest of the early Christian movement, it would be logical to conclude that the Johannine community could expect scrutiny[27] of the Gospel of John's

---

27 Whether the Gospel of John shows literary dependence or independence from the Synoptics is a long running debate in biblical research that is beyond the scope of this chapter. Nevertheless, even if the Gospel of John is viewed as totally independent of the

portrayal of Jesus's actions. The discussion concerning the relationships of the individual Synoptic Gospels to the Gospel of John in regards to the Passion Narrative[28] needs to be set in this broader context. The Johannine community faced a distinctive social and political setting. In the decades immediately after the Jewish Revolt the priority message of the Johannine community would need to focus on the life of Jesus and the social environment of the Johannine community during the Flavian era. The Gospel of John has a narrative strategy that stresses a non-violent message for its first readers in the post-Jewish Revolt environment. That is the message it prioritized to broadcast.

3 Pilate and Pressure

Jesus tells Pilate that Rome has nothing to fear but the truth in John 18:37. Now a kingdom based on truth sounds noble but it is also very abstract to a Roman aristocrat facing the concrete stresses of managing a populace as challenging as the one in Judea. Pilate needed to juggle competing interests because he was a man under pressure. The local aristocracy in John 19:12 inform Pilate that he has much to fear because he needs to be Caesar's friend. Now it is Pilate's turn to fear because he needs their support or at least their acquiescence to maintain his position. The charge of not being Caesar's friend would resonate in both the 30s CE and the 70s CE for the simple fact it was hard to know who was acting as Caesar. Whether one favors a date for the Crucifixion in 30 CE or 33 CE,[29] the Sejanus protectorate was a factor in assessing the state of internal Roman politics. If the Crucifixion was in 30 CE, Sejanus was at the height of his power. If one favors 33 CE, then Sejanus had been violently deposed less than two years earlier. Either way, Pilate would be nervous about the situation in Rome because of its ambiguity. He certainly would not want to be seen as ineffective in dealing with the local elite and facing an accusation of disloyalty. This mirrors the tension seen within the Roman empire after the accession of

---

Synoptics and the literary traditions that led to the creation of each Synoptic Gospel, the Christian communities that used the Synoptics would not be unknown to the Johannine community.

28 Raymond Brown, *Death of the Messiah*, 2 vols. (New York: Doubleday, 1994), 1:75–93. Brown provides a good starting point to the question of how the Gospel of John in its Passion Narrative compares to the Synoptics.

29 The most commonly supported dates by biblical scholarship for the Crucifixion are 30 CE and 33 CE. For a helpful discussion of the issues involved see Brown, *Death of the Messiah*, 2:1373–76.

Vespasian. Vespasian had obtained the empire by force after imperial civil war and the Jewish Revolt; the Flavian ascension was still new.

Pilate solves his own immediate problem by ordering the execution of Jesus. By doing so he creates his own distinct place in history and provides the contemporary scholar with an unambiguous anchor for understanding the biography of Jesus. The fourfold-Gospel attestation of the *titulus* provides a fixed historical point for understanding the life of Jesus. Even the staunchest critic of the Gospel of John's historical content would have difficulty doubting Jesus was executed as a messianic pretender by Pilate. Yet for the Johannine community it also provides another reason why the peaceful nature of Jesus's kingdom needs to be stressed. The Romans executed their opponents frequently; whether the Romans were always fair with their victims is another question.

The irony is that for a Jewish audience the question of whether the *titulus* spoke the theological truth about Jesus being the genuine King of the Jews was also an important issue. The synagogue was a place of controversy for the Johannine community; John 12:42 notes that a fear of expulsion from the synagogue by the Pharisees was perceived as an issue. Regardless of whether one supports the supposition that the Speakers of Smooth Things were Pharisees or not, it is evident that the Qumran community was active in polemic. In this regards the 30s CE again parallel the 70s CE. The contest of ideas within the synagogue in the post-70 CE era could involve the full spectrum of opinion on how to deal with Rome. It would also require an appraisal of the Johannine community's assertion that Jesus was the peaceful King of Israel. The priority for the Johannine community was communicating a message that explained how the Good Shepherd had an irenic message for everyone.

The fall of the Temple did not end Jewish resistance to Roman imperial rule. The Masada resistance was not meant to be unique; the group of fortress-palaces in Judea facing east toward Nabatea could provide bases for a continuing fight against Rome. Since the Jewish insurgencies in Egypt in 115–117 CE and the Bar-Kochba Revolt in 132–135 CE are still in the not too distant future, it suggests that the Johannine community would be dealing with difficult questions as it engaged the broader Jewish community. Was fighting Rome legitimate and what is the right way to follow Moses after the destruction of the Temple?

4   A Message for Its Times

The Johannine community in the years between c. 70 CE to c. 85 CE lived with the tension that followed the victory of Vespasian in the Jewish Revolt.

The Roman empire in general and Judea in particular had just been through a wrenching and bloody period of years. A visible sign of this new era was the permanent stationing of a Roman legion at Jerusalem. The Romans now considered Judea a military priority because of the danger of possible rebellion and were not subtle in how they would deal with any Jewish opposition. Whereas the Romans had used auxiliaries before the Jewish Revolt to garrison Jerusalem, now Legio x Fretensis permanently[30] occupied it. There can be no clearer representation of the imperial Roman attitude toward the Jewish population in the post-Jewish Revolt era. Any previous Roman qualms about offending Jewish religious sensibilities by stationing a legion with its standards in Jerusalem were gone. A legion that had participated in both the siege of Jerusalem and the capture of Masada was the new symbol of Roman authority in Judea.

History tells us that the Flavian dynasty brought a measure of stability to the Roman empire but that is the knowledge gained by those who are now almost two thousand years removed from this situation. For any Jew who lived through imperial civil war, the Jewish Revolt, and then the first few years of the reign of Vespasian this new stability would not have seemed so obvious. Certainly for any possible survivors of the Qumran community the immediate years after the destruction of their settlement would have proved difficult. It is indeed an irony of history that the Dead Sea Scrolls found in the caves around Qumran have given contemporary biblical scholarship an opportunity to better understand the beliefs of Second Temple Judaism(s) but only because the Qumran settlement was destroyed. Being connected to Judaism in the Roman empire in the Flavian era had now become more difficult for every shade of Jewish or Jewish-Christian belief.

So how then did the Johannine community deal with this new situation? The Johannine community responded with a message for dual audiences. The Prologue begins with language that is both Gentile friendly while still containing significant meaning for Jewish readers. For readers steeped in Hellenistic thought the Prologue uses language that would make sense to their own cultural background; it would also serve as a bridge to any member of the Greco-Roman elite curious about the message of the Johannine community. For non-Jewish readers, the language of the Gospel of John stressed the peaceful nature of Jesus's message. At the same time the Prologue leads to a discussion of Moses. For Jewish readers the Gospel of John shows an acute awareness of topics current within the wider Jewish community. Issues like proper sabbath observance and understanding the correct role of Torah are

---

30   Edward Dabrowa, *Legio X Fretensis* (Stuttgart: Franz Steiner, 1993), 14.

important but they are important in the context of the authority of Moses. The Moses motif is expounded for Jewish readers because Jesus is identified as the solution to the exegetical problem of the bronze serpent. Jesus is superior to Moses not because Moses failed but because Moses led to Jesus in the theology of the Johannine community.

The contrast between Jesus and Moses in the Prologue is not intended to be inherently adversarial; the contrast is meant to explain that in the theological worldview of the Johannine community Moses pointed to Jesus. Obviously there would have been a division of opinion in that era and today over whether the Johannine community's interpretation of Moses was correct. Nonetheless the Johannine community was convinced that it had the proper understanding of Moses and it had a duty to proclaim this message.

This suggests further historical context for understanding John 16:2. The Moses motif in the Gospel of John was written knowing that the Temple had been destroyed. Synagogue discussions on war and peace in the post-Jewish Revolt era could be expected to be highly contentious. The Gospel of John stresses the peaceful kingdom of Jesus and this is a critical point for understanding the Gospel of John as a point of contact with a wider Jewish community that suffered greatly from the Jewish Revolt. Jewish readers also needed to know that Jesus's kingdom was irenic.

5   Conclusion

The Gospel of John has another well-known name to biblical scholarship, the Fourth Gospel. Since it is written after the Synoptics, its perspective could be expected to be different from the earlier Gospels. This highlights the reality that the social situation facing the Johannine community during the Flavian era required a response that would make sense to different cultural backgrounds after the Jewish Revolt. The Johannine community needed to communicate in a social milieu that showed great similarities with the 30s CE but in an even more rigid and dangerous political environment. The message of the Johannine community was that Jesus is the Good Shepherd of a peaceful kingdom that was beyond the politics of this world. It had to communicate this message both carefully and powerfully because in the Flavian Roman empire what was now called peace arose from the demise of the Temple and dreams of Jewish independence.

CHAPTER 7

The King on the Cross: Johannine Christology in the Roman Imperial Context

Arthur M. Wright, Jr.

1   Introduction[1]

Scholars have long recognized that the Fourth Gospel displays a Christology among the highest of the New Testament writings. However, little attention has been given to the fact that a formidable obstacle to this elevated Christology exists toward the end of John's narrative: Jesus's death on a Roman cross. The crucifixion and death of Jesus present a tremendous challenge to Johannine Christology. Within the Roman imperial world, the cross sends a stark message about the meaning and identity of Jesus, one in serious conflict with the elevated Johannine vision. Roman crucifixion shames, humiliates, and defeats its victims in no uncertain terms. Yet the Fourth Evangelist manages to overcome the problem presented by the cross; indeed, John's Christology soars to an apex in the crucifixion account. In order to accomplish this, the Fourth Gospel subverts the Roman imperial meaning of the cross with its presentation of Jesus's crucifixion, death, and burial (19:16b–42). As Jesus dies on the cross, his kingship is keenly evident, even in the midst of the brutality that he endures. In effect, John *ironizes* the meaning of the cross, allowing two separate meanings to exist within the narrative. While Jesus is tortured and dies at the hands of the Romans, his crucifixion is cast as his moment of enthronement, glorification, and triumph.

2   The Folly of the Cross

Given the centrality of Jesus's crucifixion in Christian theology of the past two millennia, it is remarkable to note the brevity with which the Fourth Gospel narrates the moment: "There they crucified him, and with him two others, one on either side, with Jesus between them" (19:18). The evangelist provides few

---

[1] Parts of this article were previously published in Arthur M. Wright, Jr., *The Governor and the King: Irony, Hidden Transcripts, and Negotiating Empire in the Fourth Gospel* (Eugene, OR: Pickwick, 2019), 186–230. Used by permission of Wipf and Stock Publishers (www.wipfandstock.com).

clues to the means of crucifixion or details about the extent of Jesus's suffering. Yet the act of crucifixion would have spoken volumes to John's original audience. Ancient sources are helpful for understanding both the method of Roman crucifixion, as well as the symbolic value of this particular type of execution.

The manner in which crucifixion was carried out was not uniform, and executioners could take creative license in killing their victims. Josephus records a mass execution of Jewish rebels in the Jewish War: "the [Roman] soldiers out of rage and hatred amused themselves by nailing their prisoners in different postures; and so great was their number, that space could not be found for the crosses nor crosses for the bodies" (*J.W.* 5.451). Seneca also reports great variety in the manner with which crucifixion was carried out: "I see crosses there, not just of one kind but made in many different ways: some have their victims with head down to the ground; some impale their private parts; others stretch out their arms on the gibbet" (*Marc.* 20.3).[2] However it was carried out, crucifixion was invariably a cruel, violent, and torturous means of execution. Often its victims suffered for days before finally dying from blood loss, infection, asphyxiation, dehydration, or exposure.[3] Crucifixion was also a public spectacle by design. Victims were executed in public places to serve as a warning and deterrent to all who passed by. Quintilian explains that "when we [Romans] crucify criminals the most frequented roads are chosen, where the greatest number of people can look and be seized by this fear" (*Decl.* 274).

Crucifixion held a special place or purpose in the maintenance of control within the Roman empire. There were other means of execution in the ancient world, such as hanging, impalement, or beheading.[4] Yet the symbolic value of crucifixion made it a powerful tool of Roman imperial power. This particular manner of execution demonstrated Roman dominance and hegemony. Moreover, it humiliated, shamed, and tortured the victim as they died.

---

2   Quoted from Martin Hengel, *Crucifixion in the Ancient World and the Folly of the Message of the Cross* (Philadelphia: Fortress, 1977), 25.

3   Cilliers L. Retief, "The History and Pathology of Crucifixion," *South African Medical Journal* 93 (2003): 938–941; Frederick T. Zugibe, "Two Questions about Crucifixion: Does the Victim Die of Asphyxiation? Would Nails in the Hand Hold the Weight of the Body?" *BRev* 5 (1989): 34–43; and Raymond E. Brown, *Death of the Messiah: From Gethsemane to the Grave: A Commentary on the Passion Narratives in the Four Gospels*, 2 vols., ABRL (New York: Doubleday, 1994), 2:1090–92.

4   Brown, *Death of the Messiah*, 2:945. The 7th century writer Isidore of Seville noted that "hanging [was] a lesser penalty than the cross. For the gallows kills the victim immediately, whereas the cross tortures for a long time those who are fixed to it" (*Etymologia*, 5.27.34; quoted in Hengel, *Crucifixion*, 29).

Finally, within the Jewish context, crucifixion suggested that the victim was under God's judgment.

2.1 *Crucifixion as Instrument and Symbol of Roman Domination*

The cross was an instrument of terror intended to discourage resistance to Roman rule. Bloody, ragged figures crucified along a roadside conveyed the message that Rome could do whatever they wished to whoever they deemed a threat; Rome's agents would employ all of the violence and brutality they could muster to maintain control of a province. Furthermore, crucifixion reminded provincials of their status as conquered and subject people. Tom Thatcher explains this symbolic value of crucifixion:

> [E]very crucifixion reenacted Rome's conquest of the victim's nation. In this drama, the officiating soldiers played the role of the conquering Roman legions, while the person on the cross represented his entire people group, beaten, broken, and subjugated. In Palestine particularly, every crucifixion reenacted Pompey's conquest of the region in 63 BCE, reminding both Rome and the Jews of exactly how things came to be the way they are.[5]

A Roman cross was a visual and visceral symbol of Roman domination. Moreover, it was a graphic reminder of what happened to all who opposed Roman hegemony.

2.2 *Crucifixion as Instrument of Shame and Annihilation*

Crucifixion was such a humiliating and degrading form of execution that Roman law typically restricted this type of capital punishment to members of the lower classes, provincials, and slaves; it would have been considered uncouth to execute Roman citizens and elite members of society in such a fashion.[6] It was so offensive that ancient authors appear to have been reticent to write at length about it; Brown detects this tendency, observing wryly that "at any period of history those who practice torture are not overly communicative about the details."[7]

---

5 Tom Thatcher, *Greater than Caesar: Christology and Empire in the Fourth Gospel* (Minneapolis: Fortress, 2009), 93.
6 Brown, *Death of the Messiah*, 2:946. However, Hengel does note that Roman citizens might be crucified for especially severe crimes such as treason. See *Crucifixion*, 39–40.
7 Brown, *Death of the Messiah*, 2:946.

Shame and humiliation were part of the design of crucifixion. If the only desired outcome on the part of the executioner was the death of the victim, a number of other, simpler, more efficient options for execution were available, such as beheading or impaling. Crucifixion made a spectacle of the condemned, presenting their naked, broken, bloody, dying body in public space for all to see as they suffered and died. Even after death, bodies were often left on the cross for display. Victims were not deemed worthy of burial, and scavengers often consumed the bodies.[8]

As a shameful means of execution, crucifixion was what James C. Scott describes as a "ritual of denigration"—granted, a rather severe one—designed to strip dominated persons of their dignity and autonomy even as it killed them.[9] In crucifixion, Roman agents demonstrated their domination over bodies of subject people, inflicting physical abuse even to the point of death. Alan Kirk explains further that "torturous deaths—such as crucifixion was—can be highly symbolized forms of violence, with the disfiguring, distending, dismembering, smashing, and perforation of the human body routinized and choreographed to display and enact publicly the socially degraded status of the victim."[10] Along these lines, Tom Thatcher elucidates a deeper, symbolic meaning of death by crucifixion: "The violence of the cross went beyond physical punishment to symbolic annihilation, with the destruction of the victim's flesh narrating Rome's capacity to suppress every threat to the state's entire sovereignty."[11] Thus, the symbolic value of crucifixion extended well beyond its basic value as a means of execution.

2.3 Crucifixion as Symbol of God's Judgment

Against the backdrop of the Jewish Scriptures, crucifixion carried significant symbolic meaning, as well. Deuteronomy 21:22–23 proclaims that "anyone hung on a tree is under God's curse." Paul employs this text to explain that Christ redeems humanity "from the curse of the law by becoming a curse for us—for it is written, 'Cursed is everyone who hangs on a tree'" (Gal 3:13). A

---

8 John Dominic Crossan makes this argument on the basis that modern archaeologists have only discovered one extant skeleton fragment from a crucified man from antiquity (*The Historical Jesus: The Life of a Mediterranean Jewish Peasant* [San Francisco: Harper & Row, 1988], 391–92).

9 James C. Scott, *Domination and the Arts of Resistance: Hidden Transcripts* (New Haven: Yale University Press, 1990), 23.

10 Alan Kirk, "The Memory of Violence and the Death of Jesus in Q," in *Memory, Tradition, and Text: Uses of the Past in Early Christianity*, ed. Alan Kirk and Tom Thatcher, SemeiaSt 52 (Atlanta: Society of Biblical Literature, 2005), 192–93.

11 Thatcher, *Greater than Caesar*, 93.

crucified man would not appear as Messiah or king, but rather as one shamed, abandoned, and under God's judgment.

Paul recognizes the obstacle to proclaiming a crucified messiah when he writes that "the message about the cross is foolishness to those who are perishing" (1 Cor 1:18). He concedes that "Christ crucified" is a "stumbling block to Jews and foolishness to Gentiles" (1 Cor 1:23). Likewise, the author of Hebrews recognizes the shame and disgrace implicit in crucifixion, recalling that Jesus "endured the cross" and "disregard[ed] its shame" (12:2). The proclamation of a "crucified messiah" would have sounded utterly oxymoronic.

2.4 The Ironic Meaning of the Cross in the Fourth Gospel

Thus, in the Roman imperial world, the cross presents a daunting obstacle to the Fourth Gospel's presentation of Jesus. The Roman cross broadcasts a message of imperial power, triumph, and violent terror. Yet the Fourth Gospel presents the crucifixion account in a particular fashion so as to transform the Roman imperial meaning of the cross; Jesus's shameful death upon the cross becomes his moment of triumph and glory. The Fourth Evangelist creates an ironic presentation of Jesus's crucifixion so that Jesus appears not simply as humiliated and brutalized victim, but also as triumphal king.

Irony suffuses the Gospel of John to the extent that its author has been called a "master of irony."[12] Paul Duke offers a helpful definition of irony: "Irony as a literary device is a double-leveled literary phenomenon in which two tiers of meaning stand in some opposition to each other and in which some degree of unawareness is expressed or implied."[13] R. Alan Culpepper suggests that, in ironic communication, the "narrator means more than he says," "the characters do not understand what is happening or what they are saying," and that "the implied author smiles, winks, and raises his eyebrows as the story is told."[14] Both of these definitions of irony illuminate what is happening in the Fourth Gospel's crucifixion scene.

Two levels of meaning co-exist within the narrative; on the one hand, Jesus is crucified and dies at the hands of his Roman executioners. On the other hand, the Gospel casts this death in terms of Jesus's glorification (7:39; 12:23), moment of triumph, and return to his Father (13:1, 3; 14:12; 16:10, 28; 17:11). An

---

12   See, for example, R. Alan Culpepper, *Anatomy of the Fourth Gospel: A Study in Literary Design* (Philadelphia: Fortress, 1983), 166; and Wayne Meeks, "The Divine Agent and His Counterfeit in Philo and the Fourth Gospel," in *Aspects of Religious Propaganda in Judaism and Early Christianity*, ed. Elizabeth Schüssler Fiorenza (Notre Dame, IN: University of Notre Dame Press, 1976), 59.

13   Paul D. Duke, *Irony in the Fourth Gospel* (Atlanta: John Knox, 1985), 17.

14   Culpepper, *Anatomy*, 165–66.

element of unawareness also exists within the narrative; characters within the story appear oblivious to the deeper meaning of events as they transpire. The Roman soldiers mock Jesus, divide up his clothing, and finally pierce his dead body with a spear, with no awareness of the greater significance of Jesus's death as the Fourth Gospel presents it. Yet attentive readers and hearers of the Gospel are able to perceive the ironic meaning of Jesus's crucifixion; he is enthroned as king upon the cross, fulfills God's purposes, and draws all people to himself as he is "lifted up" from the earth. In the sections to follow, we will examine the crucifixion and burial accounts to see how the Fourth Gospel accomplishes this task.

3   Jesus's Crucifixion (19:16b–18)

The crucifixion account begins as Pilate hands Jesus over to be crucified (19:16a). Roman soldiers take him swiftly to Golgotha, the site of execution, and the actual crucifixion is narrated with brevity. Yet even within this brief scene, key Johannine themes emerge which cast Jesus as king and contest the Roman imperial meaning of the cross.

In comparison to the Synoptic Gospels, Jesus's way to the cross in John is presented in unique fashion. Luke's Gospel, for example, describes how a "great number of people" follow him, including women who beat their breasts and wail for him (Luke 23:27); John includes no such account. Within the narrative world of the Fourth Gospel, there is no reason to mourn for Jesus as he makes his way to the cross.

Likewise, there is no account of Simon of Cyrene carrying Jesus's cross. Typically, condemned persons would carry their own crossbeams to the place of execution; in this sense, it comes as no surprise that Jesus carries his own cross in John.[15] Yet Simon of Cyrene appears in each of the three Synoptic Gospels.[16] Furthermore, the omission appears to be of special significance to the Fourth Evangelist, who emphatically states that Jesus walks to the crucifixion site "carrying the cross *by himself*" (19:17; note the reflexive pronoun ἑαυτῷ). Given that the Simon tradition is well attested in early Christianity, the Fourth Evangelist appears to deliberately disregard and even contradict it to stress

---

15   See Rudolf Karl Bultmann, *The Gospel of John: A Commentary* (Philadelphia: Westminster, 1971), 668. Bultmann gives a number of primary sources which attest condemned persons carrying crossbeams to the site of execution (see 668 n. 3).
16   Cf. Mark 15:21; Matt 27:32; and Luke 23:26. In all likelihood, it is merely the crossbeam that Simon carries in the Synoptics and that Jesus carries in the Fourth Gospel.

Jesus's strength, dignity, and command of the situation as he makes his way to Golgotha.[17] Brown suggests that this is likely a "deliberate excision of the memory of Simon" on the part of the Fourth Evangelist in order to "continue the theme that Jesus went to his death as sole master of his own destiny."[18] This coheres with Jesus's earlier claim: "No one takes [my life] from me, but I lay it down of my own accord" (10:18a). Jesus appears dignified and in control of his situation as he proceeds to the cross.

Although sparse details are given as Jesus is crucified, the evangelist emphasizes the placement of Jesus on a cross between two other crucified persons. Yet the Gospel records no details about these two men, other than describing them as "two others" (ἄλλους δύο; John 19:18). In contrast, Mark and Matthew describe these two as "bandits" (λῃσταί; Mark 15:27 and Matt 27:38), while Luke indicates that they are "criminals" (κακούργους; Luke 23:33) and features a brief dialogue between them and Jesus (Luke 23:39–43). In Mark and Matthew, both of the figures mock Jesus (Mark 15:32; Matt 27:44), and in Luke, one of them does (Luke 23:39). In the Fourth Gospel, these figures do not speak; the emphasis is not on their criminality or their mockery of Jesus, but rather on their arrangement with respect to Jesus. They are placed "one on either side" (ἐντεῦθεν καὶ ἐντεῦθεν) of Jesus (19:18), and the narrator reiterates that Jesus is "between them," or more precisely, perhaps, that "Jesus [is] in the middle" (μέσον δὲ τὸν Ἰησοῦν). The evangelist emphasizes Jesus's placement as the central figure. Given that the Gospel has previously emphasized Jesus's identity as "king" in the Passion Narrative (18:33, 36–37; 19:2–3, 12, 14–15), the presentation of two crucified men on either side of Jesus mimics a royal entourage. Senior agrees, contending that these two become "part of the crucified King's 'retinue' as he takes his place on the throne of the cross."[19] Though Jesus is crucified alongside two other criminals, the narrator downplays this element and instead stresses his kingship.

Already in the crucifixion account we see how the Fourth Evangelist has highlighted Jesus's kingship while de-emphasizing the shameful, degrading aspects of his crucifixion. This presentation creates tension with the dominant meaning of crucifixion while supporting John's high Christology. Jesus is presented with regality: he is strong enough to carry his own cross and is

---

17 In fact, one wonders if this tradition may go back to an eyewitness account. Mark 15:21 notes that Simon was "the father of Alexander and Rufus," suggesting that these two may be known to the Markan community.
18 Raymond E. Brown, *The Gospel According to John*, AB 29–29A, 2 vols. (New York: Doubleday, 1966–1970), 2:917.
19 Donald Senior, *The Passion of Jesus in the Gospel of John* (Collegeville, MN: Liturgical, 1991), 103.

surrounded by a symbolic entourage as he is lifted up from the earth. Even as Jesus is crucified, the cross becomes the place of his exaltation.

4 Pilate's Inscription on the Cross (19:19–22)

After Jesus is crucified, the narrative shifts attention back to the Roman governor, Pilate. In all four Gospels, Pilate has an inscription placed upon the cross. In the Fourth Gospel, however, the scene is depicted in an ironic manner that points to the deeper reality and meaning of Jesus's crucifixion. O'Day observes that "on [a] theological level ... this inscription positions the kingship motifs from the trial before Pilate (18:28–19:16a) as the interpretive lens through which to view Jesus's crucifixion."[20] With a uniquely Johannine encounter between Pilate and the Jewish authorities regarding the wording on the inscription, this scene subverts the dominant meaning of the cross and advances the Johannine theme of Jesus's kingship. As this scene unfolds, Pilate—the principal agent of Roman imperial power in the province of Judaea—announces Jesus's kingship in ironic fashion.

Many English translations obscure Pilate's agency in writing and placing the inscription on the cross at 19:19, implying that the Roman soldiers do so.[21] Yet the Greek text emphasizes Pilate's involvement: "and Pilate also wrote an inscription and placed it upon the cross" (ἔγραψεν δὲ καὶ τίτλον ὁ Πιλᾶτος καὶ ἔθηκεν ἐπὶ τοῦ σταυροῦ; 19:19).[22] The inscription is an official charge describing why Jesus is being executed; the Greek word τίτλον, unique to John, transliterates the technical Latin term *titulus*.[23] As "the king of the Jews," Jesus is presented as an unsanctioned royal claimant and thus a threat to imperial hegemony.[24] The inscription is also an ironic declaration that Jesus is an agent of divine power and is representative of God's sovereignty; from the point of view of the Johannine narrator, Jesus really is the "king of the Jews."

---

20 Gail R. O'Day, "The Gospel of John: Introduction, Commentary, and Reflections," in *Luke, John*, NIB 9, ed. Leander E. Keck (Nashville: Abingdon, 1995), 830.
21 E.g., the NRSV reads "Pilate also had an inscription written and put on the cross."
22 The verb can be interpreted with causative force, implying that Pilate orders others to write and place the inscription. Nevertheless, with Pilate as the subject of both verbs, the text highlights Pilate's agency in this scene. Cf. 19:1, in which the Greek text reads that Pilate "flogged" Jesus (Τότε οὖν ἔλαβεν ὁ Πιλᾶτος τὸν Ἰησοῦν καὶ ἐμαστίγωσεν).
23 Mark describes this placard as "inscription of the charge" (ἐπιγραφὴ τῆς αἰτίας; Mark 15:26); Matthew and Luke simplify this as a "charge" (αἰτίαν; Matt 27:37) and an "inscription" (ἐπιγραφή; Luke 23:38).
24 A figure such as Herod, in contrast, was sanctioned by Rome to rule on their behalf as "king of the Jews" (e.g., *Ant.* 14.9; 15.409).

The placard carries additional ironic significance, for it broadcasts Jesus's sovereignty to all those who pass by: "many of the Jews read this inscription, because the place where Jesus was crucified was near the city; and it was written in Hebrew, in Latin, and in Greek" (19:20).[25] Pilate and his soldiers intend that the deaths of Jesus and the others will serve as a warning and reminder of Roman imperial power to all who pass by. The crosses broadcast the message to those who might oppose Rome that "threats to Roman rule would not be tolerated."[26] Within the narrative of the Gospel, however, the public display and inscription work against Roman sovereignty; they are ironic declarations of Jesus's kingship and his glorification. The fact that many read the inscription is suggestive that he is drawing all people to himself by means of his crucifixion. Recall Jesus's statement that "when I am lifted up [Greek: ὑψωθῶ] from the earth, [I] will draw all people to myself" (12:32; cf. 3:14 and 11:52). The Greek word ὑψόω is used ironically throughout the Fourth Gospel (3:14; 8:28; 12:32, 34), carrying a double meaning that indicates both the physical lifting of Jesus up on the cross by Roman soldiers, as well as and Jesus's symbolic exaltation as Son of Man and King. Moreover, Jesus's exaltation upon the cross makes eternal life (ζωὴν αἰώνιον) available to believers (3:15).

Of the four Gospels, John alone reports that the inscription is written in three languages: Hebrew, Latin, and Greek. O'Day observes that these are the three principal languages of the Roman province of Judaea: Aramaic was the common, everyday language of the people; Latin was the official language of the Roman empire; and Greek would have been used for business and commerce. Thus, she says this is a "universally comprehensible announcement."[27] Brown agrees, calling it a "world-wide proclamation of enthronement."[28] The Samaritan woman's proclamation that Jesus is "Savior of the world" (4:42) rings particularly true in this moment; as Jesus is glorified on the cross, the Gospel envisions that his kingship extends to all people.

The Jewish authorities dispute Pilate's choice of words for the inscription, however. They are offended and request that Pilate reconsider: "Do not write, 'The King of the Jews,' but, 'This man said, I am King of the Jews'" (19:21). Pilate taunted the Jewish authorities by calling Jesus the "king of the Jews" during

---

25   The Synoptic Gospels all lack this detail.
26   Craig R. Koester, *Symbolism in the Fourth Gospel: Meaning, Mystery, Community* (Minneapolis: Fortress, 1995), 227.
27   O'Day, "John," 830.
28   Brown, *Gospel According to John*, 2:919. Wes Howard-Brook observes that these are the "three languages of the Johannine world," and therefore are "tongues for the entire 'world' to understand" (*Becoming Children of God: John's Gospel and Radical Discipleship* [Eugene, OR: Wipf and Stock, 1994], 417).

the trial; now, as Michaels observes, Pilate is "rubbing salt in old wounds, the wounds that were opened when he repeatedly called Jesus 'the King of the Jews'" earlier (18:33, 39; 19:3, 5, 14, 15).[29] The title reminds them of their status as a subject people. Their request for an alternative inscription is also an attempt to distance themselves from the crucified man; they do not want to be associated with Jesus as he is crucified as a representative of their oppressed people. Pilate will not yield, however, and responds, "What I have written, I have written [Greek: γέγραφα]."

Pilate's statement is also ironic, for the governor unwittingly says more than he knows. Throughout the Fourth Gospel, the Greek verb γράφω is used to refer to the writings of the Jewish Scriptures (1:45; 2:17; 5:46; 6:31, 45; 8:17; 10:34; 12:14, 16; 15:25).[30] The few exceptions refer to the writing of the Fourth Gospel itself (20:30, 31; 21:24, 25). By repeatedly applying the word γράφω to describe the governor's *writing* of the charge (19:19 [2], 20, 21, 22 [2]), the inscription is invested with deeper authority, as though it were Scripture. The inscription is actually true: Jesus *is* the king of the Jews. Pilate, of course, cannot see the deeper truth of his writing. Duke describes this type of irony as "unconscious testimony."[31] It is dramatic irony, an "incongruity is between what a dramatic character says, believes, or does and how unbeknownst to that character, the dramatic reality is."[32] Pilate is an unwitting victim of irony as he bears witness to the truth: Jesus is king (cf. 18:39; 19:14, 15). The chief agent of Roman imperial power in the Roman province of Judaea announces Jesus's sovereignty to all the world; he advances the Johannine Christology and subverts the imperial meaning of the cross.

This inscription reveals the profound situational irony of John's crucifixion account: Jesus, the crucified one, is the king of the Jews and God's sovereign agent on earth. This irony contests the Roman imperial meaning of the cross as well as the imperial claim that the Roman emperor is the one who enacts the divine will on earth. The author of John presents the inscription on the cross so that, rather than simply being a charge of criminal activity, it becomes a proclamation of Jesus's kingship and true identity. Bultmann observes that, "as the Crucified, Jesus is really the king; the kingly rule, awaited in hope, is not as such destroyed, but established in a new sense; the cross is the exaltation and

---

29 J. Ramsey Michaels, *The Gospel of John*, NICNT (Grand Rapids: Eerdmans, 2010), 950.
30 Jesus himself writes on the ground in 8:8; however, the *pericope adulterae* (7:53–8:11) is not in the earliest manuscripts of the Fourth Gospel and is unlikely of Johannine origin.
31 Duke, *Irony*, 89.
32 David Wolfsdorf, *Trials of Reason: Plato and the Crafting of Philosophy* (Oxford: Oxford University Press, 2008), 246.

THE KING ON THE CROSS 137

glorification of Jesus."[33] Jesus's crucifixion is the moment he is "lifted up" and exalted; the inscription Pilate writes and places upon the cross becomes Jesus's glorious title.

5   Dividing Spoils and Fulfilling Scripture (19:23–25a)

On the heels of Pilate's response to the Jewish authorities that he will not change the inscription, the narrative describes the division of Jesus's clothing by the Roman soldiers, an event common to all four Gospels.[34] This demeaning act suits the undignified treatment of Jesus throughout the crucifixion account. Yet the Johannine Evangelist emphasizes that this division of clothing echoes Ps 22:18, thus fulfilling Scripture. Jesus is portrayed as the paradigmatic figure of Psalm 22, a righteous sufferer who will ultimately be vindicated by God.

Psalm 22 (LXX Ps 21) depicts one who is surrounded, mocked, and threatened by a number of adversaries. The psalmist despairs at this plight: "I am a worm, and not human; scorned by others, and despised by the people. All who see me mock at me; they make mouths at me, they shake their heads" (Psalm 22:6–7). At the same time, the psalmist recalls God's faithfulness and anticipates salvation: "For he did not despise or abhor the affliction of the afflicted; he did not hide his face from me, but heard when I cried to him" (Psalm 22:24). The psalmist acknowledges the reality of suffering yet expects God's sure deliverance.

In this psalm, early Christians found much to reflect on as they sought to make sense of Jesus's crucifixion. Each of the three Synoptic Gospels draws on its imagery as they narrate their own crucifixion accounts. Mark and Matthew depict various figures deriding Jesus, "shaking their heads," and mocking him (Mark 15:29–31; Matt 27:39–42). In Luke, the leaders "scoff" at Jesus; soldiers mock him, and one of the other crucified men "derides him" (Luke 23:35–39). In all four Gospels, Jesus is presented as the figure of Psalm 22 as he suffers and is mocked on the cross. Yet John downplays Jesus's suffering and his antagonists' mocking cries. There is no explicit mockery in John's crucifixion account. Nor does Jesus cry out from the cross as in Mark and Matthew ("My God, my God, why have you forsaken me?"; Mark 15:34; Matt 27:46). Moreover, what the Synoptic Gospels only hint at, the Fourth Gospel makes explicit: the division

---

33   Bultmann, *Gospel of John*, 669.
34   Cf. Mark 15:24; Matt 27:35; and Luke 23:34.

of clothing fulfills Scripture ("this was to fulfill what the scripture says" [ἵνα ἡ γραφὴ πληρωθῇ; 19:24]).[35]

The division of clothing in Ps 22:18 employs Hebrew parallelism to describe a single event: "they divide my clothes among themselves, and for my clothing they cast lots." The Fourth Gospel narrates this as two events, however: the soldiers first split four items of Jesus's clothing amongst themselves and then gamble for the tunic that remains (19:23).[36] Both of these events have been fruitful sources for much scholarly speculation;[37] yet the details within the narrative are sparse, and attention is directed toward the fulfillment motif. This attention is made by means of strong allusion to, and then direct quotation of Ps 22:18: "They divided my clothes among themselves, and for my clothing they cast lots." With this, Jesus is presented as the suffering psalmist of Psalm 22, the righteous one who will ultimately be rescued by divine intervention.

This is the first of three declarations of the fulfillment of Scripture in the crucifixion account (cf. 19:28, 36). Each of these is significant for understanding the presentation of imperial power and Jesus's identity. While crucifixion asserts Roman dominion and power, the evangelist suggests that, even as Jesus's clothing is being split between the soldiers, God's purposes are being fulfilled. In this way, "prophecy thus becomes an antidote for imperial power."[38] Jesus, in dying on the cross, is enacting God's will, not succumbing to the dominating power of Rome.

---

35 This formulaic statement appears several times throughout the Gospel, often word-for-word (12:38; 13:18; 15:25; 17:12; 19, 28, 36).

36 Brown (*Death of the Messiah*, 954) and O'Day ("John," 831) suggest that the evangelist has simply ignored the parallelism of the verse. Other scholars, however, insist that the author's treatment of the parallelism is intentional (e.g., Michaels, *Gospel of John*, 952; and Douglas J. Moo, *The Old Testament in the Gospel Passion Narratives* [Sheffield: Almond, 1983], 256–57).

37 For example, D.A. Carson speculates that the four items of clothing are a purple robe (19:2), a belt, sandals, and a typical Jewish head covering (*The Gospel according to John* [Grand Rapids: Eerdmans, 1991], 612). Furthermore, he proposes that the soldiers probably split these four pieces by lot, as well, since they would have been of unequal value. A number of scholars discuss possible symbolism of the seamless tunic (19:23), with the majority of scholars suggesting one of two options: that it is symbolic of Jesus's identity as a high priestly figure or that it symbolizes the unity of the early Christian community. Between the two, stronger emphasis in the Fourth Gospel lies on Christian unity than on Jesus's identity as high priest (Brown, *Death of the Messiah*, 2:957). Yet neither is particularly likely in the context of the narrative, since the tunic is ultimately pilfered by the soldiers (Michaels sees this as the major stumbling block for interpreting either symbolism in the tunic [*Gospel of John*, 953]).

38 Thatcher, *Greater than Caesar*, 99.

Irony is in play here. Rome's agents—the soldiers—cannot see that they are pawns in a larger cosmic drama that is unfolding. From their point of view within the narrative, they are parceling out the remaining possessions of a dying criminal. Yet their actions reveal Jesus's identity at a profound level as they unwittingly follow the script of Psalm 22.

Furthermore, the full context of Psalm 22 imbues an even deeper meaning to the events that transpire as the soldiers divide Jesus's clothing. The psalmist anticipates God's salvation, declaring "you have rescued me" (22:21), and "[God] heard when I cried" (22:24). As Jesus predicted, he will likewise be rescued: "I lay down my life in order to take it up again" (John 10:17; cf. 2:19–21). Though he will die on the cross, he will be resurrected in due time.

Though much of early Christian tradition draws upon Psalm 22 to understand Jesus's crucifixion, the presentation of the material in the Fourth Gospel is unique among the Gospels. The evangelist downplays Jesus's suffering and the mocking words of his antagonists while emphasizing the crucified Jesus as the one who fulfills the role of the figure of Psalm 22. The evangelist has turned the division of clothing, which appears to be a rather mundane moment, on its head; it signals that God's plan is unfolding in these events and that Jesus will ultimately be saved by God. On the cross, Jesus is neither defeated by Rome nor forsaken by God.

6   Words from the Cross (19:25b–27)

While the soldiers distribute Jesus's few articles of clothing, the narrator describes Jesus's interaction with his mother, other women, and the beloved disciple while he hangs on the cross. In the Fourth Gospel, these followers are "beside the cross" (παρὰ τῷ σταυρῷ; 19:25) and are close enough to talk to Jesus. Their devotion to Jesus surpasses whatever terror they might feel standing in the shadow of the cross, the threatening symbol of Roman dominance.[39] In this uniquely Johannine scene, the narrator demonstrates that though Jesus suffers on the cross, he displays control and presence of mind in this scene to ensure his mother's ongoing care.

A number of significant features can be observed about this scene. Whereas nearly all of Jesus's male followers abandoned him following his arrest, just as he predicted (16:32), these women are exemplary in their faithfulness to Jesus,

---

39   While the Synoptic Gospels also depict women observing Jesus's death, they are described as standing at a distance from the cross, perhaps because of fear (Mark 15:40; Matt 27:55; Luke 23:49).

even to the end. Even in the face of possible harassment and punishment, the women have not deserted Jesus.[40]

The symbolic import of Jesus's instructions to his mother and the beloved disciple are also significant. Jesus's words, "Woman, here is your son," and "Here is your mother" (19:26–27), echo ancient adoption formulas.[41] They suggest a new, legal bond, with the practical outcome that the beloved disciple becomes a male relative to support Jesus's mother after Jesus's death.[42]

Most noteworthy for our purposes, however, is what this scene adds to the presentation of Jesus on the cross. In spite of being crucified, Jesus appears calm and collected. Thatcher observes that "Christ possesses the power and presence of mind to care for his mother and the Beloved Disciple, even in his darkest hour."[43] Absent is the agony of the Markan Jesus, who cries out "My God, my God, why have you forsaken me?" (Mark 15:34; cf. Matt 27:46). Though Jesus must have been in excruciating pain as he suffered on the cross,[44] he has the presence of mind and lucidity to care for the needs of others.

This moment contests the Roman imperial meaning of the cross. Jesus is not in intolerable agony while on the cross; instead, it is his moment of triumph and exaltation, and he demonstrates full command of events as they transpire. Howard-Brook observes that "the Johannine Jesus uses the power of the cross to form new relationships, to heal wounds, to generate new communities just when all seems dust and ashes."[45] Jesus co-opts the cross to carve out something new in the midst of the terror, violence, and death that Roman agents intends to inflict. He thus displays the power and authority which he has received from his Father, subverting the power and authority that Rome flaunts with the cross. Moreover, the faithful presence of the women and the beloved

---

40   Gail R. O'Day, "Gospel of John," in *Women's Bible Commentary*, 3rd ed., ed. Carol A. Newsom, Sharon H. Ringe, and Jacqueline E. Lapsley (Louisville: Westminster John Knox, 2012), 527.

41   C.K. Barrett makes a similar observation (*The Gospel According to St. John: An Introduction with Commentary and Notes on the Greek Text* [London: SPCK, 1958], 459). Roland de Vaux has a brief but helpful discussion of adoption formulas in the ancient world in *Ancient Israel: Its Life and Institutions*, trans. John McHugh (New York: McGraw Hill, 1961), 112–13.

42   Jesus's brothers and father are mentioned earlier in the Fourth Gospel, yet do not appear in the latter half of the narrative. Jesus's brothers appear several times (2:12; 7:3, 5, 10), but then drop out of sight after 7:10. Joseph is mentioned twice (1:45; 6:42), but never appears in the narrative. In the narrative world of the Fourth Gospel, none of them are available to care for Jesus's mother from this point forward. Jesus thus designates a male relative, ensuring his mother's welfare, and the beloved disciple welcomes her "into his own home" (εἰς τὰ ἴδια; 19:27).

43   Thatcher, *Greater than Caesar*, 159.

44   Note that the etymological roots of the English word "excruciating" are found in the Latin word *crux* ("cross").

45   Howard-Brook, *Becoming Children*, 423.

disciple at the cross, as well as Jesus's words from the cross, bear testimony to divine love and care for one another; they contrast strongly with the violence and self-interest of Rome.

7 Jesus's Death (19:28–30)

The moment of Jesus's death on the cross is rich with christological significance. Once again, the Fourth Evangelist has crafted the narrative carefully to demonstrate that Jesus's death is not his humiliation and defeat at the hands of Rome, but rather his exaltation. Moreover, Jesus maintains command of the events that transpire all the way to the point of death. He displays no agony or pain as he dies of his own volition, appearing confident and composed. As Jesus dies, the moment is depicted in terms of his completion of his Father's work. Finally, the theme of Jesus's death as fulfillment continues. The Fourth Evangelist draws upon Psalm 69 (LXX Ps 68) to present Jesus as a righteous one who suffers, yet who remains confident of God's certain salvation.

The emphasis on Jesus's death as the completion of the divine plan and fulfillment of Scripture is especially pronounced here. The Greek verbs τελέω and τελειόω appear three times in these three verses. Aware that "all was now finished [τετέλεσται]," Jesus announces his thirst "in order to fulfill [τελειωθῇ] the scripture" (19:28).[46] After receiving wine, Jesus finally announces, "It is finished [τετέλεσται]" (19:30). The evangelist has previously employed τελειόω and related words to describe Jesus's mission to complete the work of his Father (e.g., 4:34; 5:36; 17:4). Having accomplished everything according to God's plan, Jesus can now die and return to the Father.[47]

The Fourth Evangelist signals that Jesus's dying moment fulfills Scripture by casting Jesus in the guise of the suffering figure of Psalm 69. Jesus declares "I am thirsty" (διψῶ) to evoke Scripture; it is "a profound expression of Jesus's awareness that his death is following a divine program."[48] Jesus then receives a sponge of wine (ὄξους) from his enemies. Taken together, the announcement of thirst and the offer of wine recall Psalm 69, a psalm that the Fourth

---

46 Typically, πληρόω is used by the Fourth Evangelist to indicate fulfillment of Scripture (cf. 12:38; 13:18; 15:25; 17:12; 18:9; 19:24, 36). Here, τελειόω is used as a synonym for πληρόω. See C.F.D. Moule, "Fulfillment-Words in the New Testament: Use and Abuse," *NTS* 14 (1968): 318.

47 Intentionally or not, John evokes Isa 55:1–11, and v. 11 in particular: "[S]o shall my word be that goes out from my mouth; it shall not return to me empty, but it shall accomplish that which I purpose, and succeed in the thing for which I sent it."

48 Thatcher, *Greater than Caesar*, 115.

Evangelist has employed twice before in the Gospel (cf. 2:17; 15:25). Like the psalmist who laments, "[F]or my thirst [δίψαν] they gave me vinegar [ὄξος] to drink" (Ps 69:21), Jesus is beset by enemies who give him bitter wine in response to his thirst. Jesus, depicted as this paradigmatic figure, suffers on the cross under the gaze of Roman soldiers. Yet the psalmist pleads to God for deliverance (e.g., Ps 69:13–14, 17) and maintains faith that God will surely intervene (Ps 69:30–36). Likewise, the Johannine audience can anticipate God's ultimate intervention and salvation for Jesus. Jesus's suffering will end in resurrection and life, not death, suggesting that Rome's power and cross will not have the last word. Even as Jesus dies on the cross, the events unfold according to the divine plan.

The hyssop branch from which Jesus receives the sponge of wine evokes Exodus 12 and the Passover lamb tradition. The Fourth Gospel has previously alluded to Jesus's connection with the slaughtered Passover lamb on a number of occasions (1:29; 18:28, 39; 19:14), and will allude to it again soon (19:33, 36). In the Exodus narrative, Moses directs the Israelites in Egypt to take hyssop and smear the blood from a slaughtered lamb (LXX: πάσχα) on their doorposts to identity the residents as Jewish (Exod 12:21–22). God thus spares Israelite children while passing through the land and killing the firstborn children of Egyptians. The passover event results in the liberation of the Jewish people; it provokes Pharaoh to relent and release them from captivity (Exod 11:1–12:33). In the Fourth Gospel, Jesus's blood smeared upon the cross suggests that the cross is not simply an instrument of Roman execution and terror, but rather is part of God's work for liberation.[49]

There are curious connections that bookend the beginning of Jesus's ministry in John 2 and the end of his ministry here in John 19. Most notably, Jesus's mother and wine appear in both scenes. Yet there is a distinct contrast between the quality of wines in each scene. Here, as Jesus dies, the Roman soldiers offer him ὄξος, a cheap, vinegary wine that was commonly available among the lower classes and Roman soldiers.[50] At the wedding at Cana, however, which launched his public ministry, Jesus produced good wine (καλὸν οἶνον) in abundance, thereby revealing his glory (2:10–11). In Jewish tradition, abundant wine was symbolic of the bounty and blessing of God's reign in the age to come (e.g.,

---

49 See Howard-Brook, *Becoming Children*, 424.
50 BDAG, 715. On the cheap wine common to Roman soldiers, see Carson, *Gospel According to John*, 620. Note that the immediate antecedents of the "they" who offer Jesus the vinegary wine are Jesus's mother and the beloved disciple. Nevertheless, readers should probably understand that it is the Roman soldiers who have the wine available and also direct access to Jesus as he hangs on the cross (Brown, *Death of the Messiah*, 2:1074).

Amos 9:13; Joel 3:18). The offer of common wine to Jesus on the cross contrasts with the good wine he makes available to others as a blessing.

This scene also evokes Jesus's offer of "living water" to the Samaritan woman so that she will "never be thirsty" again (4:10–15). There is irony evident in the contrast between Jesus's provision of living water for her and the cheap wine he is offered on the cross, as O'Day observes: "The world falsely attempts to assuage the thirst of the One who is himself the source of 'living water.'"[51] Moreover, Jesus's declaration to the Samaritan woman is also appropriate for the Roman soldiers: "If you knew the gift of God, and who it is that is saying to you, 'Give me a drink,' you would have asked him, and he would have given you living water" (4:10). The Roman soldiers are unable to grasp that Jesus is the true source of life and thirst-quenching drink.

When Jesus finally dies, his death is narrated with restraint. The evangelist presents Jesus's death not as a moment of agony, but as the death of one who is coherent and dignified. Jesus states simply, "It is finished" (τετέλεσται; 19:30).[52] A superficial reading of the text suggests the last desperate gasp of a dying victim, yet it is certainly much more. As Thatcher observes, "'It is finished' means nothing like 'I'm done for.'"[53] This is Jesus's pronouncement that he has accomplished the tasks set out for him by the Father. Moloney agrees, stating that Jesus's final cry is "an exclamation of achievement, almost of triumph."[54] With this, Jesus dies, bowing his head and "handing over" (παρέδωκεν) his spirit.[55] Throughout the Passion Narrative, the verb παραδίδωμι has been employed to describe Jesus's betrayal into the hands of Roman agents (see 18:2, 5, 30, 35, 36; 19:11). What began with Judas's betrayal in the garden (18:2) is now complete.[56] Ironically, however, it is neither Judas, nor the Jewish authorities, nor the Romans who ultimately control Jesus's fate. Instead, Jesus himself "hands over" his own life, validating his claim that "no one takes my life from me, but I lay it

---

51 O'Day, "John," 832.
52 In contrast, Jesus's loud cry as he dies in Mark 15:37 (cf. Matt 27:50) is presented as an "incoherent death scream" (Thatcher, *Greater than Caesar*, 115).
53 Thatcher, *Greater than Caesar*, 115.
54 Francis J. Moloney, *The Gospel of John*, SP 4 (Collegeville, MN: Liturgical, 1998), 504.
55 What the evangelist means for Jesus to "hand over the spirit" (19:30) is debatable. Some scholars such as Moloney propose that in this act, Jesus grants the Holy Spirit to his followers (*Gospel of John*, 504–5). Within the narrative of the Fourth Gospel, however, Jesus explicitly grants the Spirit to his followers at 20:22: "When he had said this, he breathed on them and said to them, 'Receive the Holy Spirit.'" Thus, at 19:30, the Greek word πνεῦμα simply describes Jesus's life force, "that which animates or gives life to the body" (BDAG, 832). Cf. Matt 27:50, which depicts Jesus's dying moment similarly.
56 Howard-Brook, *Becoming Children*, 424.

down of my own accord" (10:18). Jesus remains the master of his fate, even to his last breath.[57]

Thus, Jesus's moment of death is presented in careful fashion to emphasize key christological points. This scene contests the Roman imperial meaning of death on a cross; Jesus's crucifixion is not depicted as a shameful, humiliating death, but rather as dignified and purposeful. Jesus's words carry deep meaning. By stating "I thirst," and "It is finished," Jesus suggests that his death fulfills Scripture and completes his work on behalf of the Father. By identifying Jesus with the figure of Psalm 69, readers can anticipate that Jesus will soon be delivered by God. Moreover, each of these statements represent *double entendre*. It would not be surprising for a crucified person to request a drink and then later gasp "It is finished" while he dies. In the narrative context however, these statements convey far deeper meaning. They are profoundly ironic statements that guide attentive readers to a deeper understanding of Jesus's death on the cross. He is more than a condemned and dying criminal who has been broken by the agents of Roman imperial power; Jesus is the agent of God's saving activity who directs the course of events in accordance to the divine plan. In his death, Jesus is exalted and God's will is done.

8 Blood and Water (19:31–37)

The events following Jesus's death continue to have christological implications. The narrative presents him not as one who has been overcome by Roman imperial power, but rather as one who has died with dignity. Moreover, the Fourth Evangelist reframes Jesus's death within the context of Jewish Scripture; his death is neither haphazard nor contingent upon the will of Roman agents but occurs in accordance with the divine plan.

The Jewish authorities do not want the bodies of the crucified men left on the crosses as the Sabbath begins at sunset, so they ask Pilate to hasten the executions and have the bodies of the victims removed.[58] Pilate evidently assents, and soldiers go to break the legs of the two crucified on either side of

---

57 It is worth comparing the Synoptic accounts of Jesus's dying moment. Mark 15:37 and Luke 23:46 report simply that Jesus "expired" (ἐξέπνευσεν). After Jesus's loud cry, Matt 27:50 states that Jesus "let the spirit go" (ἀφῆκεν τὸ πνεῦμα).

58 The Jewish authorities are possibly motivated by Deut 21:22–23: "When someone is convicted of a crime punishable by death and is executed, and you hang him on a tree, his corpse must not remain all night upon the tree; you shall bury him that same day, for anyone hung on a tree is under God's curse."

THE KING ON THE CROSS 145

Jesus.[59] Imperial agents inflict further violence in order to kill these crucified victims more quickly. Jesus, however, has already died of his own volition, "giving up his spirit" in v. 30. The soldiers thus have no need to break his bones and leave his legs intact. In this way, Jesus is presented in a fashion that preserves a measure of dignity in his death.

One of the soldiers, however, stabs Jesus's body in the side with his spear, probably to confirm that he is indeed dead, and blood and water issue forth from the wound. The symbolism that the author intends with the blood and water—if any—is difficult to discern. The best explanation centers on the meaning of the flow of water from the wound.[60] Water is a pervasive image throughout the Fourth Gospel. Water is used symbolically in baptism (1:26, 31, 33) and foot washing (13:5) and provides the basis for a miraculous provision of abundant wine (2:9). Jesus walks on the chaotic sea (6:16–21) and a man seeks healing in the waters of a pool (5:2–9). Of all the occurrences of water in the Gospel, Jesus's conversation with the Samaritan woman (4:5–42) is particularly relevant to the interpretation of 19:34. After Jesus asks the woman for a drink (4:7), he in turn offers her living water (4:10), saying, "those who drink of the water that I will give them will never be thirsty. The water that I will give will become in them a spring of water gushing up to eternal life" (4:14). Jesus uses the image of water in connection with belief and the full, abundant life that he offers.

Jesus employs water imagery for another noteworthy statement during the Festival of Booths. Toward the conclusion of the festival, Jesus declares, "Let anyone who is thirsty come to me, and let the one who believes in me drink" (7:37–38). The narrator clarifies that Scripture provides the source for this statement:[61] "Out of his belly [κοιλίας] will flow rivers of living water" (7:38; my

---

59 A crucified person could potentially survive many days on a cross before succumbing to death. Breaking the legs of a crucifixion victim was known as *crurifragium*, and would hasten death by increasing blood loss and decreasing their ability to breathe. See John Dominic Crossan, *The Cross That Spoke: The Origins of the Passion Narrative* (San Francisco: Harper & Row, 1988), 163.

60 Patristic and medieval interpreters were eager to find sacramental symbolism in the blood and water: blood for the eucharist and water for baptism. See O'Day, "John," 834. For an example of this interpretation from the patristic era, see Augustine, *Civ.* 22.17. Some modern commentators also find sacramental symbolism in this incident (e.g., Moloney, *Gospel of John*, 505–6, 509). Yet the blood is to be expected from the wound; the water is the surprising element, and thus the focus of the interpretation above.

61 It is not clear what Scripture the evangelist has in mind here. Michaels has a helpful discussion regarding the text that may be in view here. He argues that Zech 14:8 is the likeliest source: "On that day living waters shall flow out from Jerusalem, half of them to the

trans.).⁶² In the Fourth Gospel, Jesus's own body provides the source of true life, symbolically presented as living water. The blood and water that flow out of his body in 19:34 visualize this reality: living water flows from Jesus's pierced side. Jesus's death on the cross thus becomes the source of true life.⁶³

Moreover, the evangelist suggests that these events happen in order to fulfill Scripture: "These things occurred so that the scripture might be fulfilled, 'None of his bones shall be broken.' And again another passage of scripture says, 'They will look on the one whom they have pierced'" (19:36–37). Once again, the evangelist frames the events surrounding Jesus's death in the context of Jewish Scripture and God's plan.

The first reference (v. 36) actually evokes two texts from the Hebrew Scriptures: Exod 12:10 (LXX) and Ps 34:21 (33:21 LXX). Exodus 12:10 (LXX) recalls the preparation of the Passover lamb before the tenth and final Egyptian plague: "You shall not let any of it remain until morning and you shall not break a bone of it" (cf. Exod 12:46; Num 9:12; *Jub.* 49:13–14). Psalm 34:20 (33:21 LXX) is a hymn of thanksgiving and praise for God's protection:⁶⁴ "He keeps all their bones; not one of them will be broken." Neither text is an exact match with John 19:36,⁶⁵ but both have implications for Johannine Christology.

---

eastern sea and half of them to the western sea; it shall continue in summer as in winter." See Michaels, *Gospel of John*, 465–66.

62   O'Day notes the translational difficulty presented by 7:38 ("John," 622–23). Because the punctuation is not clear, two primary options are possible. The NRSV interprets this text to indicate that the *believer* is the source of rivers of living water: "Out of the believer's heart shall flow rivers of living water" (7:38). It is more likely that the evangelist intends that *Jesus* is the source of the flow of water, however. Jesus has already been presented as the source of living water in 4:10–14. Water flows from his wound in 19:34 as well. Thus, in the narrative context, it is best to interpret Jesus as the source of living water in 7:37–38. Another matter of translation is noteworthy here, too: κοιλίας can be rendered as "womb" rather than "belly," "heart," or "stomach"; this brings richer meaning to the life-generative potential that flows out of Jesus.

63   The contrast between the Fourth Gospel and the Synoptics is striking. In the Synoptics, miraculous signs accompany Jesus's death: the sky darkens (Mark 15:33; Matt 27:45; Luke 23:44–45), the temple curtain is ripped in two (Mark 15:38; Matt 27:51; Luke 23:45), an earthquake occurs (Matt 27:51), and tombs open and the dead are raised (Matt 27:52–53). In the Fourth Gospel, the miraculous issue of blood and water accompanies Jesus's death, but it is localized in his body. No external signs occur.

64   O'Day, "John," 834.

65   The noun "bone" (ὀστοῦν) is singular in the Fourth Gospel, as it is in Exod 12:10 (LXX). It is plural in Ps 34:20. However, the verb συντριβήσεται is in passive voice in both John 19:36 and Ps 34:20. The verb is active (συντρίψετε) in Exod 12:10 (LXX). The evangelist may have combined these two references, presenting Jesus as both the paschal lamb and as the righteous sufferer whom God will deliver.

The Gospel has employed lamb imagery previously to describe Jesus; upon seeing Jesus, John the Baptist calls him the "Lamb of God" (1:29). Much later in the Gospel, just before Jesus is sent to be crucified by Pilate, the narrator reports that the time is "about noon" on the day of preparation for Passover (19:14). This is roughly the time when paschal lambs would have been slaughtered. The implication is that Jesus, who is also about to be slaughtered, is analogous to the paschal lambs. Like the unblemished paschal lambs, Jesus's bones remain intact. Likewise, just as the paschal lambs commemorate the Passover and God's liberation of the people of Israel from Egyptian domination, Jesus's death effects liberation. Moreover, for Johannine Christians living under the shadow of the Roman empire, the Passover evokes God's power to overcome imperial domination.

By evoking Ps 34:20, the evangelist draws on images of God's protection and deliverance. Beset by trials, the psalmist declares God's salvation: "Many are the afflictions of the righteous, but the LORD rescues them from them all. He keeps all their bones; not one of them will be broken" (Ps 34:19–20). The Johannine audience knows that God will save Jesus from Rome's cross and the power of death; Jesus will be resurrected (John 2:19–22).

The Roman soldiers unwittingly evoke Scripture when they refrain from breaking Jesus's legs and then pierce his side. By casting the events following Jesus's death in terms of Exod 12:10 and Ps 34:20, the evangelist subverts the notion that Jesus's death on the cross is his moment of defeat. Though the Jewish authorities and Roman soldiers have their own motives (namely, to maintain the sanctity of the Sabbath and to ensure Jesus's death), their actions bear witness to the divine plan as it unfolds and promote belief in Jesus. A major irony undergirds this narrative, as well: as Jesus's side is pierced and yields living water, Jesus's death is ultimately life-giving.

9 A Burial Fit for a King (19:38–42)

The removal of Jesus's body from the cross and his burial by two unlikely followers provide a fitting conclusion to the crucifixion account. Joseph of Arimathea approaches Pilate with a request for Jesus's body, and the governor permits him to take it. Nicodemus appears and together they place Jesus in a tomb after preparing his body for burial. This brief scene continues christological themes that have previously emerged in the Passion Narrative. Jesus is buried with dignity, in a manner befitting a king.

The very fact that Jesus is buried at all is noteworthy. A burial was by no means guaranteed for crucifixion victims. A quotation from Pseudo-Manetho indicates that bodies would often be left on crosses after death for animals to consume, "[as] evil food for birds of prey and grim pickings for dogs" (*Apotelesmatica* 4.198–200).[66] In similar fashion, Horace implies that victims' bodies would "feed crows on a cross " (*Epistles* 1.16.48; my trans.). The very purpose and design of crucifixion suggests that "there might be nothing left to bury at the end."[67] Roman soldiers would have incentive to leave bodies upon the crosses—it added to the humiliation for one's body to be left to rot or be picked apart by scavengers. Moreover, as a body hung on the cross for an indefinite time, it served as an ongoing reminder to onlookers that resistance to Roman rule would not be tolerated.

Concerning the historical Jesus, Crossan proposes that, in all likelihood, Jesus's body was probably either buried unceremoniously by Roman soldiers in an unmarked grave, or simply left on the cross for scavengers.[68] Brown argues that it would be unlikely for the body of a figure like Jesus to be handed over to be buried, for "Roman governors were anxious that the convicted criminal not be regarded as a hero to be imitated."[69] Whatever the historical outcome of Jesus's body, in the Fourth Gospel, the simple fact that Jesus is buried, in a marked grave—a new tomb, even—undermines the Roman meaning and purpose of the cross. Rome's agents do not wholly eliminate Jesus; instead, he is given an honorable, even regal burial in a tomb that his followers can access.

Both Joseph of Arimathea and Nicodemus are improbable undertakers who demonstrate courage and devotion by burying Jesus. Joseph is presented as a "secret" disciple who fears the Jewish authorities (19:38). Though not explicit in the Fourth Gospel, Joseph is likely a person of status and power, as he is in the Synoptic Gospels.[70] O'Day agrees, drawing a connection between Joseph and other Jewish authorities in the Fourth Gospel: "In identifying Joseph as a secret disciple of Jesus, the Fourth Evangelist links him with the Jewish authorities of [12:42–43] who, because of a fear of losing their political power and position

---

66   Quoted from Hengel, *Crucifixion*, 9.
67   John Dominic Crossan, *Jesus: A Revolutionary Biography* (San Francisco: HarperSan Francisco, 1994), 126.
68   Crossan, *The Historical Jesus*, 391–92. Crossan further proposes that wealth and power would be significant in gaining access to recover the body of a loved one following crucifixion. Thus, he suggests that the author of Mark may have invented a wealthy figure—Joseph of Arimathea—in order to explain how Jesus's followers could have recovered and buried his body (393–94).
69   Brown, *Death of the Messiah*, 2:1208.
70   Cf. Mark 15:43–46, which presents Joseph as a "respected member of the council"; Matt 27:57–60, which describes Joseph as a "rich man" who has "his own new tomb"; and Luke 23:50–53, which says he is a "member of the council."

within the synagogue, will not confess their faith in Jesus."[71] Moreover, the fact that he can gain an audience with Pilate also suggests a person of status and influence (19:38). In aligning himself with Jesus by requesting the body, Joseph risks personal status and honor.

As a "leader of the Jews" (3:1), Nicodemus also takes a risk in burying Jesus. The narrator recalls he had previously approached Jesus under the cover of darkness (19:39); here Nicodemus steps into the metaphorical daylight to demonstrate his devotion to Jesus. Though he previously supported Jesus in an ambiguous fashion to fellow Jewish authorities (7:50–52), here there is no uncertainty about Nicodemus's loyalty. Both Joseph and Nicodemus have cause to be cautious about their faith in Jesus, yet they both honor him openly by according him a dignified burial. The cross has not succeeded in terrorizing them; rather, Joseph and Nicodemus represent the first of many who will be "drawn" to Jesus as a result of him being lifted up and exalted on the cross (12:32).

The manner of the burial is remarkable, too; it is regal, stately, and excessively lavish for a simple peasant or itinerant teacher. Nicodemus brings "about a hundred pounds" of myrrh and aloes to prepare Jesus's body (19:39–40). While the purpose of spices would be to mask the stench of a decomposing body, the quantity of spices here is extraordinary.[72] Yet hyperbole is common in the Fourth Gospel, and always serves the theological and rhetorical purposes of the evangelist. It comes as little surprise following stories of abundant wine (2:1–11), a miraculous provision of bread to feed thousands (6:2–13), an expensive anointing (12:1–8), and an enormous catch of 153 fish (21:6, 11). Here, the extravagant burial suggests Jesus's identity as king. Such a burial would not be outside of the realm of possibility for royal figures. Josephus, for example, records the burial of Herod the Great in which five hundred servants carry spices (*J.W.* 1.673). In the Hebrew Scriptures, King Asa's body is placed in a tomb filled with spices following his death (2 Chron 16:14). Moreover, the location of the tomb in a garden is suggestive of a regal burial. Brown recalls that at least two Judean kings received burials in garden tombs (2 Kgs 21:18, 26), and that King David's tomb may also have been in a garden (Neh 3:16 LXX).[73]

---

71 O'Day, "John," 835.
72 The quantity of spices is so great that some scholars attempt to explain it as a mistake. For example, Marie-Joseph Lagrange imagines that, historically, the quantity must have been more modest, and a scribal error accounts for the incredulous amount reported in the Fourth Gospel (*Evangile selon Saint Jean* [7th ed.; Paris: J. Gabalda, 1948], 503). No textual variants exist in extant manuscripts, however.
73 Brown, *Death of the Messiah*, 2:1270.

F.F. Bruce even proposes—perhaps with a little too much confidence—that Joseph and Nicodemus themselves envision this as a regal burial for Jesus.[74]

Thus, the evangelist has presented the burial of Jesus in a manner consonant with his presentation elsewhere as king. Brown concludes that "John transformed the crucifixion into the triumph of Jesus; so also he has transformed the burial into a triumph. One who reigned as a king on the cross receives a burial worthy of his status."[75] Though Rome publicly humiliates and eliminates Jesus by executing him on a cross, Joseph and Nicodemus subvert Rome's purposes by honoring Jesus with a dignified burial. Rather than annihilating the threat that Jesus poses to Rome, the evangelist demonstrates that the cross is a means of drawing people to Jesus, the exalted king (12:32).

10 Conclusion

Early Christians struggled to make sense of Jesus's crucifixion in light of their theology and the meaning of the cross in the Roman imperial world. For example, Basilides, a gnostic Christian teacher, insisted that Simon of Cyrene was inadvertently nailed to the cross instead of Jesus. As reported by Irenaeus, Basilides taught that:

> [Jesus] did not himself suffer death, but Simon, a certain man of Cyrene, being compelled, bore the cross in his stead; so that this latter being transfigured by him, that he might be thought to be Jesus, was crucified, through ignorance and error, while Jesus himself received the form of Simon, and, standing by, laughed at them.
> *Adv. haer.* 1.24.4[76]

Confronted with the problem of Jesus's crucifixion, Basilides sidestepped the issue altogether by maintaining that Jesus was not, in fact, crucified.

Rather than sidestepping the issue, the Fourth Gospel ironizes the meaning of Jesus's death on the Roman cross by casting an alternative meaning for its significance. Crucifixion was a shameful, humiliating death that proclaimed

---

74 F.F. Bruce, *The Gospel of John: Introduction, Exposition and Notes* (Grand Rapids: Eerdmans, 1983), 379.
75 Brown, *Death of the Messiah*, 2:1268.
76 For other examples of how early Christians struggled to understand Jesus's crucifixion, see Brown, *Death of the Messiah*, 2:1093.

Roman domination while it eliminated threats to the imperial status quo. Yet in the Johannine vision the cross does not annihilate Jesus; instead, he is "lifted up" and exalted as king, and the cross becomes the means by which he draws all people to himself (cf. 12:32). The inscription on the cross serves not as a warning to other would-be dissidents, but rather as a worldwide proclamation of Jesus's sovereignty. The cross does not ultimately point to Rome's dominance, but to Jesus and God's. Finally, with Jesus's death, he completes the work that the Father has given to him to do. Having done so, he lays down his life willingly; throughout, Jesus is the sole master of his life and death. Rather than being an obstacle to the elevated Christology of the Johannine vision, Jesus's death on a Roman cross bolsters it.

The burial account supports these claims. Jesus is buried in a manner befitting a king by two reluctant followers who are drawn to him by his death. Joseph of Arimathea and Nicodemus provide a lavish burial for the one whom Rome has dishonored with crucifixion. And of course, neither crucifixion nor burial have the last word. Roman imperial power, in the end, is limited and cannot annihilate Jesus; he will soon be resurrected, proving that Rome holds no power over him at all.

The two opposed meanings of the cross—the imperial one and the ironic Johannine one—coexist within the Gospel narrative. Unaware readers as well as characters within the narrative still perceive Jesus's death as an experience of shame, humiliation, and defeat; he really does die. Yet attentive readers will grasp the ironic meaning and see the cross as his moment of enthronement, glorification, and return to the Father.

Finally, it is worth briefly noting the ways in which the Fourth Gospel mimics aspects of Roman imperial power even as it ironizes the meaning of the crucifixion. John presents Jesus's sovereignty in contrast to the emperor's, and God's power as an alternative to Rome's. Jesus is presented as "King" and "Savior of the World."[77] The Gospel envisions a kingdom/empire of God that extends across the entire world. Thus, the Gospel does not merely contest imperial power but adopts the language of empire in order to transform the meaning of its cross.

---

77 The title "Savior of the World" imitates titles used for Roman emperors. For an extended discussion of the way in which Jesus's title "Savior of the world" intersects with Roman imperial claims, see Craig R. Koester, "Savior of the World (John 4:42)," *JBL* 109 (1990): 665–80.

PART 3

Christology and the Literary Character of the Johannine Writings

∴

CHAPTER 8

The Narrative Structure and Flow of the Prologue to John's Gospel

Derek Morton Hamilton Tovey

The prologue to the Gospel (John 1:1–18) has been described as functioning rather like the overture to an opera, or as the threshold to a building.[1] But is it an integral part of the Gospel as a whole, or has it been added later? The question arises from a number of related textual and interpretive issues which have puzzled generations of scholars. One is the question whether we have here a piece of writing that is poetic in form, with additions in prose. Related to this is the issue whether there lies behind the prologue a hymn, which has been taken up by the evangelist to begin his Gospel. Is the prologue structurally a unity; and how well does it lead into the rest of the Gospel? Another question concerns the use of the metaphor of the *Logos*, and the question why it appears here in the prologue as such a strong image, and then does not appear in the remainder of the Gospel in this fashion.[2]

The structure of the prologue has long been a matter for scholarly analysis and debate. The proposals are many and varied. The French scholar, Léonard Ramaroson, maintains that, among those who find a structure in the prologue, there are two main proposals: those scholars who see the prologue as structured in the form of a parabola, or a chiasm,[3] and those who see the prologue proceeding in a rectilinear (or one might say, sequential) fashion.[4] In

---

1 See Peter Phillips, *The Prologue of the Fourth Gospel: A Sequential Reading*, LNTS 294 (London: T&T Clark, 2006), 2.
2 Christopher W. Skinner, "Misunderstanding, Christology, and Johannine Characterization: Reading John's Characters through the Lens of the Prologue," in *Characters and Characteriztion in the Gospel of John*, ed. Christopher W. Skinner, LNTS 461 (London: Bloomsbury T&T Clark, 2013), 116.
3 There are a number of ways in which these structures may be designated: "concentric" is one other.
4 L. Ramaroson, "La Structure du Prologue de Jean," *Science et Esprit* 28/3 (1976): 281–96, especially 281–83; see also Marc Girard, "Analyse Structurelle de Jn 1, 1–18: L'Unité des Deux Testaments dans la Structure Bipolaire du Prologue de Jean," *Science et Esprit* 35/1 (1983): 5–31, who surveys a number of the parabolic or chiastic proposals. See further R. Alan Culpepper, "The Pivot of John's Prologue," *NTS* 27/1 (1980): 1–31, who provides criteria for determining chiastic

my analysis, I adopt a rectilinear approach, insofar as the prologue is a piece of narrative (certainly the introduction to a narrative) which is to be received in a sequential manner. Writing an exegetical piece on the prologue, Gail R. O'Day has declared that the prologue is shaped by "the same narrative pattern and technique of retelling a biblical story" but that it is rarely interpreted as a narrative.[5]

Indeed, given that many who first encountered the Gospel would have heard it rather than read it, the way in which it falls on the ear is an important consideration. It is unlikely that many would have had the time to engage in the detailed source-critical analysis or to have taken up the wide background cultural and intertextual associations which are possible when scholars engage in consideration of the prologue's structure.[6] The first hearers would have been pulled along by the forward thrust of the prologue's narrative structure, as I hope to demonstrate.[7]

I argue in this chapter that the evangelist (or implied author) uses a number of techniques that not only point to its character as the beginning of a narrative, but also that the prologue is an integrated piece of writing structured to bring about the gradual revelation of the human identity of one whose identity is initially veiled under the cumulative force of a number of metaphors, the function of which is to provide an understanding of this human character as more than human. Implicature ties these metaphors with the main character, Jesus Christ, and the effect of the narrative flow is to provide a view of Jesus

---

structures. Ramaroson provides a brief description of a number of the "rectilinear" proposals, most of which divide the prologue into several sections.

5 Gail R. O'Day, "John 1:1–9 [Exegetical Perspective]," in *Feasting on the Gospels: John, Volume 1: Chapters 1–9*, ed. Cynthia A. Jarvis and E. Elizabeth Johnson (Louisville: Westminster John Knox, 2015), 3, 5 (the quotation appears on page five). O'Day sees the prologue's genre as a midrash upon Gen 1:1–5 (and "not a hymn").

6 Of course, if the hypothesis that the prologue incorporates an early Christian hymn is correct, then many hearers may already have come to their hearing of the prologue with certain understandings and expectations in place on account of their familiarity with the hymn.

7 Tom Thatcher, "The Riddle of the Baptist and the Genesis of the Prologue: John 1:1–18 in Oral/Aural Media Culture," in *The Fourth Gospel in First-Century Media Culture*, ed. Anthony Le Donne and Tom Thatcher (London: T&T Clark, 2011), 29–48, discusses the dynamics whereby hearers would have heard the prologue as an integrated piece. Some of his insights complement the argument outlined here. That notwithstanding, it remains the case that the Fourth Gospel, whatever connections it may have with oral discourse, was first received as a *written* document. It is, in my opinion, impossible to determine what differences might exist between a fully oral performance (a storyteller telling a story for instance) and the oral presentation of a written document (that is, an oral reading over against an oral telling).

both "from above" and "from below."[8] The prologue, then, introduces the reader to the character whose story is told in the remainder of the Gospel.

1 The *Logos* as a Nonsequential Sequence-Signal

The prologue begins with the strong and striking metaphor of the *Logos*, a being or an entity that is put in close association with God. The *Logos* is "with God," and *is* ("the same as") God. But it is not clear how this *Logos* should be understood. Is this *Logos* (Word) a divine being, a hypostasization—a personified quality or attribute, much as Lady Wisdom is in Proverbs—or a human character?[9] In a sense, this designation *the Logos* (*the* Word) acts as a type of "character-substitute" and as a nonsequential sequence-signal.

J.M. Backus, in an article written in 1965, defines a sequence-signal as a word "appearing in a sentence (the sequence-sentence) following another sentence that depends upon that preceding sentence for its full meaning, because the preceding sentence contains the referent for that word, or sequence-signal."[10] Take the sentences: "The man walked into the room. He was still wearing his top hat." The personal pronoun "he" in the second sentence is the sequence-signal depending upon the noun "man," in the previous sentence, for its referent. Where a story begins thus: "He walked into the room still wearing his top hat," we have an instance of a nonsequential sequence-signal, because the personal pronoun "he" lacks an immediate referent.

Backus shows that many stories begin with such nonsequential sequence-signals, often a referentless pronoun (as in the example just given). Backus

---

[8] Implicature is a term from speech-act theory which denotes the types of assumptions and calculations that hearers (and readers) engage in to make sense of what they hear (or read). Connections may be made in a discourse which are implied rather than explicitly stated.

[9] Cf. Martinus C. De Boer, "The Original Prologue to the Gospel of John," *NTS* 61 (2015): 448–49; "the Word (ὁ λόγος) ... appears to involve a personification." De Boer (in a footnote) says that "[t]his claim is an exegetical conclusion derived from considering the use of the term in its narrower and broader context. In v. 17, ὁ λόγος is explicitly identified as the person of 'Jesus Christ' and that identification already seems to be presupposed in v. 1." I would argue that, on a first reading at least, the option that the *Logos* is a human character would not present itself in v. 1.

[10] See here Derek Tovey, "Narrative Strategies in the Prologue and the Metaphor of ὁ λόγος in John's Gospel," *Pacifica* 15/2 (2002): 140–41. Also, J.M. Backus, "'He came into her line of vision walking backward': Nonsequential Sequence-signals in Short Story Openings," *Language Learning* 15 (1965): 67–83, see on this especially 67–68.

calls these referentless pronouns, "character-substitutes." Another type of "character-substitute" (closely related to the referentless pronoun) is what Backus calls the "noun-phrase." A noun-phrase is a noun that points to a specific referent by the use of the definite article, or a demonstrative pronoun, such as "this," but is a character-substitute when the specific identity of the referent is not disclosed (at least not immediately). Hence, a story that begins with the sentence: "The man walked into the room still wearing his top hat," would convey to the reader the understanding that a specific man is being referred to, but that the identity of the man is not yet revealed. The effect of the definite article would be to entice the reader to ask "What (or, 'who is this') man?" and to have his or her curiosity piqued. The reader would read on to discover the identity of the man.

The prologue, I suggest, begins in such a fashion. "The Word" or ὁ λόγος is a character-substitute in that the reader casts around for a character with whom this metaphor can be associated. It is nonsequential because nothing precedes its introduction to explain the metaphor. In other words, the reader asks "Who or What is this Word?" Nevertheless, despite being uncertain as to the exact identity of this Word, the reader is apprised of the fact that this being is the same as God, yet distinct from God. It is possible that the reader will now think that the Word is some sort of divine being.[11]

2 Deictics as Sequence-Signals

Verse two begins with a very important demonstrative pronoun: οὗτος ("this one").[12] It acts as a sequence-signal that points back to its referent in verse one: namely, the *Logos*/Word. I call this the "Johannine index finger" pointing to the *Logos* and reiterating that *this one*, this entity, was in the beginning with God. Steven Runge discusses the discourse function of the deictic demonstrative pronouns (οὗτος/ἐκεῖνος; or, "this one"/"that one") that we find in the

---

[11] There is debate amongst scholars as to the force of the use of the word θεός here: some suggest that the phrase means that "the Word was divine," though as Raymond Brown points out, there was an adjective available to make this point: θεῖος; see Raymond E. Brown, *The Gospel According to John I–XII*, AB 29 (New York: Doubleday, 1966), 5. The difficulty lies in envisaging how a Jew would receive such a statement. The rhetorical force would be such to make the reader read on to discover more about this being.

[12] English translations (see e.g. NRSV, ESV, NIV, JB, TEV) generally render these demonstrative pronouns with the third person pronoun, "he" (or provide a paraphrase translation). I translate the demonstrative "this one" to reproduce the deictic function of the demonstrative pronoun.

prologue, in terms of a "near/far" dynamic, whereby the near demonstrative pronoun (οὗτος; "this one") functions to mark the thematic role of the referent (we might say that it serves to throw the focus or "spotlight" on this referent). The far demonstrative pronoun (ἐκεῖνος; "that one") serves to render a referent "athematic" (that is to switch the focus from the most recently mentioned referent to another prior referent).[13] Earlier he writes of the "forward-pointing" function these deictic pronouns may play.[14] While it is, perhaps, a bit of a stretch to claim that the demonstrative pronouns used here in the prologue have a forward-pointing function (they rather serve the conventional function of referring back to an antecedent referent), insofar as the antecedent referent "the Word" is a character-substitute awaiting the full revelation of the one to whom the metaphor applies, the demonstrative pronoun has somewhat of a "forward-pointing" element to it.

The prologue continues to develop the functions and roles of this Word. He (or It) is the one through whom everything came into being, and what specifically came into being in him was life, a life that was (or is) the light of all people, a light which shines in the darkness and is not overcome. As is the case with the Word, there is nothing to suggest that this light is anything other than a designation for some entity or quality. Perhaps as it is associated with life, and is the light for all people, it should be understood as a metaphor for salvation.

However, the prologue then proceeds to state that there was a man sent from God, whose name was John. So here we have a human character, with a name. We are then told the role and function of this human character. Note that the Johannine index finger comes into play again: *This one* came as a witness to testify to the light. The use of this sequence-signal, this demonstrative pronoun, serves to place John in juxtaposition with the Word through the parallel use of the demonstrative pronoun. *This one* (the Word) was with God in the beginning (v. 2). *This one* (John) came as a witness (v. 7a). Note that it is not clear that what John testifies to is anything other than an inanimate quality or function, namely, light which may be salvation. But then comes a surprising turn: another demonstrative pronoun comes into play, and because the narrator wishes the index finger to point back beyond the last noun referent

---

13 Steven E. Runge, *Discourse Grammar of the Greek New Testament: A Practical Introduction for Teaching and Exegesis*, Lexham Bible Reference Series (Peabody: Hendrickson, 2010), 365–75; on John 1: 7–8, see especially 374–75.
14 Runge, *Discourse Grammar*, 61–63.

(the light) to John, the "this one" who came to testify to the light, he uses the demonstrative pronoun: "That one" (ἐκεῖνος).[15]

So the narrator, if you will, points back across the light to John, whom he says is not the light. This is where the operations of implicature come into play (what is implied rather than stated explicitly). For if John, a human person, is not the light, then by implication another human person is the light. Who can that be? We are not told immediately; rather we are told what the progress and the effects of this one who is described as the light will be. He is one who is coming into the world. This again suggests that this must be another human person. He comes to his own who do not receive him, but those who do receive him will be given power to become children of God.

3   The Function of the Metaphors Word/*Logos* and Light

If we still have doubts about whether or not the Word/*Logos* is a human person, these are dispelled by what is said in v. 14. "And the Word became flesh and lived among us." The Word, like John, is a human being. What we should also note is that now two metaphors have been used to describe this human person: The Word and the Light. Each serves to make a different point about this human person. The first that he is to be associated with God. That through him everything came into being: so he shares creative power with God. The second, that through him (as Light) salvation, understood as enlightenment and power to become children of God, comes to all who believe in his name. But we still do not have a name for this person who has been introduced under the guise of the metaphors Word and Light.[16]

John appears again. In my book *Jesus, Story of God: John's Story of Jesus*, I use the image of a spotlight illuminating characters on a stage. First the spotlight lights up a figure who is called the Word (this figure is completely shrouded—we do not know if this is a human or not). Then the spotlight shifts onto John: and we learn that he is not the Light, but a witness to the Light. Then the spotlight shifts back to the figure of the Word (now also given the designation, "the Light") and we begin to understand that this figure is also a human person. And with the repetition of the metaphor of the Word in v. 14, the shroud

---

15   Following Runge, we would say that John is thereby rendered "athematic." It is the light that is "thematic"; "that one" (ἐκεῖνος) places a thematic distance between John and "the light," while ironically drawing John briefly back into focus.

16   I shall henceforth capitalize both "Word" or *Logos*, and "Light," to indicate that they refer to a human character; and one of special significance.

drops completely, and we see that the Word/Light is indeed a human being (but he is still masked, as it were). The spotlight again illuminates John, who declares: "*This one*/οὗτος (again the Johannine index finger comes into play), this was he of whom I said, 'The one who comes after me ranks ahead of me because he was before me'" (v. 15). This is a proleptic statement, as John has not yet testified to Jesus—that testimony comes in the remainder of the chapter. Indeed, these words are repeated almost verbatim in 1:30 except that, since the prologue has fully revealed the humanity of the *Logos*, this restatement of the "one coming after" John explicitly states that he is "a man" (ἀνήρ). It is not quite like what John the Baptist says in the Synoptic Gospels: there he speaks of one "more powerful than me" coming (see Mark 1: 7//Matt 3:11//Luke 3:16). Here, the implied author evidently wants to make a point about Jesus's priority to John in terms of being, status, and rank—and perhaps even chronology.

It is worth pausing here to note the rhetorical and structural strategy of the evangelist. The use of the deictic demonstrative pronouns: "this one" and "that one" serves to set up a contrast between John and Jesus, or places them in juxtaposition to one another. But these deictics also have implicative functions: for the Word (the one first designated as "this one" in v. 2) is equated with God, but it is not clear whether he is also human. When John is designated as a witness, in the second use of the deictic "this one," we immediately also learn that he is not the Light: he simply witnesses to the Light. Thus the implication behind the fact that he is not the Light is that another human person is the Light. So this serves to set up the expectation of a human character who will be revealed, and who at the moment is being introduced under the guise of two metaphors: Word and Light.

4 The Metaphors of Light and Word/*Logos* Beyond the Prologue

The metaphor of the Light is one that is picked up in the rest of the Gospel. Jesus specifically associates himself with the Light, as in John 8:12, when Jesus says, "I am the light of the world. Whoever follows me will never walk in darkness, but will have the light of life."[17] Again, at the beginning of chapter 9, Jesus and his disciples encounter a blind man. The disciples ask whose sin, the blind man's or his parents', has caused the man's blindness. Jesus says that neither is the case, but that this man's blindness will provide an occasion for the works of God to be revealed. He goes on to say: "As long as I am in the world, I am the light of the world" (John 9:5). Clearly, this metaphor is associated with

---

17 Quotations of the biblical text are from the NRSV, unless otherwise stated.

Jesus's life-bringing, life-enhancing, salvific activities. It relates also to the challenge to accept the revelation of God that Jesus brings. In John 12:35, 36 Jesus challenges the Jews to respond positively to him when he says: "The light is with you for a little longer. Walk while you have the light, so that the darkness may not overtake you. If you walk in the darkness, you do not know where you are going. While you have the light, believe in the light, so that you may become children of light."

Many scholars contend that the metaphor of the Word (*Logos*), however, does not appear in quite the same way as in the prologue.[18] It is never used of Jesus again, to describe who he is. In fact, some might argue that it perhaps should not be seen as a metaphor. It is rather a reference to a being, or entity, in its own right. One that shares the nature of God, and then is revealed as having become a human being. It is perhaps more correct, then, to say that the eternal Word becomes Jesus, the human person. It is not merely a descriptor of Jesus.

I suggest, however, that the referent in view *is* the human character, Jesus. That is, the prologue is building to the revelation of the identity of the Word, or *Logos*, as Jesus. Again this is done cleverly, by the use of implicature (implication), as a description of qualities of the Word ("grace and truth") are taken up again in 1:17 where it is said that "grace and truth came through Jesus Christ." Notice how the name is dropped into the narrative casually, and almost incidentally. But the effect is, as it were, to remove the mask from the face of the figure of the Word. We now know not only that this is a human person, but that he has a specific name, Jesus Christ, and therefore a specific identity.

The metaphor of the Word, with which Jesus is introduced into the story, is so strong that it dominates scholarly thinking and discussion of the prologue. It seems strange, then, that it does not appear again in the Gospel. Such is the consensus amongst scholars. However, I would argue that having planted this strong metaphor in the mind of the reader, the implied author (or, the evangelist) at a number of points in the Gospel intends this sense to resonate in the reader's mind. I provide only three examples.[19]

In John 6 Jesus has been speaking about himself as the bread of life, and saying how people must eat his flesh and drink his blood in order to find true

---

[18] See here, C.H. Dodd, *The Interpretation of the Fourth Gospel* (Cambridge: Cambridge University Press, 1953), 267; Elizabeth Harris, *Prologue and Gospel: The Theology of the Fourth Evangelist*, JSNTSup 107 (Sheffield: Sheffield Academic, 1994), 196; Harris states that "the figure of the Logos ... affects the presentation of Jesus in [the] Gospel." See also Phillips, *The Prologue*, 73; Phillips himself contends that the *Logos* becomes redundant after the introduction of the "historic individual" Jesus, because it has done its job in leading up to the revelation of Jesus as the fulfiller of "the concept" (see pp. 140–41).

[19] For a fuller discussion, and an examination of more instances, see Tovey, "Narrative Strategies."

life. Many of his disciples take offense at this; and they say: "This teaching is difficult; who can accept it?" (John 6:60, NRSV), or "This is a hard saying; who can listen to it?" (RSV). The Greek might be more literally rendered: "Difficult is the word, this one. Who can listen to it?" Here we have the same phrase as is found in the prologue: the Greek is ὁ λόγος οὗτος (the Johannine index finger is in play again); and because the pronoun (αὐτοῦ) translated "it" in the phrase "Who can listen to it" may be either masculine or neuter, we could understand the whole statement as saying: "This Word is difficult: who can listen to him?"

In John 8, Jesus gets into a very tense and difficult argument with some Jews who believe in him, over who he is and what it means to truly be his disciple. Jesus accuses them of trying to kill him. He says, "… you look for an opportunity to kill me, because there is no place in you for my word" (John 8:37). The noun-phrase, ὁ λόγος, occurs here: "my word" might almost be understood as a self-reference and the exchange underlines the claim in the prologue that the Word came to his own people, and found no place amongst them (1:11). The use of the nominative form here, while not a reference to "the Word" of the prologue, is evocative of it, and I would argue that the strong metaphor of the prologue echoes in the mind of the reader at this point.

As a final example, we may note John 17:17, where Jesus prays for his disciples that they may be sanctified in the truth. Then he says, "Your word is truth." The phrase in the Greek includes the noun phrase, and reads: ὁ λόγος ὁ σὸς ἀλήθειά ἐστιν. Given that Jesus has earlier said that he is "the truth" (14:6) and has described the One who sent him as true (ἀληθής), and with whom Jesus's discourses to this point have forged a strong association (that is, between "the Father" and himself, as "the Son"), the use of the noun-phrase here might well evoke the Word/*Logos* of the prologue. Indeed, we may recall that the *Logos* was described as full of grace and truth; and that the association between the *Logos* and Jesus Christ was strengthened by making the statement that grace and truth came through Jesus Christ in 1:17.[20]

5 The Implied Author's Rhetorical Strategy in Using Metaphors and Deictic Pronouns

The thrust of this chapter, then, is to argue that the narrative flow of the prologue, which builds towards vv. 17 and 18 and the final revelation of Jesus Christ as the character to whom the preceding metaphors of Word/*Logos* and Light apply, is structured by the rhetorical devices of using deictic demonstrative

---

[20] See here Tovey, "Narrative Strategies," 151–52; and for further examples, and discussion of the instances given here, see 145–52.

pronouns both to tie the Word/*Logos* to the metaphor of the Light, and to place John in juxtaposition with this being, the Word/*Logos*/Light. This has the effect, also, of implying that the Word/*Logos*/Light is another human being, who follows John chronologically, but ranks ahead of him in status. This rhetorical strategy has the purpose of introducing Jesus (whose name is finally revealed in v. 17) gradually, under cover of these metaphors. The operations of implicature, whereby connections between the Word/*Logos*/Light and Jesus are made implicitly, throw an air of mystery over Jesus (as well as clearly indicating that his origins are more than merely human). There are other implicit connections made: as, for instance, when the phrase "grace and truth" is associated both with the Word/*Logos* and with Jesus. These are, in fact, but some of the exegetical considerations that can be brought into play to demonstrate the sequential, cumulative rhetorical operations in this prologue.[21]

Having, in 1:17, revealed the name of Jesus Christ, the narrator makes one further claim about him. In 1:18, he states that this Jesus, who may also be known as the only Son,[22] has revealed God. In a sense, this returns us to the beginning of the prologue, for it is because Jesus was with God as the Word/*Logos*, that he can make God known. But a new aspect of this connection is revealed, in that it is the close relationship between God, now identified as "the Father," and Jesus that enables him to make God known. As Jesus resides close to the Father's heart (NRSV: Greek, κόλπος, "chest," or "breast") he is able to "exegete" God. This will be done, by sign and through discourse, in word and in action, in the story to follow.

6 Three Implications of the Implied Author's Rhetorical Strategy

What are some of the implications for a reading of the prologue in view of this rhetorical strategy? There are three which I wish to briefly outline here. First of all, the prologue is a unity. I am inclined to agree with C.K. Barrett, who stated long ago that "[t]he Prologue is not a jig-saw puzzle but one piece of solid theological writing. The evangelist wrote it all ..."[23] Even if he drew on prior sources, such as a Logos hymn, he has so thoroughly integrated these into his writing, that it is difficult now to detect the seams and splices.

---

21 For further instances, refer to Phillips, *The Prologue*, chapter six.
22 The manuscript evidence is quite mixed here: some read "[the] only God."
23 C.K. Barrett, "The Prologue of St John's Gospel," in his *New Testament Essays* (London: SPCK, 1972), 48.

One of the latest attempts to isolate a poem in the prologue, that of Martinus de Boer, appears to lend support to the argument I make here, I would suggest, although in an implicit way.[24] De Boer wishes to argue that John 1:1–5 (and only these verses) constitute the original prologue because the narrative appears to begin at v. 6 with the introduction of John (de Boer draws a parallel between the Septuagintal form of 1 Sam 1:1 and John 1:6). Hence, it is the (largely) narrative nature of vv. 6–18 that forms a plank in de Boer's argument.

Further, vv. 1–5 display the most marked poetic form of all the first eighteen verses. That this is so seems to come down mostly to the (admittedly strongly marked) staircase parallelism in these verses.[25] Nevertheless, there are sufficient qualifications in the argument to suggest that it is *possible* but not certain that the first five verses constitute an original poetic prelude to a narrative. To give but one example, de Boer concedes that the "boundaries between poetry and prose … are fluid in the prologue."[26] De Boer is quoting Ridderbos here, but earlier he has stated that "[a]t first sight the Prologue seems to be a stylistic unity but upon closer examination the Prologue appears to be a peculiar, even confusing, combination of poetic and prosaic elements."[27] The whole of the prologue, then, might well be taken as a narrative introduction to the Gospel, even if we were to concede de Boer's point that this narrative begins in a poetic fashion (or with a piece of poetry at its head).[28]

Second, the view of Jesus is one that is both "from above" and "from below." It is "from above" because the prologue begins by speaking of the divine nature of the Word/*Logos*, who is pre-existent with God from the beginning. But it is

---

24   De Boer, "Original Prologue." He discusses the view that the prologue contains a hymn (see 455–60), but it is not clear (to me, at least) whether he would so designate vv. 1–5, or whether he simply sees them as having a poetic quality.

25   De Boer, "Original Prologue," 449–50, 59–60. De Boer only briefly discusses the exegetical issue of whether v. 2 originally forms part of the poem; and here what he says is ambiguous. In the main text he describes it as "an appendage" (463), in a footnote he states that its function "becomes clear" as that of closing off the first strophe (De Boer, "Original Prologue," 463 n84).

26   De Boer, "Original Prologue," 459.

27   De Boer, "Original Prologue," 454. I do not consider de Boer's argument that the "romantic, nineteenth-century view" of the prologue as "the product of a solitary genius" is untenable as a sufficient argument against Barrett's view of the prologue as "a prose introduction," see p. 458. Nevertheless, I wholly concur that the prologue may appear as an admixture of poetry and prose.

28   There is a strong consensus that vv. 1–5 belong to a *Logos* hymn (with some doubt about v. 2 in particular); thereafter opinion varies more widely. On this see E.L. Miller, *Salvation-History in the Prologue of John: The Significance of John 1:3–4*, NovTSup 110 (Leiden: Brill, 1989), 6; and Gérard Rochais, "La Formation du Prologue" (Jn 1, 1–18)," *Science et Esprit* 37/1 (1985): 7–9; also Brown, *The Gospel According to John I–XII*, 22.

also "from below" because the divine being and nature of the central character is captured in the human story of Jesus Christ. The prologue introduces the reader to this human character progressively and gradually under cover of a series of metaphors. But I would argue that the fact that this human character is clearly linked with the Word/*Logos*, and the Light, through the operations of implicature examined above, means that the whole prologue is subsequently read (or heard) through the "lens" of the incarnation. To put it another way, the use of deictics, the juxtaposition of John with the Word/*Logos*/Light, pulls the reader's understanding of the identity of the Word/*Logos*/Light forward to the point at which the prologue reveals this figure as human, and bearing the name Jesus Christ.

That this is the case may be illustrated by the debate amongst scholars about the point in the prologue at which the incarnation may be said to have first appeared. Some claim that this first occurs in v. 9; others would push the reference back as early as v. 4.[29] It is arguably the case that this is because the revelation of the Word/*Logos* as σάρξ (or a human being) throws its light backward, as it were, upon the previous discussion of the Word/*Logos*. Were v. 14 to be removed from the prologue, would an incarnational reading of vv. 4 or 9 resonate so strongly in scholars' minds? Nevertheless, it is possible to argue, I contend, that the incarnation may be seen *implicitly* within these verses (most certainly v. 9, and possibly in v. 4).[30]

---

[29] A cogent argument for reading John 1:4 as the first reference to the incarnation is provided by Miller, *Salvation-History*, 76–89. He writes that 1:4 "is to be translated something like, 'That which appeared in him was life, and the life was the light of men,' and that it expresses the Johannine belief that salvific life and light has appeared to men in the historical advent of the incarnate Logos. In John 1:4 we have, therefore, the first reference in the Prologue, and thus in the Gospel of John, to the Incarnation" (77). Nevertheless, I would argue, this consideration would not even arise, necessarily, without the explicit mention that the Word became flesh in v. 14, and Miller's reference to the fact that "salvific life and light has appeared to men in the historical advent of the incarnate Logos" in fact shows that the whole human story of Jesus must be implicitly in mind. One might also argue that an incarnational understanding of v. 9 must similarly rest on knowledge of what follows. It is the rising expectation of a human referent for the Word/*Logos*/Light prompted by implicit understandings set up by the juxtapositions of John with the figure of the Word/*Logos*/Light through the use of deictics that leads to these interpretations.

[30] It should be noted that v. 5 is also proposed as the first mention of the incarnation, see for instance, Ruth B. Edwards, *Discovering John: Content, Interpretation, Reception*, 2nd ed. (London: SPCK, 2014), 101. Interestingly, after discussing a number of options for the point at which the incarnation is first mentioned in the prologue, she writes: "Perhaps John deliberately left Jesus's entry on the scene ambiguous, using 1.5, 9, 11 as pointers to it before proclaiming it unequivocally in 1.14" (102).

Third, and finally, the prologue is an integral part of the Gospel. It truly serves as an overture, or a threshold to the building. In the prologue are foreshadowed many of the themes to be developed in the body of the Gospel. Its integration with the Gospel is also seen in the way that the metaphors of light and life are taken up in the body of the Gospel to further explicate the meaning and identity of Jesus. I have argued that the metaphor of the Word/*Logos*, which strikes the reader of the prologue so strongly, would also resonate, at least implicitly, at other times in the Gospel, especially when the noun phrase, ὁ λόγος, appears, and most particularly where the general context also echoes claims or statements about Jesus's nature and identity. Furthermore, the figure of John and his testimony is also evoked in the prologue. This testimony is to form the first part of the narrative as it gets under way, and, indeed, John 1:15 provides a proleptic disclosure of his testimony as found in v. 30. What is interesting is that in both of these verses, the testimony is said to have taken place at some time prior, a function perhaps of the generally retrospective character of the evangelist's own witness.[31]

7   The Implied Author's Rhetorical Strategy and Jesus's Relationship with God

There is a final, theological point to make about the prologue as a narrative introduction to the Gospel. It is an introduction to a narrative about a human character, Jesus of Nazareth. This human character makes bold and surprising claims about his relationship with God. The reader is prepared for these by the prologue. So, for example, when Jesus says to his Jewish interlocutors: "Very truly, I tell you, before Abraham was, I am" (8:58), or "The Father and I are one" (10:30), the reader finds this congruent with the presentation of the Logos in the prologue. Jesus Christ, the prologue tells the reader for its part, is the one

---

31   In v. 15 "testified" (μαρτυρεῖ) is an historic present—somewhat typical of this evangelist's style. The prior testimony to Jesus's precedence to John might be found in his words in v. 27 (cf. Matt 3:11/Mark 1:7/Luke 3:16). John's words in v. 26, "Among you stands one whom you do not know," are intriguing: their surface, or plain meaning, is that Jesus is already on the scene although not yet known or recognized. It hints at his hidden presence, yet I cannot help but wonder whether there is not an ironic ring to John's words (in v. 30): "He who comes after me ranks ahead of me *because he was before me.*" In other words, Jesus is prior to John chronologically as well as being above, or ahead of, him in rank. In the Greek, this would be conveyed by the phrase, ὃς ἔμπροσθέν μου γέγονεν. This is true not only in terms of actual chronology (Jesus as the Word/*Logos* existed with God in the beginning) but also in terms of narrative progression: as the Word/*Logos*, Jesus has entered the story before John.

who makes God (the Father) known (1:18). Later in the Gospel story we have the poignant scene where, on the eve of Jesus's departure, Jesus's disciple Philip makes this request: "Lord, show us the Father, and we shall be satisfied" (14:8). To this request, Jesus replies: "Have I been with you all this time, Philip, and you still do not know me? Whoever has seen me has seen the Father" (14:9a).

The prologue builds to the revelation of the name of this human person for, as the prologue has it, the *Logos* became a human person. It is the human person that defines the *Logos*, and not the other way around. It is as if the question with its answer is not: "Who is Jesus?" "He is the *Logos*." Rather the question is: "Who is the *Logos*?" with its answer, "The *Logos* is Jesus." This Jesus of Nazareth is one who may be also be understood as *Logos*, and Light, and "only begotten" (Son), and the same as God. The narrative structure and flow of the prologue is designed to introduce the human character about whom these other things may also be said. To miss the dynamic of this narrative beginning is to risk missing the intent of the implied author's story.[32]

---

[32] Something of what I say here (both the theological import and the function of the prologue) is conveyed by Oscar Cullmann, "The Theological Content of the Prologue to John in Its Present Form," in *The Conversation Continues: Studies in Paul and John in Honor of J. Louis Martyn*, ed. Robert T. Fortna and Beverly R. Gaventa (Nashville: Abingdon, 1990), 295–98. I find it significant that Cullmann maintains that "the main theological point of the prologue ... is expressed in the *alternating juxtaposition*" (Cullmann's emphasis) of what is asserted about John and Jesus (or the *Logos*; 296). Cullmann concludes by stating that "[a]s an integrating element of the theological framework of the Gospel of John," the prologue is "indispensable" (298).

CHAPTER 9

John's Portrayal of Jesus as the Divine-Adamic Priest and What It Means for the Temple Cleansing in John 2:13–25

Chris S. Stevens

The artistic and literary dimensions of the Gospel of John have always provoked the fascination of the Christian church and biblical scholars. The unique features of the Gospel have provided endless opportunities to explore christological details. Significant themes run through the Gospel that are either absent or minimally present in the Synoptics. From the famous "I am" sayings, to the motif of Light, or the Logos in the prologue, John contains many aspects that intrigue readers. In this paper, I draw attention to the innovative and theological creativity of John 1–2; specifically, the ways John depicts Christ as the Divine-Adamic priest.

In his first two chapters, John portrays Christ as architect and executor of recreation in divine terms and imagery. John then portrays Jesus as the new Adam. Taking the two together, we see that John presents readers of his Gospel with a literary masterpiece of heightened Christology. The paper will demonstrate that John uses Gen 1–3 as his literary and theological source text. The design of John 1–2 is so extensively interwoven with themes from the original creation account one might call it Genesis Part II: The Continuing Drama. Furthermore, reading John 1–2 with the support of Gen 1–3 offers clarity concerning the temple episode of John 2:13–25. The paper contends that Jesus, as the Divine-Adamic priest, is pictured as carrying out his duty to purify and cleanse the temple of matters unbefitting the sanctity of the place of worship and communion with God.

1   Method

The initial requirement in pursing the thesis is to establish formal parallels between Gen 1–3 and John 1–2. A common method is to look for typological connections. However, there is little in the way of formal criteria for typology.[1]

---

1   A seminal work on typology is Leonhard Goppelt, *Typos: The Typological Interpretation of the Old Testament in the New* (Grand Rapids: Eerdmans, 1982). More recent use is described by

Hugenberger notes that typological methods need greater rigor to achieve a controlled and sober application.[2] In order to establish formal literary and conceptual connections I propose the use of two criteria from the field of modern linguistics. The first is examining linguistic frames or scenarios, and the second is examining transitivity structure.

The examination of linguistic scenarios reveals what Westfall calls "an extended domain of reference," which look at specific settings and situations of the narrative.[3] Next the examination of the lexicogrammatical transitivity network distinguishes clauses into participants (Actors or Agents), actions (Processes), and outcomes (Goals or Medium).[4] In simple terms, transitivity focuses on who does what to whom. Transitivity analysis will highlight the similarities of the Actors and Processes in the two narratives. Taken together, the scenario and transitivity structure that John adopts from Gen 1–3 portrays Jesus as analogous to both θεός as divine creator and Adam as priest in Gen 1–3.

2   First Scenario and Transitivity Analysis

Hambly and others readily acknowledge that John "deliberately institutes a parallel to the creation narrative" of Gen 1–2.[5] Many further recognize that the

---

W. Edward Glenny, "Typology: A Summary of the Present Evangelical Discussion," *JETS* 40 (1997): 627–38.

2   G.P. Hugenberger, "Introductory Notes on Typology," in *The Right Doctrine from the Wrong Texts? Essays on the Use of the Old Testament in the New*, ed. G.K. Beale (Grand Rapids: Baker, 1994), 333–34, 336.

3   Cynthia Westfall, "Messianic Themes of Temple, Enthronement, and Victory in Hebrews and the General Epistles," in *The Messiah in the Old and New Testaments*, ed. Stanley E. Porter (Grand Rapids: Eerdmans, 2007), 212. A similar approach is used by Wally V. Cirafesi, "The Priestly Portrait of Jesus in the Gospel of John in Light of 1QS, 1QSA and 1QSB," *JGRChJ* 8 (2011–2012): 86, 88–92. Scenarios and scripts are formally explained in Gillian Brown and George Yule, *Discourse Analysis*, CTL (Cambridge: Cambridge University Press, 1983), 236–56.

4   I am using transitivity as part of the Ideational metafunction in Systemic Functional Linguistics. For a thorough explanation, see M.A.K. Halliday, *Halliday's Introduction to Functional Grammar*, rev. Christian M.I.M. Matthiessen, 4th ed. (London: Routledge, 2014), 333–46. For an application to the NT, see Gustavo Martín-Asensio, *Transitivity-Based Foregrounding in the Acts of the Apostles: A Functional-Grammatical Approach to the Lukan Perspective*, JSNTSup 202 (Sheffield: Sheffield Academic, 2000).

5   W.F. Hambly, "Creation and Gospel: A Brief Comparison of Genesis 1,1–2,4 and John 1,1–2,12," in *Studia Evangeica Vol. V*, ed. F.L. Cross (Berlin: Akademie-Verlag, 1968), 69; T.E. Phillips, "'The Third Fifth Day?' John 2:1 in Context," *ExpTim* 115 (2004): 330; Ernst Haenchen, *John: A Commentary on the Gospel of John*, Hermeneia, trans. Robert Walter Funk (Philadelphia: Fortress, 1984), 109; Donald A. Carson, *The Gospel According to John*, PNTC (Grand Rapids: Eerdmans, 1991), 113; Craig A. Evans, *Word and Glory: On the Exegetical and Theological*

Johannine timeline invites comparison with the creational week. The thrice-repeated phrase, "the next day," leads to "on the third day," depicting the first miracle of the wedding at Cana occurring on either the sixth[6] or seventh day.[7] The general features of the two stories have obvious relations, but further linguistic examination of the scenario displays more formal literary connections.

The most obvious connection is John choosing the opening phrase ἐν ἀρχῇ to mimic the Genesis account and immediately summon Genesis imagery to the minds of readers. However, John does not stop at a general connotation with creation; rather he fills his message with creational words and activities.[8] John uses κόσμος in John 1:9, 10, and 1:29, similarly to the manner Genesis uses γῆ forty-six times and אֶרֶץ twenty-nine times.[9] Also, οὐρανός is used sixteen times in Genesis and in John 1:32 and 1:51. Furthermore, there are comparable references to tree (συκῆ Gen 3:7 and John 1:48, 50), flesh (σάρξ in Gen 2:21, 23–24 and John 1:13–14), and the Spirit in motion (πνεῦμα Gen 1:2 and John 1:32).

John does more than simply adopt lexical similarities. He also adapts the material from Genesis and creatively combines features. In Gen 1–2 there is an interaction of life ζωή and light φῶς shining forth φαίνω into darkness σκοτία,

---

Background of John's Prologue, JSNTSup 89 (Sheffield: JSOT Press, 1993), 77–79; B.F. Westcott, *The Gospel According to St. John: The Authorized Version with Introduction and Notes* (Grand Rapids: Eerdmans, 1958), 2; Stanley E. Porter, *John, His Gospel, and Jesus: In Pursuit of the Johannine Voice* (Grand Rapids: Eerdmans, 2015), 43; Martin Hengel, *The Johannine Question*, trans. John Bowden (London: SCM, 1989), 71, 106.

6   Craig S. Keener, *The Gospel of John: A Commentary*, 2 vols. (Peabody: Hendrickson, 2003), 1:496; Hambly, "Creation," 71. Others believe mention of the third day is merely a temporal marker for narratological purposes. See Haenchen, *John*, 172. While Westcott believes the travel of sixty miles from Nazareth to Cana was a three-day journey, Westcott, *John*, 36.

7   Rudolf Schnackenburg, *The Gospel According to St. John*, trans. Cecily Hastings, Francis McDonagh, and David Smith, 3 vols. (New York: Seabury, 1980), 1:325; Carson, *John*, 166–68; J.N. Sanders, *A Commentary on the Gospel According to St. John*, HNTC (New York: Harper & Row, 1968), 107–8; Ernest Wilhelm Hengstenberg, *Commentary on the Gospel of St. John*, 2 vols. (Edinburgh: T&T Clark, 1865), 116; Alan R. Kerr, *The Temple of Jesus' Body: The Temple Theme in the Gospel of John*, JSNTSup 220 (Sheffield: Sheffield Academic, 2002), 70.

8   Some would argue for an eschatologically influenced New Creation imagery. See Kerr, *Temple of Jesus' Body*, 70–77, 132–33.

9   Greek citations are from Kurt Aland et al., *Novum Testamentum Graece* (Stuttgart: Deutsche Bibelgesellschaft, 2012); Alfred Rahlfs, *Septuaginta* (Stuttgart: Württembergische Bibelanstalt, 1935). The OT passages presented as parallels with John are according to the Greek text, which the early church and apostles used. See Martin Hengel, *The Septuagint as Christian Scripture: Its Prehistory and the Problem of its Canon*, trans. Mark E. Biddle (Edinburgh: T&T Clark, 2002), esp. 41–49, 108–11; Stanley E. Porter, "Septuagint/Greek Old Testament," *DNTB*, 1101–1102; Mogens Müller, "The Septuagint as the Bible of the New Testament Church," *SJOT* 7 (1993): esp. 122–95; Mogens Müller, *The First Bible of the Church: A Plea for the Septuagint*, JSOTSup 206 (Sheffield: Sheffield Academic, 1996).

σκότος. In John, the four themes—using the same lexical roots—are interwoven in John 1:4–5. Such lexical and thematic parallels demonstrate, alongside the overarching chronological depiction, the explicit intent of John to create a scenario of a cosmic creation in John 1 similar to Gen 1–2.

The transitivity analysis offers further parallels by focusing on the details of the participants, their roles, and their actions. First, there are two important verbs used in the corresponding creation accounts: ποιέω and γίνομαι. Gen 1–3 uses forms of ποιέω seventeen times with θεός as the Actor. In John, ποιέω is used six times with Jesus as Actor. Particularly important is the Genesis narrative using ποιέω and γίνομαι to depict acts of creation or creational configuration. Gen 1:1 presents θεός as the Actor who makes ἐποίησεν everything; the maker of the heavens and the earth. Similarly, in John 1:3 and 1:10, the middle verb ἐγένετο in intransitive clauses presents Jesus as the Agent who creates all things. In both accounts, the role of Actor and Agent are equally held by θεός, λογός, Ἰησοῦς, or an appropriate relative pronoun.

The shared creational scenario depicts Jesus as the Actor and Agent of divine creational acts. Consequently, John intends readers to see Jesus as a divine agent of creation.[10] While this conclusion is not substantively different than what is commonly understood, the method of using scenario and transitivity analysis demonstrates how formal connections are made. The same method will now be used to examine connections between Jesus and Adam.

3 Second Scenario Connection

At various places in the New Testament, comparison is made between Adam and Christ, especially in the writings of Paul.[11] The parallels between Jesus and Adam in the opening chapters of John are less discussed. However, the shared scenario is multilayered. Some connections are overt, such as the centralization of Jesus in the storyline and actions he performs. Other connections are subtle, requiring a biblical-theological understanding of the imagery. Examining these connections will establish a firm link between the two figures.

To begin, the creation week contributes to a shared scenario connecting Jesus with Adam. The cosmic creation week is the setting for introducing

---

10 Meredith G. Kline, *Kingdom Prologue: Genesis Foundations for a Covenantal Worldview* (Eugene, OR: Wipf and Stock, 2006), 31; Carson, *John*, 118; George R. Beasley-Murray, *John*, WBC 36 (Nashville: Thomas Nelson, 1999), 11.

11 Rudolf Karl Bultmann, "Adam und Christus nach Rm 5," *ZNW* 50 (1959): 145–65; Morna Dorothy Hooker, *From Adam to Christ: Essays on Paul* (Cambridge: Cambridge University Press, 1990).

Adam and his actions. So also Jesus arrives in the narrative scene during the chronological week in John.

Another overt connection is the absence of genealogy. John presents the origin of Jesus as equivalent to that of Adam, namely without descent. Irenaeus notes that just as the Father alone formed Adam, so John depicts Jesus as being begotten by the Father alone.[12] The approach by John is in contrast to the Synoptics. While the Gospels of Matthew and Luke both contain a genealogy and birth narrative, Mark contains neither. In contrast, Genesis and John agree in their omission of the genealogy and birth narrative and instead have origin accounts. Adam is made ἐποίησεν in Gen 1:27 and Jesus is begotten ἐγένετο in John 1:14, again using the words of creation. The accounts link the characters through the direct divine involvement in their origins.

Another shared element of the scenario derives from how Adam and Jesus are spoken about prior to their becoming active within the narrative scenes. The external narrator and active characters function as focalizers directing attention to the focalized, namely Adam and Jesus.[13] In Gen 1:26, God speaks to his royal court about Adam before making him. Also, God speaks blessings and gives directives to the humans in Gen 1:28–30 while they remain inactive and speechless. God again acts upon and speaks to Adam in 2:15–19, but it is not until 2:20 that Adam finally becomes an active character in the narrative.

Likewise, in the Gospel the narrator and John the Baptist talk about Jesus in John 1:14–18 and 26–27. The external narrator and the internal characters are pointing forward to Jesus and focalizing him. However, it is not until 1:29 that Jesus becomes an active character and not until 1:38 that he speaks. Unmistakably the Gospel of John adopts the narrative focalization method of Genesis. John highlights and focalizes Jesus by producing expectation of his arrival.

Further centralization of Adam and Jesus is accomplished by their equivalent active and passive actions. In Gen 2:19 animals are brought to Adam and he looks upon them and names them, ἤγαγεν αὐτὰ πρὸς τὸν Αδαμ ἰδεῖν τί καλέσει. Gen 2:22–23 uses nearly identical language concerning the woman being brought to Adam, who rejoices and calls her Eve, ἤγαγεν αὐτὴν πρὸς τὸν Αδαμ … κληθήσεται γυνή. Adam is centralized through the directional prepositional phrase and his role as Actor in the naming.

John centralizes Jesus in the same manner. In John 1:42 Simon is brought to Jesus who then looks at him and names him, ἤγαγεν αὐτὸν πρὸς τὸν Ἰησοῦν

---

12   Irenaeus, *Adv. Haer.* 3.21.10 (ANF[1] 1.454).
13   For an explanation of various focalization methods, see Mieke Bal, *Narratology: Introduction to the Theory of Narrative* (Toronto: University of Toronto Press, 1985), 100–110.

ἐμβλέψας ... κληθήσῃ.[14] The parallels are lexical and grammatical. Additionally, the same action is performed. The difference emerges in a heightening of the authoritative position of Jesus. While Adam names animals and Eve, who have no prior names, Jesus is presented as having the authority to rename Simon as Peter. The authoritative act is analogous to the authority displayed in the Sermon on the Mount, in which Jesus uses the repeated "You have heard it said … but I say," to display his authority to change current thoughts and give authoritative teaching.[15]

It is worth noting that the shared scenario is not a historical accident. John was not forced by historical details to record his opening chapters by referencing Genesis. For instance, the Synoptics do not record the renaming of Simon as Peter. In Mark 3:16 and Luke 6:14 the name of Peter is mentioned offhand, without any reportage of the scene of renaming. While Matt 16:16 is the closest parallel to John, the context of the situation is entirely different. Most importantly, the Synoptics do not use the lexical items John and Genesis share, namely ἄγω, ἐμβλέπω, or καλέω.[16] Furthermore, the Synoptics do not record Peter, or any other, being led to Jesus for renaming. Therefore, John crafts the narrative scene to depict the renaming of Peter as an Adamic-Christological parallel with shared authoritative roles.

The phrase "Son of Man" marks further links between Jesus and Adam. The phrase is used thirteen times in John; most importantly, for the purposes of this paper, is John 1:51. Sahlin concludes that John wants readers to see Jesus as an Adamic figure in both his role and actions. As Sahlin says, "Er [Jesus] ist der von Gott gesandte neue Adam, der 'Sohn Gottes' in ganz speziellem Sinn."[17] A growing body of literature connects Jesus, Son of Adam, and Son of Man, with the theology in Gen 1–4, Daniel 7, various Psalms, and the Gospel of Mark.[18]

---

14 John does not intend to picture Andrew as parallel to God, though he is the one bringing Peter to Jesus. The centralization is upon Jesus not Andrew. Furthermore, John 1:46–47 uses similar lexical items for Philip bringing Nathaniel to Jesus, who in turn refers to his seeing of Nathaniel.

15 Ἠκούσατε ὅτι ἐρρέθη ... ἐγὼ δὲ λέγω is repeated in Matt 5:21–22; 27–28, 33–34, 38–39, 43–44.

16 Mark 3:16 contains the noun phrase ὄνομα τῷ Σίμωνι Πέτρον, while Luke has the verbal form ὠνόμασεν Πέτρον.

17 Harald Sahlin, "Adam-Christologie im Neuen testament," *ST* 41 (1987): 23 (*trans*. He is God's new Adam, the 'Son of God' in a very special sense).

18 For a recent review of scholarship connecting the Adamic portrayal of Son of Man with Jesus see Andrew Streett, "From Marginal to Mainstream: The Adamic Son of Man and the Potential of Psalm 80," *CTR* 13 (2016): 77–98. See also J. Marcus, "Son of Man as Son of Adam," *RB* 110 (2003): 38–61; J. Marcus, "Son of Man as Son of Adam. Part II: Exegesis," *RB* 110 (2003): 370–86; Simon Gathercole, "The Son of Man in Mark's Gospel," *ExpTim* 115 (2004): 366.

These parallels show that John continues to adopt a shared scenario with Gen 1–3 to create a correlation between Adam and Jesus. Both narratives create expectation and focalization. Both narratives also focalize their characters through grammatical and lexical parallels, including the actions they perform. Examining the shared scenario elements between the two narratives achieves a more formal ground of connection than many typological approaches. We can, therefore, make a summary statement of how John portrays Jesus in the opening of his Gospel, namely as a figure where divine and Adamic elements merge. In systematic theology, the term God-man is used to depict Jesus as both divine and human.[19] John, however, uses the biblical theology of contemporary Judaism to unite divine and Adamic elements into a single figure.[20] According to John, Jesus is the Divine-Adam.

The Gospel of John not only portrays Jesus as the Divine-Adamic figure, but also uses Gen 1–3 as the theological and narrative background to write his opening chapters. Therefore, we should use Gen 1–3 as the interpretive lens for John 1–2, which will offer new intertextual imagery for a reexamination of the temple episode.

4 Motivation Behind Temple Episode of John 2:13–25

Much debate exists concerning the motives of the actions displayed in Herod's Temple. Malina and Rohrbaugh note that "scholars have been unable to decide whether this incident represents an attempt at reforming the temple ... or a prophetic action symbolizing the temple's destruction."[21] Unsurprisingly, there are even more interpretive options. Herzog divides opinions into four primary categories: religious, messianic, prophetic, and political.[22] The position of

---

Kirk also contends the Adamic Christology of Paul as equivalent to the Markan portrayal of Jesus as the Son of Man. See J.R. Daniel Kirk, "Mark's Son of Man and Paul's Second Adam," *HBT* 37 (2015): 170–95.

19   Berkhof says Jesus is the union of the Logos and humanity, the God-man. See Louis Berkhof, *Systematic Theology* (Grand Rapids: Eerdmans, 1938), 329; Herman Bavinck, *Reformed Dogmatics: Sin and Salvation in Christ*, trans. John Bolt (Grand Rapids: Baker, 2006), 343.

20   Andrew Chester, "High Christology—Whence, When and Why?" *EC* 2 (2011): 31.

21   B.J. Malina and R.L. Rohrbaugh, *Social-Science Commentary on the Gospel of John* (Minneapolis: Augsburg Fortress, 1998), 73.

22   W.R. Herzog, "Temple Cleansing," *DJG*, 820. *Religious* means cleansing the temple of impurities, represented by Bruce Chilton, *The Temple of Jesus: His Sacrificial Program within a Cultural History of Sacrifice* (University Park, PA: Pennsylvania State University Press, 1992), 91–111; Cirafesi, "Priestly Portrait of Jesus," 102–3; Craig A. Evans, "Jesus' Action in the Temple: Cleansing or Portent of Destruction?," *CBQ* 51 (1989): 269; Carson, *John*, 179;

religious motivation has the most proponents and many of the better arguments. Moreover, this paper puts forth an entirely new argument for seeing Jesus as cleansing the temple of religious impurities.

While in an exhaustive hermeneutical approach, all social and historical features require exploration, I believe intertextual matters are far too underdeveloped in many current analyses. If John intends for readers to understand what he is writing, then his writing likely gives clues as to what the appropriate interpretive framework is. Looking for interpretive clues within the text itself does not remove the possibility of ambiguity, homophoric reference, or even John being a bad writer.[23] However, as the above examination shows, John crafted his Gospel using explicit and implicit connections to Genesis. The temple episode continues this direct connection with Gen 3. Therefore, I will use Gen 1–3 as the informational lens to reexamine the motivation for the temple episode. Before doing so relevant imagery in Gen 1–3 needs further consideration.

5 The Garden-Temple and Adam's Role

The first matter to explore is the biblical imagery of the temple in Gen 1–3. Fletcher-Louis contends there is a "most-widely—if not universally—accepted" thesis that "both accounts of creation in Genesis 1–3 describe the contents and order of creation in terms of ancient temple building."[24] The creation narrative does not depict the construction of an ancient Near Eastern

---

Beasley-Murray, *John*, 39–40. Though Domeris finds commercial activity to be the immediate focus of Jesus, the goal is maintaining holiness in the temple, William Domeris, "The 'Enigma of Jesus' Temple Intervention: Four Essential Keys," *HTS* 71 (2015): 72. *Messianic* means the inclusion of the Gentiles. *Prophetic* means announcing destruction of the temple, represented by Jacob Chanikuzhy, *Jesus, The Eschatological Temple: An Exegetical Study of Jn 2,13–22 in the Light of the Pre-70 CE Eschatological Temple Hopes and the Synoptic Temple Action*, CBET 58 (Leuven: Peeters, 2012), 327–28; E.P. Sanders, *Jesus and Judaism* (Philadelphia: Fortress, 1985), 4. *Political* views the commercial activities as oppressive, represented by Neill Quinn Hamilton, "Temple Cleansing and Temple Bank," *JBL* 83 (1964): 365–72.

23 Homophoric reference is insider language of knowledge presumed shared by author and audience. It is possible John is referring to matters commonly understood by his audience that are not recoverable by modern interpreters. See J.R. Martin and David Rose, *Working with Discourse: Meaning Beyond the Clause* (New York: Continuum, 2007), 170; Halliday, *Functional Grammar*, 371, 631.

24 Crispin Fletcher-Louis, "God's Image, His Cosmic Temple and the High Priest," in *Heaven on Earth: The Temple in Biblical Theology*, ed. T. Desmond Alexander and Simon Gathercole (Carlisle, UK: Paternoster, 2004), 82.

piece of farmland. Rather, the author of Genesis intends for readers to discern, according to Wenham, the garden as "an archetypal sanctuary, that is a place where God dwells and where man should worship him."[25] In concise terms, Shimoff explains the "Pardes, the Temple, the Holy of Holies, are all one."[26] Gen 1–3 portrays the creation of a sacrosanct garden sanctuary or a garden-temple where the first humans dwelled in the presence of God.

Later passages in the OT confirm a garden-temple interpretation. For instance, in Gen 3:24 the Cherubim are the guardians of the garden-temple. As Kline explains, "those holy beings who attend the divine Presence" are tasked with guarding the garden-temple.[27] The Cherubim are also depicted as guardians of the presence of God on the ark in Exod 25:18–22. They appear on the tabernacle veil in Exod 26:31. Later on, the Cherubim are used in the inner temple sanctuary in 1 Kgs 6:23–28 and placed on the walls in 1 Kgs 6:29.

The garden-temple is also the place God walks with his people, as seen in Gen 3:8. As Wenham explains, "the Lord walked in Eden as he subsequently walked in the tabernacle."[28] The same word is used in Lev 26:12 to describe his personal and direct presence.[29] Additionally, Exod 3:5, 2 Sam 7:6–7, and Deut 23:14 portray the place where God walks and moves as one of holiness.

The garden-temple interpretation is also found outside the Hebrew Bible. The book of *Jubilees* mentions various features linking to temple motifs. Ruiten concludes that Jubilees conceives of Eden "as a holy place, more holy than any land (*Jub.* 3:12), it is a sanctuary (*Jub.* 4:26). In fact, Eden is the prototype of the

---

[25] Gordon J. Wenham, "Sanctuary Symbolism in the Garden of Eden Story," in *'I Studied Inscriptions from before the Flood': Ancient Near Eastern, Linguistic Approaches to Genesis 1–11*, ed. Richard S. Hess and David Toshio Tsumura (Winona Lake: Eisenbrauns, 1994), 399. See also Gordon J. Wenham, *Genesis 1–15*, WBC (Dallas: Word, 1998), 61; Lifsa Schachter, "The Garden of Eden as God's First Sanctuary," *JBQ* 41 (2013): 74–75; John A. Davies, "'Discerning Between Good and Evil': Solomon as a New Adam in 1 Kings," *WTJ* 73 (2011): 42–43; Kline, *Kingdom Prologue*, 47–49; Moshe Weinfeld, "Sabbath, Temple, and the Enthronement of the Lord: The Problem of the 'Sitz im Leben' of Genesis 1:1–2:3," in *Melanges bibliques et orientaux en l'honneur de M Henri Cazelles*, ed. A. Caquot and M. Delcor (Kevelaer: Butzon & Bercker, 1981), 501–3.

[26] Sandra R. Shimoff, "Gardens: From Edem to Jerusalem," *JSJ* 26 (1995): 155. In very similar terms, Kline (*Kingdom Prologue*, 49) says, "the garden of Eden was a microcosmic, earthly version of the cosmic temple and the site of a visible, local projection of the heavenly temple." See also C.T.R. Hayward, "The Figure of Adam in Pseudo-Philo's Biblical Antiquities," *JSJ* 23 (1987): 7.

[27] Kline, *Kingdom Prologue*, 48.

[28] Wenham, "Sanctuary Symbolism," 401. See also Kline, *Kingdom Prologue*, 47.

[29] Gen 3:8 περιπατοῦντος parallels Lev 26:12 ἐμπεριπατήσω.

Temple."[30] Eden as the prototype is most pointedly observed in the garden-temple construction resurfacing in the instructions given to Moses for building the tabernacle in Exod 25–40.[31]

Appreciating Eden as the original garden-temple helps elucidate the role Adam serves in it. A temple entails a priest, perhaps even requires one. Kline contends that "as a sanctuary of God it presented man with a cultic vocation of priestly guardianship."[32] Thus if Adam is in the prototypical garden-temple with unparalleled access to the presence of God, his responsibility is to be the prototypical priest.[33] The priestly character of Adam is attested through various details.

First, the charge in Gen 2:15 given to Adam is indicative of his priestly role.[34] The verbs often translated as work and keep are better translated as work and guard, and they are the same tasks assigned to the Levites for guarding the tabernacle in Num 3:7–8; 8:26; 18:5–6.[35] Adam is the archetypal Levite.[36]

Furthermore, Ezek 28:13 mentions Adam being covered with the same precious stones on the breastplate of the high priest in Exod 28:17–20. The priestly position of Adam is also attested outside the Hebrew Bible, which portrays Adam as building an altar and offering sacrifices.[37] Taking these and other

---

30 J. van Ruiten, "The Garden of Eden and Jubilees 3:1–31," *Bijdr* 57 (1996): 311. See also Gary Anderson, "Celibacy or Consummation in the Garden? Reflections on Early Jewish and Christian Interpretations of the Garden of Eden," *HTR* 82 (1989): 129; John H. Walton, *The Lost World of Genesis One: Ancient Cosmology and the Origins Debate* (Downers Grove: Intervarsity, 2009), 108.

31 Features connecting the prototypical garden-temple with the tabernacle include, among other things, the priestly jewels, gold, menorah and the tree of life, entrance from the east, and most importantly the presence of God. See Fletcher-Louis, "God's Image," 89; Gordon J. Wenham, *Exploring the Old Testament: The Pentateuch*, Vol. 1 (London: Society for Promoting Christian Knowledge, 2003), 76; Weinfeld, "Sabbath," 503, even says Gen 1–3 and Exod 39 are typologically identical.

32 Kline, *Kingdom Prologue*, 66.

33 See also Schachter, "Garden of Eden," 7; Wenham, "Sanctuary Symbolism," 401; Davies, "Discerning Between," 4; Walton, *Lost World*, 104–10; G.K. Beale, *A New Testament Biblical Theology: The Unfolding of the Old Testament in the New* (Grand Rapids: Baker, 2011), 33; Matthew Habib Emadi, "The Royal Priest: Psalm 110 in Biblical Theological Perspective" (PhD diss., Southern Baptist Theological Seminary, 2016), 33.

34 Tg. Ps.-J. 2.15 similarly portrays the charge to Adam as fulfilling the law and commandments in the garden-temple.

35 ἐργάζεσθαι and φυλάσσειν and לְעָבְדָהּ and וּשְׁמְרָהּ. Schachter, "Garden of Eden," 7; Walton, *Lost World*, 105–7; Kline, *Kingdom Prologue*, 85–86. Similar statements are in 1 Chron 23:32 and Ezek 44:14.

36 Wenham, "Sanctuary Symbolism," 401.

37 Tg. Ps.-J. 8.20 mentions Adam building an altar. *Jub.* 3:26–27 mentions Adam making an altar sacrifice. Similarly, *Apoc. Mos.* 29:3–6 depicts Adam burning spices on an altar. In b.

evidences into account, Hayward concludes there was a "widespread tradition that he [Adam] was a priest and offered sacrifice."[38]

Additionally, the precise grounds for the expulsion of Adam from the garden-temple support the view of his prototypical priestly role. To appreciate his distinctive failure requires distinguishing between the role of Adam and Eve since both are expelled and both are clothed in animal garments for their disobedience in partaking of the forbidden tree. However, the description of the curse and expulsion reveals a failure unique to Adam.

Before expulsion, as mentioned above, Adam is assigned the priestly task of working and guarding the garden-temple in Gen 2:15. However, when Adam is expelled from the garden-temple he is stripped of his priestly protector role.[39] Adam is no longer to guard and protect the garden-temple; rather, as Gen 3:17 and 23 indicate, he is to only work the cursed ground. The role of guardian and protector is turned over to the Cherubim.[40] Thus the distinguishing mark between Adam and Eve is the failure of Adam to carry out his priestly responsibilities of guarding and protecting the garden-temple.

On account of the holy presence of God, Adam was required to be pure and to guard the garden-temple of impurities. His responsibility was to remove anything that was impure or unholy. Deut 23:14 offers a succinct portrayal of this type of responsibility. God explains that on account of his presence within the camp, the entire camp must be holy and anything unclean must be removed, including the latrine.[41]

If the wandering people were to keep the entire camp pure, the responsibility of Adam to keep the garden-temple pure was much greater. When the serpent arrived, trying to return the good garden to chaos—the cosmological *Chaoskampf*—and lure humans away from allegiance to God, the responsibility of Adam was evident. In the words of Kline:

'Abod. Zar. 8a Adam offers up a one horned steer, and Gen. Rab. 34.9 also mentions the altar built by Adam used after his death. Ben Sira 49:16 also makes a connection between Adam and the high priesthood.

38 Hayward, "Figure of Adam," 7. Focusing on the work of Pseudo-Philo, Hayward ("Figure of Adam," 20) further explains there was an Adam tradition that viewed him as a priest, sacrificer, and Patriarch.

39 Davies, "Discerning Between," 4; Beale, *Biblical Theology*, 38; G.K. Beale, "Eden, the Temple, and the Church's Mission in the New Creation," *JETS* 48 (2005): 8; Emadi, "Royal Priest," 33, 48.

40 Kline sees Ezek 28:14, 16 as a reference to the event of the Cherubim replacing Adam. See Meredith G. Kline, *Images of the Spirit* (Eugene, OR: Wipf & Stock, 1999), 36.

41 Jeffrey Tigay, *Deuteronomy*, JPS Torah Commentary (New York: The Jewish Publication Society, 1996), 214. He explains that the idiom *'ervat davar* in Deut 23:14 is broad enough to indicate, "virtually anything offensive."

> The hour had come for the priest-king of Eden, robed in his God-like dignity, to declare the righteous judgment of his holy Lord. The blaspheming profane serpent must be trampled under foot. This was the task which, by the Creator's appointment, lay at the threshhold (sic.) of man's historic mission ... The faithful priest must hallow God's name and defend God's sanctuary.[42]

The responsibility to protect the purity of the garden-temple necessitated killing the usurping serpent. When the serpent transgressed that purity and was tempting others to do likewise, Adam should have exercised authority over creatures (Gen 1:26, 28) and executed a priestly judicial verdict.[43]

As Deut 17:6–7 requires, there were two witnesses available against the serpent, and thus it should have been put to death and the evil purged from the garden temple. However, Adam did not execute his responsibility as the priest and was thus stripped of his priesthood. He and Eve subsequently ate of the forbidden fruit, thereby further contradicting the explicit command of God, and were driven out. Adam failed at being a priest and was removed from the garden-temple.

6 John 2:13–25 and the Temple Cleansing

When the imagery of the garden-temple and priestly biblical details from Gen 1–3 are used as a background for John 2, an entirely new picture emerges. For starters, the biblical imagery in Gen 1–3 gives a more precise explanation of how John is portraying Jesus. As shown above, John uses Gen 1–3 to create intimate connections between Jesus and God and Jesus and Adam. Therefore, since Adam is the prototypical priest, readers of John are intended to understand Jesus as the new priest, an Adamic-priest.[44] With this in mind, we are now in a position to reexamine the temple scene of John.

First, there are chronological similarities. Prior to John 2:12 the narrative presents a clearly defined chronology. As mentioned above, John mimics the Genesis narrative of a seven-day cycle. However, at John 2:12 there is

---

42   Kline, *Kingdom Prologue*, 121, 123.
43   Wenham, *Genesis 1–15*, 75; Beale, *Biblical Theology*, 34, 38; Crispin Fletcher-Louis, "Jesus as the High Priestly Messiah: Part 1," *JSHJ* 4 (2006): 159.
44   Others also note the priestly Christology in John. Cirafesi, "Priesty Portrait of Jesus," 104–5; John Paul Heil, "Jesus as the Unique High Priest in the Gospel of John," *CBQ* 57 (1995): 729–45.

the vague turn of οὐ πολλὰς ἡμέρας, not many days.⁴⁵ Such vagueness is also in Gen 3:1. After a clear demarcation of a seven-day cycle, there is no mention of the chronological gap between the union of Adam and Eve and the arrival of the serpent.

While it is not necessary to mention the exact number of days, the sharp contrast with the preceding narrative is an interesting element in Gen 3:1 that John adopts. The literary parallel is remarkable. Adam and Eve celebrate union and then there is an unspecified timeframe before the next scene. Likewise, Jesus is at a wedding uniting two people in marriage and then there is an unspecified timeframe before the next scene in the narrative.⁴⁶

A second connection is that the chief setting in both narratives is in a temple. While Adam has been in the garden-temple his whole life, this marks a new development in the Gospel of John. Dramatically, John places Jesus, the new Adam, in the temple after a wedding, and after a vague time gap. Moreover, both priestly characters are involved in a dramatic temple scene.

A third connection is the respective priests in both narratives encounter unholy characters and activities in the temple. The priest is confronted with those engaged in actives that are not devoted to God. Using Gen 1–3 as the interpretive lens, therefore, we can better understand the provocation of Jesus. As the second Adam, Jesus is faced with the same type of scenario as the first Adam. While the first Adam failed to act and render his priestly verdict, Jesus responds by driving out the animals and workers. The choice is between executing his priestly duties or not doing so. Jesus is motivated to execute his Adamic-priestly role in the temple of God. While Haenchen argues that "Jesus' actions appears to lack a biblical base," in light of the Genesis connection, the biblical base is clear that where the first Adam failed the second Adam now triumphs.⁴⁷

A difference between the two scenes concerns the severity of the unholy agents in the situation and the appropriate response. Adam was faced with the serpent trying, according to Kline, "to persuade man to violate the basic covenantal demand for wholehearted devotion."⁴⁸ Faced with a direct assault against God, his garden-temple, and his people, Adam should, therefore, have killed the serpent.

---

45   Carson, *John*, 176.
46   This paper lacks space to address the wedding at Cana. However, the celebratory wedding and wine are paralleled in the Genesis narrative with the union of Adam and Eve and the Sabbath rest. They are at least placed in similar chronological order.
47   Haenchen, *John*, 184.
48   Kline, *Kingdom Prologue*, 120.

Jesus, however, does not encounter the same type of unholy activity. The commercial activity is not necessarily a direct assault on the character and presence of God. Instead, the noise of cattle, sheep, and commerce describes a scene devoid of wholehearted devotion.[49] Thus commercial activity is not equated with sin or idolatry.[50] Instead of the priestly verdict of death to the animals and workers, Jesus declares and enacts purification.[51] Rather Jesus declares the contrast between a "house of my father" versus a "house of trade"; meaning something sacrosanct is transformed into something not. Commerce is not an assault on God's presence; it simply has no place in the temple confines. Therefore, instead of a judicial priestly verdict of death, Jesus simply drives them out. He removes unholy things and activities from the temple. Jesus cleanses the temple by driving out everything that is unholy. The priest stays in the temple but the unholy characters are driven out, just as God did to Adam and Eve.

Lastly, using Gen 1–3 as the interpretive lens also offers insights into John 2:19–25. When Jesus calls for destruction of the temple, the omniscient narrator explains in 2:21 that Jesus is referring to his body. The interaction represents the climax of John's use of temple imagery from Gen 1–3.

The temple represents the place people meet with God, and John is representing Jesus as the very embodiment of that meeting place; Jesus is the better temple. As Cirafesi explains, John depicts Jesus as "the realization of the Holy of Holies in which the priestly service is carried out."[52] In John 1:14, Jesus is said to tabernacle ἐσκήνωσεν with the people.[53] John makes explicit that Jesus is the replacement of the old temple.[54]

When the totality of the scene is put together, a seamless storyline of John 1:1–2:25 mirrors the theological imagery and drama of Gen 1–3. God made a pure garden-temple for his people to commune with him. Adam was charged

---

49 Carson, *John*, 179. Beasley-Murray (*John*, 39) points out the "wrath was directed not against those engaged in or leading worship, but against those detracting from it."

50 Hamilton exaggerates the significance of the commercial and temple banking system in the cleansing episode. See Hamilton, "Temple Cleansing," esp. 368–70. The commercial activity should not occur within the confines of the temple. See B.G. Schuchard, *Scripture within Scripture: The Interrelationship of Form and Function in the Explicit Old Testament Citations in the Gospel of John* (Atlanta: Scholars Press, 1991), 24; Kerr, *Temple of Jesus' Body*, 80.

51 The conclusion of purification contradicts Sanders' contention that the actions of Jesus are symbolic for the destruction of the temple. See Sanders, *Jesus and Judaism*, 61–76.

52 Cirafesi, "Priesty Portrait of Jesus," 105.

53 Exod 25–40 repeatedly uses σκηνή (or miškān) to describe the tabernacle or mobile temple.

54 There are also overtones of replacing the Passover. See Porter, *John, His Gospel*, 211–13.

to keep himself and the garden-temple pure. When the serpent arrived challenging that charge, Adam failed to carry out his duties. In fact, he not only allowed the serpent to speak against God and lead Eve astray but participated in the defilement of the garden-temple. John wants readers to see that Jesus, in contrast to Adam, is the better Adamic priest doing precisely what the former failed to do, namely cleansing the temple,[55] as the Divine-Adamic priest Jesus drives out what is unholy from the temple.

7   Further Application

The use of Gen 1–3 as the background for John offers a number of insights into the Johannine story besides a better understanding of the temple cleansing. Here, I draw attention to two additional debates where this information is pertinent.

First, Bultmann offers a counter-proposal to the thesis of using Gen 1–3 as the primary source for the theological imagery and storyline of the Gospel of John. He contends that the imagery of the exalted character in the story of John 1–2 is adopted from pre-Christian Gnostic material. Specifically, the incarnation of a redeemer figure, in the words of Bultmann, "is itself originally Gnostic, and was taken over at a very early stage by Christianity."[56] This "archetypal man" is a product of Gnostic and Greek material adopted from the Orient.[57]

There are some inherent problems with the proposal. For starters, others indicate that the material Bultmann draws upon is later than the writing of John, and was likely influenced by Christian thought.[58] Evans puts it bluntly, there is "no evidence for the existence of a first-century Primal Man myth" or Wisdom mythology.[59] Furthermore, as this paper demonstrates, the material Bultmann is trying to draw upon is entirely unnecessary for the interpretation of John. The details of Gen 1–3 serve as the literary, biblical-theological, and imaginative paradigm for John 1–2.

Furthermore, when attempting to situate the motivation for the cleansing of the temple, the parallel with Gen 1–3 is sufficient for background information. While Evans is likely correct that the corrupt aristocratic priests would also

---

55   Others see the temple cleansing as a priestly act. See Cirafesi, "Priesty Portrait of Jesus," 103.
56   Rudolf Karl Bultmann, *The Gospel of John: A Commentary*, ed. G.R. Beasley-Murray, trans. R.W.N. Hoare and J.K. Riches (Philadelphia: Westminster, 1971), 26.
57   Bultmann, *John*, 26 n3.
58   Porter, *John, His Gospel*, 102–7; Evans, *Word and Glory*, esp. 47–76.
59   Evans, *Word and Glory*, 193.

have provoked Jesus, as is revealed by Jesus's confrontation with the Pharisees throughout John, the understanding of the scene in John 2 is not dependent on such information.[60]

A second area of debate concerns how the temple cleansing compares with the Synoptic accounts. There remains the continual question of whether there are two cleansings or one. Porter contends for two cleansings since "the Johannine account is sufficiently different that it has very little in common with the Synoptic accounts."[61] Many others believe John records the same event as the Synoptics in a dischronologized fashion.[62] While this paper does not intend to solve the debate, it does contribute an important bit of information, namely the motivated narrative framework.

John 1–2 follows the order of events of Gen 1–3 in such a remarkable manner that one should conclude that John narrates the temple cleansing after the creation week and wedding to mirror Genesis. John is mirroring Genesis to make explicit connections with the prototypical priest to present Jesus as the new and better Adamic-priest. However, this does not absolutely require a dischronologization of the historical events. It is possible that there were two cleansing events. Perhaps the Synoptics chose to record the latter one to create a crescendo in their Gospels, while John chose to record the neglected event for the literary parallels.

8 Conclusion

John wrote a literary masterpiece in recording the story and message of Jesus. The depth and literary character is perhaps the best in the New Testament, at least it is for this reader of the New Testament. This paper has tried to join the chorus in drawing out the theology of John embedded in his literary techniques. Examining the linguistic details of John 1–2 makes evident that John creates scenarios that intimately connect with Gen 1–3.

John creates a scenario of cosmic creation to present Jesus as the divine architect who arrives in the creation he made. John intends for his readers to see Jesus as divine. After the climactic turn in John 1:14, John creates a

---

60 Evans, "Jesus' Action," 255–63.
61 Porter, *John, His Gospel*, 78. While Carson (*John*, 177) agrees, he points out that "only a very few judge it likely that there were two temple cleansings." See also Leon Morris, *The Gospel according to John*, NICNT (Grand Rapids: Eerdmans, 1995), 188–91.
62 Haenchen (*John*, 187) contends for a dischronologized order and says it is the position of "the majority of scholars." See also Schnackenburg, *John*, 1:370; Raymond Edward Brown, *The Gospel According to John*, AB (Garden City: Yale University Press, 1966), 1:118.

scenario—structured as a creation week—with the central figure being the new Adam. Jesus, as new Adam, does similar things as the first one but Jesus does them better and more authoritatively. The cumulative picture is Jesus presented as the Divine-Adamic priest. Unlike the first Adam, the Divine-Adamic priest cleanses the temple of all things unfit to be in the place where God communes with his people. Where the first Adam wavered in his allegiance to God and was unwilling to exercise his priestly duty to purify the garden-temple, the second Divine-Adamic priest is unwavering for pure worship in the house of God. His zeal to be a perfect priest consumed him.

The use of the Gen 1–3 as the primary model and literary background for John 1–2 makes interpretation more lucid and recourse to tangential texts unnecessary. This thesis in no way restricts the reflective theological creativity of John. In fact, this paper highlights the literary originality of John who used texts familiar to his audience in new ways to situate the Gospel of Jesus within the religious narrative of contemporary Judaism.

CHAPTER 10

Jesus, the λόγος, and Recognition: a Study of Concealed and Revealed Identity in John's Gospel

Adam Z. Wright

1 Introduction

A truly fascinating feature of John's Gospel is that Jesus's identity goes largely unrecognized throughout the narrative despite a number of revealing dialogues and miracles. This could mean one of two things: either that Jesus was unconvincing in his attempts to reveal his true identity, which could also mean that the crowds lacked the necessary insight to understand; or that the concealment of Jesus's identity is a feature that has a purpose in the narrative. The first option is rather questionable because one would then have to answer why a writer would choose to tell a story about a Messiah that was unsuccessful in his efforts. If the second option is viable, then we have to ask why and for what purpose the concealment of his identity is a valid feature in the narrative.

This essay will examine the relationship between concealment and recognition in the Gospel of John. Specifically, it will be argued that recognition was a common literary motif that appeared in many different ancient genres, and that there are discernible criteria that can be established in order to examine such motifs. This also raises a question concerning genre, and so this essay will also explore the concept of ancient genre and access a number of possibilities with regard to John's genre. Recognition functions in John's Gospel similar to how it functions in ancient drama, specifically tragedy. Further, it is the essential element that characterized drama, particularly tragedy, and the same can be said of John's Gospel.

These questions are linked to one of the more observable traits of John's Gospel—that is, the author's tendency to create dichotomies, or opposites. This is important because everything in the field of time is dual: light and dark, past and future, dead and alive, is or is not. The perception of this discrepancy leads to beliefs about the discrepancy and then action towards either end of the spectrum. This is the basis of ethics, and thus the creation of that which is good and that which is evil. To be within time is to experience and struggle with these dualities and therefore to be human, and the λόγος has entered time. This, as we will see, is important because the λόγος must bridge the experience between that which is eternal and that which is not by teaching how to think and how to live. This creates the ultimate dichotomy, which is that the λόγος has created the world and has now entered into it but the world is unable to recognize him (John 1:10).[1] This means that recognition of the creator and saviour of the world is at the centre of the Gospel.

2   Concealment and Recognition

Linguistically speaking, recognition is a decoding process by which an uttered statement is received and interpreted by a listener, a process known as *discourse utterance*. The way that a listener interprets the statement is based on how he or she incorporates the uttered statement into what they already know. Thus, recognition becomes less about learning something completely new and more about altering what someone already knows.[2]

This is best illustrated in the following scenario:

> A rich man enters a hotel owned by an elderly couple where he rents a room. After the man falls asleep, the elderly couple decides to enter the room and steal his money after they murder the man. Picking up the man's wallet to steal his money, the elderly couple discover a photograph and realize that the man they had just murdered was their long-lost son.

Returning to what was said above, the moment of recognition was an alteration of knowledge: to the elderly couple, the rich man *appeared* as a stranger but was really their son. This creates an aspect of concealment and recognition that we call "secrecy"; being and yet not appearing. It also creates two

---

1   There is some question here as to whether the λόγος simply embodies Jesus and works through him or whether Jesus and the λόγος are the same. Lindars points out this distinction and blames it on the idea that Wisdom is embodied in the Law of Moses (Eccl 24:23). Lindars point is well taken here; however, it appears that Lindars is more concerned with the denotation of the term λόγος rather than the connotation. The λόγος connotes that which is beyond human contemplation; the eternal God who lives in the Spiritual Realm according to Bruce. Human beings, however, are visible and observable. This is why Tragedy is an appropriate genre for John's Gospel, and that is because it serves as a poetic, or symbolic, representation of the surreal. See R. Alan Culpepper, Barnabas Lindars, Ruth B. Edwards, and John M. Court, *The Johannine Literature* (Sheffield: Sheffield Academic, 2000), 86; F.F. Bruce, *The Gospel of John: Introduction, Exposition, and Notes* (Grand Rapids: Eerdmans, 1983) 13.
2   A.J. Greimas and J. Courtes, "The Cognitive Dimensions of Narrative Discourse," *NLH* 8 (1976) 433–47, 440.

categories of perception, or points of view, which Greimas and Courtes call *cognitive positions*: the point of view of the elderly couple and that of the son.

Yet another aspect of concealment and recognition can be illustrated in an additional scenario:

> A king promises the marriage of his daughter in exchange for killing a dragon. A hero accepts this offer and kills the dragon, but he is killed during the battle. An onlooker, who had witnessed the hero's death, returns to the king and claims that it was he who overcame the dragon thereby claiming the king's daughter for himself.

What is illustrated here is what we call "illusion": the onlooker appears to be the hero to the king but, in reality, is not. These cognitive positions allow the audience to recognize the deception even if the king does not, creating another aspect of not being and yet appearing.

These two aspects then create categories of truth and falsehood, and these cognitive positions can be illustrated in the following diagram (see figure 10.1):[3]

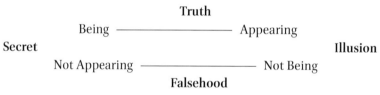

FIGURE 10.1   Comparison of truth, falsehood, secret, and illusion

The prologue of any drama, and certainly true of John's Gospel as well, is essential to the process of recognition and concealment. Without prior knowledge of the protagonist's true identity, the irony of the drama cannot take full effect and the overall message of the drama is lost.[4] John's Gospel, like other examples of tragedy, masterfully creates certain expectations in its opening lines, and allows the audience to establish certain presuppositions in their minds with regard to the protagonist, the λόγος.

---

3   This diagram is taken from Greimas and Courtes, "Dimensions," 440.
4   Although not certain, this could be what Aristotle refers to as *catharsis*, a releasing of *pity* and *fear* in the audience. In order for a drama to be essentially dramatic, the audience must be granted some form of pre-knowledge that is altered at some point in the drama. Doing so challenges certain expectations and presuppositions which is the most important part of drama. See Aristotle, *Poetics* 1385b 12–16, 1382a 21–25; Gregory Nagy, *The Ancient Greek Hero in 24 Hours* (Cambridge, MA: Belknap, 2013), 64–65; Michael Davis, *Aristotle's Poetics: The Poetics of Philosophy* (Lanham, MD: Rowman & Littlefield, 1992), 39.

3   Some Brief Comments on the Tragic Genre

Tragedy is the appropriate generic category for John's Gospel for two major reasons, the first is related to the character of Jesus and his experiences and the second to the concept of his resurrection. With regard to Jesus's character and experiences, a number of things should be noted. Tragic heroes suffer in order to bring about some form of social or religious change. These heroes can be mortal or divine, but their suffering is inevitable and quite voluntary. In the example of John's Gospel, Jesus is presented as a paradox: he is entirely mortal and yet entirely divine. He is a God of a dual nature, a child of both the divine and mortal realm—a twice-born God in a sense—which makes him especially enigmatic and worthy of considerable thought because it forces us to consider the nature of immortality mixed with the inevitable consequence of mortality. He is, therefore, a God who must suffer and die as he lives within the constraints of human existence and, as such, embodies the fullness of life and the violence of death. Such an enigmatic figure forces one to consider the duality of such a paradox which prompts one to consider the nature of reality itself. And this is certainly the purpose of John's Gospel: to advocate a dual existence of heaven and earth as well as flesh-out the paradox of suffering as a means of attaining heaven. One is thus forced to accept this duality of this nature—both of Jesus and of reality—or fall completely into ignorance and darkness as the prologue suggests.

The second reason why tragedy is an appropriate genre for John's Gospel is the result that it produces within the audience. Aristotle perhaps first attempted to articulate this phenomenon by introducing to us the term *catharsis*, which is a purging of the emotions through the viewing of a tragic drama. But how exactly does this work? The answer is that tragic life circumstances have the potential to breed life. This is, of course, not always true but the potential for growth or—I daresay a resurrection—can result from tragic events. When something tragic occurs, we have two options. We can choose to surrender, a result which could very well result in our death. Such a reaction reduces the amount of serotonin produced within the brain and results in continued feelings of depression and loss. But the actions displayed by Jesus within John's Gospel are quite different. They illustrate a Jesus who does not cower in the face of his inevitable death. Instead, they illustrate a Jesus who stands firm and faces down death and suffering in order to achieve the resurrection. This becomes a valuable lesson for the audience who face similar circumstances. One is consistently faced with the dangers of existence and must find a way to endure such suffering. The lesson that Jesus teaches—and is taught in all tragedy—is that suffering is a necessary experience of the human condition and that such suffering is necessary for growth, both psychologically and spiritually. When a person undergoes a terrible experience, that person is forced to rectify the experience and move beyond it—damage may occur, but it is necessary for growth. The same thing can be said of a belief system as well. For example, we may subscribe to a particular way of thinking, but in order to grow and survive, we must put to death certain beliefs and go through a time of uncertainty, after which we can be resurrected, so to speak, into a new way of thinking that is more conducive to our survival. What Jesus does, therefore, is model a pattern of thinking and being that embraces suffering and death with the aim of being resurrected into something better. This, I believe, is what Aristotle means by *catharsis*.

This applies directly to the circumstance of the first-century Christian audience, particularly to the Judaeo-Christian portion of that audience. Assuming that John's Gospel was written post AD 70, the Jewish population would have been mourning the destruction of Israel's centre of worship, the Temple.[5] Not only this, but functional practice of worship would have been radically altered through its destruction. Such an experience could, no doubt, be equated to a kind of death, certainly the death of a religious system that had existed for hundreds of years. But Jesus represents a new kind of thinking that allowed one to access God, or more specifically, contend with one's sin in the presence of God, by means of something other than the sacrifice of something external. Instead, one must learn to sacrifice oneself; a process that would have resulted in an extensive amount of time spent in uncertainty. Such a process would have led to a change in thinking—a resurrection of the mind.

This plays out in John's Gospel in two ways. First, in order to understand the reasons why an ancient author depicts a God in a certain way, one needs to consider the world in which the author lives or the worldview that an author has. In John's Gospel, Jesus is depicted as a healer and miracle worker who confounds the leaders of the social system through a series of dialogues. He is persecuted because of his words and actions and is then crucified after which he is resurrected from the dead. Jesus is thus presented as the divine archetype of a triumphant hero and, at the same time, as the suffering and dying God. This contrast is particularly tragic and is symbolic of the tragic nature found within all things, most certainly life itself. As the prologue states, Jesus embodies contrast and harmony, creation and destruction, and even life and death. These things are inseparable from one another, and they represent a true awareness

---

5   Bruce notes that this point in time marked the "cessation" of sacrificial worship. In the time thereafter, debates between the synagogue authorities and the Christians would have revolved around how proper worship should work. See Bruce, *John*, 15.

of the nature of things. Jesus is an affirmation of the totality of being where, for example, suffering and death are not seen as something to avoid but rather a completion of the totality of the life of an early Christian. This view of life, tragic though it may be, is desirable and leads to a fuller appreciation of life. That is to say: to view the darkness of death while at the same time acknowledging the bliss of eternal life leads one to a greater sense of consciousness and a more pleasurable psychological state.

Second, merely by merit of a doctrine of resurrection, one can speculate that the biggest challenge to John's audience was the threat of death or death itself. The earliest Christians faced immense persecution. John's Gospel depicts a Messiah who embodies the fullness of life while at the same time suffers the violence of death. Death then becomes a means by which one gains access to eternity, and, in some senses, a divine rite-of-passage to life; pain and suffering is therefore necessary to attain life. The story of Jesus in John's Gospel is a justification of pain and suffering, a suffering which precedes creation. This leads one to affirm death and suffering as a highly desirable part of life. Since Jesus can both fathom and entertain the most dreadful and ecstatic aspects of life simultaneously, he becomes a hero of the highest order; the tragic hero.

In what follows, the chapter will discuss one of the most prominent features of tragedy and, by extension, John's Gospel, namely recognition scenes and their function within the story of Jesus. I will be working with the theory of Greimas and Courtes as used in their article "The Cognitive Dimensions of Narrative Discourse." This will help us understand the nature of recognition and the purpose it serves in the narrative.[6]

4   John's Prologue and Other Forms of Tragic Drama

Tragic drama contains within it the motif of recognition, and the reason for this is to generate a sense of irony for the audience. Irony is essentially tragic, and the reason for this is because the tragic hero is destined to suffer for the good of the many. In the cases discussed below, a god aims to restore something that is lost or to change something fundamental about society but, in order to do so, he or she must suffer. In one sense, then, the choice of a particular god to subject him or herself to degradation for the common good *is* tragedy. In John's Gospel, it is too much for the world to be confronted with the instrument of creation in a direct way; to do so would rob the narrative of its potency. Instead, the hero, or λόγος, must at first remain disguised as he conducts himself and

---

6   Greimas and Courtes, "Cognitive Dimensions."

suffers within the world. Recognition then comes to those who are able to see correctly, supposedly influenced by the λόγος.

Much like the *Bacchae* of Euripides, John's prologue informs the reader of what will come. Not only this, but each protagonist is introduced in such a way as to create a level of irony throughout the drama. In the *Bacchae*, Dionysus appears to the audience and announces that he has come to reinstitute the proper worship of himself within the city of Thebes. He reveals his godly character to the audience and then conceals this character behind a mask, appearing as a lowly beggar. Doing so prevents the people in Thebes to recognize him immediately thereby creating the *raison d'être* of drama: concealment.[7] Concealment is therefore integral to drama or else the story has no reason to continue: the arrival of a god within the city would presumably overwhelm the people and have no dramatic quality about it. A concealed god, however, creates a level of irony that builds tension as the concealed god interacts with his unknowing subjects.

John's prologue functions this way. The audience is introduced to the protagonist, the λόγος. The λόγος does not speak directly to the audience as Dionysus does, but he is described as "being with God in the beginning" and having created the world which he now inhabits. Each of these statements brings credibility to the λόγος and announces his status as being both divine and creatively all-powerful. What is more, the λόγος enters the world, which he has created, but those whom he has created do not recognize him (ἔγνω).[8] *Why* is no one able to recognize such divinity and power? The answer is because, much like Dionysus, the λόγος conceals himself in low social status which prevents him from being recognized (1:46).[9] As a result, concealment in John's Gospel functions much like it does in the *Bacchae*: an all-powerful deity is present amongst

---

7 A similar recognition trope appears in Homer's *Odyssey*. After Odysseus returns home from his adventures, he enters his home as a beggar who goes unrecognized by his family and friends. It is not until he sits in a bath that his true identity is discovered by means of a recognizable scar on his leg (*Od.* 19.528–538). More will be made of this below.

8 This is a cognate of γινώσκω and should be translated as "recognize" (John 1:10) and appears 80 times throughout the Gospel.

9 According to Malina and Rohrbaugh, Mediterranean people thought in terms of stereotypes. Persons were, therefore, not known by their "psychological personalities and uniqueness, but by general social categories, such as place or origin, residence, family, gender, age, and the range of other groups to which they might belong." Because the crowds can identity Jesus, they have difficulty understanding what he says in light of the stereotypes. Since Jesus is from Nazareth or a disreputable Galilean (7:52), he is not to be taken seriously which adds an incredible ironic dimension to the Gospel. See Bruce J. Malina and Richard L. Rohrbaugh, *Social-Science Commentary on the Gospel of John* (Minneapolis: Fortress, 1989), 165–66.

his people but his people are unable to recognize his true identity because he has concealed himself as a person of low social status.

Each of these examples follows closely with our proposed methodology. Both Jesus and Dionysus appear as a "Secret" because their true identities are present though do not appear. Through a series of interactions, their characters slowly move from "Secret" to "Truth" as their persons are recognized.

5 Recognition in John's Gospel

Various aspects of John's Gospel revolve around recognition. What follows will begin with a discussion of the λόγος as the basis for all recognition in the Gospel. It will then discuss the "I AM" statements as well as the post resurrection recognition scenes, particularly that of Thomas.

5.1 The λόγος

The term λόγος contains within it a large amount of currency in the ancient world, and it is without doubt that the author of John's Gospel purposefully chose this term.[10] It was used within Judaism, early and late Christianity, and a variety of Greek philosophical traditions.[11] It would be too great a task, however, to outline each of the various nuances of the term in this article.

---

[10] The consequences of John's use of the term λόγος were astounding. By using Greek philosophy to explain a foreign religious system like Judaism, John was able to create a blueprint for Christian theology that would make sense to a Graeco-Roman culture. This God also transcended several presuppositions about the gods and added new perspective to the philosophical systems of Plato and Aristotle. Doing so made Plato's Forms more real by adding the incarnation, and by recording the actions of the λόγος in the world, believers "will have eternal life in His name" (John 20:31). Arthur Herman, *The Cave and the Light: Plato Versus Aristotle, and the Struggle for the Soul of Western Civilization* (New York: Random House, 2014), 151.

[11] Because of what John had done, later church Fathers were able to relate Christian doctrines with the rest of the world. Clement understood the coming of the λόγος as the final step in the journey begun by Socrates. Because the earliest church Fathers understood John's λόγος as such, a large backlash began when Neo Platonists took offence to how Christians were abusing Plato's philosophical systems. Celsus, a student of the Neo-Platonist Plotinus, launched a brutal attack on Christianity in his work "The True λόγος." He thought that the idea of a poor Jewish boy being the λόγος was absurd, something that both Origen and Augustine responded to in time. In *The True Logos*, Celsus states, "Did not Plato say that the Architect and Father of the universe is not easily found?" On this point, Herman adds, "How likely would it be that His (the Father's) son would turn up in a despised corner of the world like Galilee?" See Herman, *Cave and the Light*, 154.

However, a few comments with regard to how it functions within John's Gospel will suffice.[12]

The metaphorical functions of λόγος in John's Gospel are parallel to those found in the earliest chapters of Genesis. In Genesis, we are told that God created the world out of chaos through speech—through λόγος—after which He speaks light into existence. As a metaphor, this sequence represents the creation of human consciousness—a movement from the darkness of ignorance into the light of understanding. Because of its early placement in the creation sequence, Light is an extremely prominent aspect of creation. The reason for this could be because light plays an integral part in human existence, particularly with regard to how humanity understands the world around it. This is a necessary condition since humanity relied on light to help it avoid the world's dangers which could lead to death and destruction. Light, then, becomes synonymous with life and, subsequently, darkness with death, and it is God's λόγος that delivers a person to the former from the latter.

John continues this literary tradition by introducing the λόγος as the chief instrument of creation (1:3). John also makes the λόγος synonymous with Light and it is fair to suggest that John is continuing the metaphor of creating consciousness. The λόγος rescues a person from chaos, or ignorance, by providing the proper understanding necessary to live well. This is important to John's narrative because it allows Jesus to be the source from which all true knowledge comes into the world, thus providing the premise for all of the dialogues throughout the narrative.

This is also important with regard to the tragic genre because the hero must be well-established within the traditions of his ancestors. Since John does not provide a genealogy for Jesus that links him to the heroic past of kingship or

---

12 According to Herman, "the triumph of Christianity does *not* mark the end of ancient philosophy ... instead, it depended and broadened the Greek imprint on Western culture. It allowed familiar features to stand out in striking new ways." The Greek philosophical tradition was steeped in λόγος tradition ranging from Heraclitus to Plato, Plato to Aristotle, Aristotle to the Stoics, and the Stoics to the earliest Christian Fathers. It was used to describe a divine essence that pervaded the universe, known as "immortal, λόγος, Aeon, Father, Son, God, justice and ruler of the universe. John makes it clear that this same λόγος who had made the world and everything in it had now come into the world as a fleshly being. It is also worth noting that John was not the first Jewish writer to connect the Jewish God to the Greek philosophical system. Over one hundred years earlier, Philo of Alexandria had established the same line of thought, identifying the λόγος as the offspring of Plato's *Demiurge* in the *Timaeus.*" See Herman, *Cave*, 151; Alexander Kohanski, *The Greek Mode of Thought in Western Philosophy* (Rutherford, NJ: Fairleigh Dickinson University Press, 1984), 92; John Dillon, *The Middle Platonists: A Study of Platonism 80 BC to AD 220* (London: Gerald Duckworth, 1977).

patriarchal descent like Matthew does, John links the λόγος to the beginning of time and creation, assuming a crucial link between the λόγος and God himself. The λόγος has thus come into the world to correct what has gone wrong and reestablish the proper and truthful way of thinking and conducting oneself in the world (18:37).

5.2 The "I AM" Statements

There are six "I AM" statements in John's Gospel and each pertains to how Jesus (the λόγος) reveals his identity through an interpretation of Old Testament Scripture. This is a different approach from Thomas's recognition, as we will see, because Jesus's true identity remains concealed throughout his presentation. This means that Jesus continues to occupy the cognitive position of *Secret* though he intends his audience to understand that Scripture is properly interpreted *in light of* himself.

The purpose of each "I AM" statement is to create a mode of thinking within the audience which reflects a metaphorical pattern of dying, coping, and resurrection. The first function serves to equate Jesus (λόγος) with God by alluding directly to God's self-description found in Exod 3:14 thereby granting a high level of authority to Jesus's words. The second function is to provide a new pattern of interpretation for Scripture, one that reflects the nature of Jesus's life and ministry. The third function is to illustrate a metaphorical process by which someone dies to an old way of thinking, exists in a state of uncertainty, and is then resurrected into a new way of thinking. This metaphorical pattern is based on the idea that God created order (λόγος) from chaos in Genesis and, as the λόγος, Jesus is inviting his listeners to partake in the sacred imitation of moving from death into life—from uncertainty into certainty—as he himself does through his death and resurrection. In what follows, I will describe the context of each of the statements as it pertains to the Old Testament and then connect each of these to the proposed methodology above.

The first "I AM" statement is found in John 6:35 in which Jesus declares that he is the Bread of Life. This alludes to Exodus 16 in which God speaks to Moses and offers the Israelites bread from heaven for sustenance on their 40-year sojourn through the wilderness to the Promised Land. The Israelites had just escaped from Egypt and were concerned that they may have made the incorrect choice by abandoning a certain level of comfort and following Moses into the wilderness, a place where they may ultimately die (v. 3). The wilderness often represents a place of disorder or chaos, a kind of hell, while the Promised Land represents unlimited potential, which relates to a person's psychological state of uncertainty and inner turmoil juxtaposed with hope. The purpose of the story in Exodus 16 is to showcase how God provides hope to a person in the midst of their chaotic position, be it psychologically or physically. In other words, God's purpose is to provide the means by which one moves from uncertainty into certainty or from death into life, so to speak.

The Bread of Life statement functions the same way. The Israelites approach Jesus and ask him to reveal the proper way to live (John 6:28), a question that reveals some perceived discrepancy in how they were conducting themselves, and they are interested in hearing what Jesus will suggest. At this point, Jesus points out their lack of recognition of his true character as the eternal λόγος (vv. 36, 42) and explains how eating his kind of bread will lead to eternal life (vv. 38–40). This confuses his listeners because they are unable to recognize who Jesus really is and his function as the λόγος.

Such is the purpose of the first "I AM" statement. Jesus is teaching that a person is able to move from uncertainty to certainty—from death to life—by recognizing who he is and what he provides. Jesus continues the metaphor by insisting that his followers "eat of his flesh and drink his blood" (vv. 53–58). This may be an allusion to the institution of the Eucharist, but it may also be an insistence that one must continually partake in the sacred imitation of death and resurrection that occurs when a person dies, exists in uncertainty, and is resurrected into a new pattern of thinking.

In the second "I AM" statement, Jesus refers to himself as the "light of the world" (8:12). This statement can perhaps be most closely associated with the Feast of Tabernacles, during which water and light were used as symbols commemorating water from the rock and the pillar of fire that guided the Israelites through the wilderness.[13] Light is also a trope that was used in a variety of other contexts. For example, light is one of the first creations (Gen 1:3); it is a guide (Exod 13:21–22; Ps 78:14); and can even refer to God himself (27:1). Light can even be equated with cognitive illumination (Prov 8:22) and with ethics (Ps 119:105). A number of scholars have even equated this passage to Isaiah 9, in which the Messiah is prophesied to bring light to a people living in darkness (also see Isa 12:46).

This particular "I AM" statement is important because it is found in a broader discussion of who Jesus is (8: 21–29). Those who are listening to Jesus are unable to recognize him for who he is as the λόγος, and Jesus continues to talk as one who has always existed, even before Abraham (v. 58). This raises a number of concerns among his listeners, but it creates a segue for the "I AM" statement. Again, this statement reflects a pattern of dying to a way of thinking, living in uncertainty, and being resurrected into a new way of thinking, and by suggesting

---

13   B.E. Simmons, "A Christology of the 'I am' Sayings in the Gospel of John," *Theological Educator* 38 (1988): 97.

that he can provide a means by which a person no longer walks in darkness, Jesus is saying that he can provide a level of consciousness that a person could not otherwise achieve without the help of the λόγος. This statement fits with the act of creation itself. I argue here not only that the act of creation in Genesis stands for the creation of the physical universe and its properties, but that it also stands for the creation of human consciousness. Such an act of creation moves a person from ignorance into knowledge. Jesus is talking about the same thing in John, but also that moving from ignorance into knowledge—from darkness to light—requires that one recognize Jesus as the λόγος.

The statements "I am the gate" (10:7) and "I am the good shepherd" (10:8) allude to an archetypal image of a deity keeping watch over his people (Isa 63:11; Jer 31:10). In addition, the Patriarchs (Gen 47:3; 4:2); Moses (Ps 77:21); and David (2 Sam 5:2; Ps 78:70–71) were all considered to be as shepherds to the people of Israel. In this instance, Jesus is continuing with these archetypes by stating that his teaching is the only way that one can learn the truth thereby achieving eternal life (v. 9). In addition, Jesus juxtaposes his teaching with others, presumably the Pharisees, who are unable to teach the truth. If we consider these things in respect to the death, uncertainty, resurrection process mentioned above, Jesus is stating that it is only through his teaching that one is able to achieve the resurrection portion of the process. To listen to the Pharisees, for example, is to continue in uncertainty and engage in false interpretation of Scripture. Jesus buttresses his position by pointing out that his eventual death and resurrection are the proofs needed to justify his ability to tell the truth, but also verify the three-point process mentioned here.

However, as with each of the "I AM" statements listed so far, there is a level of confusion as to what Jesus could mean because his audience is unable to recognize Jesus as the λόγος. Some of his listeners go so far as to suggest that he is demon possessed because of his claims, especially with regard to his resurrection.

The statements "I am the resurrection and the life" (John 11:25) and "I am the way the truth and the life" (14:6) appear within the story of Lazarus's resurrection and during the Last Supper discourse, respectively. As for the resurrection statement, it is clear that Mary subscribes to a belief that a resurrection will occur (v. 24), but she is unable to recognize Jesus as the λόγος or as the one who granted life to his creation in the beginning. Jesus corrects Mary with the "I AM" statement here, assuring her that *he* is the resurrection and the life. Jesus then proceeds to raise the physical body of Lazarus from the dead after which he expounds on how belief in him will produce eternal life even though a person may die (v. 25). This certainly points to the promise of a resurrection that will occur for those who believe in *who* Jesus is, but it also points to the three-stage process discussed above. The way and truth statement adds a similar sentiment, stating that Jesus as the λόγος is the only method by which someone can be resurrected, either physically or cognitively.

The death of Lazarus must then be understood on two levels. The first level is as a physical resurrection. The second level is as a metaphorical representation of how a person dies to a particular way of thinking, lives in uncertainty, and is then to be resurrected into a new way of thinking. Lazarus then represents the first level of interpretation here, while Mary represents the second. She believes that some form of resurrection will occur, but she does not understand why Jesus would let her brother die. This level of uncertainty is then changed when she sees how Jesus, as the λόγος, is able to resurrect the dead. We are then told that several people who came to see Mary began to recognize who Jesus was and understand his character properly (v. 45) while certain others reported to the Pharisees what had happened, a sequence that begins to push Jesus towards his ultimate death. Herein lies the irony of the Gospel: as Jesus is properly recognized as the eternal λόγος, it brings about his ultimate death.

The final "I AM" statement, "I am the true vine" (John 15:1), alludes to a large number of Old Testament passages in which Israel is referred to as a vine that is planted and tended by God (Hos 10:1–2; Isa 5:1–7; Jer 2:21; 12:10–11; Ezek 15:1–5; 17:1–6; 19:10–14; Ps 80:8–18). The statement appears within a discourse that appears rather suddenly after the Last Supper discourse, so it is difficult to discern the context of the discussion. However, this final "I AM" statement fits well within the proposed method here, perhaps being the most notable.

Jesus begins his discussion by pointing out that branches that do not produce good fruit will be discarded while those that do will be pruned in order to produce even more (15:2). The question of what "good fruit" means is answered in v. 7: if a person is able to do what Jesus says, that person will produce the metaphorical fruit. Given that Jesus is the λόγος, it is fair to suggest that Jesus is asking his listeners to align themselves with his proposed way of thinking. What is more, Jesus will be asking his disciples to suffer in the ways that he suffers if they follow his way of thinking (vv. 18–25). Since this is so, it follows that Jesus is asking his disciples to follow the pattern of cognitive death and resurrection that his teaching embodies and that his ministry will eventually produce. If one is able to continually follow this pattern, that person will produce fruit that will last (v. 16). Alternatively, if one does not follow this pattern, that person will presumably be discarded (v. 6). This could be referring to a state of punishment that God will carry out if things are not being done properly. It could also refer to a person whose mind has gone stagnant, so to speak. This person is not growing and changing like a flourishing vine, but is instead stuck in a state of perpetual uncertainty, or chaos, as described above. Jesus could be combining the concept of hell with a continued state of chaos since he describes it like being subjected to burning.

The "I AM" statements are an integral part of how Jesus reveals his true character as the λόγος. Some of the statements bring about a great level of uncertainty, while certain others are accepted and understood. This is best understood as a pattern of dying to a way of thinking, living in uncertainty, and then being resurrected to a new way of thinking. As mentioned, this pattern embodies the earthly ministry of Jesus as he approaches the Passion narrative, but it also embodies the process by which the λόγος begins to change the perspectives or mindsets of those who choose to listen which leads to life. Alternatively, symbolic death comes to those who do not follow the process laid out by the λόγος. This is illustrated most clearly by the Pharisees who only grow angrier with Jesus as they remain in a state of uncertainty or chaos, a position that leads to murder and death rather than life and love as communicated by the vine statement.

5.3 Thomas's Recognition of Jesus

Thomas's recognition of Jesus (20:24–29) is an important feature of our discussion since it represents an occasion on which one of Jesus's disciples recognizes the true character of Jesus.[14] Referring to our proposed method, this recognition scene moves Jesus from *Secret* to *Truth*. In what follows, the recognition scene will be discussed in reference to other recognition scenes that occur by way of a token: a person is able to recognize another by a visible and characteristic token that is unmistakable.[15]

Recognition by token is common within tragedy, and the prototypical recognition scene by way of token appears in the *Odyssey*. After twenty years away from his wife Penelope and his son Telemachus, Odysseus returns only to find his home occupied by suitors keen on marrying Penelope and obtaining Odysseus's property. For twenty years these suitors have ravaged the land waiting for Penelope to accept the death of her husband and choose one from amongst them to be her new husband. Odysseus appears again, but inconspicuously as a beggar. After revealing himself to Telemachus and making a plan to murder the suitors and reclaim his kingdom, Odysseus finds himself, still

---

14   Larsen notes that this recognition scene is the "climax" of recognition and is "as far as full recognition is possible within the story-world" (Kasper Bro Larsen, *Recognizing the Stranger: Recognition Scenes in the Gospel of John* [Leiden: Brill, 2008], 186). Larsen also notes a "Seeing, Telling, Hearing" formula that accompanies recognition (*Recognizing*, 187–92).

15   The scar is a token-motif of recognition as explained by Aristotle. See *Poetics* 1454b 23–24.

in disguise, in the presence of his wife and old nurse Eurycleia. As Eurycleia provides a customary bath for the stranger, she notices a scar on his thigh that reminds her of her old master Odysseus. After remembering how Odysseus received the scar during a boar hunt, she finally recognizes that the stranger is, in fact, her master:

> That scar—as the old nurse cradled his leg and her hands passed down she felt it, knew it, suddenly let his footfall—down it dropped in the basin—the bronze clanged, tipping over, spilling water across the floor. Joy and torment gripped her heart at once, tears rushed to her eyes—voice choked in her throat she reached for Odysseus' chin and whispered quickly, "Yes, yes! You are Odysseus—oh dear boy—I could not know (ἔγνων) you before ... not till I touched the body of my king!
> *Od.* 19.528–538

Much like Odysseus, John's prologue makes it clear that the λόγος is concealed within a mortal body and that its true identity is unrecognizable as such. We have observed that deities sometimes conceal themselves in this way, especially in tragedy, in order to convey a level of irony throughout the narrative. John's narrative contains a large number of dialogues during which Jesus conveys his true character—as in the "I AM" statements discussed above—but he does so by remaining concealed in his earthly disguise, so to speak. When we come to Thomas's recognition, Jesus has been crucified and resurrected and has shed his mortal body taking on the characteristics of a non-mortal body: one that can appear and disappear much like the gods of myth.[16]

John's Gospel, like the *Odyssey*, contains within it a series of events that lead to Thomas's ultimate recognition. This progression can be understood as a means of elevating the dramatic tension while maintaining the *Secrecy* of concealment. For example, Mary Magdalene is unable to recognize Jesus when she encounters him despite having spent a considerable amount of time with him (20:14). In addition, several others were unable to recognize Jesus after his resurrection (20:20; 20:27–28) despite their familiarity with him. This tells us that Jesus's mortal body has changed in some respect, further alluding to the idea that he has shifted to a non-mortal body. Even with the doors shut and locked,

---

16 It is not uncommon for a god to appear or disappear, remain concealed or disclose themselves at will to mortals. In Acts 14, Paul and Barnabas are mistaken for gods who have come down from heaven (Acts 14:11–12). Another example includes Athena who remains invisible to Telemachus while appearing to Odysseus. See *Od.* 16.182; Jean-Pierre Vernant, "Mortals and Immortals: The Body of the Divine," in *Mortals and Immortals: Collected Essays* (Princeton, NJ: Princeton University Press, 1991), 27–49.

Jesus appears amongst his disciples (20:26). At this point, the disguise of flesh has been completely removed due to its death, and the λόγος is revealed for what it really is: an immortal being. Referring once again to our methodology, the disciples have moved from the cognitive position of *Secret* to that of *True* after their encounters in chapter 20.[17] This means that the disciples are now on the same level of recognition as the reader, and the narrative must end.[18]

6 Conclusion

The purpose of this chapter has been to illustrate the ways in which recognition functions at several levels within the Gospel of John and to argue that John's Gospel is to be read as a form of ancient tragedy. The proposed methodology, as introduced in Greimas and Courtes, lays the foundation for how recognition scenes work in literature. This chapter has extended this method to the Gospel of John and shown how recognition scenes function within the Gospel. From there, it was shown how recognition functions within the "I AM" statements and Thomas's recognition of the resurrected Jesus.

The key component to understanding recognition in John's Gospel is through the information presented in the prologue. In it, Jesus is introduced as the λόγος, the instrument by which the entire world was created. In addition, we are told that the λόγος came into the world and that his own creation did not recognize him. It was observed that this kind of introduction is similar to that of Dionysus in the *Bacchae* who introduces himself to the audience as a god but then conceals himself as a beggar. Likewise, Jesus appears as a

---

[17] Lincoln notes that all of the earliest manuscripts contain chapter 21 and that it should not be seen as interpolated material (Lincoln, *Gospel*, 508). Larsen disagrees and suggests that chapter 21 was added as a secondary postscript to the original ending at 20:31 (Larsen, *Recognizing*, 211). Though Lincoln admits that the recognition content of chapter 21 does not necessarily match chapter 20, he maintains its authenticity and suggests that it may reflect specific issues that arose at a late stage of the Gospel's composition (509). Bultmann insists on the ending of the Gospel at 20:31, also bringing the Gospel full-circle with respect to the prologue (see Bultmann, *John*, 697–99). Whitacre suggests that the content of chapter 21 may have been intended as a conclusion, not an epilogue. His logic is that John frequently summarizes his material (12:36–37; 1 John 5:13; Rev 22:5), making chapter 21 a possible summary conclusion (see Rodney A. Whitacre, *John* (Downers Grove, IL: IVP, 2010) 489). Raymond Brown suggests that chapter 21 serves as an epilogue, dealing with matters left unresolved by the original Gospel (see Brown, *Introduction*, 310).

[18] According to Larsen: "[It is the] moment where the cognitive level of a character from the story-world finally reaches the level of knowledge presented to the reader in the prologue." See *Recognizing*, 208.

lowly person from Nazareth. From there, both attempt to correct the behaviors and thinking of their people, but, because their people are unable to recognize them, dramatic irony increases.

As the narrative progresses, Jesus begins to reveal his true character as the λόγος through a number of dialogues. These function as a way for Jesus to be recognized, but few do recognize Jesus because they do not have the same level of recognition as that of the reader. Recognition in the "I AM" statements functions differently from that of Thomas. In the "I AM" statements, Jesus begins to reveal who he is through dialogue while keeping his true identity concealed. This creates a level of dramatic irony because the reader is more aware of Jesus's true identity as the λόγος than those within the narrative. Thomas's recognition moves the characters within the narrative to the same level as that of the reader thereby ending the concealment completely and thus ending the narrative.

CHAPTER 11

The Effusion of Blood and Water for Purity and Sanctity: Jesus's Body, the Passover Lamb, and the Red Heifer in Johannine Temple Christology

Tat Yu Lam

The incident of the piercing of Jesus's side following with the effusion of blood and water (John 19:34) is distinctive and remarkable in the Johannine Passion narrative. Additionally, the description is specified as a true testimony given by an eye-witness so that people may believe (John 19:35). This enunciates its theological significance. In the past, scholars have attempted to unfold the meaning of this text. Complex and diverse interpretations of the blood and water have resulted, which may be summarized into three main categories: (1) a symbolic reference to sacraments,[1] (2) the account of a natural event,[2] and (3) symbolical of other soteriological concepts.[3] Although the sacramental

---

1   The sacramental interpretations view the reference of blood and water as natural and spiritual life which underlie the meaning of eucharist and baptism. B.F. Westcott, *The Gospel According to St. John: The Greek Text with Introduction and Notes* (Grand Rapids: Eerdmans, 1954), 279–86; Rudolf Karl Bultmann, *The Gospel of John* (Philadelphia: Westminster, 1971), 677–78; Edwyn Clement Hoskyns, *The Fourth Gospel* (London: Faber and Faber, 1947), 532–36; C.K. Barrett, *The Gospel According to St. John*, 2nd ed. (Philadelphia: Westminster, 1978), 556–57; R.H. Lightfoot, *St John's Gospel: A Commentary* (Oxford: Clarendon, 1983), 319–20; Raymond Edward Brown, *The Gospel According to John*, AB 29–29A (Garden City: Doubleday, 1966–1970), 948–52; J.N. Sanders and B.A. Mastin, *The Gospel According to St. John* (Peabody: Hendrickson, 1968), 411–12; Peter F. Ellis, *The Genius of John: A Composition-Critical Commentary on the Fourth Gospel* (Collegeville, MN: Liturgical, 1984), 275–76; Ernst Haenchen, *John 2: A Commentary on the Gospel of John 7–21*, trans. Robert W. Funk (Philadelphia: Fortress, 1984), 195; Thomas L. Brodie, *The Gospel According to John: A Literary and Theological Commentary* (New York: Oxford University Press, 1993), 552–53; Francis J. Moloney, *Glory Not Dishonor* (Minneapolis: Fortress, 1998), 148–49; Dwight Moody Smith, *John* (Nashville: Abingdon, 1999), 363–64.
2   This view emphasizes the event as the evidence of Jesus's humanity or merely a fact not a miracle. See J.H. Bernard, *The Gospel According to St. John* (Edinburgh: T&T Clark, 1928), 2:647–48; D.A. Carson, *The Gospel According to John* (Grand Rapids: Eerdmans, 1991), 623; Smith, *John*, 363–64; H.N. Ridderbos, *The Gospel According to John* (Grand Rapids: Eerdmans, 1997), 619.
3   Some scholars propose several possible interpretations. Some share similar views on blood or water but seldom agree with each other on both. For the symbolic meaning of blood related to the Lamb of God, see Hoskyns, *The Fourth Gospel*, 532–36; Ellis, *The Genius of John*, 275–76; Urban C. von Wahlde, *The Gospel and Letters of John*, vol. 2 (Grand Rapids: Eerdmans,

interpretations have long been accepted based on assumptions such as the presence of redaction and associations from an ecclesiastical background, arguments for them lack internal evidence.[4] Even though some scholars view the flowing of blood and water as a natural event, most of them hold a secondary symbolical interpretation.[5] Isolated passages from the Gospel such as John 1:29 and 6:53–56 are used to shed light on the interpretations of blood, and John 7:37–39 (cf. John 1:31, 33; 2:6; 3:5; 4:14; 5:2; 9:7; 13:5) on the interpretation of water. Other passages are adduced outside the Gospel including 1 John 5:6–8, Exod 7:15–21, and Exodus 17.[6] One of the difficulties of narrowing down the symbolic meaning of the effusion of blood and water is their seemingly separate and independent development in the Gospel before they appear together in John 19:34.[7] Any attempt to handle these variously arrayed occurrences of blood and water by induction will produce an ambiguous interpretation. An alternative method is to scrutinize the symbolic meaning through three interrelated contexts that to some extent manifest Johannine Temple Christology.[8]

2010), 817–20; and Passover Lamb, see Barrett, *The Gospel According to St. John*, 556–57; R. Alan Culpepper, *Anatomy of the Fourth Gospel: A Study in Literary Design* (Philadelphia: Fortress, 1983), 237; Craig S. Keener, *The Gospel of John* (Peabody: Hendrickson, 2003), 2:1152–54; Andreas J. Köstenberger, *John* (Grand Rapids: Baker Academic, 2004), 552–53. The interpretation of water is associated with purification, life, and spirit. Others view blood as death and water as spirit; see C.H. Dodd, *The Interpretation of the Fourth Gospel* (Cambridge: Cambridge University Press, 1953), 438–39; Rudolf Schnackenburg, *The Gospel According to St. John* (New York: Crossroad, 1982), 3:289–94; G.R. Beasley-Murray, *John*, WBC (Dallas: Word, 1987), 355–58; Brodie, *The Gospel According to John*, 552–53; J. Ramsey Michaels, *The Gospel of John* (Grand Rapids: Eerdmans, 2010), 969.

4 Malatesta lists 14 different interpretations of the blood and water in John 19.34. Although he admits that the citations of the Scriptures are the key to interpreting this symbolism, he emphasizes the ecclesiastical background of this text. A detailed table of patristic citations on the symbolism of John 19:34 is offered at the end. Edward Malatesta, "Blood and Water from the Pierced Side of Christ (Jn 19:34)," in *Segni E Sacramenti Nel Vangelo Di Giovanni*, Studia Anselmiana 66 (Rome: Editrice Anselmiana, 1977), 166–81.

5 Except for Ridderbos. Ridderbos, *John*, 619–20.

6 See Köstenberger, *John*, 552–53; Keener, *John*, 2:1152–54; von Wahlde, *The Gospel and Letters of John*, 2:817–20.

7 With one exception (John 19:34), "blood," αἷμα, occurs totally six times distributed in chs. 1, 6, 19 (John 1:13; 6:53, 54, 55, 56; 19:34) and "water," ὕδωρ, occurs 21 times mainly within chs. 1 to 13 (John 1:26, 31, 33; 2:7, 9×2; 3:5, 23; 4:7, 10, 11, 13, 14 3×, 15, 46; 5:7; 7:38; 13:5). In his published dissertation in 2012, Carnazzo studies blood and water in John 19:34 by induction using a narrative-critical method and the assumption of sacraments of Eucharist and baptism. Sebastian A. Carnazzo, *Seeing Blood and Water: A Narrative-Critical Study of John 19:34* (Eugene, OR: Wipf and Stock, 2012), 82–87.

8 The significance of the temple theme in John's Gospel has been recognized by commentators and scholars such as Hoskyns, Brown, and Koester, to name a few. Monographs on this topic

The first is the thematic context of the temple where Jesus's body, the source of the blood and water, is claimed as the New Temple (John 2:21). The second is the double OT fulfillment quotations in the immediate co-text regarding "not a bone of his will be broken" and the "pierced one" (John 19:36–37; cf. Exod 12:46; Num 9:12; Psalm 34:20; Zech 12:10; 13:1). The third is the literary relationship between the "two" first signs—the juxtaposed first sign of changing water into wine at Cana and the temple cleansing in Jerusalem—and the climax of *the* sign, Jesus's crucifixion, in the Passion narrative (John 2:1–25 and 19:23–37).

1 Jesus as the New Temple and the Uses of the Blood and Water in God's Dwellings

The term "body," σῶμα, occurs six times in John and all denote Jesus's body. The first use appears in the pericope of the Temple Cleansing during the first Passover, where Jesus's body refers to a New Temple at the beginning of his ministry (John 2:21). The other uses point to his crucified, dead, and buried body at the end, the last Passover (John 19:31, 38×2, 40 and 20:12). Jesus's body seems to cohere with the Passover to frame his ministry as a New Temple.

In the prologue, Jesus, the *Logos*, is portrayed as the "enfleshed Tabernacle" (John 1:14).[9] In John 2, Jesus's body is the New Temple (2:21). In John 4, new worship is in truth and spirit through Jesus which is beyond Jerusalem and Samaria (John 4:21–24). In John 5–12, Jesus takes up the roles of the feasts as the New Temple. On the one hand, as W.D. Davies observes, Jesus seems "disengaged" during the Feast of Dedication. In saying so, Jesus was fully engaged in the pericope of Temple Cleansing (John 2:12–22) in the first Passover but attending the Feast of Tabernacles in the middle of it (John 7:14) and, standing in the portico of Solomon which is actually outside the temple proper in the Feast of Dedication (John 10:23). But Jesus gradually departs because of the heightening of the conflicts with the Jews.[10] On the other hand, Jesus takes over the role of the feasts. He is portrayed as greater than the Sabbath (John 5:9, 9:14, 19:31)

---

include, Mary L. Coloe, *God Dwells with Us: Temple Symbolism in the Fourth Gospel* (Collegeville, MN: Liturgical, 2001); Alan Kerr, *The Temple of Jesus's Body: The Temple Theme in the Gospel of John* (JSNTSup 220; London: Sheffield Academic, 2002); Paul M. Hoskins, *Jesus as the Fulfillment of the Temple in the Gospel of John* (Milton Keynes: Paternoster, 2006); Stephen Um, *The Theme of Temple Christology in John's Gospel* (London: T&T Clark, 2006).

9   Hoskins, *Jesus the Fulfillment*, 124.
10 W.D. Davies, *The Gospel and the Land: Early Christianity and Jewish Territorial Doctrine* (Berkeley: University of California Press, 1974), 289–92.

through the redemptive work of God on Sabbath (John 5:17; cf. 7:22–24); greater than the Feast of Tabernacles by being the light and source of living water in the Tabernacle (John 7:1–8:59); greater than the Feast of Dedication (ἐγκαίνια, John 10:22–39) through consecration to replace the Temple and the sacrifice (cf. John 17:19);[11] and greater than the Passover by becoming the Passover lamb (John 1:29; 2:13; 6:4; 13:1; 19:36; cf. 11:55; 19:14, 31).[12] In John 13–21, Jesus purifies and sanctifies his disciples through the examples of foot-washing (John 13), vine pruning (John 15), and his prayer to God (John 17:17, 19×2; cf. John 10:36). In fact, it shows the mutual indwelling, the union, between the presence of the Father and his children through Jesus, the New Temple.

The uses of blood and water in God's dwellings seem closely related to purification and sanctification because of the presence of God. Particularly, the roles of the blood of the Passover lamb and the water of the red heifer ashes are fundamental to establishing a relationship with God. The first Passover was observed in Egypt. Although "blood" in Exodus represented a *sign* (σημεῖον, LXX) of God's judgment to the Egyptians when the water of the Nile is changed to blood (Exod 4:9; 7:17–18, LXX), it also represents a *sign* for the judgment of God to "pass-over," to set apart the Israelites from the Egyptians (Exod 12:13; cf. Exod 12:1–36). The smeared sign of the blood of a Passover lamb marks the deliverance of the Israelites as well as a new era as God prescribes the month for observation of the Passover as the first month of the year (Exod 12:1–2). After the Israelites have been delivered from Egypt, blood was used to ratify the covenant for them to become the holy nation of God (Exod 19, 24).

God's presence among his people is manifest by his abode, the Tabernacle. Its "tripartite division" reflects the restrictiveness of purity. Thus, the blood of sacrifices is used to purify and sanctify the priests, the Levites, the Israelites, and the altar (Exod 29:10–21, 35–37; Lev 1–7; 8:14–30; 16:1–28; Num 8:8–13). Furthermore, a close connection between the Passover and the Tabernacle is established as the celebration and commemoration of Passover is then tied to one place, a dwelling for the name of God (Deut 16:1–8). It signifies that Israel, the whole family of God, celebrates Passover together in God's house as a union.[13] Since observing the Passover is obligated (Num 9:13), those who are defiled by a dead body are granted a second chance on the same day of the second month (Num 9:6–12).

---

11 Hoskins, *Jesus the Fulfillment*, 173–74; Bauckham, "The Holiness," 106 and J. McCaffrey, *The House with Many Rooms* (Rome: Gregorian, 1988), 234.

12 For more detail on Jesus replacing the feasts, see G.A. Yee, *Jewish Feasts and the Gospel of John* (Wilmington, DE: Michael Glazier, 1989).

13 Peter C. Craigie, *The Book of Deuteronomy* (Grand Rapids: Eerdmans, 1976), 242.

A close connection between Passover and the temple cleansing is reflected in Hezekiah's reformation (2 Chr 29–30). It is notable that Hezekiah's zeal of purifying the temple resonates with Jesus's zeal.[14] The cleansing process started with the consecration of the priests and Levites so that they could enter to cleanse the temple (2 Kgs 16:10–18). After rededicating the temple, Hezekiah reunified Israel to celebrate the Second Passover so that the priests, Levites, and Israelites had enough time to consecrate themselves (ἁγνίζω, 2 Chr 30:1–4). Differing from the instruction of Passover prescribed in Exodus, where Paschal blood is smeared on the door frame, Paschal blood is passed by the Levites and tossed by the priests in Hezekiah's time (2 Chr 30:16, cf. 35:11).[15] Thus, Hezekiah did not only cleanse God's house but also God's household by reuniting the Israelites to consecrate themselves and celebrate the Passover. Even in the dedication of the Second Temple, Passover was celebrated with the concern of communal purity of the Jews (Ezra 6:19–22). Since the exiles had lost their religious practice while living abroad, when they returned to Jerusalem without a king, the hierarchy of the temple and the ceremonial purity became their identity.[16]

Similarly, the uses of water are part of the purification process in preparation for the indwelling of God among his people. Whereas the Paschal blood was a sign for the judgment of God to "pass-over" among his people in Egypt, the water of the Red Sea was the judgment of God to "wash" away the Egyptians (Exod 14:27–28). After the setting up of the Tabernacle "water" is used to purify the priests, Levites, and Israelites (Exod 19:10–11, 15) through washing and bathing, and is used to cleanse the offering. However, the purification water of red heifer ashes (Num 19) is outstanding, as it is used to purify the Levites in their installation (Num 8:7),[17] and to cleanse corpse impurity in general and before observing Passover in particular (Num 9:6–7).

---

14   Raymond B. Dillard, *2 Chronicles*, WBC (Dallas: Word, 1987), 237.
15   Sarah Japhet, *The Ideology of the Book of Chronicles and Its Place in Biblical Thought* (Winona Lake, IN: Eisenbrauns, 2009), 188–89. Whereas the blood is specified to be tossed by the priests, its recipient is omitted. Some English translations supply the recipient as an "altar" (e.g. CEV and NLT). Regarding the practice of tossing the Paschal blood, see Jacob Neusner, *The Comparative Hermeneutics of Rabbinic Judaism: Introduction and the Hermeneutics of Berakhot and Seder Mo'ed* (Binghamton: Global, 2000), 1:272.
16   Knute Larson and Kathy Dahlen, *Holman Old Testament Commentary-Ezra, Nehemiah, Esther*, ed. Max Anders (Nashville: B&H, 2005), 71.
17   Milgrom contends that this purification water refers to the water of red heifer ashes, but Levine disagrees. See Jacob Milgrom, *Numbers. The JPS Torah Commentary: The Traditional Hebrew Text with the New JPS Translation* (Philadelphia: Jewish Publication Society, 1990), 61, 159; Baruch A. Levine, *Numbers 1–20: A New Translation with Introduction and Commentary*, AB (New York: Doubleday, 1993), 274–75, 463–64.

The red heifer ritual is unique in several ways among all animal sacrifices, and its impact is long lasting. First, a "red cow" is chosen; it may symbolize "life in blood."[18] Second, the whole cow, including hide, flesh, blood, and dung is burnt with cedar wood, hyssop, and scarlet thread outside the camp (Num 19:5–6). Third, whoever participates in preparing the ashes is defiled, but after living water is added to the ashes, it purifies the most contagious impurity, the impurity of the death (Num 9:7–10; 19:1–22). Milgrom uses the rabbinic apothegm to capture this paradox: "They purify the defiled and defile the pure."[19] The ritual of the red heifer is prescribed as a permanent ordinance (Num 19:10), and its practice is described in the Jewish tractate of Parah (Cow) in Mishnah and its supplementary literature Tosefta. Further, its influence has not ceased. Nowadays, the Temple Institute in Jerusalem is still searching for a qualified red heifer to reinstall this ritual so that the Jews can be ceremonially purified to enter the Temple Mount.[20]

Although the uses of blood and water are crucial for purity and sanctity in God's dwellings, including the eschatological temple in Ezekiel (Ezek 40–48) and Zechariah (Zech 1:16; 2:10; 3:7; 6:12–15; 8:9; 10:6; 12:7; 14:20–21),[21] does this accord with the focus of John's Gospel?

Apparently, the themes of purity and holiness do not stand out in John. J.R. Michaels points out that the word καθαρισμός (purification) occurs only twice in the Gospel (John 2:6, 3:25).[22] And Bauckham argues that this Gospel does not seem to focus on the theme of "holy church" as the word ἅγιος (holy) only occurs four times to describe the Father (John 17:11), Jesus (John 6:69), and the Spirit (John 14:26; 20:22) and the word ἐκκλησία (church) is not mentioned at all. However, if the contexts of the verb ἁγιάζω (to make holy), which occurs

---

18   Milgrom points out that according to the priestly code, a female sacrifice is chosen representing an individual for purification of sin (חטאת, Lev 4:22–35; Num 15:27–29). Furthermore, the size of a cow could produce a maximum amount of ashes. Milgrom, *Numbers*, 439–40.

19   Milgrom, *Numbers*, 438.

20   Inbari Motti, "Messianic Religious Zionism and the Reintroduction of Sacrifice: The Case of the Temple Institute," in *Rethinking the Messianic Idea in Judaism*, ed. Michael L. Morgan and Steven Weitzman (Bloomington: Indiana University Press, 2014), 256–57; S. Sizer, "The Temple in Contemporary Christian Zionism," in *Heaven on Earth*, ed. Desmond T. Alexander and Simon J. Gathercole (Milton Keynes: Paternoster, 2004), 259.

21   Whereas Ezekiel's eschatological temple is more concrete (Ezek 40–48), Zechariah's seems diffuse (Zech 2:4–5). David L. Petersen, "Zechariah's Visions: A Theological Perspective," *VT* 34 (1984): 195–206.

22   J.R. Michaels, "By Water and Blood: Sin and Purification in John and First John," in *Dimensions of Baptism: Biblical and Theological Studies*, ed. S.E. Porter and A.R. Cross, JSNTSup 234 (Sheffield: Sheffield Academic, 2002), 150.

four times (John 10:36; 17:17, 19×2) are scrutinized, the result would show that the holiness of disciples indeed is significant and is closely connected to the holiness of Jesus.[23] Further, John uses ἁγνίζω (purify) to enrich the color of purity and holiness. This verb occurs 34 times in the LXX, seven times in the NT, and only *once* among all the Gospels (John 11:55).[24] Out of 34 times in the LXX, 16 times are used in Hezekiah's reformation (2 Chron 29–31) related to the consecration of the priests and Levites for cleansing the temple, and the Israelites for observing the Second Passover.[25] Since this rendering is also used for describing the purification of contracted corpse impurity by the purification water of the red heifer (Num 19:12; 31:19, 23), the consecration in Hezekiah's reformation probably follows the same practice. Thus, John uses ἁγνίζω (John 11:55) to reveal the significance of purification before the Passover, probably using the purification water of the red heifer in Jewish practice. Together with words like μιαίνω (defile) (John 18:28); ἐγκαίνια (dedication or inauguration) (John 10:22); νίπτω (wash) (John 9:7, 11, 15; 13:5, 6, 8, 10, 12, 14); λούω (bathe) (John 13:10); καθαρός, "clean" in the foot-washing scene (John 13:10×2, 11) and vine pruning scene (John 15:3), the setting of two cleansing pools, κολυμβήθρα (John 5:2 Bethzatha; John 9:7 Siloam), the overtone of purification is constructed in John's Gospel. Thus, it is possible that the effusion of the blood and water in the New Temple is closely related to the purity and sanctity of God's people in John. Whether the blood and water are related to the Passover lamb and red heifer will be discussed below.

2 The Uses of Blood and Water in Light of the Fulfillment of Jesus as the Passover Lamb and the Pierced One in John 19:36–37

The effusion of blood and water is explicitly depicted after Jesus's death when he is pierced by a soldier (John 19:34). It is presented as the solemn truth (John 19:35) and further fulfills the OT Scriptures (John 19:36–37). This link of double formulaic quotations to Jesus's death in the Passion Narrative is unique in John, compared with the Synoptics where OT Scriptures are only implicitly referenced.[26] Further, Porter observes that John's use of the OT formulaic

---

23 Bauckham, "The Holiness," 95.
24 The seven occurrences in NT: John 11:55; Acts 21:24, 26, 24:18; Jas 4:8; 1 Pet 1:22; 1 John 3:3.
25 Exod 19:10; Num 6:3, 8:21, 11:18, 19:12, 31:19, 31:23; Josh 3:5; 1 Sam 21:6; 1 Chr 15:12, 14; 2 Chr 29:5×2, 15, 16, 17×2, 18, 19, 34×2, 30:3, 15, 17×2, 18, 31:18; Isa 66:17; Jer 12:3; 2 Macc 1:33, 12:38; 1 Esd 7:10, 11×2.
26 Matt 27:9–10 regarding the "field of blood" (Jeremiah; more likely from Zech 11:12–13); Mark 15:34 (Ps 22:1); Luke 23:46 (Ps 31:5).

quotations is well structured and developed.²⁷ Thus, the double formulaic OT fulfillment quotations most probably are the key to interpreting the unique event of the "coming out of blood and water" in John's Gospel.

John uses the fulfillment quotation formula ἵνα ἡ γραφὴ πληρωθῇ to introduce the two concluding OT Scriptures that refer to the fact that "Jesus's leg was not broken" (John 19:36) and "he was pierced" (John 19:37). Although the specific way of using different OT quotation formulae between the first (γράφω, John 2:17) and second part (πληρόω, John 12:38) of the Gospel is noticed by scholars, Porter notes the neatness of the inclusio of the double OT quotations in both the beginning of the fulfillment motif (John 12:38–40; cf. Isa 53:1; 6:9) and the climax at the end (John 19:36–37).²⁸ With a total of three direct fulfillment quotations of the OT in ch. 19 (John 19:24, 36, 37, πάλιν), one of them being the fulfillment of the Passover lamb, Porter argues for the great significance of the fulfillment quotations of the OT in John 19:36–37 and states that here we have the convergence of the fulfillment and Passover motifs of the whole Gospel.²⁹ Thus, we now focus on the "Passover Lamb" and "Pierced One."

2.1 The Blood of the Passover Lamb

Admittedly there is no single OT text that is totally matched with the composite quotation, ὀστοῦν οὐ συντριβήσεται αὐτοῦ (John 19:36). The various possible sources for this quotation include Exod 12:46 (v. 10 LXX), Num 9:12, and Ps 34:20 (LXX: 33:21, MT: 34:21). However, according to the linguistics and contextual evidence, Porter contends that the reference to the fulfillment quotation of 19:36 more likely is from Num 9:12.³⁰ Although the Passover motif is prominent in John's Gospel and many scholars agree that Jesus points to the Passover lamb symbolically, not everyone is convinced.³¹ The allusions of Jesus to the Passover lamb, as Porter attests, include John 1:29–36; 2:13–25; 6:1–14, 22–71; 11:47–12:8;

---

27 Stanley E. Porter, "Exodus 12 and the Passover Theme in John," in *Sacred Tradition in the New Testament: Tracing Old Testament Themes in the Gospels and Epistles* (Grand Rapids: Baker Academic, 2016), 147.

28 Stanley E. Porter, "Can Traditional Exegesis Enlighten Literary Analysis of the Fourth Gospel: An Examination of the Old Testament Fulfilment Motif and the Passover Theme," in *The Gospels and the Scriptures of Israel*, ed. Craig A. Evans and Richard Stegner (Sheffield: Sheffield Academic, 1994), 403.

29 Porter, "Can Traditional Exegesis Enlighten Literary Analysis," 418–21; see also Porter, "Exodus 12," 127–51.

30 Porter, "Exodus 12," 149.

31 Ridderbos argues that Jesus's death is not related to Passover. Thus the OT quotation refers to Ps 34:20. Ridderbos, *John*, 617, 622–23.

13:1–17:26 and 19:13–42.³² He adduces four main observations to support the climactic development of the Passover motif in the Passion Narrative regarding the specific day, the hour of Jesus's death, the use of hyssop, and the OT fulfillment, which point to Jesus as the Passover lamb.³³ A subsidiary evidence will be offered concerning the use of προσφέρω (John 19:29) which may point further to the Passover sacrifice.

The mention of hyssop reveals "theological symbolism."³⁴ Whereas the Gospels of Matthew and Mark use "reed," κάλαμος, as a tool and the verb "give drink," ποτίζω (Matt 27:48; Mark 15:36) to describe the action of giving sour wine to Jesus, John uses "hyssop," ὕσσωπος and the verb προσφέρω instead (John 19:29). Freed admits that it would have "theological or symbolic significance" but the meaning is uncertain.³⁵ The word προσφέρω is frequently used in the LXX to render the Hebrew verbs for offering a gift or sacrifice (קרב or עלה, Lev 1:2). It occurs altogether 158 times in the LXX, of which 134 are in the canonical books; of these in turn 100 are in Leviticus and Numbers (Lev: 69; Num: 31), which are the two books representing the law of holiness and sacrifices.³⁶ As "hyssop" is first mentioned in the Passover in Egypt and is also used for ritual cleansing and the purification water of red heifer ashes (Exod 12:22; Lev 14:4, 6, 49, 51, 52; Num 19:6, 18; Ps 50:9; Heb 9:19), by using προσφέρω together with "hyssop," the sacrificial and purification overtone is profound. Possibly, John associates the moment of offering the sour wine to quench Jesus's thirst with the process of sacrifice. This association of Jesus with sacrifice points further to the Passover by another link of προσφέρω to another passage in the Gospel.

In John, προσφέρω appears only twice (John 16:2; 19:29). In John 16:2, λατρείαν προσφέρειν refers to "service to offer." Brown points out that, "the Greek has 'to offer λατρεία to God,' a somewhat redundant expression, for λατρεία by itself means the service of offering worship to the deity."³⁷ Brown is right, as προσφέρειν and τῷ θεῷ seem to be added after δόξῃ λατρείαν. Perhaps, it is done on purpose to form a link. The word λατρεία occurs nine times altogether in the LXX. Five of these nine are in the canonical books, and three of these are in Exodus. All three occurrences in Exodus relate the "service" to the need for the Israelites to observe Passover and the Feast of Unleavened Bread (Exod 12:25,

---

32 Porter, "Traditional Exegesis," 405–21. Besides, Porter adds one more section from 8:31–47 on the basis of Hoskins' claim on the relation between freedom, slavery, and Passover. Porter, "Exodus 12," 140–41.
33 Porter, "Exodus 12," 144–50.
34 Brown, *The Gospel According to John*, 930.
35 Edwin D. Freed, *Old Testament Quotations in the Gospel of John* (Leiden: Brill, 1965), 107.
36 It occurs totally 47 times in NT, of which 20 times are in Hebrews.
37 Brown, *The Gospel According to John*, 691.

26; 13:5). If a link of προσφέρω to λατρεία is intended and λατρεία refers to the service of Passover or Feast of Unleavened Bread, and προσφέρω connects to Jesus, a possible link is formed between Jesus and Passover. Remarkably, λατρείαν προσφέρειν appears in a context where Jesus forewarned his disciples to remember (μνημονεύω; John 16:4) that the one who kills them will think he is offering service (Passover or Feast of Unleavened Bread) to God. However, earlier, Jesus also told his disciples to remember (μνημονεύω) that if people persecute him, they will also persecute them (John 15:20). In other words, Jesus implies that he will be persecuted first by being killed as offering Passover service. This result accords with the previous arguments that the blood of Jesus, which is the Paschal blood, sets apart God's people, so that fellowship between them becomes possible.

2.2   *The Water Related to the Pierced One*

The second fulfillment quotation refers to the Pierced One in Zech 12:10. John uses καὶ πάλιν ἑτέρα γραφὴ λέγει to link the quotation of John 19:37. The context of Zech 12:10 lies within the focus on the house of David (Zech 12:7, 8, 10, 12×2; 13:1) where its glory will be manifested (Zech 12:7), the spirit of grace and supplication will be poured out (Zech 12:10), and a fountain will be opened to cleanse the sin and impurity of David's house (Zech 13:1). Although the blood of the Pierced One is not mentioned,[38] the consequence of his death is immense as it leads to the opening of a fountain to cleanse the sin (חטאת) and impurity (נדה) of the house of David and the people in Jerusalem after their mourning of the Pierced One (Zech 13:1). Some scholars point out that the purification water of this fountain, in fact, refers to the potent purification water of the red heifer ashes, which was prescribed for purifying the Levites and impurity such as skin diseases, discharges, and corpses (Num 8:7; 19:1–31; 31:23; cf. Ezek 36:25).[39] These two words, "sin" and "impurity," appear together again only in Num 19:9 regarding the purification water of red heifer ashes.[40] Conrad's comment about this fountain captures precisely the paradox of the scene that Zech 13:1

---

[38]   In the Hebrew text, the use of the personal pronoun "to me," אלי, specifies the pierced one is God. C.H.H. Wright, *Zechariah and His Prophecies* (Minnesota: Klock & Klock Christian, 1980), 389.

[39]   David L. Petersen, *Zechariah 9–14 and Malachi: A Commentary* (Louisville: Westminster John Knox, 1995), 123; Edgar W. Conrad, *Zechariah* (Sheffield: Sheffield Academic, 1999), 184; Carol L. Meyers and Eric M. Meyers, *Zechariah 9–14: A New Translation with Introduction and Commentary*, AB (Garden City: Doubleday, 1993), 362; Ralph Lee Smith, *Micah-Malachi* (Dallas: Word Books, 1984), 280. For the discussion of the relationship between these two purification waters, see Milgrom, *Numbers*, 61, 159; Levine, *Numbers 1–20*, 274–75, 463–64; R. Dennis Cole, *Numbers* (Nashville: B&H, 2000), 149.

[40]   Mark J. Boda, *The Book of Zechariah* (Grand Rapids: Eerdmans, 2016), 724.

"rounds off the section with one who was slain (Zech 12:10–14) by speaking about the LORD as opening a fountain of waters to cleanse those who have been in contact with a corpse, the one whom they have slain (Zech 12:10)."[41] Jesus's death echoes this scene as well as the paradox of the red heifer ritual as purification water flowing out from Jesus's dead body to purify the defiled.

It is, therefore, quite possible that the OT fulfillment quotations allow us to conclude that the blood and water from Jesus's body may refer to the blood of the Passover Lamb and the purification water of the red heifer ashes. The following discussion will buttress this conclusion further.

3 The Uses of Blood and Water in the Pericopae of the Wedding at Cana and the Temple Cleansing and Their Literary Relationship to the Passion Narrative (John 2:1–25; 19:23–37)

The juxtaposition of the pericopae of the Wedding at Cana and the Temple Cleansing stand out from the Synoptics. Although the pericope of "Temple Cleansing" occurs in all four Gospels,[42] it is placed at the beginning of Jesus ministry in John instead of in the Passion week. Whereas the first miraculous sign (σημεῖον, John 2:11) was manifested in a family festive wedding at Cana, the Temple Cleansing was the first public act performed in the Gospel's first Passover feast in Jerusalem, which points to the sign (σημεῖον, John 2:18) of rebuilding the temple by Jesus's body through his death and resurrection. If these two pericopae are meant to be put side by side to form a unit, the water in the six purification stone jars, in fact, is related to the blood of Jesus, his death, which is implied in Temple Cleansing.[43] This relation will be shown as follows.

Besides the juxtaposition (John 2:1–25) and the link about a sign (John 2:11, 18, σημεῖον), others links are found between the pericopae of the Wedding at Cana and the Temple Cleansing. First is the use of "third, three" (John 2:1 τρίτος; 2:19, 20 τρεῖς). The Wedding at Cana takes place on "the third day" (John 2:1). By counting the sequence of the days from day one (John 1:19), Carson and Morris contend that "the third day" points to day seven.[44] However, John uses "the third day" on purpose. Moloney suggests that "the third day" may refer to the time in Jewish tradition while the Israelites were preparing for the revelation

---

41 Conrad, *Zechariah*, 184.
42 Matt 21: 12; Mark 11: 15; Luke 19:45; John 2:14–15.
43 Koester, *Symbolism*, 83.
44 Carson, *John*, 168; Morris, *John*, 156.

of God at Sinai (Exod 19:16, the Targums, Mekilta).[45] This suggestion may be too far removed from the text. A more plausible one is Keener's suggestion that it may allude to the resurrection of Jesus on the third day. Since Jesus declares that he can rebuild the temple in "three days," and "third" and "three" occur only here in the Gospel, it links the pericopae of the Wedding at Cana and the Temple Cleansing together. Keener affirms: "the sign of John 2:1–11 thus points to the ultimate sign of the resurrection (John 2:18–19), and Jesus's assault on the institution of the temple must be read in the setting aside of the ceremonial pots in John 2:1–11."[46] Second is the overtone of Jesus's death and resurrection through the first occurrence of "my hour" which points to Jesus's death in the pericope of the Wedding at Cana (John 2:4) and "to raise" which points to Jesus's resurrection in the Temple Cleansing (John 2:19). Third, the parallel details of the stone jars for purification (John 2:6) and the sacrificial animals in the temple (John 2:14–16) are both exclusively stated in John, pointing to the rituals, one for water purification and the other for blood sacrifices. Fourth, at the concluding end of the Cana to Cana cycle (John 2:1–4:54), the narrator recapitulates side by side the events of what "Jesus did during the feast in Jerusalem" (John 4:45) and "changing water into wine at Cana" (John 4:46). In light of these close connections, the implication of blood and water in these two pericopae will be discussed below.

3.1 Blood for Restoring Worship in the Temple Cleansing Pericope (John 2:12–25)

The implied reference to blood is shown through the literary structure and the OT quotation in the Temple Cleansing pericope. M. Coloe points out that Jesus's action of cleansing the temple (John 2:14–17) and his speech of rebuilding the temple (John 2:18–22) are separately recorded in the Synoptics,[47] but they are combined and framed with a similar structure to form a unit in John.[48] The section is opened and closed by the marker of the festival of Passover (John 2:13; 2:23). Inside this Passover *inclusio*, the two parts are linked by the same imperative verb form ἄρατε and λύσατε (John 2:16 and 2:19, both aorist active). At the end, both have a clause with the verb μιμνήσκομαι (John 2:17; 2:22).[49] This precise arrangement conjoins Jesus's zeal for restoring pure worship in the house of God (Ps 69:9; Zech 14:21) to his plan of raising up

---

45 Moloney, *John*, 77.
46 Keener, *John*, 1:496–98.
47 Action of temple cleansing: Matt 21:12–13; Mark 11:15–19; Luke 19:45–48; speech of rebuilding the temple: Matt 26:61; Mark 14:58.
48 Coloe, *God Dwells*, 70.
49 Coloe, *God Dwells*, 70.

another temple in three days (John 2:19). This arrangement brings out at least two implications through the OT references.

Firstly, it signals that Jesus is the sacrifice, the Passover lamb. As John 2:17 said, "Zeal for your house will consume me." This OT reference is from Ps 69:9. Although the original tense form of "consume" is in aorist in the LXX, John uses a future tense form to look forward to Jesus's death, as a sacrifice.[50] Furthermore, in the action scene, the details of animals and birds (John 2:14–16) in the temple are absent from the Synoptics but vividly described in John. This highlights the rituals of sacrifices that are prescribed in Leviticus for worshipping God.[51] Hence, by driving away those animals and speaking about rebuilding the temple, it is implied, Jesus would "consume" himself to restore the whole sacrificial worship in the new temple. Since the structural unit is enclosed by Passover and Jesus's first title, the Lamb of God (John 1:29, 36), is developed throughout the Gospel,[52] Porter contends that the focus of this pericope is to institute a new Passover in which Jesus himself is the Passover lamb.[53] The recognition of Jesus as the Passover lamb coheres with the fulfillment quotation of John 19:36 which refers to Jesus as the one without a broken bone (Exod 12:10, 46; Num 9:12). Hence, this theme of the Passover lamb is probably linked and fulfilled in the Passion Narrative.

Secondly, it signifies Jesus's physical cleansing of his Father's house, οἶκος (John 2:16–17) and designates a spiritual cleansing of sacrificial worship and people, which is equivalent to rebuilding the temple (John 2:19–21). This claim can be demonstrated through the dual reference to "house," οἶκος, and the context of the OT references. First, the word οἶκος or בית can refer to both "household" and "house." One of the examples is in Nathan's prophecy. When King David desires to build a house for the LORD (2 Sam 7:5), the LORD promises to build the household of David (2 Sam 7:11). When Jesus uses οἶκος in John 2:16–17 he possibly has both in mind. Further, when Jesus prohibits those dove sellers from making his Father's house a house of merchandizing, μὴ ποιεῖτε τὸν οἶκον τοῦ πατρός μου οἶκον ἐμπορίου (John 2:16), he rebukes both the dove sellers

---

50 Bultmann, *The Gospel of John*, 124. For the uses of the future tense form, see Stanley E. Porter, *Idioms of the Greek New Testament*, 2nd ed. (Sheffield: Sheffield Academic, 1994), 43–45.

51 Koester, *Symbolism*, 83.

52 For the discussion whether Jesus as the Lamb of God is equivalent to the Passover Lamb, see Paul M. Hoskins, "Deliverance from Death by the True Passover Lamb: A Significant Aspect of the Fulfillment of the Passover in the Gospel of John," *JETS* 52.2 (2009): 286–89; Bruce H. Grigsby, "The Cross as an Expiatory Sacrifice in the Fourth Gospel," *JSNT* 15 (1982): 66; Porter, "Traditional Exegesis," 411.

53 Porter, "Traditional Exegesis," 412.

and their act. This clause may paraphrase Zech 14:21 (cf. Mal 3:1, 3) regarding the eschatological expectation of the house of the LORD.[54] The larger context of Zech 14:21 denotes the coming of "the day of the LORD" (Zech 14:20–21). The restoration of the holy worship and sacrifices is anticipated for all clans (Zech 13:1; 14:8, 17–21; Mal 3:1, 3) in the new temple.[55] Moreover, in the context of Ps 69:9, although the zeal of God's house had consumed David, he was confident that God would save and rebuild Judah (Ps 69:35–36). Thus, the house of God, including his servants, children, and those who love his name, will be rebuilt and restored so that they can worship God.[56] Köstenberger claims that the temple will be "a restoration of worship centered on the 'temple' of Jesus's body."[57] In other words, through Jesus's blood, i.e. his death, he rebuilds the temple, the worship center, by purifying and sanctifying the priesthood, sacrifices, and his people.

3.2 Water for Purification in the Wedding at Cana (John 2:1–11)

The implied significance of water in the pericope of the Wedding at Cana is hinted at in John 2:6. The containers for the water are described as six stone jars, each holding two to three measures (μετρητής), which are about twenty to thirty gallons, and they are used for Jewish ceremonial washing (καθαρισμός). Although these details do not seem to ring any bells for people living in another culture and centuries later about the kind of purification that is in mind, the first audience of the Gospel would have known directly about the occasion, location, type of vessels, and volume of water. Neusner points out: "in correct volume, deriving from the appropriate source, water also has the power to diminish or even remove uncleanness, still water the former, flowing water the latter."[58] In the setting of a wedding feast, water may be used for hand washing (cf. Mark 7:1–4) and specific utensils.[59] The source of the water is not mentioned. Some scholars suspect it is drawn from a well, as ἀντλέω, draw, is used when it is presented to the master of the feast (John 2:8–9; cf. John 4:7; 15).[60]

---

54 Dodd, *Interpretation*, 300. The MT uses "not a Canaanite" (a merchant) will be in the house of the LORD. For the definition of "paraphrase," see Porter, *Sacred Tradition*, 36.
55 Brown, *The Gospel According to John*, 121 and Andreas J. Köstenberger, "John," in *Commentary on the New Testament Use of the Old Testament*, ed. G.K. Beale and D.A. Carson (Grand Rapids: Baker Academic, 2007), 433.
56 Köstenberger, "John," 432–33.
57 Köstenberger, "John," 434.
58 J. Neusner, "Contexts of Purification: The Halakhic Theology of Immersion—Mishnah—Tosefta Tractate Miqvaot in the Context of Tractates Tebul Yom and Parah," *Review of Rabbinic Judaism* 61 (2003): 68.
59 Morris, *John*, 160; Barrett, *John*, 192. Köstenberger, *John*, 96.
60 Barrett, *John*, 192. Westcott, *John*, 84.

Though it is uncertain whether it is drawn from a well or a cistern, John may only want to give an impression of "drawn water."[61] According to Neusner, drawn water is less potent than flowing water in purification and can be used for general cleanness and hand washing.[62] Through the mention of the purification water as ordinarily drawn water but not the more potent flowing water (e.g. Jordan River, pools of Bethzatha and Siloam), John may be trying to strengthen the contrast of the miracle from changing the *so-so* purification water into *choice* wine. The consequence of the first miraculous sign is Jesus's disciples believing in him, and Jesus's glory is revealed (φανερόω, John 2:11). The abundance of the wine itself may be a sign of the messianic age (Gen 49:11; Isa 25:6; Amos 9:13–14; Jer 31:12–14; Joel 3:18).[63] Whereas calling this the "first" (ἀρχή) sign would also mean that it is "beginning" or "primary," the first sign in Cana becomes the foundation of the creative and transforming work of Jesus.[64] Linking to "the hour has not yet come" (John 2:4), it implies that greater glory, grace, and joy will be revealed when the hour has come which is Jesus's death, the shedding of the blood of the Passover Lamb.

3.3 *The Literary and Thematic Links between the Pericopae of the Wedding at Cana, the Temple Cleansing, and the Passion Narrative*

In the discussion of the fulfillment quotations of John 19:36–37 in section 2, it was shown that the implications of the blood and water are expressed through the Passover Lamb and the Pierced One who leads to the opening of the fountain of the purification water of the red heifer ashes. A similar result is obtained in the juxtaposed signs in John 2 in which Jesus changes the purification water to choice wine and consumes himself as the Passover sacrifice to restore worship. Thus, two thematic links are formed that link the element of blood to the blood of the Passover lamb and the water to purification water. However, could this purification water relate to the purification water of red heifer ashes? The answer is hidden in the literary parallels between the pericope of the Wedding at Cana and the Passion Narrative.

The relationship between the pericope of the Wedding at Cana and the Passion Narrative is the climactic development of the sign. We noted that in the Wedding of Cana Jesus transformed purification water into choice wine to begin his ministry. Ironically, he was offered sour wine when he completed his

---

61 Köstenberger suggests it does not necessarily refer to drawing water from a well. Köstenberger, *John*, 97–98.
62 Neusner, "Contexts of Purification," 70.
63 Köstenberger, *John*, 97; Ridderbos, *John*, 108.
64 Barrett, *John*, 193; Ridderbos, *John*, 113.

ministry (John 19:28). If these two scenes are scrutinized further, some literary parallels are found.

The scene of offering Jesus sour wine (i.e. vinegar) in the Passion Narrative is the consequence of fulfilling the Scripture introduced by the word τελειωθῇ and completed after Jesus saying "I am thirsty" (John 19:28; Ps 69:21). As previously stated, John uses "hyssop" and the verb προσφέρω to enhance the sacrificial overtone when the sponge soaked in sour wine is lifted to Jesus. Moreover, Freed points out, "John adds to the account that 'a vessel full of vinegar stood there' (κεῖμαι, John 19:29; cf. 2:6), a fact certainly implied in the Synoptic narrative."[65] The point is that, in John's Gospel, other vessels are also described as "standing" (κεῖμαι), namely the six stone jars in John 2:6. Further, a comparatively obvious link between the Wedding at Cana and the Passion Narrative is the participants, the remarkable one is Jesus's mother, and the rest include Jesus and his disciples (John 2:1–11; 19:25–27). Jesus's mother appears only in these two pericopae (μήτηρ; John 2:1, 3, 5, 12; 19:25×2, 26×2 and 27).[66] In both pericopae, Jesus addresses his mother as "woman" (γυνή; John 2:4; 19:26). Some similarities and contrasts between these two pericopae are listed below (see table 11.1).

The points of comparison between the two pericopae are in similarities (//) and contrasts (vs.).[67] The table below tries to demonstrate the links between the first sign in the Wedding at Cana and the Passion Narrative. At the beginning of the ministry, the first sign Jesus did is to turn the least potent purification water to choice wine (see section 3.2). Ironically, at the end of his ministry, Jesus was offered sour/cheap wine (John 19:29), and blood and water came out when he was pierced. According to the fulfillment quotations in John 19:37, the water points to the most potent purification water of red heifer ashes, the fountain for removing sin and impurity (Zech 13:1; Num 19).

Additionally, the essential elements that are to burn with the red heifer are subtly presented in the Passion Narrative. As mentioned previously, John mentions "hyssop and a vessel" when the sour wine is presented to Jesus (John 19:29). Moreover, Jesus himself carries the cross in John (John 19:17) instead of Simon of Cyrene (Matt 27:32; Mark 15:21; Luke 23:26). Whereas in the Synoptics Jesus's purple robe is stripped off (Matt 27:31; Mark 15:20; Luke 23:11),[68] John's Gospel

---

65   Freed, *Old Testament Quotations*, 107.
66   Scholars who would view these two passages as related include Carson, *John*, 618; Koester, *Symbolism*, 86 and Barrett, *John*, 190.
67   Jones also supports the parallel between the Wedding at Cana and the crucifixion in the manifestation of Jesus's glory and the belief of disciples. Larry Paul Jones, *The Symbol of Water in the Gospel of John* (Sheffield: Sheffield Academic, 1997), 62.
68   In the Gospel of Luke, royal clothing is used instead of the purple robe (Luke 23:11).

TABLE 11.1 Comparison of John 2:1–11 and John 19:25–37

Points of Comparison	The Wedding at Cana (John 2:1–11)	The Passion Narrative (John 19:25–37)
Participants: Jesus, Jesus's mother & disciples // Jesus, Jesus's mother and relatives, beloved disciple **Place:** Wedding vs. Cross **Direct speech:** Questioning vs. caring **Time:** time not yet come vs. while realizing everything was completed	v.1 **Wedding:** Jesus's mother, Jesus and his disciples v.4 Jesus replied to his mother, "Woman why are you saying this to me? *My time has not yet come.*"	v.25–26 beside Jesus's **cross** were his mother, his mother's sister Mary the wife of Clopas, and Mary Magdalene, and his beloved disciple v.26 Jesus said to his mother, "Woman, look, here is your son! v.28 After this Jesus, realizing that *everything was completed* ..."
Container + verb (κεῖμαι): Jewish ceremonial washing water vs. Roman soldier's sour wine	v.6 six stone water jars (ὑδρίαι) for Jewish ceremonial washing **lying/setting** (κείμεναι from κεῖμαι).	v.29 a vessel (σκεῦος) **was laid/ set** (ἔκειτο from κεῖμαι) containing Roman soldier's sour wine
The fullness of the container(s): up to brim/very top // full (ἕως ἄνω // μεστόν)	v.7 "Fill the water jars with water." So they filled them up to the **very top** (ἕως ἄνω).	v.29 a vessel **full** (μεστόν) of sour wine, a branch of hyssop wrapped with a sponge **full** (μεστόν) of sour wine
Verb of bring/take φέρω // προσφέρω	v.8 "Now draw some out and take it (ἤνεγκαν from φέρω) to the head steward." (to drink)	v.29 bring forward/held/ (προσήνεγκαν from προσφέρω) it to his mouth (to drink)
Transformation: water in purification jars through Jesus's words → choice wine vs. sour wine in Roman soldier's vessel through Jesus's mouth and death → flow out blood and water	v.9–10 water turned to **choice wine,** the servants know where it came from but not the head steward.	**sour wine** to his mouth → v.30 completed, handed over his spirit. v.34 → flow out blood and water (purification water)
Glory and Belief Jesus's glory revealed and the disciples believe // true witnesses and many people believe	v.11 First sign, in Cana of Galilee. He revealed his **glory,** and his disciple **believed** in him.	v.35 The person who saw has testified and his testimony is true, and the one knows that he is telling the truth, so that you also may **believe.**

is silent (John 19:2). In other words, the purple robe is not off the scene. Brown states that "John indicates that the crown and cloak were kept on during the latter part of the trial and, indeed, never mentions that Jesus was allowed to put on his own clothes again."[69] If the picture is of Jesus wearing the purple cloak, carrying the cross, nailed on the cross outside the city (John 19:20), and being offered the hyssop (John 19:29), these three distinctive features in John may create the overtone of the elements that are burnt together with the red heifer outside the camp. As this ritual requires the "scarlet fiber, hyssop, cedar wood" (Num 19:6), in Jesus's case, we have the purple robe (John 19:2), hyssop (John 19:29), and the cross (John 19:17). In other words, the sacrificial overtone is built up particularly in John 19:29, where Jesus is wearing the purple cloak and nailed on the cross, is offered (προσφέρω) cheap wine with hyssop. It explains the use of "hyssop," which is used not only for sprinkling the Paschal blood but also in the preparation of red heifer ashes for purifying the impurity of a corpse and purification before observing Passover.

The contrast in changing cheap wine to the most potent purification water from Jesus's body is indeed dramatic. Moreover, it is ironic that the Jewish leaders tried to avoid contracting impurity from the dead bodies and asked Pilate to have the victims' legs broken and the bodies taken down (John 19:31; cf. John 11:55). What the Jews thought of as impure, namely Jesus's body, indeed, was the source of purification water for the impurity of dead bodies. However, a greater impact is created by the revelation of the glory. If the first sign of changing purification water to choice wine revealed glory and people believed in him (John 2:11), how much more glorious would it be when cheap wine, poured by the Roman through Jesus's mouth and dying body, came out as the most potent purification water for all people?[70] Therefore, the solemn truth that is declared in John 19:35, on the one hand, is parallel to John 2:11. On the other hand, this parallel leaves a gap for readers to experience by themselves how glorious it is when Jesus on the cross turns cheap wine into the most potent purification water for the world. Such an impact cannot be made by another literary device.

Wai-Yee Ng has pointed out that there is "a subtle but worth noting" allusion in the flowing of blood and water to the red heifer sacrifice. She notices that Jesus's death was specified outside the city and there was a flow of blood and water from his body, which aligns with two of the elements used in the red heifer ritual. Thus, she suggests that here is an "implicit fulfillment" of Mosaic

---

69   Brown, *The Gospel According to John*, 875.
70   Koester wrote, "The presence of Jesus's mother at Cana and the cross reinforces the idea that the glory manifested in the wine and in Jesus's death must be understood together ... Jesus's messiahship would lead to Golgotha, and his glorification would be accomplished through crucifixion and resurrection. The divine favor revealed by his gift of wine was a prelude to the gift of his own life." Koester, *Symbolism*, 86.

Law concerning sin purification through Jesus's death.[71] As it has been shown, the fulfillment of the red heifer sacrifice is as expressive as the fulfillment of the Passover lamb in that they fulfill the OT quotations from the prophecy of Zechariah (Zech 12:10 and 13:1 in John 19:37). With the use of the fulfillment quotations, the literary parallels to the purification water in the Wedding at Cana, and the symbolic counterparts (purple robe, hyssop, cross) of the three elements (scarlet fibre, hyssop, cedar wood) in the Passion Narrative (John 19:29), John highlights the flowing out of purification water of red heifer ashes to purify the impurity of death, the sin of the world. The significance of this purification water in Jewish tradition has been mentioned in section 1. In addition, this water, the water of purification *par excellence*, of which the ritual is recorded in Mosaic law (Num 19), the tractate Parah (Cow) under Tohorot (Purities) in the Mishnah and the Tosefta, is also mentioned in the Dead Sea Scrolls,[72] and in the book of Hebrews in the New Testament (Heb 9:13). The site of ashes is indicated in the list in the Copper Scrolls (3Q15) as a hidden treasure.[73] The search for a red heifer is still going on nowadays as a prerequisite for entering the Temple Mount.[74] Although seven (R. Meir) or nine heifers (rabbis) had been burnt according to the Mishnah (Par. 3:5) with the tenth or last heifer being burnt by the Messiah as recorded in the medieval rabbinic literature (Yad, Parah Adummah 3:4),[75] whether the ritual of the red heifer contains any typological significance is a topic for further study.

4 Conclusion: the Effusion of the Blood and Water for Purity and Sanctity in Light of Johannine Temple Christology

The purity and sanctity of God's people and the temple is significant in John's Gospel. By putting the pericope of the first sign in the Wedding at Cana (John 2:1–11) side by side with the Temple Cleansing (John 2:12–25) where Jesus promised to do the sign of rebuilding the temple by his body, the symbolism

---

[71] Wai-Yee Ng, *Water Symbolism in John: An Eschatological Interpretation* (New York: Peter Lang, 2001), 169–70.

[72] E.g. MMT 4Q394 3–7i, 395 and 4Q276–7 (4QTohorot Bª), see G. Vermes, *The Complete Dead Sea Scrolls in English-kindle version* (London: Penguin Books, 2004), location 1188–95; 5029–46; 5234–52. The 4Q276 is dated to the first century BCE.

[73] Daniel C. Browning, "The Strange Search for the Ashes of the Red Heifer," *Biblical Archaeology* 59 (1996): 74.

[74] Browning, "The Strange Search," 75.

[75] *Encyclopedia Judaica*, 1974 ed., s.v. "red heifer" by A. Strikovsky. Although the rabbinic literature "Yad" (Mishnah Torah) is the medieval Jewish literature by Rabbi Moses Maimonides (Rambam), its content may originate from an earlier oral tradition or reflect the influences of the practices and beliefs of early Judaism.

of water in the Wedding at Cana is linked to the implied symbolism of blood from Jesus's body in the Temple Cleansing pericope. It reflects a close linkage between "water" and "blood" where "water" refers to purification water and "blood" symbolizes the blood of the Passover lamb. This "water-blood" link reaches its climax in the Passion Narrative where the blood and water comes out from Jesus's body. A connection between the first sign in the Wedding at Cana and the climactic sign in the Passion Narrative is established on the basis of the theme of purification water and the literary structure of parallelism. This parallelism dramatically connects the "water" from Jesus's body to the most potent purification water of the red heifer ashes. The glory of Jesus in turning cheap wine to the most potent purification water on the cross far exceeds the glory of changing water into choice wine. At the same time, another connection between the Temple Cleansing pericope and the Passion Narrative is built thematically on the Passover and rebuilding the temple by Jesus's death. Whereas the purification water of the red heifer ashes is the most potent purification water, the blood of the Passover lamb plays a significant role in salvation history to set apart God's people.

Furthermore, according to the double fulfillment quotations of the OT (John 19:36–37), Jesus fulfilled the role of the Passover lamb and the Pierced One. Whereas the former figure conveys the thought of Paschal blood for setting apart the house of God to worship him as a union, the latter expresses the eschatological expectation of purification by the purification water of the red heifer ashes. At first sight, water symbolism does not seem to have any relation to the Passover theme and OT fulfillment motif.[76] However, if the implications of the fulfillment quotations are traced further and more attention is paid to the ritual practice of Passover, then a close relation between water, fulfillment quotations, and the Passover theme can be seen. In fact, the effusion of blood and water from Jesus's body is incorporated with the Passover theme and OT fulfillment quotations to demonstrate the glory and functions of the New Temple.

By means of portraying Jesus as the New Temple, the OT fulfillment quotations, the thematic development of Passover, and the literary parallelism of "sign," John implies that the blood and water from Jesus's body, the New Temple, is the counterpart to the blood of the Passover lamb and the purification water of red heifer ashes to purify and sanctify his people to restore worship so that they might be in union with God through the Holy Spirit.

---

76 For example, Ng attests that the "water symbol does not come close to any direct OT citations in John and does not cross paths with the OT fulfillment theme that Porter proposes … it does not have any significant part in the Passover." Ng, *Water Symbolism*, 92–93.

CHAPTER 12

The Person of Christ in John's Revelation and Gospel

Stephen S. Smalley

1   Introduction

I am honoured by the invitation to contribute to this volume of essays, and begin by offering my broad proposals, argued in detail elsewhere, about the genre, date, purpose and theology of the Johannine Apocalypse and Gospel. On that basis I will proceed to an examination of the nature of Jesus, as it appears in both documents, since I regard this as a feature central to John's thought.

1.1   *Genre and Date*

The Revelation to John is not a Gospel, nor is it simply a letter, even if it includes (in Rev 2–3) material that is epistolary in character. It is (so Rev 1:1) an ἀποκάλυψις, a dramatic and divine disclosure to the prophet-seer about God's purposes and rule throughout his creation in the present as well as in the future.[1] It is apocalyptic deepened by prophetic insight, as well as prophecy intensified by apocalyptic vision.[2] I date John's Revelation to 70 CE and suggest that it was written by John the Apostle just before Jerusalem fell to Titus, the son of the Emperor Vespasian.[3]

John's Gospel exemplifies a distinctive literary form. It is not a straightforward biography, but a work that combines an historical basis with narrative interpretation. The Fourth Gospel has its center in a developed Christology and, more than any other document of its kind, consistently views the author's

---

1 See S.S. Smalley, *Thunder and Love: John's Revelation and John's Community* (Milton Keynes: Nelson Word, 1994; Eugene, OR: Wipf and Stock, 2012), 23–31. Also S.S. Smalley, *The Revelation to John: A Commentary on the Greek Text of the Apocalypse* (London: SPCK; Downers Grove: IVP, 2005), 6–8.
2 Smalley, *Revelation*, 8.
3 Smalley, *Revelation*, 2–3.

understanding of the life and ministry of Jesus as a drama.[4] Members of John's circle probably published the final edition of the work around 80 CE.[5]

1.2 Purpose

I regard the chief intention of John's Revelation as a dramatic presentation of the theme of God's salvation, working through his judgement, to a community infected with falsehood. Its members were drawn to inadequate belief, notably about the person of Jesus, and therefore to wrong conduct. Encouraged by a surrounding pagan society, they were tempted to compromise with the truth, and to misuse power. The prophet-seer thus warns his readers about the dangers of idolatry in any form: political, ecclesiastical, or economic. John urges his Christian adherents instead to worship God, rather than the beast, and to reject the wiles of Satan by following closely the exalted Lamb (14:1).[6]

The purpose of the Gospel of John fits into such a framework. My thesis suggests that three groups of believers within the Johannine community found it increasingly difficult to co-exist: those from a Jewish environment who could not easily accept the *divine* nature of the Christ; individuals whose derivation was Hellenistic (including Jewish Christians of Grecian origin) and who were not in sympathy with the notion that Jesus was fully *human*; and a third party consisting of those whose Christology was more balanced, in that they saw Jesus as neither just a man nor simply God-like, but as both fully *human and divine*. Addressing such a volatile situation, John emphasises both the need for equilibrium in doctrine, and also the desirability of unity in the approach to others.[7]

1.3 Theology

John the Divine's Revelation is full of apocalyptic symbolism, and the meaning of his symbols is always greater than the symbols themselves. But like the fourth evangelist, who develops this teaching later, John understands that the concept of human salvation through divine judgement is not only pictured but also made real. So, the destruction of Babylon (Rev 17–18), for example, is not simply an evocation of God's wrath in response to rebellious humanity; it

---

[4] See S.S. Smalley, *John: Evangelist and Interpreter*, 2nd ed. (Carlisle: Paternoster Press, 1998; Eugene, OR: Wipf and Stock, 2012), esp. 141–54.
[5] Smalley, 90–93, esp. 93 n74.
[6] See further Smalley, *Revelation*, 4–6, esp. 6.
[7] Smalley, *Revelation*, 4–5. The story of John's community may, on this showing, be traced from the Apocalypse through the Fourth Gospel to the Letters of John. See further S.S. Smalley, *1, 2, 3 John*, WBC 51, rev. ed. (Nashville: Thomas Nelson, 2007), xx–xxix.

also demonstrates what actually takes place in society when systemic evil and idolatry prevail.[8]

The theology of John's Gospel flows naturally from this approach. The evangelist uses vivid and varied symbols to illustrate his understanding of the Christian narrative, but he also draws on a dimension that may best be termed the "sacramental." That is to say, John takes ordinary facts of created existence, such as bread, water, and life itself, and perceives them not merely as representative of the spiritual and the divine, but also as their medium. Since the incarnation, the spiritual is decisively given and received through the material. This principle controls John's thought in all sections of his Gospel. He sees clearly, as a result, that the coming of Jesus is climactic, and the highest expression of the truth that God gives himself to humanity through flesh and blood themselves.[9]

1.4 *Conclusion*

It has already become clear that, as so often in the Johannine literature of the New Testament, the view of the person and work of Jesus, and his place in the outworking of God's purposes for his creation in both time and eternity, belong together in both the Revelation and Gospel that bear his name. But crucial to John's perception of the salvation of the world is his Christology: his fundamental belief that it is above all in the person of Christ himself that humanity has received the possibility and gift of eternal life.[10]

To that distinctive christological perspective, we now turn.

2 The Person of Christ

2.1 *Revelation*

There is a consistent symmetry in the presentation of the nature of Jesus by the author of the Apocalypse. The prophet-seer, with careful balance, sees Jesus as one in being with the Father, but also as identified with humanity. Such equilibrium stems from John's characteristic cosmology, in which the material and spiritual worlds are conjoined (John 1:51). Since the Word became flesh (John 1:14), that is to say, the physical dimension has been invaded by the metaphysical in such a way that matter can become the carrier of spirit.

---

8   See further Smalley, *Revelation*, 13–15; Smalley, *Thunder and Love*, 157–60.
9   See further Smalley, *John*, 232–38.
10 Note Smalley, *John*, 238.

This balance, between the earthly and the heavenly, is typical of the Christology in the Revelation. The Jesus of the Apocalypse is the one who was crucified in history, but now is alive and exalted in eternity (Rev 1:18); he is the first and the last, but currently active in the life of the church (1:8,17; 2:1–7); he is the Lion who is also the Lamb (5:5–6), the messianic Lord of earth as well as heaven (12:9–10), and the glorified Christ who sends his angel to the angels of the local churches with a testimony for them (22:16).

Significantly, John ascribes to Jesus the attributes of God himself (see 1:12–20[11]). Thus, both God and Jesus are confessed as Alpha and Omega (1:8; 22:13); Christ, like the Father himself, is seen in Revelation as the mediator of creation, redemption, and the final kingdom (3:14; 5:5–14; 19:11–16); and the kingdom of the world is described as becoming jointly "the sovereign realm of our Lord and of his Messiah" (11:15).

At the same time the exalted Christ, who is in some sense as one with God, is also human. Although clothed in the vesture of majesty, he appears as a "son of man figure" (1:13).[12] He keeps close to the congregations of Asia and promises to come to them soon (2:16; 3:11), while still sharing with God himself the eternal throne of sovereignty (22:3). In John's Apocalypse there is a Christology that is noticeably high.[13]

2.2 John's Gospel

The Christology of John's Gospel goes beyond that of the Synoptic Gospels. John sees Jesus as the functionary of God, his earthly agent who was sent to accomplish the Father's work (John 4:34; 5:36; 17:4). The Johannine interpretation of the person of Christ in Revelation is developed even further, and the prophet-seer now understands that in the saving purposes and work of Jesus are brought together elements that are both human and divine (so Rev 1:17–18).

In the Fourth Gospel, John acknowledges that there is a complete unity at the level of being, which existed before time, between Jesus-the-Word and God.[14] In this new context, Jesus is aware of the special relationship between himself and God. For example, he knows about the glory that he shared with the Father before the world existed (John 17:5). Now, by his very presence in creation, Jesus is able to reveal that glorious character in the world, and so

---

11 See also Smalley, *Revelation*, 52–59.
12 Cf. the literature cited at Smalley, *Revelation*, 53–54.
13 Smalley, *Revelation*, 11–13.
14 Note the high christological implications of the designation θεός ("God"), as used of Jesus in this Gospel (1:18, s.v.l.; 20:28; cf. 1 John 5:20).

continue God's salvific work among his people (5:17). The life of God himself is not only present in the ministry of the Son, but also mediated by him (10:30; 14:28).

Secondly, and at the same time, John also sees Jesus as being one with us. There is a familiar stress in this Gospel on the humanity of Christ. As in the Synoptic tradition generally, Jesus shares with the creation in a fully human existence. Beyond this view, however, John is aware both of the genuine humanity of the Son of God, and also of his unity of being with the Father. He is sensitive to the fact that the divine nature of God is communicated *through* the human nature of Jesus. In the flesh of Jesus, that is, the grace and truth of God—and thus the potential, salvific gift of eternal life—are finally and fully revealed (1:14–18).

2.3 *Conclusion*

The evidence surveyed so far suggests that, notably in his Gospel, John's Christology stands alone as a courageous theological development in primitive Christianity. John does not merely state the fact that Jesus shared fully in two natures; he also points the way towards a resolution of the tension that such a Christology involves.[15] He goes beyond the view of Christ's person presented in Hebrews, where the writer describes Jesus as a "Son," through whom God has spoken to his creation, and "through whom he has also created the worlds."[16] Equally, John's Christology progresses further than that of Paul, who sees Jesus as "the image of the invisible God, by whom all things in heaven and on earth were created."[17]

Among the New Testament writers, it seems apparent that John alone is the first to identify the concept of the "Word" of God, which in biblical and even philosophical contexts may appear at times less than personal,[18] as not only intensely personal, but also recognisable as an individual human being: in Jesus of Nazareth himself. I conclude by testing such a claim in the light of the broad Johannine theme of God's dwelling on earth.

---

15 Cf. A.T. Hanson, *Grace and Truth: A Study in the Docrine of the Incarnation* (London: SPCK, 1975), 73–74. It was from John, probably, that the early Fathers took the lead when they eventually formulated their own "two natures" Christology at the Council of Chalcedon in 451 CE.
16 Heb 1:2, s.v. 1.
17 Col 1:15–20, et al.
18 Cf. Smalley, *John*, 130–31.

3   John's Christology as God's Earthly Dwelling

We may approach this aspect of John's total theology by considering his use in the Revelation and Gospel of three significant symbols. Each of these fits easily into an apocalyptic framework but may at the same time be regarded as suited to the general context of normative Johannine thought.

3.1   *The Voice*

The Jesus of the Apocalypse arrives attended by the full range of apocalyptic imagery, including a brilliantly white head of hair, fiery eyes, and burnished feet (Rev 1:1–16). In Revelation he is also seen as a victorious and sovereign Lamb, seated on a white horse, dispensing terrifying justice with the assistance of the armies of heaven (19:11–16).[19] In John's Gospel, by contrast, Jesus appears as a much "quieter" figure. Admittedly, in the cleansing of the temple pericope (John 2:13–22), found only in this Gospel, when he drives out the money changers with a "whip of cords," and commands them sternly to take their wares away and stop treating his Father's house as a marketplace, the demeanour of Jesus is stern and unyielding. And, on occasions, as in the course of a discussion with the Jews at the pool of Bethesda (John 5), he refers to (himself as?) the Son in eschatological language that has about it a distinctly Synoptic resonance.[20] But these touches do not obscure the general presentation of Jesus in John's Gospel as one who is calm and in control.

A similar diversity is evident in the dominical manner of speech recorded in Revelation and the Fourth Gospel. In the Apocalypse Jesus rarely speaks, except in the oracles of chapters 2–3, where a "son of man figure" (1:13) makes divine pronouncements through the prophet-seer to the angels of the seven churches. Beyond those addresses, however, the exalted Christ is virtually silent, except when he is heard to proclaim, and repeat twice, the promise that he is "coming soon" (22:7, 12 and 20; see 2:16; 3:11).

Interestingly, the announcement in Revelation 22 is associated in the second of these three instances with a warning (22:12, the "reward" [ὁ μισθός] is "to repay all people according to their deeds"; note 22:11). However, even in this text (v. 12) the language and thought may not be entirely negative and threatening, but include as well the positive idea of generosity (see

---

19   Cf. I. Boxall, "From the Apocalypse of John to the Johannine 'Apocalypse in Reverse': Intimations of Apocalyptic and the Quest for a Relationship," in *John's Gospel and Intimations of Apocalyptic*, ed. C.H. Williams and C. Rowland (London: Bloomsbury T&T Clark, 2013), 73–74.

20   Note, in particular, vv. 25–29.

Luke 6:37–38; and note the parallels in Matt 7:2*b*=Mark 4:24*b*).[21] And the promise of the Son's imminent advent in Rev 22 comes, in the other two occurrences, with a benediction (v. 7, "happy is the one who obeys the message of this prophetic document"; and v. 21, "the love of the Lord Jesus be with you all").

Given that Revelation is a visionary work, the eschatological statement, "I am coming soon," is surprisingly personal (note the repeated use of the first person singular pronoun), and undoubtedly reassuring. The risen Son comes near to his people and deals specifically with them (so 3:20) + "The Voice," on these occasions, is loud enough to be heard throughout the universe (as in 21:3), but sufficiently quiet to connect with individual human beings.

Meanwhile, in John's Gospel, Jesus is represented as engaging in extensive dialogues and delivering long discourses, especially to his disciples, most notably in the Farewell Discourse of John 14–17. The Johannine prose of these intimate talks is uniquely solemn and, as in the Wisdom literature, even quasi-poetic.[22] In this way it also reflects the synonymous, synthetic, and antithetic parallelism of Old Testament poetry.[23] The dominant theme of the teaching of Jesus in these speeches, controlled no doubt by the situation within the Johannine community itself, is the need for love and unity (as in John 17:20–26).

3.2   *The Shekinah*

This concept features strikingly in the opening verses of John's Gospel: "And the Word became flesh and lived (ἐσκήνωσεν, literally 'tented,' or 'tabernacled') among us" (John 1:14). Precisely the same Greek term is also found, even if used differently, in Rev 21:3. During the visionary narrative of the holy city of the New Jerusalem descending from heaven, a loud voice issues a proclamation: "God's dwelling place (ἡ σκηνή, literally 'tent') is with human beings. He will make his home (σκηνώσει) among them, and they will be his people." The passage in the Apocalypse, that is to say, uses the same verb as in John 1:14 (σκηνόω), as well as the cognate noun, denoting precisely the wilderness tabernacle of ancient Israel.[24]

---

21   See further I.H. Marshall, *The Gospel of Luke: A Commentary on the Greek Text*, NIGTC (Exeter: Paternoster, 1978), 267.

22   See further R.E. Brown, *An Introduction to the Gospel of John*, ed. F.J. Moloney, AB (New York: Doubleday, 2003), 284–87.

23   So John 3:11; 8:44; 9:39, et al.

24   See J. Frey, "God's Dwelling on Earth: *Shekhina*-Theology in Revelation 21 and in the Gospel of John," in *John's Gospel and Intimations of Apocalyptic*, ed. C.H. Williams and C. Rowland (London: Bloomsbury T&T Clark, 2013), 79. The parallel Hebrew abstract noun is not attested beyond 70 CE, when it is used as a technical term in Rabbinic theology and the Targums (87).

The marked similarity in the diction of these two texts in John's Revelation and Gospel establishes a sound basis on which to compare the theology, and indeed the Christology, of both documents. The verb σκηνόω ("tent") is used elsewhere in the Apocalypse to mean simply living on earth (Rev 12:12) or in heaven (13:6), and at 7:15 to signify the idea of God dwelling among or "above" (ἐπί) the redeemed members of his community, who remain in front of God's throne, and "serve him day and night in the sanctuary." But only here in the New Testament (Rev 21:3 and John 1:14) is this verb employed to mean specifically God in person, "setting up his tent" among his people. The use of the noun σκηνή in the Apocalypse is equally significant. Apart from the present text (21:3), the term occurs only twice in Revelation, to represent the heavenly dwelling of God, blasphemed (13:6) and revealed (15:5).[25] The terminology does not appear elsewhere in the New Testament.

The general background to the imagery of divine "dwelling," in the two Johannine passages under consideration, appears to be common. Nevertheless, this motif is clearly received from different biblical contexts. The scene presented in the dramatic climax of Rev 21:1–8, which alone in the visionary material of the Apocalypse includes words spoken by God himself (vv. 5–8), is followed by a detailed description of the New Jerusalem (vv. 9–27).

The earlier verses in Rev 21 (1–8) reflect sayings drawn primarily from Isaiah and Ezekiel.[26] In v. 3 itself, the writer brings together in an eschatological setting the idea of God "making his home" among human beings, and the Judaic theme of the covenant (God will be with his peoples, and they will be with him).[27] The scope of this logion is markedly universal: God's presence in the future will no longer be simply with his own people, Israel, but with all humanity. The covenant once expressed in the wilderness tabernacle will be fulfilled throughout creation in an eschatological communion between God and his people, as well as by the "immediate and eternal presence of God" on earth.[28]

On the other hand, the background to the notion of "tabernacling" (שׁכן) in John 1:14 is to be found in the wisdom tradition, and notably in the Praise of Wisdom herself seen at Sirach 24. In this passage, the imagery of "finding a resting place" (Sir 24:7, 11) is allocated to Wisdom, rather than to God (note also Prov 8:1–9:6 and Wis 18:14–16, as well as the problematic allusion to [divine?] wisdom at Luke 11:49). And while the eschatological perspective

---

25   But cf. Mark 9:5 par.; Luke 16:9; Acts 7:44; 15:16; also 2 Cor 12:9.
26   See esp. LXX Isa 52:1b; 61:10; 25:8; 43:19; Ezek 34:30.
27   As in Ezek 37:27; note also LXX Lev 26:11–12; Zech 2:14–15.
28   So Frey, "God's Dwelling on Earth," 101.

of the Revelation is more "future" than that of the Fourth Gospel, which emphasises the present possession of divine salvation (although the overlapping between the two is evident), the message is ultimately the same: God's dwelling in his world has been finally and fully accomplished in his incarnate and exalted Christ.[29]

3.3   *The Word*

The Greek phrase, "The word of God" (ὁ λόγος τοῦ θεοῦ), is found five times in John's Apocalypse (1:2, 9; 6:9; 19:13; 20:4), and also, in the plural, at 17:17; 19:9.[30] Both forms refer to the content of the Christian gospel, where the genitive "of God" is probably to be construed not only as subjective but also as objective.[31]

The description, "[his name was called] 'The Word of God,'" is used as a title for Jesus the Christ in Revelation only at Rev 19:13. This language may seem to resonate with the reference to the pre-existent Christ as Logos in John 1:1–2, and also with the "tabernacling" of the Word at John 1:14 (see above). However, the ascription of "Word" to Jesus in Rev 19:13 is not related, as it is in the Johannine prologue, to the notion of God's self-disclosure in his Son, a human being. It has much more to do with God's salvific activity and the fulfilment of his restorative purposes of judgement, which in this context concern discrimination against the nations (19:15). The association between the high Christology of both the Revelation and Gospel of John (for the latter note John 1:1–14) may be established through the theology of the hypostatic "Voice" (Rev 1:12), rather than in terms of "Word" imagery as such (as in Rev 19:13).[32] See above.

It is interesting that the figure of Christ who appears in the preceding verses of this section of Revelation (19:11–12) is presented as a warrior-like King and Lord (so eventually v. 16), and yet now (in v. 13), as one "robed in a garment soaked in blood."[33] The graphic imagery of a triumphant conqueror is

---

29   Note e.g. Rev 5:12; 22:1–2. *Contra* Frey, "God's Dwelling on Earth," 101–3, who suggests that making historical connections between the divine "indwelling" theologies of the Apocalypse and John's Gospel is difficult. He concludes that, in the presentation of this motif, different versions of it exist, and that these are shared within primitive Christianity, and even within the Johannine corpus itself (103).

30   Cf. the related "true words" of prophecy at 21:5 and 22:6.

31   Note a similar ambiguity in the phraseology of "the word of life" in 1 John 1:1, suggesting both person and proclamation. Cf. Smalley, *1, 2, 3 John*, 4–6.

32   So, Smalley, *Revelation*, 492. P. Prigent, *Commentary on the Apocalypse of St John*, rev. ed. (Tübingen: Mohr Siebeck, 2001), 545, suggests that the title "Word of God" for the Messiah, in the context of Rev 19:13, should be construed not as a proper noun, but more as a confession of faith.

33   The Greek text at this point (using βεβαμμένον, "soaked," or "dipped") has strong MS support, and best accounts for the variants.

drawn from the oracle of vengeance in Isa 63:1–6 (note v. 4); but see also Exod 15:11–18 and Zech 14:1–21, et al. The "blood" associated with the garment worn by the victorious messianic rider in this scene (v. 11) does not therefore primarily evoke that of a sacrificial victim.[34]

Nevertheless, the sacrificial overtones of the "blood," to which reference is made in this text (Rev 19:13), would not have been entirely lost on the prophet-seer or his audience, particularly in view of the associations between αἷμα ("blood") and the atoning death of Jesus to which allusion is made elsewhere in John's Revelation (see 1:5; 5:9; 7:14; 12:11). So even if the figure of the avenging judge is dominant in this passage, and the idea of the redeeming Christ is subordinate,[35] it becomes clear that true divine justice is finally revealed in the salvific and personal activity of the Lamb (as in 19:9–10), who is called God's Word.

John's thinking about the Word of God in the Fourth Gospel moves forward the teaching on this subject in the Apocalypse. Almost at the beginning of the Prologue (John 1:14) comes the pivotal announcement that "the Word became flesh." The use of the verb γίνομαι ("became") here implies entry into an entirely new condition. By becoming flesh, that is to say, the Logos of God participates fully in the creaturely vulnerability of humanity.[36]

In that state of human weakness, the writer continues in v. 14, the Word "set up his tent" among us, so that "we" could gaze upon his divine glory. For the leading concept of God "dwelling" in creation, see the preceding section. For the "glory" of God in John's Revelation and Gospel, see Rev 15:8; 18:1; 21:11, 23; John 2:11; 8:54; 11:4, 40; 12:43; 17:5, et al. The language evokes the disclosure of God's glory in the Exodus narrative, notably at the tent of meeting pitched by Moses outside the Israelite camp (Exod 33:7–11). The Exodus associations are intentional, in that they link the cross and exaltation of Jesus with the hope finally promised in a *second*, eschatological deliverance.[37]

The emphatically corporate yet also highly individualised reference to the testimony of eyewitnesses, as first-hand evidence of Christ's person and work, is marked in John 1:14. "*We* saw his glory" (using the aorist, ἐθεασάμεθα) in that statement refers not simply to the quality of spiritual insight, although it must include it. John is thinking in this testimony of the literal perception of divine glory by the first followers of Jesus in his signs (John 2:11), death (19:35),

---

34   Note the similarly complex associations, both military and piacular, in the representation of Jesus as the "Lamb" of God by John the Baptist in John 1:29, 36.
35   Prigent, *Apocalypse*, 544.
36   G.R. Beasley-Murray, *John*, WBC 36 (Waco: Word, 1987), 13–14.
37   Beasley-Murray, *John*, 14.

and exaltation (20:24–29) and, as such, this must have derived uniquely from "*God's* one and only Son."[38]

This section of the Johannine Prologue (John 1:1–18), speaking first of the Word of God and creation (vv. 1–5), and then of the reaction to the Word in the world (vv. 9–13), comes to a climax when John refers to the incarnation of the Word, visibly "tented" and glorified in the flesh of humanity, as being filled with "grace and truth" (χάρις καὶ ἀλήθεια). Such a phrase is often used in the LXX to describe God's covenant love (as in Exod 34:6).

The two words in the Hebrew version of that phrase (חסד ואמת) are closely related in meaning, and signify God's "loyalty and faithfulness to his covenant and covenant people."[39] The idea of "truth" (ἀλήθεια) is prominent in the Gospel of John. The word combines its Hebraic background, meaning stability and personal trustworthiness, with a Greek understanding of the term as "eternal reality," or the disclosure of that reality to humanity.

In the LXX, חסד is often translated in the Greek as ἔλεος, meaning God's undeserved love, or favour.[40] In John's Gospel, the term χάρις is found only in the Prologue (1:14 and 16, 17). But the very fact of its threefold repetition in this passage,[41] and in verses that are close together, indicates the centrality of the concept in John's theology. When the writer begins to speak in the opening section of the Johannine Gospel of the Word as incarnate, the language suddenly assumes a more Christian coloring. God's glory is shown by the truth that he acts in faithfulness to his own character, which nature reveals itself as love.[42]

4   Summary and Conclusions

The imagery used in both John's Apocalypse and Gospel to describe the dwelling of God in his creation, discussed above, has the potential in its original context and in later reception to be understood in personal and indeed human terms.

In the opening vision of Revelation, John "turns round to see whose *voice* was speaking" to him (1:12). James Charlesworth has argued convincingly that

---

38   See also 1 John 1:1–3. Cf. Beasley-Murray, *John*, 14.
39   C.K. Barrett, *The Gospel According to St John: An Introduction with Commentary and Notes on the Greek Text*, 2nd ed. (London: SPCK, 1978), 167.
40   Barrett, *Gospel*, 167.
41   The composition of the Johannine Prologue is debatable. But, as with the Fourth Gospel as a whole, its thought may well reflect the situation of the Johannine community itself. See Smalley, *John*, esp. 135–38.
42   Barrett, *John*, 167.

in Jewish and Christian apocalyptic literature "the voice," as in Rev 1:12, is used to designate a divine creature.[43] So the seer encounters here not a disembodied vocal sound but a visible being, revealed as both the exalted Son of God, and also as a son of man figure (verse 13; see John 1:14). John the Divine remits his hypostatic embodiment in a Christian and personal mode, while John the evangelist presents his Christology by using the concept of *Logos*.[44]

Although deriving from varied backgrounds, the precise image of God, in person, "setting up his *tent*" among his people, or in his creation, appears in the New Testament only at Rev 21:3 and John 1:14. The "tabernacling" metaphor embraces a wealth of biblical and theological ideas, and may perhaps be regarded as a leading component of Johannine thought. For it expresses John's fundamental understanding that God's dwelling in creation has been finally and fully accomplished in the human "tent" of his incarnate and exalted Christ.

Such imagery points towards, and indeed surrounds, the third way used by John to represent God's dwelling on earth that has been considered in this chapter: namely, in the *Word* made flesh. By sharing in humanity and vulnerability, the Word of God participates in a complete and redemptive act of new creation. But we have noticed that the way into this theological perception has already been prepared by the presentation of the "voice" imagery in Rev 1:12, and the scene in Rev 19:11–16, where the kingly "Word" of God appears in a blood-soaked robe.

It may be concluded that the images appearing in John's Revelation and Gospel to describe the essential being of Jesus the Christ, as Voice, Tent and Word, all graze the edge (at least) of the process of divinity invading humanity,

In this context, it is noteworthy that the statement in John 1:14, ὁ λόγος σὰρξ ἐγένετο (literally, "the Word flesh became"), is followed immediately by the equally breath-taking disclosure, καὶ ἐσκήνωσεν ἐν ἡμῖν ("and pitched his tent among us"). The images of "Word" and "Tent" here, it may be suggested, are virtually identical in their theological significance. They are fully inclusive and echo one another completely in their Christology. Such an understanding, it may be proposed, is anticipated in John's thinking by his earlier use of motifs describing God's decisive indwelling in his creation.

We may use the (very biblical) analogy of a mountain. At the base, in christological terms, we have intimations of divine indwelling, in such symbols as angels, and the crucial pattern of light overcoming darkness (as in Rev 10:1–3; 1:12–18; John 1:51; 1:4–5, et al.). On the ascent, and tapping the christological

---

43   J.H. Charlesworth, "The Jewish Roots of Christology: The Discovery of the Hypostatic Voice," *SJT* 39 (1986): 19–41.
44   Cf. Smalley, *Revelation*, 52–53.

roots already identified, we discover the typically Johannine language of the "Voice," in association with the sovereign Christ and his discourse teaching.

Peaking at the summit, Jesus the Christ is finally revealed in flesh as together both "Tabernacle" and "Word." That is to say, notions which have been sown as part of a seemingly impersonal Christology, accompanied on the way by creative theological ideas, eventually flower as the Johannine expression of Jesus, the salvific Messiah of God, becoming flesh for that purpose in a crucified but now exalted individual human being. John alone, it seems, both in his Apocalypse and Gospel, has in the end made that remarkable identification clear.

PART 4

The Application of Christology for the Johannine Audience and Beyond

∵

CHAPTER 13

Jesus in Word and Deed through the Ritual Activity of Tabernacles in John 7:1–10:21

Sherri Brown

In the Gospel of John, Jesus's public ministry is recounted across John 1:19–12:50. This first half of the body of the Gospel is commonly known as the Book of Signs due to the evangelist's distinctive use of the Greek word σημεῖα, or "signs," to designate Jesus's miraculous deeds.[1] This word choice seems to be a deliberate indication that these miracles are not ends in themselves. Rather, they are signs that point beyond both Jesus and the immediate situation to the God whom Jesus calls "Father" and in whose name he lives out his mission—much like the "signs and wonders" either performed by Moses or indicated by God to *signify* the *wondrous* power of God in the Exodus and beyond.[2] These signs, along with the dialogues and discourses of John 1:19–12:50, are regularly contextualized by central feasts of the Jewish ritual calendar.[3] Two-plus years' time in the narrative passes, indicated by Passover in John 2, then marked temporally by the Sabbath (5:1–47), Passover (6:1–71), Tabernacles (7:1–10:21), Dedication (10:22–42), until the third Passover is announced at 11:55. Indeed, this final festival contextualizes the remainder of the body of the Gospel (through 20:31).

In the Jewish Scriptures, the feasts of Israel are presented as a *zikaron* (זכרון), a "memorial," of God's past active presence in the lives of his chosen people (Lev 23:24). Leviticus 23:1–44 narrates God's appointment of these feasts through Moses. Celebrating the ritual activity of the festival then manifests that past presence among the people in the current age.[4] If, as many scholars

---

1 John 2:11, 18, 23; 3:2; 4:48, 54; 6:2, 14, 26, 30, 7:31; 9:16; 10:41; 11:47; 12:18, 37; 20:30; R.E. Brown, *The Gospel according to John*, 2 vols., AB 29–29a (New York: Doubleday, 1966–1970), 1:cxl–cxli. Unless otherwise indicated, all translations are taken from the NRSV.

2 Exod 7:9; 11:9,10; Deut 6:22; 7:19; 11:3; 13:2, 3; 28:46; 29:2. For uses of "signs" alone in the same sense, see Exod 3:12; 4:8, 9, 17, 28, 30; 7:3; 8:23; 10:1, 2; 12:13; 13:9; 31:13, 37.

3 This process begins with the feast of Pentecost as the theological canvas behind the portrait of the wedding at Cana (John 2–4; see S. Brown and F.J. Moloney, *Interpreting the Gospel of John: An Introduction* [Grand Rapids: Eerdmans, 2017], 193–216 for a discussion of this claim). In John 5–10, the evangelist turns to Sabbath, Passover, Tabernacles, and Dedication.

4 F.J. Moloney, *Signs and Shadows: Reading John 5–12* (Minneapolis: Fortress, 1996), 1.

suggest, the Johannine Christians had been, or are even just feeling, marginalized from the synagogues at the end of the first century CE, they were not simply being excluded from these celebrations (a social experience), they may have felt that they were losing contact with the God of creation and God's saving action in history (a religious experience).[5] As believers in the saving action of the Christ event, they had been taught that relationship with God is engendered through the Word of Jesus; but this presents the problem at hand: what about these festivals and the experience of God's presence they facilitate? Not only must the evangelist care for the community members pastorally, he must also show God's fidelity to them and God's continuing presence in their lives as members of the new community of Christ.[6]

Reshaping the experience of God in the life of the community is therefore the particular background for the "feasts section" in John 5–10. The evangelist renders "christological" the feasts of Judaism: he teaches that God has sent Jesus the Christ to complete and embody these ritual acts.[7] Now, says he, it is Jesus the Christ who renders God present in the ongoing lives of the community. We see this reflected in the narrative as the spark of conflict between Jesus and "the Jews" catches fire across these chapters. This issue of ritual also presents the central conflict of this segment of the Gospel. The evangelist teaches that ritual must incorporate both action and meaning. Likewise, the action must be open to the very meaning it claims to facilitate, including God acting precisely the way he has in the past again, *now*, in Jesus. The inability of Jesus's opponents to grasp what he is doing leads first to profound misunderstanding then to rejection of Jesus as the incarnation of the rituals. This both parallels the experience of the early community and drives the mission of Jesus as Christ and Son of God forward to its inevitable climax.

All of John 7:1–10:21 takes place in the context of the Festival of Tabernacles and the ritual celebrations of the festival not only form the sensory backdrop of this lengthy passage but also provide the interpretive key for its exegesis. John 7–8 forms a unified whole in terms of Jesus's teaching and being viewed

---

5   Brown and Moloney, *Interpreting the Gospel of John*, 217–20.
6   I posit that the intended audience of this Gospel was ethnically Jewish and believed that Jesus was the Christ but found themselves suffering alienation from their larger community, indicated anachronistically by 9:22, 12:42, and 16:2. Rethinking the celebrations of God's presence was not exclusive to them. Post-First Jewish War Judaism was shifting from temple to synagogue-centered worship such that ritual and piety were in a state of transition. See Gale Yee, *Jewish Feasts and the Gospel of John* (Wilmington: Michael Glazier, 1989), 21.
7   Moloney, *Signs and Shadows*, 2. Yee (*Jewish Feasts*) uses "replacement" language, a concept which the evangelist never employs, an unfortunate marring of an otherwise top-notch resource. In the evangelist's vocabulary, Jesus "completes" or "fulfills" the purpose of the festal rituals.

through the lens of Tabernacles,[8] while John 9–10 narrates *how* Jesus is *what* he teaches about himself in John 7–8. Jesus is, therefore, presented as the embodiment of the ritual activity of Tabernacles for a fledgling Jewish Christian community struggling to reconstitute the presence of God in its ritual life.

1 The Feast of Tabernacles

The festival of Tabernacles was the most popular of the three pilgrimage feasts, known as the "feast of YHWH" (Lev 23:39; Num 29:12; Judg 21:19) or simply "the feast" (1 Kgs 8:2; Ezek 45:25; Neh 8:14). The Jewish historian Josephus describes Tabernacles as "especially sacred and important to the Hebrews" (*Ant.* 8.101).[9] This feast, designated the feast of Ingathering in the earliest liturgical calendars (Exod 23:16; 34:22) and later the feast of Booths/Tabernacles (*sukkot*; Deut 16:13, 16; Lev 23:34), was originally an autumn celebration of the grape and olive harvest that seems to have included dancing and partaking of the yield's new wine (so Judg 21:19–23; 1 Sam 1–19). This annual festival was later historicized and associated with the Sinai covenant and God's care and guidance during the wilderness experience. In Leviticus 23, God commands Moses to share details of the ritual:

> Now, the fifteenth day of the seventh month, when you have gathered in the produce of the land, you shall keep the festival of the LORD, lasting seven days; a complete rest on the first day, and a complete rest on the eighth day. On the first day you shall take the fruit of majestic trees, branches of palm trees, boughs of leafy trees, and willows of the brook; and you shall rejoice before the LORD your God for seven days ... You shall live in booths for seven days; all the citizens in Israel shall live in booths so that your generations may know that I made the people of

---

8 Andrew Lincoln, *The Gospel According to Saint John*, BNTC (London: Continuum, 2005), 241, observes that "smaller units" of Jesus's teaching are here "given a certain cohesiveness through their present setting in relation to the festival and through the sense of mounting conflict ..., including the note of increasing threat to Jesus's life (cf. 7.1, 19, 25, 30, 32, 44; 8:37, 40, 59)."

9 The summary presentation that follows is culled from information found in: H. Danby, *The Mishnah: Translated from the Hebrew with Introduction and Brief Explanatory Notes* (Oxford: Oxford University Press, 1933), 172–81; G. Bienaimé, *Moïse et le Don de l'Eau dans la Tradition Juive Ancienne: Targum et Midrash*, AnBib 98 (Rome: Biblical Institute Press, 1984); P. Goodman, *The Sukkot and Simkah Torah Anthology* (Philadelphia: Jewish Publication Society, 1963); G.W. MacRae, "The Meaning and Evolution of the Feast of Tabernacles," *CBQ* 22 (1960): 251–76; Moloney, *Signs and Shadows*, 65–116; Yee, *Jewish Feasts*, 70–77.

> Israel live in booths when I brought them out of the land of Egypt: I am
> the LORD your God.
>
> LEV 23:39–43

Nehemiah 8 shares how the post-exilic generation learned of the command to keep the festival through Ezra's study of the Torah (8:13–14). Following the injunction to go out "to the hills and bring branches of olive, wild olive, myrtle, palm, and other leafy trees to make booths" (v. 15), the people prepare to recommit themselves to the Torah and covenant with God.

> So the people went out and brought them, and made booths for themselves, each on the roofs of their houses, and in their courts and in the courts of the house of God, and in the square at the Water Gate and in the square at the Gate of Ephraim. And all the assembly of those who had returned from the captivity made booths and lived in them … And there was very great rejoicing. And day by day, from the first day to the last day, he read from the book of the law of God. They kept the festival seven days; and on the eighth day there was a solemn assembly, according to the ordinance.
>
> NEH 8:16–18

Elsewhere we find indications that these branches were also carried during the rituals of the feast (2 Macc 10:6–8; Ps 118:27). By the end of the prophetic age and into NT times, the feast had also been eschatologized such that the celebration included explicit hopes for the coming of the Messiah and messianic age.[10] We see this in Zechariah 14 with a further focus on light and water in the form of rain (appropriate for an autumn festival after the dry summer months).

> On that day there shall be neither cold nor frost. And there shall be continuous day … not day and not night, for at evening time there shall be light. On that day living waters shall flow out of Jerusalem, half of them to the eastern sea and half of them to the western sea; it shall continue in summer and in winter. And the LORD will become king over all the earth; on that day the Lord will be one and his name one.
>
> ZECH 14:6–9

---

10   Lincoln, *Saint John*, 242; Moloney, *Signs and Shadows*, 66. For more detail on the eschatological component of the celebration, see Bienaimé, *Moïse et le Don de l'Eau*, 200–229.

In its later evolution, Tabernacles became an eight-day pilgrimage feast to the temple in Jerusalem. The festival worshippers looked expectantly to God for a time when life-giving waters flowed from the temple which served as a beacon of light to the world.[11] The Mishnah, dated to the second century CE, after the standing of the temple, presents the laws for Tabernacles in the tractate *Sukkah* in the second division *Moed*.[12] The festival still began on the fifteenth day of the seventh month, Tishri (September–October) and was highlighted by building shelters, representing the nomadic experience of the Israelites in the wilderness. For seven days, the men celebrating the festival ritual sleep and eat in their shelters. After the initial seven days, an additional eighth day specifically recalls God's protection in the wilderness.

Looking back, the rabbis further indicate three major elements form the festival celebration in the temple area. The daily ritual begins with the Water Libation Ceremony (*m. Suk.* 4.9–10). At the dawn of each day a procession accompanied by blasts of the shofar moves down to the pool of Siloam to gather water in a golden container before returning through the Water Gate. This gate marked the source from which the waters of life, issuing from the temple, would flow in the messianic age (*t. Suk.* 3.2; *Gen. Rab.* 28.18; *m. Sheq.* 6.3; *m. Mid.* 2.6). Singing psalms (the Hallel, Pss 113–118), the procession arrives at the altar where the water is mixed with wine and allowed to flow out onto the altar (*m. Suk.* 4.5). The ritual was thus linked with both the giving of rain in the wilderness and current messianic expectations (so Ezek 47:1–5; Zech 14:8, 20; Joel 4:18).[13] This linked the Messiah with both a Moses-like teacher and the definitive gift of water from the well of Torah, the ultimate perfection of the Law (*m. Suk.* 3.3–9; *Eccl. Rab.* 1.8). The second component of the ritual is the Ceremony of Light (*m. Suk.* 5.1–4). Four huge candelabra are placed at the center of the Court of the Women. Again, to the sounds of Psalms (120–134), celebrations under these lights last most of the night each of the seven days of the feast. The temple then also becomes the beacon that looks back at God's guidance in the wilderness through the pillar of fire and forward to the

---

11   Yee, *Jewish Feasts*, 76.

12   The following description is necessarily speculative. On the value of using this material for insight into John 7–10, see Frédéric Manns, *L'Evangile de Jean à la Lumière du Judaïsme* (Jerusalem: Franciscan, 1991), 185–94; Moloney, *Signs and Shadows*, 66–67; G. Vermes, "Jewish Literature and New Testament Exegesis: Reflections on Methodology," in *Jesus and the World of Judaism* (London: SCM Press, 1983), 74–88. Yee asserts, "there is no question that some of [the Mishnah's] legislation reflected a much earlier period when the temple was still in operation" (*Jewish Feasts*, 74).

13   Yee (*Jewish Feasts*, 75) notes that *t. Sukk.* 3.11–12 understands Moses' sign that creates water from the rock (Exod 17:1–7; Num 20:8–13) to be the progenitor of the Tabernacles water ritual.

pillar's expected return in the messianic age (Exod 13:21; Isa 4:5; Bar 5:8–9; *Song Rab.* 1.7). The daily celebration culminates with the Rite of Facing the Temple (*m. Suk.* 5:2–4). At cockcrow of each of the seven days of the feast the men proceed to the east gate of the temple and face toward the east, away from the temple. At sunrise they turn, face the temple, and recite, "Our fathers when they were in this place turned *with their backs toward the Temple of the Lord and their faces toward the east, and they worshipped the sun toward the east*; but as for us, our eyes are turned toward the Lord."[14] This ritual greeting of the light of the new day affirmed that God is the one true God to whom all honor, glory, and obedience are due. On the last and greatest day of the festival, the priests process through the Water Gate and circle the sacred altar not once, but seven times with the waters drawn from the pool of Siloam as a final libation rite of completion (*m. Sukk.* 4.9).[15]

First-century Tabernacles celebrations were therefore marked by increased messianic expectation coupled with profound symbolism of God's covenantal action in Israel, manifested in facing God through the temple, lighting of great candelabra, and water rituals around the altar as the locus of the dwelling presence of God. This is the sensory backdrop of Jesus's encounters in the temple area recounted in John 7:1–10:21.

2 The Flow of the Narrative

The narrator opens John 7 with a word about the threat rising in Judea against Jesus as the Jewish festival of Tabernacles draws near that results in questions about whether Jesus will attend (vv. 1–13). The narrative shift in tempo and tone and the temporal marker μετὰ ταῦτα ("after these things") indicates that the entirety of John 7:1–10:21 takes place in the context of Tabernacles (v. 2).[16] Once Jesus arrives, the narrative falls into two major segments. The first is primarily dialogue as Jesus uses Tabernacles as the canvas for his teaching of himself as the living water and light of the world that brings about the integration and fulfillment of their scriptural history (7:14–8:59). The encounters that ensue between Jesus, "the Jews," and "the crowds" unfold in two major scenes: the dialogue that occurs "about the middle of the festival" (7:14–36); and the dialogue

---

14 This translation of the proclamation in *m. Sukk.* 5.4 is found in Danby, *Mishnah*, 180, emphasis in the original; see Ezek 8:16.
15 Yee, *Jewish Feasts*, 79.
16 I. de la Potterie, *La Verité dans Saint Jean*, 2 vols., AnBib 73–74 (Rome: Biblical Institute Press, 1977), 816–19; Lincoln, *Saint John*, 241; Moloney, *Signs and Shadows*, 65–66; L. Schenke, "Joh 7–10: Eine dramatische Szene," ZNW 80 (1989): 172–92.

engaged "on the last day of the festival" (7:37–8:59).[17] The second major segment takes place in the aftermath of these dialogues (9:1–10:21) and focuses first on Jesus's healing of a man born blind and its consequences (9:1–41). This sign provides for Jesus's self-identification as both the Sheep-Gate and the Good Shepherd who will lay down his life for his own (10:1–21). The temporal markers and thematic shifts lead to the ensuing outline:

> 7:1–10:21 Jesus and the Festival of Tabernacles
>   7:1–13 Introduction: Will Jesus go up to the Feast?
>   7:14–8:59 The Dialogues during Tabernacles: Who and What Jesus is
>   7:14–36 Scene 1: Dialogues on Middle Day of the Festal Week
>   7:37–52 Scene 2a: Dialogues on the Last Day of the Festal Week
>   [7:53–8:11 The Woman Caught in Adultery]
>   8:12–59 Scene 2b: Dialogues Conclude: Jesus, Light of the World
>   9:1–10:21 The Action during Tabernacles: How Jesus is the Fulfillment
>   9:1–41 Jesus as the Giver of Sight to the Blind through Living Waters
>   10:1–21 Jesus as the Sheep-Gate and Good Shepherd

This flow of the narrative further highlights the shift from dialogue to action in terms of Jesus's teaching about himself through first word then deed. It is also our guide to further analysis.

3 Jesus and the Festival of Tabernacles (7:1–10:21)

A close exegetical analysis of the entirety of this series of encounters is beyond the scope of the present study.[18] Our focus lies instead upon the christological

---

17 For more detail on the Tabernacles dialogues scenes, see C. Cory, "Wisdom's Rescue: A New Reading of the Tabernacles Discourse (John 7:1–8:59)," *JBL* 116 (1997): 95–116; and F.J. Moloney, "Narrative and Discourse at the Feast of Tabernacles: John 7:1–8:59," in *The Gospel of John: Text and Context*, BINS 72 (Leiden: Brill, 2005), 193–213.

18 The encounter between Jesus, the Pharisees, and the woman caught in adultery is in square brackets in the diagram and not mentioned in the overview. This signifies the textual issue that underlies the placement of this scene. Scholars generally agree that this episode was a free-floating tradition that found its canonical place amid the Tabernacles dialogues late in the tradition and thus lies outside both the evangelist's narrative flow and our concern for the role of Tabernacles ritual across 7:1–10:21. See C.K. Barrett, *The Gospel According to St. John: An Introduction with Commentary and Notes on the Greek Text*, 2nd ed. (Philadelphia: Westminster, 1978), 589; Brown, *John*, 1:332–38; Lincoln, *Saint John*, 242; Moloney, *John*, 259; S.R. Pickering, "John 7:53–8:11: The Woman Taken in

presentation of the effect of Jesus's teaching in the dialogue of John 7–8 upon his action in John 9–10 and vice versa.

3.1 Introduction: Will Jesus Go Up to the Feast? (7:1–13)

The narrator opens by articulating the rising conflict in Judea as the Jewish festival of Tabernacles drew near (vv. 1–2). After an interaction between Jesus and his brothers about how he should manifest himself "to the world" (vv. 3–9), Jesus goes up in secret to Jerusalem. The narrator's additional remark that even his brothers did not believe him (v. 5) continues the theme of Jesus having to reconstitute "his own" family based on believing (1:11–13). His absence to this point had caused a schism among "the crowds," though fear of "the Jews" had kept such speculation private (vv. 10–13). We must take care to contextualize this language historically as the evangelist uses the term "the Jews" in multifaceted ways across his narrative. In 7:1–10:21, in particular, he uses this group as a foil for Jesus, to represent those who are on the opposite side of the christological debate that Jesus is waging.[19] It is not, therefore, a general rejection of the group as a whole, but a caricature of a closed system. Jesus goes up, but not until the middle of the festival. He seems to want to go and teach on his own terms, not those of the "world."

3.2 The Dialogues during Tabernacles: Who and What Jesus Is (7:14–8:59)

John 7–8 is one of the most difficult movements in all the Gospel narratives. The encounter brings the people in the story (and audiences of the story) to a crisis, to a point where they are forced once again to begin to make decisions about where they stand in the mounting christological conflict between Jesus and the Jewish authorities. Is Jesus the Christ, or is he just crazy? The conflict is now public and will soon become terminally violent.

Scene 1: Dialogues on Middle Day of the Festal Week (7:14–36)

The initial encounter that takes place "about the middle of the festival" (7:14–36) is marked by two dialogical exchanges (vv. 14–24; vv. 32–36) that frame a

---

Adultery," *New Testament Textual Research Update* 1 (1993): 6–7. For detailed textual analysis, see Bruce Metzger, *A Textual Commentary on the Greek New Testament*, 2nd ed. (New York: United Bible Societies, 1994), 187–89. For the pericope's transmission history, see J. Rius-Camps, "The Pericope of the Adulteress Reconsidered: The Nomadic Misfortunes of a Bold Pericope," *NTS* 53 (2007): 379–405.

19 Note that Jesus, "the crowds" (τοῖς ὄχλοις, v. 12), and "the Jews" (τῶν Ἰουδαίων, v. 13) are all ethnically Jewish. See J. Ashton, *Understanding the Fourth Gospel* (Oxford: Clarendon, 1991), 131–59; Moloney, *Signs and Shadows*, 74 n33.

narration of the division among the people that Jesus's teaching in the temple area causes (vv. 25–31).[20] Imagery of Moses, including questions of Jesus's relationship to Moses and the Torah, dominates as Jesus brings the history of the festival to bear on his teaching about himself in terms of the Sinai covenant (vv. 19–24). When they are astonished at the boldness of his teaching, Jesus claims that it comes from "the one who sent" him (vv. 16, 28, 33). He refers to his healing on the sabbath in chapter five and urges them to use "right judgment" (vv. 22–24), leading to questions regarding his origin and destiny. Ultimately, Jesus presents himself as the messianic figure of the prophet like Moses. Even those who are positive focus on his signs, however, and struggle with his claims to be like Moses and more, the Son of God the Father (vv. 25–31). Concerns culminate in a thwarted attempt to arrest Jesus for such disturbances (v. 32). Violence threatens.

Scene 2a: Dialogues on the Last Day of the Feast (7:37–52)
The encounters at Tabernacles begin to reach their climax "on the last day of the festival, the great day," when Jesus reveals that he personifies the water rite of the feast (vv. 37–39). Jesus is standing in the temple area where the priests are pouring the water from the Pool of Siloam, the source of living waters, over the altar both in homage to Moses the giver and teacher of Torah and in messianic expectation.[21] Paraphrasing Zechariah 14, Jesus beseeches all those who are thirsty to come to him and have their thirst sated spiritually, "Let anyone who is thirsty come to me, and let the one who believes in me drink. As the scripture has said, 'Out of the believer's heart shall flow rivers of living water'" (vv. 37–38). Craig Koester notes that, if in dialogue in the middle of the festival Jesus identified himself as "one whose teaching is consistent with the law," the invitation to drink the living water flowing ἐκ τῆς κοιλίας αὐτοῦ (from his "heart," literally, "belly"; v. 38) is an offer "to partake of divine wisdom."[22] The significance of the metaphor emerges as audiences bring to bear both the cultic activity of Tabernacles and depictions of God as the giver of physical and spiritual water in the Jewish scriptures (e.g., Exod 17:1–7; Num 20:1–13; Ps 42:1–2; 63:1;

---

20   For more on the structure of John 7, see J. Schneider, "Zur Komposition von Joh 7," *ZNW* 45 (1954): 108–19; E. Bammel, "Joh 7:35 in Manis Lebensbeschribung," *NovT* 15 (1973): 191–92.
21   In Jewish tradition, water symbolism is multifaceted, including representing the wisdom of the Law (Prov 13:14; Sir 15:3; 24:21–26; Zech 13:1); see Craig R. Koester, *Symbolism in the Fourth Gospel: Meaning, Mystery, Community*, 2nd ed. (Minneapolis: Fortress, 2003), 192–200.
22   Koester, *Symbolism*, 194.

Isa 55:1).[23] Stories about Moses providing the gift of water pervade the festival, and, through this statement, the evangelist identifies Jesus as the prophet like Moses.[24] This claim, to be the embodiment of the living waters in fulfillment of Torah, creates a crisis of judgment and a schism among the people, particularly as to whether Jesus is the expected Messiah (vv. 40–44). Jesus's origins are the focus here. Indeed, the call to come and drink from his living water is an identification of Jesus's divinity.[25] The rituals of the festival recall God's saving action in the past in the gift of water to the Israelites in the wilderness, but they also anticipate future blessings, and Jesus's words have the very universal scope that Zechariah originally envisioned: "anyone" (τις; v. 37) who is thirsty is invited to drink. By claiming to be the incarnation of rituals of the Festival of Tabernacles, Jesus is claiming for himself the roles of Messiah, source of divine wisdom, and prophet like Moses. The primary question for the people comes into clearer focus: could Jesus's claims about himself be true regardless of their traditional expectations?

When the arresting party from the previous scene must account for their failure to the chief priest and Pharisees, they exclaim their awe at Jesus's teaching (vv. 45–46). For their part, the Pharisees defer to authority to condemn Jesus without further hearing, indicating that the crowds are easily swayed by such talk (vv. 47–49). Nicodemus, who came to Jesus by night in chapter 3 and is now standing with these fellow Pharisees, takes a step forward into the light and refers to this same authority in defense of Jesus. He reminds his colleagues that the Law requires an investigation before such verdicts are cast. The accused must be heard, and what he does must be seen. Regardless, Nicodemus is shut down quickly as they dismiss the possibility of a prophet coming from Galilee (vv. 50–52). The encounter comes to a halt for the moment.

Scene 2b: Dialogues Conclude: Jesus Light of the World (8:12–59)
As the Tabernacles dialogues proper resume, they flow to their climax.[26] In 8:12–30, Jesus resumes the teaching begun at 7:37–39 and claims to be the

---

23 Dorothy Lee, *Flesh and Glory: Symbolism, Gender and Theology in the Gospel of John* (New York: Crossroad, 2002), 18.
24 See Deut 18:15–18 for the promise that God will raise up a new prophet like Moses.
25 Koester, *Symbolism*, 196.
26 Scholars have noted the forensic nature of this encounter between Jesus and "the Jews," and gleaning the trial motif that pervades all of John 8:12–59 can be elucidating. See J.H. Neyrey, "Jesus the Judge: Forensic Process in John 8:21–59," *Bib* 68 (1987): 509–42; "The Trials (Forensic) and Tribulations (Honor Challenges) of Jesus: John 7 in Social Science Perspective," *BTB* 26 (1996): 107–24; A. Lincoln, *Truth on Trial: The Lawsuit Motif in the Fourth Gospel* (Peabody: Hendrickson, 2000), esp. 82–96. The groundbreaking study on the trial motif in the Gospel of John in general remains A.E. Harvey, *Jesus on Trial*

fulfillment of additional symbolism in this feast: "I am the light of the world" (8:12). This stage of the dialogue is integral to the fundamental divide between Jesus and his opponents (vv. 12–20), followed by open debate about Jesus's origins and destiny (vv. 21–30). Jesus and his opponents come closest to a meeting of hearts here (v. 30). Then, however, Jesus characteristically begins to challenge those who profess belief in him further, beyond their earthly, more comfortable, categories, and the interaction takes the next, potentially violent, step (vv. 31–59).

John 8 presents the most extended verbal interaction between Jesus and any interlocutors of the Gospel. Although Jesus retains center stage throughout this dialogue, his conversation partners are also very involved, with considerable opportunity for questions and responses of their own. Nonetheless, Jesus continues to lead the discussion with teaching about himself and the representation of the experience of God in the feast of Tabernacles through what God the Father has done and is doing through the Son. The impact for John's first-century audience to hear and visualize Jesus standing in the Temple area on this last and greatest day of the feast with the huge candelabra quite possibly framing his stance, and proclaiming, "*I* am the Light of the World" (ἐγώ εἰμι τὸ φῶς τοῦ κόσμου; 8:12) cannot be overstated.[27] Further, "the light of life" is available to any and all who "follow" him (ὁ ἀκολουθῶν ἐμοὶ οὐ μὴ περιπατήσῃ ἐν τῇ σκοτίᾳ, ἀλλ' ἕξει τὸ φῶς τῆς ζωῆς; 8:12). In this sense, the metaphor becomes the message itself. Dorothy Lee observes how audiences both in and of the Gospel are "challenged to move from the literal level (the sun) to the metaphorical or spiritual meaning: Jesus gives human life its true meaning, providing spiritual guidance through self-knowledge and the knowledge of God."[28]

(London: SPCK, 1976). The evangelist's use of a trial structure allows for a dual function: organization of both the plot and the experience of the audience who is called to decision (Jo-Ann A. Brant, *Dialogue and Drama: Elements of Greek Tragedy in the Fourth Gospel* [Peabody: Hendrickson, 2004], 141).

27 Use of the pronoun in the proclamation "ἐγώ εἰμι" suggests emphasis on the agency of Jesus.

28 Lee, *Flesh and Glory*, 17. "Jesus' functions as the tenor and 'light' as the vehicle [of the metaphor], creating new meaning within the Johannine text. While being grounded in Old Testament metaphors of either God or Torah as light (e.g., Pss 27; 36:9; 43:3; 119:105; Prov 6:23; Isa 60:1, 19–20), as well as the cultic framework of the feast of Tabernacles, the metaphor also possesses a universal quality ... The movement from the literal to the metaphorical begins at the point where the reader recognizes the inadequacy ... of the literal level (in this case its absurdity, since Jesus is not literally the sun) and seeks a second-level meaning ... moving beyond the 'is not' of the first level to the metaphorical 'is.' In order to perceive the metaphorical, however, the reader needs to retain a sense of the literal meaning" (17–18).

By 8:30, Jesus's testimony has led many to believe in him. Audiences of the narrative thus far, however, have learned that these early stages of belief that remain in preconceived religious categories are not rooted in the abiding word necessary for full faith. Therefore, it is not surprising that at 8:31, Jesus begins to challenge those "who had believed in him" to let go of those categories and take root in his word.

This leads to a conflict concerning the identity of the true children of God based on the progeny of Abraham that takes up the rest of the passage (8:31–58). With the temple as his backdrop, Jesus challenges "the Jews" verbally to abide in the truth and see the presence of the Father in him, the Son.[29] Abiding in the word of Jesus allows those who are his disciples to come to know the truth (γνώσεσθε τὴν ἀλήθειαν), which will in turn set them free (ἡ ἀλήθεια ἐλευθερώσει ὑμᾶς; v. 32).[30] Believing and knowing the truth are therefore neither "blind acceptance of dogma" nor "esoteric knowledge in mystagogical teaching."[31] Rather, faith is an ongoing action that surrenders the previous self-understanding of knowledge to openness to God and God's revealer.[32] For their part, "the Jews" verbalize their misunderstanding of the existential component of the freedom Jesus offers in the truth of the gift of himself. They respond in terms of slavery. Although they are standing in the temple area on the culminating day of the feast of Tabernacles and celebrating the experience of the care of God in the Sinai wilderness following the Exodus from Egyptian slavery, "the Jews" reach back beyond Moses to Abraham and bring in progeny as the link to their freedom. They assert themselves not to be Jesus's disciples (see v. 31) but to be "descendants of Abraham" (v. 33). The claim is that by virtue of being the seed of Abraham they have never been enslaved by anyone. By their self-designation as the descendants of Abraham, they do, however, enter

---

29 On the covenantal aspect of "abiding" in the Johannine literature, see Edward Malatesta, *Interiority and Covenant: A Study of εἶναι ἐν and μένειν ἐν in the First Letter of Saint John*, AnBib 69 (Rome: Biblical Institute Press, 1978).

30 Moloney (*John*, 227) notes the particle ἐάν followed by the aorist subjunctive indicates Jesus's desire that an action already begun come to fruition; see BDF §373. On these verses as the "truth" of the "eternal existence and saving mission of Jesus" established in the prologue, see Barrett, *St. John*, 344. Brown (*John*, 1.355) notes in early rabbinic writing the idea that the study of the Law liberates one from worldly care: "Thus, we *may* once again have an implicit contrast between the power of Jesus's revelation and that of the Law" (emphasis in the original).

31 Rudolf Bultmann, *The Gospel of John: A Commentary*, trans. G.R. Beasley-Murray (Philadelphia: Westminster, 1971), 435.

32 Bultmann, *John*, 435. He prefaces these observations with the statement that the "promise of knowledge of the ἀλήθεια therefore is actually identical with the promise of ζωή" (434).

into the dialogue of covenant with Jesus which preserves the relevance of the Tabernacles backdrop.[33]

The first exchange of this portion of the Tabernacles dialogue, vv. 31–38, establishes the initial criterion for identifying the disciples of Jesus: they have Jesus's word. The next two exchanges establish the criterion for identifying authentic children of God in the line of Abraham's response: conduct.[34] Their father cannot be Abraham whose openness to the word of God characterized his life and journey of faith (Genesis 12–22), but someone else whose works they are emulating. Jesus states, "You are doing the works of your father" (ὑμεῖς ποιεῖτε τὰ ἔργα τοῦ πατρὸς ὑμῶν, v. 41a). This is their opportunity to respond positively to God's action of sending his Son by embracing and abiding in the word of Jesus. But they are rebuffing it. By rejecting Jesus, they are rejecting the spiritual fatherhood of that very God (ἐκεῖνος) they claim for their own (v. 42). The two issues at stake here are hearing the word of God and the action that results from abiding in that word. Truth and freedom, the concepts with which Jesus opened these verses (vv. 31–32) are found, somewhat paradoxically, in openness and obedience to the dynamic word of God. Obedience, in turn, is lived in active response to that word, as modeled by Abraham (vv. 39–40). This is the process of faith in action: "believing" (πιστεύετε).[35] They must be open to the movement of God in history *now*. The freedom found in Jesus's gift of truth, the power to become children of God (so 1:12), can be realized only by hearing the word of God when they hear the word of Jesus, by seeing God when they see Jesus. This is the believing that abides. All else is rejection, and all else is sin. And this they cannot do. The evangelist presents this refusal to see, hear, and know Jesus as tantamount to a breach of covenant and rejection of Jesus's challenge through his word. Further, through the mouth of Jesus, the evangelist seems to be challenging the role of the ritual—and the very purpose of a ritual that is closed to the potential action of God in the present even while it is celebrating that same action in the past.

---

[33] Lincoln (*Truth on Trial*, 90–91) further notes the irony on the political level that they make such a claim while under Roman occupation. The positive expression would be of their internal religious freedom "on the basis of their relation to God through the covenant with Abraham."

[34] R. Alan Culpepper, "The Pivot of John's Prologue," NTS 27 (1980): 1–31, here 28.

[35] Careful readers notice that "belief" as a noun (πίστις) does not occur in the Gospel, but forms of the verb "to believe" (πιστεύω/πιστεύομαι) occur regularly and often (98 times). Thus, faith in the Gospel of John is always an action and is rightly described in terms of a process, or better, a journey. Jesus facilitates these journeys of believing in those he encounters across his ministry.

This portion of the dialogue continues through v. 47, when the tension has increased such that Jesus pronounces that they "are not from God." "The Jews" begin to respond and it becomes apparent just how wide the gulf is between them (v. 48).[36] Jesus's interlocutors are identified again for the first time since v. 31, but now none remain who believe in Jesus. Identified simply as "the Jews," they verbalize their fierce rejection of Jesus through their certainty that he is insane (v. 48). Jesus proclaims that their decision to reject him as the true Son of God the Father is determinative of the future presence of God in their lives and in their temple. He responds by renouncing their accusations directly (ἐγὼ δαιμόνιον οὐκ ἔχω) and returning the focus to the issue of fatherhood and the right conduct of children in the same familial relationship (vv. 49–50). He introduces the concept of honor and dishonor (τιμῶ … ἀτιμάζετε) and asserts his right action in relation to the Father as it correlates to the false action of "the Jews" in rejecting him as insane (v. 49). The concept of honor leads to the notion of glory (δόξα). Jesus does not seek his own glory but points to the Father as the one who seeks and judges (v. 50). He implies that it is God the Father who seeks the glory of Jesus the Son.[37] Beginning with the double-Amen formula, he astounds them by asserting, "Whoever keeps my word shall not see death" (v. 51).[38] Returning to the directive with which he began this challenge, Jesus affirms that it is ongoing life in his word that is itself life-giving. As living water flows from within him, eternal life flows from his word. As the Father seeks the glory of the Son, the Son overcomes death and gives life to all who receive his word and become children of God. The evangelist teaches that ritual must be dynamic and active such that it does not simply memorialize a past event, but recognizes that same activity in the ongoing lives of a community of believers. Jesus, he teaches, embodies the saving action of God, precisely what the people are seeking at the festival of Tabernacles.

His opponents react to Jesus's new turn in the dialogue toward giving life with further certainty of their rejection of what he has to offer. They say,

---

36   Moloney (*John*, 283) notes this is "a genuine dialogue" in the sense of an in-depth interaction in which two points of view clash. "The Jews" interrogate (vv. 48, 53, 57), affirm their point of view (v. 52), and react (v. 59a). Jesus answers their questions (vv. 49, 54–55), affirms his point of view (vv. 50–51, 56, 58), and reacts (v. 59b).

37   Brown, *John*, 1:359. He suggests an echo here of Isa 16:5: A throne shall be set up in covenant love [חסד], and on it shall sit in truth [אמת] one who passes judgment and seeks justice.

38   Using the emphatic negation (θάνατον οὐ μὴ θεωρήσῃ), Jesus rules out the idea as being a possibility. In Greek, οὐ μή plus the aorist subjunctive "is the most decisive way" of negating something in the future (BDAG, s.v. μή). Daniel Wallace notes that "a *soteriological* theme is frequently found in such statements, especially in John …" (*Greek Grammar Beyond the Basics* [Grand Rapids: Zondervan, 1996], 468–69; italics in the original).

"Now we know (ἐγνώκαμεν) that you have a demon" (v. 52). It is the "closedness" of both their belief (in terms of "knowledge") and ritual activity that prevents the necessary openness. As Jesus challenges his opponents beyond their expectations and rigid worldview to understand his being as the incarnate Son of the one Father, they retreat to their former position and no longer venture even a partial belief. They once again reach back to Abraham and the prophets for their authority, without regard for the openness to God's continuing word found in Abraham and the prophets that Jesus has been trying to impress upon them. In their repetition of Jesus's claim, they once again misquote him. The rhetorical effect of the grammatical difference between the two statements reinforces the growing disconnection between the dialogue partners.[39] As Jesus speaks of life from above, "the Jews" conceive of merely physical death in the world below.[40]

The spiritual separation between the two parties is confirmed as "the Jews" continue to claim Abraham as their father and ask Jesus, "Are you greater than our father Abraham, who died?" (v. 53a).[41] Their construction μὴ σὺ μείζων εἶ assumes the answer no. The irony in their misunderstanding is unmistakable to audiences who have read the prologue and know the answer to be a "yes" that is clearly beyond the ken of these interrogators. They follow with, basically, "Who do you think you are?" (τίνα σεαυτὸν ποιεῖς; v. 53b). The Greek colloquial construction using the verb ποιέω deepens the irony of their rejection, as Jesus has been pointing to precisely what he "does" in the name of God the Father and "does not" do of himself throughout this Tabernacles dialogue. His dialogue partners have proven themselves unable to "hear" the answers he gives. Jesus then takes the additional step of claiming what God does for the Son: "It is my Father who glorifies me" (v. 54). He distinguishes his knowledge of God from their failure to know God and recognize God in him. Jesus, by contrast, is the Son who is the "I AM" (ἐγὼ εἰμί): the incarnation of God and fulfillment of messianic expectation (v. 58).[42] The physical reaction of "the Jews" to

---

39 See Brant, *Dialogue and Drama*, 112, for the dialogical technique of redundant narration. For the custom in biblical literature of verbatim repetition to indicate understanding and integrity, see Robert Alter, *The Art of Biblical Narrative* (New York: Basic Books, 1981), 182.
40 Brown, *John*, 1:366.
41 Note the similarity of their query to that of the uncomprehending Samaritan woman who questioned how Jesus could be "greater than our father Jacob" (4:12). She eventually opens to the word of Jesus. At this point in the dialogue, these "Jews" are, by contrast, confirming their rejection of Jesus and his word.
42 E.D. Freed, "Who or What Was before Abraham in John 8:58," *JSNT* 17 (1983): 52–59. Andrew Lincoln ties the "I am" sayings across the Gospel and here in the culminating statement of 8:58 with the covenantal lawsuit of Isa 44:6–8 in which Israel puts God on trial and God testifies on his own behalf (*Truth on Trial*, 43–50). In Isaiah, the purpose of

their verbal encounter (an attempted stoning for blasphemy) leads Jesus, who would reveal God's presence in himself, to hide himself and leave their midst.

As John tells it, "the Jews" "stand outside the world of the prologue" and this word of Jesus leads not to reconciliation and salvation for them but to the shock and dismay of blasphemy.[43] Apparently reacting based on the prescribed punishment for blasphemy (Lev 24:16), "the Jews took up stones that they might throw at him" (v. 59). They have no words left for Jesus; their response to him now is purely physical, fully rejecting Jesus's self-revelation and covenantal challenge. Jesus, too, must respond physically. The one who has taken such pains to reveal his true self to his dialogue partners at the feast of Tabernacles must now hide himself from their midst. Jesus leaves the temple precincts and thus leaves their presence so that God's plan for the Son, the hour of his lifting up in true glory, may be fulfilled.

3.3 The Action during Tabernacles: How Jesus is the Fulfillment (9:1–10:21)

Despite the physical violence with which the dialogues end, the second major segment of action and response continues unencumbered through the Tabernacles festival. The sign of the healing of the man born blind (9:1–41) and Jesus's Good Shepherd discourse (10:1–21) continue to facilitate the schism that is forming amongst the crowd about Jesus. Could he be the Messiah? His background does not fit the expectations of many and they voice the negative. His signs and teachings, however, have many others leaning toward the positive. During the sign, Jesus continues to teach of himself as the Light of the World (9:5), but now relates this metaphor to the challenge of blindness and sight through his action. In the discourse, he turns his attention to the new community he is forming through his mission and ministry by teaching of himself as both the Gate (i.e., the way in; 10:7, 9) and the Good Shepherd (i.e., the one who cares for the new community; 10:11). Jesus continues to push everyone he encounters beyond their easy answers and closed categories to a new openness to how God is acting through him in the present.

---

the lawsuit is to demonstrate that although God's sovereignty has been called into question by the Babylonian conquest and exile, God is in full control. In the Gospel of John, the crucifixion and death of Jesus likewise put this sovereignty into question, requiring that God's agent, Jesus, take the stand. For more on this discussion, see Brant, *Dialogue and Drama*, 140.

43 Moloney, *John*, 285.

3.3.1   Jesus as Giver of Sight to the Blind through Living Waters (9:1–41)

As Jesus and his disciples walk away from the temple area, they encounter a man who is blind from birth.[44] The insistence that he is not sightless simply from some passing illness or injury but from some sort of "permanent" injury from birth persists across this passage. The point is that Jesus is doing something beyond even the typical healers of the time. The disciples voice an ancient understanding of God and sin that illness and misfortune are the result of sin—some sort of breach of the covenant with God (see, e.g., Deut 6–9; 11:26–28; 28).[45] Even by the centuries prior to the life of Jesus, however, the sages were teaching that this sort theology did not hold weight. Both God and human life are more complex than this scheme allows. Jesus gives voice to this later understanding when he indicates in vv. 3–5 that the disciples have asked the wrong question.[46] The purpose of this encounter, rather, is to further reveal that Jesus is the Light of the World and Life-Giving Water. The connection with the Tabernacles dialogues is made explicit when Jesus reminds his disciples, "As long as I am in the world, I am the light of the world" (ὅταν ἐν τῷ κόσμῳ ὦ, φῶς εἰμι τοῦ κόσμου; 9:5). He then makes use of "living waters" and brings this man into the light. Jesus "spat on the ground and made mud with the saliva and spread the mud on the man's eyes, saying to him, 'Go, wash in the pool of Siloam' (which means Sent)" (9:6–7).[47] As the passage proceeds, we see that through its telling, the evangelist reveals how humans should respond to

---

44   Detail of this masterpiece of Johannine storytelling focuses on key encounters: Jesus and the disciples (9:1–5), Jesus and the man (9:6–7), the man and his neighbors (9:8–12), the man and the Pharisees (9:13–17), the Pharisees and the man's parents (9:18–23), the Pharisees and the man (9:24–34), Jesus and the man (9:35–38), and Jesus and the Pharisees (9:39–41).

45   The teaching, often called Deuteronomistic Theology, suggests those who keep the covenant will be blessed, but those who break the covenant will be cursed in some way. History, however, had shown that many who do not live good lives nonetheless succeed and many who do live in right relationship with God suffer. Initially, it was taught that misfortune can therefore transcend generations; i.e., a child could suffer from the parents' sin, hence the question in v. 2.

46   For a spot-on discussion of how these verses should be translated and exegeted, see Jaime Clark-Soles, "Love Embodied in Action: Ethics and Incarnation in the Gospel of John," in *Johannine Ethics: The Moral World of the Gospel and Epistles of John*, ed. S. Brown and C.W. Skinner (Minneapolis: Fortress, 2017), 91–116.

47   On the pool of Siloam and its impact on the study of the Gospel of John, see Urban C. von Wahlde, "The Pool of Siloam: The Importance of the New Discoveries for Our Understanding of Ritual Immersion in Late Second Temple Judaism and the Gospel of John," in *John, Jesus, and History, Volume 2: Aspects of Historicity in the Fourth Gospel*, ed. P.N. Anderson, F. Just, and T. Thatcher (Atlanta: Society of Biblical Literature, 2009), 155–74.

this light.[48] He also teaches audiences how Jesus lives out his teaching in the previous dialogues by quite literally shining a light in darkness by way of living waters.[49] This darkness is embodied physically by the man who is blind from birth, but is also embodied spiritually by those who are more concerned with rules and empty ritual than the potential for new life. Jesus forms a salve with dirt and his own saliva, but then sends the man off to wash and complete the healing in the Pool of Siloam, the same pool from which the priests have recently drawn the water for the Tabernacles ritual. This man does as he is told, but the crowd is amazed and begins to question him, eventually bringing him before some Pharisees (vv. 9–13). Only at v. 14 does the narrator reveal that all this occurred on a Sabbath.[50]

A trial ensues as they formally question first the man, then his parents, then the man again about his background and what he has experienced (vv. 15–34). The narrator mentions once again that the people and the leaders are divided about Jesus (v. 16). For his part, the newly sighted man responds to the questioning with the truth as he knows it so far: "he is a prophet" (v. 17). Not only is this not sufficient for his interrogators, they begin to question the honesty of his claims. They call in his parents who confirm both his identity as well as the veracity of his lack of sight from birth, but they wish to stay out of the current situation.[51] At this point the narrator provides hints at the world behind the story: those who confess Jesus to be the Messiah would be expelled from the synagogue (v. 22). In the end, it is the man who must make his stand alone. He does so, in magnificent fashion, claiming, "Never since the world began has it been heard that anyone opened the eyes of a person born blind. If this man were not from God, he could do nothing" (9:31–33). For his trouble, he is duly expelled (v. 34). Through this scene as a whole, the evangelist teaches not only how Jesus lives out what he claims about himself in Tabernacles dialogues (7:14–52; 8:12–59), but also the consequences for those who are open to who he really is and choose to stand accordingly. Finding meaning in this world may

---

48 The seminal work on this passage as the discourse of the evangelist in terms of a "two-level drama" remains J.L. Martyn, *History and Theology of the Fourth Gospel*, 3rd ed. (Louisville: Westminster John Knox, 2003). For his reading of John 9:1–41, see 39–66.

49 C. Koester notes both the "christological significance of water and its implications for discipleship are developed in the story of the man born blind in John 9" (*Symbolism*, 200).

50 Audiences are likely thinking, "here we go again!" as these leaders grumble about just who this man and his healer think they are. Much as he did with the crippled man in chapter 5, Jesus approaches this man who does not request a healing and sets to work.

51 The parents confirm the "man" is "of age" to "speak for himself" (9:21). That his parents are alive to testify coupled with their confirmation suggests this "man" may well be a teenager—an interesting paradigm for the community the evangelist may be instructing through this narrative.

well be difficult and they may find themselves at odds with the very system that has heretofore formed both their identity and their ritual lives. What happens next, therefore, is crucial.

The episode does not conclude without Jesus once again coming to the man and affirming his decision and stand (vv. 35–38). Jesus affirms his own identity as the Son of Man, the one whom the man can see and hear, and the newly sighted man likewise affirms his belief and worships Jesus (ὁ δὲ ἔφη· πιστεύω, κύριε· καὶ προσεκύνησεν αὐτῷ; v. 38). Here we see the link to the Tabernacles Rite of Facing the Temple: "but as for us, our eyes are turned toward the Lord." Jesus resolves the man's experience of the trial and alienation from his tradition by confirming that he made the right choice. This is what it means to see by the Light that comes from God embodied in Jesus the Christ. The evangelist is teaching audiences of the Gospel how to "stand trial" for their faith, the realities of "blindness" and "sight," as well as the ongoing presence of Jesus in their lives as both the living waters and the light sought in the rituals of the festival. John 9 concludes with Jesus continuing to challenge the "closedness" of religious systems that claim knowledge and clarity instead of openness to God's action (vv. 39, 41).

3.3.2 Jesus as the Sheep-Gate and Shepherd (10:1–21)

Jesus's "Amen, Amen …" introductory formula for his next statement indicates the significance of the teaching to come as well as how it links to what has just occurred (10:1–5; see 9:40–41).[52] Jesus shares a metaphor about the behavior of good and bad shepherds, but the Pharisees do not understand. He then describes himself first as the gate through which anyone can enter the way to nourishment, life, and security, in contrast to thieves and bandits who have no care for the sheep; then as the Good Shepherd who is known by his own and God the Father (vv. 7–15). His extended use of the shepherd imagery to describe himself resonates with God's self-characterization in the words of the prophet Ezekiel. There God calls himself the "shepherd" who will seek out and care for his sheep so that "they will know that I am God" (Ezek 34:15–31). By employing the shepherd imagery at the conclusion of the events in the context of the feast of Tabernacles, Jesus reverberates the declarations of God in Ezekiel.

In the final section, Jesus makes no further reference to the bad sheep, but describes how and why he is the Good Shepherd. As always with Jesus, who he is and what he does depends upon his oneness of love with his Father. Because of this he will give his life for his sheep, and he will take up his life again, an

---

52 See Brown and Moloney, *Interpreting the Gospel of John*, 147–53, esp. 149–50, for Jesus's teaching style in the Gospel and the "Amen, Amen …" formula introducing key teachings.

indication of the oncoming death and resurrection of Jesus. For the first time, the theme of "gathering" appears, a further reference to the harvest celebrated at the festival. Jesus will not only lay down his life for his own flock, but also for "other sheep that do not belong to this fold" (v. 16). As so often in this Gospel, Jesus's self-revelation as the light of the world, the living water, and now the Good Shepherd who gathers together all God's "flocks" creates division among the people (v. 19). Some regard him as out of his mind (v. 20: "he has a demon"), while others recognize that he is bringing goodness into the world (v. 21) both of which further connect this segment with the dialogues with which this Tabernacles episode began. Jesus pushes all those he encounters out of their comfort and toward a new realm of believing and relationship with the Father and Son as one. By presenting himself as both the way in (the Gate) and the caretaker (the Good Shepherd) for God's true flock, Jesus culminates his teaching and action during the festival of Tabernacles by taking on the role of a messianic figure who remains present in the lives of the community. This may well be the culmination of the evangelist's teaching on the new life in the light of Christ in this section: an intimate relationship that is at once both familiar to their traditions and newly envisioned through a community made up of all who choose to enter cared for by one who is always present.

4 Conclusion: Jesus in Word & Deed through the Ritual Activity of Tabernacles

What separates Jesus and his opponents at the feast of Tabernacles is a profound *closedness*. Audiences of John 7–10 have the prologue resonating in their ears as they listen to Jesus's teaching in this most heated segment of his public ministry. They know of the glory of God's action in the world through the covenantal gift of truth manifest in Jesus. Thus, when Jesus verbalizes and actualizes what God is doing through him in the tenor of his own voice, there is room for his word and deed. "The Jews," as characters who stand outside the world of the prologue and represent the opponents of a new community formed by Jesus, are ultimately not open to hearing and seeing God the Father in the voice and person of Jesus the Son.[53] Although many come to a partial faith in the messianic mission of Jesus when it rings familiar to their long-standing religious system, they cannot take root and abide in his word when he reveals the full implications of the light- and life-giving truth of his messiahship. They cannot appreciate nor participate in the openness of the very figures of their

---

53 Moloney, *John*, 285. They necessarily judge him a blasphemer and prepare to stone him.

religious history to which they appeal. Thus, the evangelist teaches, even as authentic progeny, they choose to remain outside the covenantal realm of the children of God.

For his part, Jesus stands in the temple area in the midst of the feast of Tabernacles that celebrates the experience of God's care for the children of Israel in the wilderness at Sinai and presents himself as the covenantal mediation of the experience of God's life-giving care now and from now on. As the participants in the Tabernacles celebration relive their ancestors' experience of God through rituals of water and light, Jesus shows himself to be the living water and true light that reveals God to all who would open themselves to him and take root in his word, thus empowering them to become children of God. He first makes the claims on his own terms (7:14–52; 8:12–59), then further embodies these claims first in witness to his disciples (9:1–5), then, once the stake is claimed through action, to the one who stood strong in the new life of light (9:35–41), and finally to all who could accept him as both the Gate who ushers in and the Good Shepherd who is actively present and caring (10:1–21). The evangelist therefore teaches that the power of ritual that is intended to render the past saving action of God present in the current community lies in its openness to that same action in new, dynamic, and intimate ways in the ongoing lives of real people who struggle to live in this light. Through the dialogue and action of the festival of Tabernacles, John likewise reveals that all that is accomplished in that annual feast is perfected in Jesus through word and deed as the messianic prophet like Moses in the covenantal love between the true Son and the living Father.

CHAPTER 14

Elevated Christology and Elusive Ethics: Unity and Identity in the Gospel according to John

Lindsey Trozzo

1   Introduction

We need not look far for signs of elevated Christology in the Fourth Gospel.[1] The narrator introduces Jesus as the Word who was God and was with God in the beginning, the creative agent through whom all things came into being. Though this Word became flesh and came to dwell on earth, the Johannine narrative certainly does not present Jesus as an average human being.[2] He knows things impossible for a human to know (1:48[3]), performs miraculous signs, and teaches with divine authority. Not only did he claim to do the Father's work and have knowledge from the Father, he explicitly proclaimed, "I and the Father are

---

[1]   Studies describing the elevated status of the Johannine Jesus include: Raymond Edward Brown, *The Community of the Beloved Disciple* (New York: Paulist, 1979), 36, 109; J. Louis Martyn, *History and Theology in the Fourth Gospel*, 3rd ed., NTL (Louisville: Westminster John Knox, 2003); Boy Hinrichs, *"Ich bin": Die Konsistenz des Johannes-Evangeliums in der Konzentration auf das Wort Jesu*, Stuttgarter Bibelstudien 133 (Stuttgart: Katholisches Bibelwerk, 1988); Jerome H. Neyrey, *The Gospel of John in Cultural and Rhetorical Perspective* (Grand Rapids: Eerdmans, 2009); John Ashton, *Understanding the Fourth Gospel*, 2nd ed. (Oxford: Clarendon, 2007); Alicia D. Myers, *Characterizing Jesus: A Rhetorical Analysis on the Fourth Gospel's Use of Scripture in Its Presentation of Jesus*, LNTS 458 (London: T&T Clark, 2012). Myers also helpfully calls attention to Jerome H. Neyrey, "'Without Beginning of Days or End of Life' (Hebrews 7:3): Topos for a True Deity," CBQ 53 (1991): 439–55, who notes three common characterizations of divinity in Hellenistic philosophy—being eternal, ungenerated, and uncreated (440). Cf. Theophilus, *ad Autol.* 1.3; Diod. S., *Hist.* 1.12.10; 6.1.2; Sextus Empiricus, *Adv. Phy.* 1.45; Diog. Laert., 7.137; Philo, *Leg. All.* 1.51; *Cher.* 86; *Spec. Leg.* 2.166; Josephus, *Ag. Ap.* 2.167.
[2]   The Fourth Gospel presumes Jesus's humanity and includes human aspects of characterization. Marianne Meye Thompson, *The Humanity of Jesus in the Fourth Gospel* (Philadelphia: Fortress, 1988). Johannine Christology can be seen to fit within the context of first-century Jewish monotheism, maintaining Jesus's subordination to God. James F. McGrath, *The Only True God: Early Christian Monotheism in Its Jewish Context* (Urbana: University of Illinois Press, 2009), 55–70.
[3]   Wherever I cite the Fourth Gospel, I will simply give chapter and verse. For other primary sources, I will list the book title. When quoting, I will either provide my own translation or draw upon the NRSV.

one" (10:30); "the Father is in me and I in the Father" (10:38); "The one who sees me sees the One who sent me" (12:45); "The one who receives me receives the One who sent me" (13:20). Because of his words and actions, he was accused of making himself to be equal with God (5:18)—the charge that would ultimately lead to his execution (19:7). These elements have led to an impression of elevated Christology in the Fourth Gospel, perhaps most famously expressed in Käsemann's description of the Johannine Jesus as "God going about on earth."[4] Though Johannine scholarship has since come to recognize the tensions that keep the Fourth Gospel's elevated Christology from rising to the point of "naïve docetism,"[5] we cannot help but notice that the Johannine presentation of Jesus appears much more elevated than does the Synoptic Jesus.[6]

---

4 Ernst Käsemann, *The Testament of Jesus: A Study of the Gospel of John in the Light of Chapter 17*, trans. Gerhard Krodel (Philadelphia: Fortress, 1978), 9. Cf. "Der auf Erden wandelnde Gottes Sohn oder Gott," from Wilhelm Bousset, *Kyrios Christos: Geschichte des Christusglaubens von den Anfängen des Christentums bis Irenaeus* (Göttingen: Vandenhoeck & Ruprecht, 1964), 159.

5 For a helpful and thorough discussion of the tensions in Johannine Christology, see Paul N. Anderson, *The Christology of the Fourth Gospel: Its Unity and Disunity in the Light of John 6* (Eugene, OR: Cascade Books, 2010), which approaches the issue from the viewpoint of developmental psychology to explain the christological tension as emerging from the dialectical thinking of the Evangelist. Cf. James W. Fowler, *Stages of Faith: The Psychology of Human Development and the Quest for Meaning* (San Francisco: Harper & Row, 1981); James E. Loder, *The Logic of the Spirit: Human Development in Theological Perspective* (San Francisco: Jossey-Bass, 1998). Anderson helpfully outlines the major approaches to Johannine Christology in the history of scholarship: Rudolf Bultmann, *Theology of the New Testament* (Waco: Baylor University Press, 2007). Cf. also C.K. Barrett, *The Gospel According to St. John: An Introduction with Commentary and Notes on the Greek Text* (New York: Macmillan, 1955); Peder Borgen, *Bread from Heaven: An Exegetical Study of the Concept of Manna in the Gospel of John and the Writings of Philo*, NovTSup 10 (Leiden: Brill, 1965); Raymond Edward Brown, *The Gospel According to John*, 2 vols., AB (Garden City, NY: Doubleday, 1966); Rudolf Bultmann, *The Gospel of John: A Commentary*, trans. George R. Beasley-Murray (Philadelphia: Westminster, 1971); Barnabas Lindars, *The Gospel of John* (London: Oliphants, 1972). He also includes three interpreters of John 6: Robert Kysar, "The Source Analysis of the Fourth Gospel: A Growing Consensus?," *NovT* 15 (1973): 134–52; Rudolf Schnackenburg, *The Gospel according to St. John* (New York: Crossroad, 1982); C.K. Barrett, "'The Father Is Greater than I' (John 14:28): Subordinate Christology in the New Testament," in Barrett, *Essays on John* (Philadelphia: Westminster, 1982), 19–36; Barrett, "Christocentric or Theocentric? Observations on the Theological Method of the Fourth Gospel," in Barrett, *Essays on John* (Philadelphia: Westminster, 1982), 1–18; Raymond Edward Brown, "The Theology of the Incarnation in John," in *New Testament Essays* (New York: Doubleday, 2010), 132–37; C.K. Barrett, "The Dialectical Theology of St. John," in Barrett, *Essays on John* (Philadelphia: Westminster, 1982), 49–69.

6 James D.G. Dunn, "Let John Be John: A Gospel for Its Time," in *The Gospel and the Gospels*, ed. Peter Stuhlmacher (Grand Rapids: Eerdmans, 1991), 301. T.E. Pollard, *Johannine Christology and the Early Church*, SNTSMS 13 (London: Cambridge University Press, 1970), 6.

It is precisely this elevated Christology that some have found troublesome for the pursuit of Johannine ethics.[7] Because the Fourth Gospel lacks the expected forms of moral instruction (gnomes, maxims, paraenetic sections), many have looked instead to imitation ethics, that is, to the presentation of Jesus's life for a model of behavior. However, the elevated presentation of Jesus seems to suggest a christological agenda rather than an ethical one.[8] Though Jesus experiences a human fate, the way he handles his death reveals that he is no mere human. If the Johannine Jesus is "neither a man among others, nor the representation of the people of God or of the ideal humanity, but God, descending into the human realm and there manifesting his glory,"[9] the audience is perhaps less likely to see the Johannine Jesus as a replicable pattern for their own moral formation and more likely to respond, "He has been ranked ahead of me," or even, "My Lord and my God" (20:28)! Hence, the tension between elevated Christology and ethics in the Fourth Gospel.

This essay will take three topics in turn. First, I will demonstrate that the Fourth Gospel incorporates the rhetorical topics for encomium (a formal speech of praise) to show that Jesus exceeds even the highest expectations for an honorable hero in the ancient world. Importantly, the analysis will reveal that Jesus's exalted status is grounded in his connection with God. Next, I will describe how and why the elevated presentation of Jesus can be problematic for those seeking to articulate Johannine ethics. This section will also attend to the audience of the Fourth Gospel and the rhetorical exchange between the story and the audience. Finally, I will demonstrate how the encomiastic topics are extended to the followers of Jesus and the Johannine audience, revealing the theme of unity as a bridge between the elevated Christology and elusive ethics in the Fourth Gospel.

---

7 Many scholars have helpfully pointed out that the Fourth Gospel does balance its presentation of Jesus. For example: Barrett, "Christocentric or Theocentric"; A. Feuillet, *Le Mystère de l'amour divin dans la théologie johannique*, Études bibliques (Paris: J. Gabalda, 1972); Pamela E. Kinlaw, *The Christ Is Jesus: Metamorphosis, Possession, and Johannine Christology*, Academia Biblica 18 (Leiden: Brill, 2005); William Loader, *The Christology of the Fourth Gospel: Structure and Issues*, Beiträge zur biblischen Exegese und Theologie (Frankfurt: P. Lang, 1989); Brown, "The Theology of the Incarnation in John," 132–37. Although the Johannine presentation is not exclusively elevated the Fourth Gospel's unparalleled emphasis on Jesus's elevated status might make the audience less likely to see the Johannine Jesus as an imitable model for human behavior.

8 Wayne A. Meeks, "The Ethics of the Fourth Evangelist," in *Exploring the Gospel of John: In Honor of D. Moody Smith*, ed. R. Alan Culpepper and C. Clifton Black (Louisville: Westminster John Knox, 1996), 317–26. Meeks famously suggests that his assigned topic, "The Ethics of the Fourth Evangelist," "either poses a question that cannot be answered, or it is an oxymoron."

9 Käsemann, *The Testament of Jesus*, 12–13.

As we will see, the theme of unity does rhetorical "double duty" within the narrative. Just as Jesus's connection with the Father forms the basis of his actions, the believers' connection to God through Jesus becomes the basis for their actions. More than that, unity with God involves a transformational shift in identity for the believer. Proper living would not be possible without the connection to God brought about by belief in Jesus. Thus, while the emphasis on elevated Christology may at first seem to overshadow ethics in the Fourth Gospel, our study will show that Christology is a fundamental element of Johannine ethics. Indeed, Johannine Christology reveals the determining factor for Jesus's actions and for Johannine ethics: unity with God.

2 Elevated Christology as Presented in the Encomiastic Topics

As we have seen even in this brief introduction, the Fourth Gospel's presentation of Jesus appears elevated from the very beginning. Because of this, some scholars have spoken of a "high" Christology or a "Christology from above" in the Fourth Gospel.[10] In the following section, I will show how Johannine Christology corresponds to the rhetorical tradition by utilizing the encomiastic topics, demonstrating two important points. First, the presentation of the Johannine Jesus transcends the rhetorical expectations for characterization of a lauded hero. Second, Jesus's unity with the Father is consistently the foundational element for his elevated status.

2.1 *The Encomiastic Topics in the Fourth Gospel*

Encomium is defined as one of the three types of epideictic rhetoric, which centers on praise and blame (Theon, *Progymnasmata*[11] 109 [Kennedy, 50];

---

10   Rudolf Schnackenburg, *Jesus in the Gospels: A Biblical Christology* (Louisville: Westminster John Knox, 1995), 219. The idea that the Fourth Gospel presented an elevated Christology, especially in comparison with the Synoptic Jesus, is long standing. See K.G. Bretschneider, *Probabilia de Evangelii et Epistuarum Joannis, Apostoli, Indole et Origine* (Leipzig, 1820); G.P. Wetter, *"Der Sohn Gottes": eine Untersuchung über den Charakter und die Tendenz des Johannes Evangeliums, zugleich ein Beitrag zur Kenntnis der Heilandsgestalten der Antike*, FRLANT 26 (Göttingen: Vandenhoeck & Ruprecht, 1916); Emanuel Hirsch, *Das vierte Evangelium in seiner ursprünglichen Gestalt verdeutscht und erklärt* (Tübingen: Mohr Siebeck, 1936). See a more recent discussion in Ashton, *Understanding the Fourth Gospel*.

11   The progymnasmata, or "preliminary exercises" that formed the curriculum for Greek rhetorical training, provide a relevant rubric for the gospel writings because presumably every person who learned to write in the Graeco-Roman world would have been trained in them. George Alexander Kennedy, *Progymnasmata: Greek Textbooks of Prose*

Aristotle, *Rhet.* 1.3; Quintilian, *Inst.* 3.7.6–22). An encomium focuses on "revealing the greatness of virtuous actions and other good qualities belonging to a particular person" and is carried out by the discussion of certain topics.[12] Though the Fourth Gospel is not a formal encomium,[13] the appearance of the encomiastic topics amounts to a set of "textual clues" that guide interpretation.[14]

Composition and Rhetoric, Writings from the Greco-Roman World (Atlanta: SBL, 2003), ix. Four extant progymnasmata are available: Theon (first century CE), Ps.-Hermogenes (c. third or fourth century CE), Aphthonius (fourth century CE), and Nicolaus (fifth century CE), and all arguably preserve curricula originating from no later than the first century BCE. Though the examples in these texts come in the context of strict exercises, the principles they teach can be applied to many literary forms, including the narrative of the Fourth Gospel. On the relevance of these for studying first-century writings, see Michael W. Martin, *Judas and the Rhetoric of Comparison in the Fourth Gospel* (Sheffield: Sheffield Phoenix, 2010), 37. See also Neyrey, *The Gospel of John*, x.

12 Theon divides these into three broad categories based on relation to (1) mind and character, (2) body, and (3) external things (Theon 109 [Kennedy, 50]). The first two of these find correspondence to the categories laid out by Plato (*Phaedr.* 270b; cf. Nicolaus the Sophist 50 [Kennedy, 156]), and all three correspond to Cicero's traditional "goods of mind, body, and estate" (Cicero, *Tusc.* 5.85; cf. Arist., *Rhet.* 1.9.33). A similar presentation is also given in *Rhetorica ad Herennium* (3.7.13–3.8.15). For various articulations of the topic lists, see Michael W. Martin, "Progymnastic Topic Lists: A Compositional Template for Luke and Other Bioi?" *NTS* 54 (2008): 18–41.

13 David Edward Aune, "Encomium," in *The Westminster Dictionary of New Testament and Early Christian Literature and Rhetoric* (Louisville: Westminster John Knox, 2003), 146–47. See also Heinrich Lausberg, *Handbook of Literary Rhetoric: A Foundation for Literary Study*, ed. David E. Orton and R. Dean Anderson, trans. Matthew T. Bliss, Annemiek Jansen, and David E. Orton (Leiden: Brill, 1998), §243. Encomium and narrative are distinct rhetorical forms (Theon 112 [Kennedy, 52]). The distinction is even clearer in the Armenian tradition, which is included in Patillon's Greek text: "La narration en effet est le proper des historiens" (Theon, *Prog.* 112 [Patillon, 77]). Aelius Theon, *Progymnasmata*, trans. Michel Patillon and Giancarlo Bolognesi (Paris: Les Belles lettres, 2002). English translations are taken from Kennedy, *Progymnasmata* unless otherwise noted. However, the rhetorical tradition indicates a great deal of flexibility within narrative and encomiastic discourse. Nicolaus the Sophist 47–48, 54–57 [Kennedy, 154–55, 159–60]. Cf. Isocrates' *Panegyricus* who utilized the topics in service of deliberative discourse and Demosthenes' *On the Crown* who utilized encomium in service of judicial discourse. Much like the epicheirematic topics make up formal argumentation in the rhetorical handbooks, the encomiastic topics can contribute to various forms of persuasive discourse (John of Sardis 117 [Kennedy, 207]). *Rhet. Her.* 2.18.27–28; Cicero. *Inv.* 1.30.50–37.67; Quintilian, *Inst.* 5.5–13. Though encomium is "a self-contained and complete logos" that stands apart from narration (John of Sardis 118 [Kennedy, 207]), the topics may be used in different ways. Cf. *Rhet. Her.* 3.9.17.

14 Ancient authors expected their audiences to be familiar with the rhetorical topics. Martin, "Progymnastic Topic Lists," 30–31. For more on "textual clues" for interpretation, see David Edward Aune, "Genre Theory and the Genre-Function of Mark and Matthew," in *Jesus, Gospel Tradition and Paul in the Context of Jewish and Greco-Roman Antiquity: Collected Essays II*, WUNT 303 (Tübingen: Mohr Siebeck, 2013), 25–56. For more on how genre

Below, encomiastic topics from each of the progymnasmata have been considered and synthesized with a view to their appearance throughout the Fourth Gospel.[15]

2.2 *Origin*

The progymnasmata describe origin in terms of "good birth," including the topics of geography and family ancestry.[16] While the Fourth Gospel does not begin with Jesus's geographical or ancestral origin (like the formal genealogy of Matthew or Luke), it approaches the discussion in its own unique way[17]—with a *prooemion* describing Jesus as the pre-existent Word. The "good birth" of the Johannine Jesus is presented in his being from the beginning with God (1:1), begotten from the Father (1:14, 18), the Son of God (1:34, 49).[18] John 6:42 presents an objection concerning Jesus's origin: "Isn't this Jesus, the son of Joseph, whose father and mother we know? How now does he say 'I have come down from heaven'?"[19] The emphasis on Jesus's preexistence and divine origin in the prologue counters the potential invective that would accompany such rejection.[20] Coinciding with Aristotle's teaching that it is honorable to be

---

affects interpretation, see my essay, "Genre, Rhetoric, and Moral Efficacy: Approaching Johannine Ethics in Light of Plutarch's *Lives* and the *Progymnasmata*," in *Johannine Ethics: The Moral World of the Gospel and Epistles of John*, ed. Sherri Brown and Christopher W. Skinner (Minneapolis: Fortress, 2017), 221–38.

15 These categories and their descriptions follow the entries on encomium from the four progymnasmata: Theon 109–12 [Kennedy, 50–52], Ps.-Hermogenes 15–18 [Kennedy, 81–83], Aphthonius 36–40 [Kennedy, 108–11], Nicolaus 47–58 [Kennedy, 154–62], and John of Sardis 116–42 [Kennedy, 206–10]. The progymnasmata are supplemented, where appropriate, with examples from other rhetorical handbooks. For many of the Johannine references and ancient parallels I am indebted to Martin, "Progymnastic Topic Lists"; Martin, *Judas and Rhetoric*, 92–106; Neyrey, *The Gospel of John*, 7–28; Myers, *Characterizing Jesus*.

16 See, for example, Aphthonius's encomium of Thucydides (Aphthonius 36–37 [22R–23R] [Kennedy, 108–109]) and the beginning of the Life of Alcibiades (Plutarch, *Alc.* 1.1a–b).

17 *Bioi* typically present the ancestral lineage of the hero and/or the noteworthy place of their birth. The Fourth Gospel's use of this topic is unique. Rather than a typical origin story, the hero is presented as the preexistent *Logos*. "In the beginning" and other allusions to the Genesis story maintain the theme of "origin," but the presentation is more elevated than typical uses of this topic. See the discussion in Myers, *Characterizing Jesus*, 61–75.

18 This praiseworthy origin also creates a new family line, extending also to those who are born again/from above (John 3:3, 7), born of the Spirit (John 3:8; 10:36–38), born of God: "But to those who received him, he gave them power to become children of God, to those believing in his name, who were born not from blood nor from fleshly desire nor from the will of a man, but of God" (John 1:12–13).

19 Unless otherwise indicated, all translations are my own.

20 Menander Rhetor (2.369.18–370.5) explains that the author of an encomium should be strategic in presenting the origin of the hero, emphasizing the elements that convey the most honor. Cf. Theon 111 (Kennedy, 52).

ancient (Aristotle, *Rhet.* 1.5.5), the Fourth Gospel claims that Jesus is from "the beginning" (1:1) and presents Jesus in close connection with God (1:2).[21] The rest of the narrative, presenting Jesus as the unique "Son of God" (1:34, 49; 3:18; 11:4, 27; 19:7; 20:31) confirms his honorable family line. Presenting Jesus's heavenly preexistence and divine family heritage, the Fourth Gospel takes up the topic of Jesus's origin and casts its subject in a thoroughly encomiastic light, emphasizing his connection with the Father.

2.3 Nurture and Training

The topic of nurture/training includes the subject's upbringing and education (Ps-Hermogenes 16 [Kennedy, 82]).[22] Nicolaus the Sophist famously addresses this topic with an example of the tradition concerning Achilles: "that he was fed on the marrow of deer and taught by Cheiron and all the things told him in turn" (Nicolaus the Sophist 52 [Kennedy, 157]; cf. Homer, *Il.* 11.832 and Plato, *Rep.* 3.391c). Similarly, the nursing imagery from the phrase in the Johannine prologue, ὁ ὢν εἰς τὸν κόλπον τοῦ πατρός, informs the audience that Jesus received nourishment, knowledge, and authority from his connection to his Father.[23] Cicero also suggested that discussions of training should include "in what tradition and under whose direction" the subject was reared (Cicero, *Inv.* 1.24.35). Though the author of the Fourth Gospel does not discuss Jesus's younger years, the topic of training is addressed nonetheless. By showing that Jesus received knowledge from the Father (3:31–35; 7:16–18; 12:47–50), followed the Father's example, was granted authority from the Father (5:19–24), came from the Father, and learned from him (6:45–46; 8:26–28), the Fourth Gospel presents the unique nurture and training of its subject. Again, the Fourth Gospel transcends the traditional category, focusing on Jesus's heavenly "training" that flowed from his connection with his Father.

2.4 Pursuits, Deeds, and Other External Goods

The topic of pursuits includes first the "official position" and reputation of the subject, what he set out to accomplish, and for what accomplishments he was known (Theon 110 [Kennedy, 50]).[24] Deeds, which Pseudo-Hermogenes and Aphthonius call the "most important" and the "greatest heading" of the encomiastic topics, are also included here (Ps.-Hermogenes 16 [Kennedy, 82];

---

21 The world's rejection was even anticipated in the prologue: "He was in the world, and the world came into being through him; yet the world did not know him. He came into what was his own, but the ones who were his did not receive him" (1:10–11).
22 See an example of this topic in Philo, *Mos.* 1.18–23.
23 Myers, *Characterizing Jesus*, 66.
24 See, for example, Philo, *Mos.* 1.32–50.

Aphthonius 36 [Kennedy, 108]). Theon calls them "fine actions,"[25] and these deeds correspond to the Johannine signs that show who Jesus is and elicit the response of believing in him (10:36–38; 20:30–31).[26]

The Fourth Gospel's use of titles for Jesus[27] corresponds to Theon's suggestion that honor can be draw from names and nicknames (Theon 111 [Kennedy, 51]).[28] In addition to these formal titles, references to Jesus as the one "sent" from the Father are quite prominent in the Gospel, occurring in forty different verses.[29] As the "Sent One" Jesus's mission and status are based on his having come from the Father.[30] Thus, his deeds flow out of his connection with the Father.[31] Notice his own words concerning his deeds in John 5:19–20:

---

[25] While some of Jesus's deeds bring accusations against Jesus, the narrative presents witnesses that testify favorably about Jesus's deeds: John the Baptist (John 5:33–36; cf. 1:32–34), Jesus's actions themselves (John 5:36; cf. 3:2; 9:31–33), the Father (John 5:37–38), Israel's Scripture (John 5:39), and Moses (John 5:46–47). See the expanded discussion in Neyrey, *The Gospel of John*, 175–78.

[26] Jesus's death and resurrection fit more appropriately into the topics of Noble Death and Events After Death, so they will be treated in those sections below.

[27] "Son of God" in 1:34, 49 and 11:27, "Messiah" in 1:41; 7:41; 11:27; 20:31, "King of Israel" in 1:49 and 12:13, "King of the Jews" in 18:39 and 19:19, along with more general designations (teacher in 1:38; 3:2; 11:28; 13:13; 20:16; savior in 4:42; prophet in 4:19; 6:14; 7:40; 9:17).

[28] Neyrey, *The Gospel of John*, 424. For more on the significance of the titles in the Fourth Gospel, see the following resources: H.C. Kee, "Christology and Ecclesiology: Titles of Christ and Models of Community," *Semeia* 30 (1984): 171–92; Martin Karrer, *Der Gesalbte: die Grundlagen des Christustitels*, FRLANT 151 (Göttingen: Vandenhoeck & Ruprecht, 1991); Yolanda Dreyer, *Institutionalization of Authority and the Naming of Jesus* (Eugene, OR: Pickwick, 2012); John M. McDermott, "Jesus and the Son of God Title," *Gregorianum* 62 (1981): 277–318; R. Leivestad and D.E. Aune, *Jesus in His Own Perspective: An Examination of His Sayings, Actions, and Eschatological Titles* (Minneapolis: Augsburg, 1987); Otto Betz, "The Names and Titles of Jesus: Themes of Biblical Theology," *Theologische Literaturzeitung* 94 (1969): 202–3; J. Harold Ellens, *The Son of Man in the Gospel of John*, NTM 28 (Sheffield: Sheffield Phoenix, 2010); Delbert Royce Burkett, *The Son of the Man in the Gospel of John*, JSNTSup 56 (Sheffield: JSOT Press, 1991); Van Shore, "The Titles of Jesus," in *Content and Setting of the Gospel Tradition* (Grand Rapids: Eerdmans, 2010), 417–36; Ferdinand Hahn, *The Titles of Jesus in Christology: Their History in Early Christianity* (London: Lutterworth, 1969); Francis J. Moloney, *The Johannine Son of Man*, 2nd ed. (Eugene, OR: Wipf & Stock, 2007).

[29] John 3:34; 4:34; 5:23, 24, 30, 36, 37, 38; 6:29, 38, 39, 44, 57; 7:16, 18, 28, 29, 33; 8:16, 18, 26, 29, 42; 9:4; 10:36; 11:42; 12:44, 45, 49; 13:20; 14:24; 15:21; 16:5; 17:3, 8, 18, 21, 23, 25; 20:21.

[30] "Deeds" can also include "Deeds of Fortune" or other external goods not involving fine actions, but rather consisting of one's power, friends, and fame. An encomium can thus convey honor by including "the judgment of the famous" (Theon 110 [Kennedy, 51]). The Fourth Gospel conveys honor in this way in John 5:19–24 and 8:54 when Jesus says that the Father has given him authority or power, as well as when powerful characters like Pilate, Nicodemus, and Joseph of Arimathea (18:38; 19:4, 19–22; 19:38–41) speak favorably of him or act on his behalf.

[31] "Above all, Jesus knows and is saturated with the doing of God's will." Myers, *Characterizing Jesus*, 132.

Truly, truly, I say to you, the Son is able to do nothing by himself, except what he sees the Father doing; for whatever he does, the Son also does these things likewise. For the Father loves the Son and shows him all that he himself is doing; and he will show him greater works than these, so that you will be astonished.[32]

2.5 Death and Events after Death

For an encomium, it is important that the subject's honor continue through his death (Theon 110 [Kennedy, 50]).[33] The designation, "noble death," usually used in reference to Greek funeral orations and reserved for heroes slain in battle, was granted if the hero's death met certain criteria. In his discussion of the commonplace of noble death found in Greek rhetoric, Jerome Neyrey outlines seven distinct characteristics of noble death: (1) it benefited others, (2) it served the cause of justice (i.e. democracy), (3) it was done voluntarily, (4) it was somehow victorious (even though the subject died, his death procured some triumph), (5) it was unique (in that the cause was more noble, the challenge more demanding, or the strength and courage unparalleled by the responses of others), (6) it was celebrated with posthumous honors such as games or monuments, (7) it led to immortal glory.[34]

John's Passion Narrative, with its trial, beating, and cross carries a shameful tenor that is anything but encomiastic on the surface. This episode invited descriptors like "folly," "madness," and "the worst death."[35] In the ancient

---

32 See also John 4:34; 5:36; 6:38.

33 The progymnasmata attributed to Hermogenes suggests that an encomium should outline how the subject died, whether fighting in battle or in the midst of other significant events (Ps.-Hermogenes 16 [Kennedy, 82]). The traditional "noble death" is seen, for example, in Isocrates, who writes, "death is the sentence of all mankind, but to die nobly is the special honor which nature has reserved for the good" (*Demonicus* 43 [Norlin and Van Hook, LCL]).

34 Neyrey, *The Gospel of John*, 282–312. These seven characteristics come from the presentations of noble death in funeral orations as outlined in Demosthenes (*Epitaph.*), Thucydides (*History* 2.42–44), and Plato (*Menex.* 237, 240e–249c). They correspond closely with the discussions of noble death in the progymnasmata attributed to Hermogenes (16), as well as with the criteria for noble deeds in life as presented in Aristotle (*Rhet.* 1.9.16–25) and Theon (*Prog.* 110). Neyrey also demonstrates that this rhetorical tradition can be found in the literature of Israel, namely in the books of Maccabees. See especially 1 Macc 4 and 9, 2 Mac 6–7, 4 Macc 5–11, and Josephus, *A.J.* 17.152–154, 295–300.

35 Saint Augustine, *City of God*, trans. David S. Wiesen, LCL (London: W. Heinemann, 1960), 19.23; Martin Hengel, *The Cross of the Son of God* (London: SCM, 1986), 94–96. Cf. 1 Cor 1:18 and Justin's, *Apology* 1, 13.4.

world, the shameful tenor of death by crucifixion was inescapable.[36] However, in the Passion Narrative, where the Fourth Gospel might be expected to depart from its otherwise encomiastic structure, it does not. Though the typical noble death included fighting courageously in the face of death (see in Plutarch, *Caes.* 66.4–7 how Caesar fought bravely and wounded many of his murderers as they attacked), the hero in the Fourth Gospel does just the opposite. Still, the Johannine Passion Narrative significantly corresponds to several details outlined in the discussion of encomiastic topics in the Greek rhetorical tradition on noble deeds and noble death. Thus, the Johannine presentation unexpectedly glorifies and honors the subject, transforming the traditional "status degradation ritual" of crucifixion into a "status elevation ritual."[37]

The Fourth Gospel accomplishes this "alchemy" (Theon 111 [Kennedy, 52])[38] by presenting Jesus's crucifixion in a way that corresponds to the rhetorical expectation for "fine actions" and "noble death." Theon describes encomiastic "fine actions" as those "done for others rather than ourselves." He says, "the toil is that of the doer but the benefit is common, " and states that actions are specifically to be praised if they are done "alone" (Theon 110 [Kennedy, 51]). Prudence, the exercise of one's own volition rather than simply following what comes by chance (Theon 111 [Kennedy, 52]), is to be praised. These characteristics are seen in the Johannine portrayal of Jesus heading toward his death. Before the Passion Narrative, the Fourth Gospel shows Jesus accepting his impending death as an action done for others (10:11; 12:27ff.). Within the Passion Narrative, Jesus is seen as taking this "fine action" alone (18:8; 19:17) and willfully (10:18; 18:4, 11; 19:17).[39]

In the Fourth Gospel, Jesus has full knowledge of his future and is the initiator of his fate.[40] The Johannine narrative lacks the Synoptic's famous plea to escape death in Gethsemane (Matt 26:36–46; Mark 14:32–42; Luke 22:39–46). John 12:27 contains the only hint of torment in the Johannine narrative: "now my soul is troubled." Though he is realistic, the Johannine Jesus knows his purpose and would not dare ask to escape the suffering. Note the vivid display of

---

36   Josephus (*J.W.* 7.203 [Thackeray, LCL]) calls it "the most wretched of deaths." Historians like Tacitus (*Hist.* 2.72, 4.11) record that it was reserved for the lowly—robbers, traitors, and slaves. In short, there was nothing honorable about it. Bringing shame to the convict was as important as inflicting physical suffering and death.
37   Neyrey, *The Gospel of John*, 413–14.
38   Neyrey, *The Gospel of John*, 418.
39   Bultmann, *John*, 637.
40   The statement in John 18:4, εἰδὼς πάντα τὰ ἐρχόμενα ἐπ' αὐτόν, sets the stage for the Passion Narrative (cf., 12:27; 13:1), which goes on to demonstrate Jesus's initiative. Neyrey, *The Gospel of John*, 419.

volition: "And what should I say—'Father, save me from this hour'? But because of this I have come to this hour" (12:27b–c). Indeed the Johannine Jesus was resolved to the end, approaching the arresting party ("Whom are you seeking?"[41]), handing himself over ("I am he"), and forbidding any resistance ("Put your sword back into its sheath. The cup which the Father has given to me, shall I not drink it?") (18:4–5a, 10–11).[42] Such a perspective coheres well with the description in *Rhetorica ad Herennium*: "Again, from an honourable act no peril or toil, however great, should divert us; death ought to be preferred to disgrace; no pain should force an abandonment of duty ... it behoves us to brave any peril and endure any toil" (3.3.5 [Caplan]; cf. 3.5.9). In contrast to the Synoptic Jesus, anguishing over his fate but ultimately surrendering to God's will, the Fourth Gospel portrays Jesus as an eager and victorious martyr who knowingly approaches his destiny.[43] Stepping into the Passion by his own initiative and controlling the entire episode, Jesus appropriates the ultimate, "fine action," a noble death fitting of an encomiastic narrative. Once again, the Fourth Gospel links these characteristics to his unity with the Father. The comment, "Knowing that the Father had given all things into his hands, and that he had come from God and was going to God" (13:3; cf. 3:35), signals the narrative turn to Jesus's Passion. Thus, the Fourth Gospel presents Jesus's Passion as a noble death flowing from Jesus's unity with the Father.

Theon explains that in an encomium, any statement said against the subject should be left unmentioned or should be disguised or hidden since charges against the subject would invite blame (Theon 112). Interestingly, in the Johannine portrayal of the high priest's questioning of Jesus, no formal invective is included. The charges are only implicit and assumed (18:19).[44]

---

41   The absence of Judas's kiss portrays Jesus as a willing martyr, in control of the situation, even approaching the arresting party himself (18:4).
42   Jesus's control of the situation is further demonstrated as he commands his followers not to resist (18:10–11) and his captors to let his disciples go (18:8).
43   The response ἐγώ εἰμί (which the Markan/Lukan Jesus made during his trial; Mark 14:62; Luke 22:70) not only has theological implications (based on the response of the crowd who draw back and fall to the ground) but also shows Jesus's initiative to give himself over willingly of his own accord. The posturing in the episode also conveys honor, which is pertinent to the Fourth Gospel's encomiastic tenor. Ignace de La Potterie, *The Hour of Jesus: The Passion and the Resurrection of Jesus according to John: Text and Spirit*, trans. Gregory Murray (Middlegreen, Slough, UK: St Paul Publications, 1989), 29; Neyrey, *The Gospel of John*, 419. Cf. Ezek 1:28; 44:4; Dan 2:46; Rev 1:17.
44   "No witnesses appear, and no definite accusations are lodged; the saying of Jesus about the temple plays no role. In particular, the question of the High Priest about the Messianic claim of Jesus and Jesus's answer to it are lacking. Consequently, there is not a word

In the Johannine presentation of the exchange with Pilate, the Jewish leaders initially avoid issuing a formal accusation (18:30). Only after Pilate has affirmed Jesus's innocence no less than three times (18:38; 19:4, 6) do the leaders state a formal accusation against him—"We have a law, and according to that law he ought to die because he made himself the Son of God" (19:7).[45] This accusation is reminiscent of the narrative's first indication that there is a threat against Jesus's life. "Because of this then, the Jews were seeking to kill him even more, because he was not only breaking the Sabbath, but was also calling God his own Father, making himself equal to God" (5:18).[46] Thus, the very reason for Jesus's arrest and crucifixion centers on his unity with the Father.[47]

An additional encomiastic feature can be found at the moment of Jesus's death. The Johannine Jesus gives up his spirit but goes beyond his Synoptic counterparts declaring, "It is finished." Jesus's action in giving up his spirit is

about the results of the session, or of the death sentence." Bultmann, *John*, 642. This is striking considering that the other Passion accounts treat this element of the narrative as an official court session illustrating the charges levied against Jesus (Matt 26:61–65; Mark 14:58–63; Luke 22:66–71). The shameful elements in this scene—that Jesus is subjected to questioning and even slapped in the face—are counterbalanced by Jesus's honorable responses: "I have spoken openly to the world ... I have said nothing in secret" (18:20) and "If I have spoken wrongly, testify concerning the wrong. But if well, why do you strike me?" (18:23). Similarly, Jesus's response to Pilate denotes his honor. Rather than remaining in the position of the one being questioned, the Johannine Jesus responds to Pilate with a question of his own, taking an authoritative rhetorical posture and challenging Pilate's authority: "Are you saying this from yourself, or did others tell you about me?" Jesus also affirms his authority and status using Pilate's own words. He also clarifies that his is not an empty claim to earthly kingship, but a divine claim to heavenly kingship (18:34–37). Neyrey, *The Gospel of John*, 424–25.

45   Further solidifying the encomiastic presentation, the accusation levied against Jesus is not inherently negative. A claim to be the Son of God is only negative if the claim is false. From the point of view of the author or an informed audience member, Jesus does nothing wrong in claiming to be the Son of God, since the narrative presents him as such. Jesus refuses to answer Pilate's questions and directly challenges Pilate's authority: "You have no power over at all except what was given to you from above" (19:11–12). Pilate affirms Jesus's innocence and continually attempts to release him, and only when the religious leaders bring a political threat does Pilate resign to allow an innocent man to be crucified (19:12–16).

46   Cf. 10:33 where the Jewish leaders explain to Jesus why they are attempting to stone him: "because you, though only a human being, are making yourself God."

47   The encomiastic presentation of Jesus continues through even the crucifixion, where Jesus honorably carries the cross by himself (19:17) and his title "King of the Jews" is affirmed by Pilate (19:19, 21–22). Jesus's exaltation is also seen in the wordplay describing his placement on the cross; he is "lifted up" (ὑψόω) as if enthroned, an image foreshadowed in John 3:14; 8:28; 12:32–34.

reminiscent of his words from John 10:18, "No one takes [my life] from me, but I lay it down of my own accord ... I have received this command from my Father."[48] Here, Jesus's exercise of his own will and his connection to his Father is made explicit even at the moment of his death.[49] The shepherd imagery recalled from John 10 further emphasizes Jesus's unity with the Father.[50] The image of the Good Shepherd recalls Num 27:16–17, presenting Jesus as a leader and caretaker like Moses or Joshua.[51] Another important image is found in Ezekiel 34,[52] which implies that Jesus is not only *a* good shepherd, he is *the* good shepherd, the awaited servant called David (Ezek 34:23).[53] Further still, in Ezekiel 34 YHWH promises to seek out Israel himself, to gather Israel and provide for them (Ezek 34:13–14). The claim is most forceful in vv. 11 and 15:

---

48 In the accounts of Mark and Matthew, Jesus cries with a loud voice and dies with one last exhale (Mark 15:37; Matt 27:50). This manner of death communicates no volition on the part of Jesus; he is but a victim. Luke, retaining the manner of death in Mark and Matthew, adds words to Jesus's cry, "Father, into your hands I place my spirit" (Luke 23:46).
49 Neyrey, *The Gospel of John*, 433.
50 Jesus's statement that he is the gate to "pasture" and abundant life further demonstrates that his death is noble, benefitting others (10:9–11).
51 Moses prays for YHWH to send someone: "who shall go out before them and come in before them, who shall lead them out and bring them in, so that the congregation of the LORD may not be like sheep without a shepherd." D. Moody Smith, *John*, Abingdon New Testament Commentaries (Nashville: Abingdon, 1999), 204–9. The verbal links are quite strong. In Num 27:17 YHWH replies that Moses should select Joshua (Ἰησοῦς in the LXX). In addition to the reference to sheep, the link between Jesus and Joshua is clear, and the description of Joshua in LXX 27:18 (ὃς ἔχει πνεῦμα ἐν ἑαυτῷ) is very nearly replicated in John the Baptist's description of Jesus: τεθέαμαι τὸ πνεῦμα καταβαῖνον ὡς περιστερὰν ἐξ οὐρανοῦ καὶ ἔμεινεν ἐπ' αὐτόν (John 1:32; cf. 33). Three verbs from this Johannine section (ἐξελεύσεται, εἰσελεύσεται, and ἐξάξει) are also found in the description of the leader Moses requests: ὅστις ἐξελεύσεται πρὸ προσώπου αὐτῶν καὶ ὅστις εἰσελεύσεται πρὸ προσώπου αὐτῶν καὶ ὅστις ἐξάξει αὐτοὺς καὶ ὅστις εἰσάξει αὐτούς, καὶ οὐκ ἔσται ἡ συναγωγὴ κυρίου ὡσεὶ πρόβατα, οἷς οὐκ ἔστιν ποιμήν (LXX Num 27:17).
52 Hartwig Thyen, *Das Johannesevangelium*, HNT 6 (Tübingen: Mohr Siebeck, 2005), 486; Frederick Dale Bruner, *The Gospel of John: A Commentary* (Grand Rapids: Eerdmans, 2012), 629. With this background in mind, John 10 sets up a contrast between Jesus and "false shepherds" who do not care for or feed the flock (Ezek 34:1–6). C.H. Dodd, *The Interpretation of the Fourth Gospel* (Cambridge: Cambridge University Press, 1968), 358–61. The Johannine discourse sets up Jesus as the genuine caretaker, whereas the thieves, bandits, and hired hands do not protect the sheep but allow them to be scattered and destroyed. In the literary context, the allusion to bad shepherds almost certainly comments on the Pharisees who, as was shown in chapter 9, did not care for the blind man but rather drove him out.
53 This image of the awaited shepherd, a branch of David, resounds throughout the Hebrew Bible in the Psalms and the Prophets (Ps 78:70–72; Jer 23:4–6; Mic 5:2–4).

"For thus says the Lord GOD: I *myself* will search for my sheep, and will seek them out... I *myself* will be the shepherd of my sheep."[54] With this background in mind, Jesus's claim, "I am the Good Shepherd," shows that his life and death will be for the benefit of the sheep, that he is a good shepherd in the tradition of leaders like Moses and Joshua, that he is the awaited shepherd from the line of David—but it also establishes and emphasizes his unity with God who claims that he *himself* will act on behalf of his sheep.[55] It is almost as if, in the good shepherd discourse, believers can hear Jesus saying: "You are my sheep ... and I am your God" (Ezek 34:31). This interpretation, lest it should seem too far-reaching, is supported by Jesus's unequivocal claim in the same chapter, "The Father and I are one" (10:30).[56]

The Fourth Gospel takes the unmistakably shameful nature of the arrest, trial, and crucifixion and uses it to honor the subject, causing virtue to shine forth especially in misfortune (Theon 111 [Kennedy, 52]).[57] Illustrating Jesus's prudence and volition, making the accusations against Jesus implicit, couching the formal accusations within the context of an authoritative figure confirming Jesus's innocence, and emphasizing the benefit his death had for others,[58]

---

54 YHWH is invoked as shepherd especially in the Psalms, when Israel is called his flock (Ps 79:13; 80:2; 95:7; 100:3).
55 See Smith, *John*, 207.
56 The Gospel anticipates this shocking statement already, since it has already called Jesus the Word who both was *with* God and who *was* God (1:1). Jesus is certainly distinguishable from God, but he is also in unity with God and thus able to manifest God's presence in a way that God's people had never experienced. Smith, *John*, 211; Bruner, *The Gospel of John*, 630; D.A. Carson, *The Gospel according to John* (Leicester: Inter-Varsity, 1991), 381–82; Thyen, *Das Johannesevangelium*, 486.
57 Neyrey, *The Gospel of John*, 418.
58 That the suffering of the Passion Narrative was for the benefit of others can also be seen in John the Baptist's foreshadowing statement at the beginning of the Fourth Gospel where Jesus is called "the Lamb of God who takes away the sin of the world" (John 1:29). While many theories have been proposed as a background for this imagery, its extension into the Passion Narrative indicates that the Passover Lamb is a promising proposal. The Passover imagery is also recalled in the Fourth Gospel's chronology. In contrast to the Synoptic chronology, the Fourth Gospel reports that Jesus's crucifixion coincided with the slaughter of the paschal lambs (18:28; 19:14). Mention of the hyssop branch and that none of Jesus's bones are broken also serve to support this connection (19:29, 19:36; Exod 12:46). Neyrey, *The Gospel of John*, 434. For alternative readings of the Johannine chronology and discussion of the ancient Jewish calendar, see Annie Jaubert, *La Date de la Cène: Calendrier biblique et Liturgie chrétienne* (Paris: J. Gabalda, 1957); Eugen Ruckstuhl, *Chronology of the Last Days of Jesus: A Critical Study* (New York: Desclee, 1965), 50–55, 136–39. As the Lamb of God, Jesus's noble death transforms the negative situation of humanity into a positive one. Jesper Tang Nielsen, "The Lamb of God: The Cognitive Structure

the Fourth Gospel maintains its encomiastic tone as the narrative brings the hero to his noble death. In this way, the Fourth Gospel characterizes Jesus's lasting significance and honor by showing the glory of his death.[59] This glory is linked to Jesus's unity with the Father, since his unity with the Father incited the hostility that led to his death, the charge against him is his claim to be one with the Father, and his claim to be the Good Shepherd mirrors YHWH's promise to act on behalf of his sheep.

According to the progymnasmata, the encomiastic presentation of noble death should also include events after death, like a proper burial, games held in the hero's honor or oracles about his death, vindication of wrongful death through the words of respected men, deeds of retribution, or supernatural phenomena (Ps.-Hermogenes 16–17 [Kennedy, 82]). These elements follow the records of death for many significant figures: festivals and buildings for Timoleon, public projects for Demosthenes, postmortem praise for Cicero, and divine vindication for Caesar.[60] The events after Jesus's death in the Fourth

---

of a Johannine Metaphor," in *Imagery in the Gospel of John: Terms, Forms, Themes, and Theology of Johannine Figurative Language*, ed. Jörg Frey, Ruben Zimmermann, and Jan G. van der Watt, WUNT 200 (Tübingen: Mohr Siebeck, 2006), 256. See also Raymond Edward Brown, *The Death of the Messiah: From Gethsemane to the Grave, a Commentary on the Passion Narratives in the Four Gospels*, 2 vols. (New York: Doubleday, 1994), 2:895–96. For a survey of other suggestions for the Lamb of God imagery, see Nielsen, "Lamb of God," 225–26.

59   Jurgen Zangenberg, "'Buried According to the Customs of the Jews': John 19,40 in Its Material and Literary Context," in *The Death of Jesus in the Fourth Gospel*, ed. Gilbert van Belle, BETL 200 (Leuven: Leuven University Press, 2007), 874.

60   For example, Plutarch records the elaborate burial of the beloved Timoleon, which included a decree of future contests, festivals, and building projects (Plutarch, *Tim.* 39 [Perrin, LCL, 353–55]). Similarly, women observed Demosthenes' death by fasting in the temple and erecting his statue in bronze, decreeing that the eldest of his house should have public maintenance in the prytaneium (Plutarch, *Dem.* 30.4–5 [Perrin, LCL, 77]). Plutarch also said that the wrongful murder of Cicero by Antony was vindicated postmortem through the words and actions of Caesar, recording that Caesar called him, "a learned man and a lover of his country" and chose Cicero's son as his colleague in the office (Plutarch, *Cic.* 49.3–4 [Perrin, LCL, 209]). Plutarch also records that after Caesar himself was murdered, the senate voted to give him divine honors and to retain the majority of the policies he had instilled during his rule. Further, the will of Caesar was an ongoing testament to his generosity, demonstrating his honorable character even postmortem (Plutarch, *Caes.* 68.1). The account goes on to show how Caesar's "great guardian genius" (δαίμων) continued to work toward his ultimate vindication, tracking down his killers and punishing them (Plutarch, *Caes.* 69.1–2 [Perrin, LCL, 605]). Adding even more honor to the presentation, Plutarch records how both natural and supernatural events surrounding Caesar's murder further vindicated and glorified him (Plutarch, *Caes.* 69.3 [Perrin, LCL, 605–7]). A vision further demonstrated that the gods saw Caesar's murder as an unjust tragedy (Plutarch, *Caes.* 69.5–8 [Perrin, LCL, 607–9]; cf. *Brutus*, 36; 52).

Gospel lend a similarly encomiastic tenor to the closing chapter of the hero's story. Though a shameful burial would be expected for victims of a crucifixion,[61] the statement in John 19:40 that Jesus's body was handled "according to the burial customs of the Jews" makes a striking contrast to this dishonorable expectation. Two important men are responsible for this intervention, Joseph of Arimathea, who requests Jesus's body from Pilate, and Nicodemus.[62] This initiative for Jesus on the part of reputable men (Theon 110; John of Sardis 123) brings the encomiastic tenor even to the events after the hero's death. In the Fourth Gospel Jesus is given not only a "proper" Jewish burial, but an overtly honorable one with a large amount of spices and a brand new tomb (19:39–41).

In the conclusion to the Fourth Gospel, Jesus rises from death to greet and comfort his followers.[63] The resurrection vindicates Jesus, showing that he overcame death and validating his predictions from earlier in the narrative.[64] This again recalls Jesus's words in John 10:17–18: "I lay down my life in order to take it up again. No one has taken it from me, but I lay it down of my own accord. I have power to lay it down, and I have power to take it up again." And again, Jesus's honorable prudence and volition is linked to his unity with the Father: "I have received this command from my Father." Jesus's resurrection appearances continue to emphasize his unity with the Father. Appearing first to Mary Magdalene, the resurrected Jesus tells her, "I am ascending to my Father and your Father, to my God and your God" (John 20:18). The encomiastic presentation of the events after the hero's death have the risen hero continuing

---

[61] The expected "burial" for the hero in the Fourth Gospel, a victim of crucifixion, was the antithesis of honorable or praiseworthy. At best, the bodies of convicts would be buried together indiscriminately and in an unmarked grave; and at worst, they would have been tossed in a pit for scavengers. Zangenberg, "'Buried According to the Customs of the Jews,'" 876. Neyrey, *The Gospel of John*, 434.

[62] Both of these were men of considerable importance. The narrative had already described the latter as a Pharisee and leader of the Jews, and the former is now described as one in high enough position to have access to Pilate—and to have his request granted. Zangenberg, "'Buried According to the Customs of the Jews,'" 877–78.

[63] His actions after death include miraculous appearances (20:19, 26), commissioning the disciples and giving the Holy Spirit (20:21–23), facilitating a miraculous catch of fish (21:4–8, 10–11), preparing a meal for his disciples (21:9, 12–14), and reinstating Peter (21:15–19).

[64] In John 2:19, Jesus says to the Pharisees, "Destroy this temple, and in three days I will raise it up." The narrator clarifies that Jesus was not speaking of the Jerusalem temple, rather, he was using "the temple" as a metaphor for his body. The additional explanation links this prediction with Jesus's resurrection: "When, therefore, he was raised from the dead, his disciples remembered that he had said this" (2:22).

to act for the benefit of others and continuing to emphasize his unity with the Father.[65]

In striking resemblance to the conclusion of the encomium of Thucydides—"Many other things could be said about Thucydides, if the mass of his praises did not fall short of telling everything" (Aphthonius the Sophist 38 [Kennedy, 110])—the Fourth Gospel concludes with the statement: "But there is more that Jesus did; if every one of these events was recorded, I suppose that the world itself could not contain the books that would be written" (21:25).

2.6   *Summary*

The Fourth Gospel's use of the encomiastic topics demonstrates that unity with God, expressed in Jesus's origin, training, mission and deeds, suffering and death, formed the basis of his exalted status. Unity with God was the determining factor for Jesus's identity, his authority, and his actions in the world.

3   Elusive Ethics in the Fourth Gospel

The Fourth Gospel's use of the rhetorical topics brings attention to Jesus's unity with the Father as foundational for his exalted status and as an indispensable concept for understanding Jesus's life orientation. Before diving into the tension between the elevated Christology and ethics in the Fourth Gospel, it will be helpful to briefly sketch the pursuit of Johannine ethics to see why it has often been characterized as "elusive."

3.1   *Johannine Ethics in the History of Scholarship*

Broadly speaking, the ethics of the Fourth Gospel is a neglected field of study in both New Testament and Johannine scholarship.[66] New Testament scholars

---

65   This unity with the Father is grounded in Jesus's divine origin as expressed in the prologue. The Gospel began by depicting the Word's descent from the Father to the world, and it is concluding with Jesus's words that he will return to the Father. These verses also move the rhetorical trajectory forward, bringing the believers into the unity shared between Jesus and the Father ("my Father and your Father, my God and your God" and "as the Father sent me, so I send you"). This idea will be unpacked in the "Theme of Unity" section below.

66   Currently, there are no monographs dedicated to the ethics of the Fourth Gospel within the field of Biblical Studies. Theological approaches to ethics provide some engagement with the Johannine material. Natural law ethics builds upon the Johannine prologue (e.g., Aquinas's understanding of the natural law as the expression of the eternal law in creation). The Alexandrians also utilized the logic of the *logos* in similar ways. The Fourth

routinely give only sparse attention to the Fourth Gospel in their discussions of New Testament ethics,[67] preferring the more explicit hortatory material in the Pauline epistles or the Synoptic sermons to what Heinz-Dietrich Wendland called "an enormous reduction of ethical questions and statements" in the Fourth Gospel.[68] Noting the christological and theological value of the Fourth Gospel, these scholars have abandoned the topic of ethics in its own right.[69] In his recent assessment of the state of the question, Ruben Zimmermann claimed that, despite the controversy typical in our field, "New Testament scholarship appears to find consensus on one subject—there is general agreement that the Fourth Gospel contains no ethics."[70] Until the last decade this was largely true of Johannine scholarship, which either neglected the topic

---

Gospel's dualistic language indirectly influenced the "two ways" language of both early (e.g. *Didache*) and later catechetical and ethical texts. The 19th/20th-century Protestant fixation on *agape* is indebted to the Fourth Gospel's flexible presentation of ethics (e.g., Kierkegaard's *Works of Love*, Anders Nygren's *Agape and Eros*, and Reinhold Niebuhr's Christian realism).

[67] Heinz-Dietrich Wendland, *Ethik des Neuen Testaments: Eine Einführung*, 3rd ed., NTD 4 (Göttingen: Vandenhoeck & Ruprecht, 1978); Willi Marxsen, *"Christliche" und christliche Ethik im Neuen Testament* (Gütersloh: Gütersloher Verlagshaus Gerd Mohn, 1989); Frank J. Matera, *New Testament Ethics: The Legacies of Jesus and Paul* (Louisville: Westminster John Knox, 1996).

[68] Wendland, *Ethik des Neuen Testaments*, 109.

[69] Rudolf Schnackenburg, *The Moral Teaching of the New Testament* (New York: Seabury, 1973), 148–92; Eduard Lohse, *Theological Ethics of the New Testament* (Minneapolis: Fortress, 1991), 166–70; Georg Strecker, *Theology of the New Testament*, ed. Friedrich Wilhelm Horn and M. Eugene Boring (New York: Westminster John Knox, 2000); Russell Pregeant, *Knowing Truth, Doing Good: Engaging New Testament Ethics* (Minneapolis: Fortress, 2008). For example, J.L. Houlden, *Ethics and the New Testament* (London: T&T Clark International, 2004), 35–40, suggests that the Fourth Gospel's contribution is solely christological, and Wolfgang Schrage, *The Ethics of the New Testament* (Philadelphia: Fortress, 1988), 297, suggests that it belongs only to New Testament theology.

[70] Ruben Zimmermann, "Is There Ethics in the Gospel of John? Challenging an Outdated Consensus," in *Rethinking the Ethics of John: "Implicit Ethics" in the Johannine Writings*, ed. Jan G. van der Watt and Ruben Zimmermann, WUNT 291 (Tübingen: Mohr Siebeck, 2012), 44–88. See also the following reports: Walter Rebell, "Neutestamentliche Ethik— Anmerkungen zum gegenwärtigen Diskussionsstand," *ZEE* 32 (1988): 143–51; Petr Pokorný, "Neutestamentliche Ethik und die Probleme ihrer Darstellungen," *EvT* 50 (1990): 357–71; Friedrich Wilhelm Horn, "Ethik des Neuen Testaments 1982–1992," *TRu* 60 (1995): 32–86; Werner Zager, "Neutestamentliche Ethik im Spiegel der Forschung," *ZNT* 11 (2003): 3–13; Richard B. Hays, "Mapping the Field: Approaches to New Testament Ethics," in *Identity, Ethics, and Ethos in the New Testament*, ed. Jan G. van der Watt, BZNW 141 (Berlin: Walter de Gruyter, 2006), 3–19.

of Johannine ethics[71] or deemed it an extremely limited presentation, given the scarcity of expected forms of moral instruction (e.g., maxims, paraenetic sections, or sermons with practical instructions).[72] Johannine scholarship has recently begun to explore new possibilities for a Johannine ethic, recognizing

---

71   See Klaus Scholtissek, "Johannine Studies: A Survey of Recent Research with Special Regard to German Contributions I," *CurRBS* 6 (1998): 227–259 and Klaus Scholtissek, "Johannine Studies: A Survey of Recent Research with Special Regard to German Contributions II," *CurRBS* 9 (2001): 277–305, which survey German commentaries including Schenke, Wilckens, and Schnelle and suggest that recent scholarship has focused on the relationship to the Synoptics, Christology, and eschatology. Aside from one reference to the foot washing, this extensive survey does not mention Johannine ethics. Zimmermann, "Is There Ethics in the Gospel of John?," 45, examines recent commentaries—Wengst, Dietzfelbinger, Thyen, Theobald, Carson, Moloney, Keener, Köstenberger, and Lincoln—for which the subject of ethics is "of practically no importance." See also Udo Schnelle, "Ein neuer Blick: Tendenzen der gegenwärtigen Johanneforschung," *BTZ* 16 (1999): 29–40; Paul Anderson, "Beyond the Shade of the Oak Tree: The Recent Growth of Johannine Studies," *ExpTim* 119 (2008): 365–73; Francis Moloney, "Recent Johannine Studies: Part One: Commentaries," *ExpTim* 123 (2012): 313–22; Moloney, "Recent Johannine Studies: Part Two: Monographs," *ExpTim* 123 (2012): 417–28.

72   The Fourth Gospel does reference Jesus's "commands" (10:18; 13:34; 14:15, 21; 15:10, 12, 14). Some take this as referring to the Torah (Jey J. Kanagaraj, "The Implied Ethics of the Fourth Gospel: A Reinterpretation of the Decalogue," *TynBul* 52 [2001]: 33–60), while others take it as referring to the more explicit ethical teaching of the Synoptic tradition (D. Moody Smith, *John among the Gospels*, 2nd ed. [Columbia: University of South Carolina Press, 2001]). More appealing is the suggestion that the referents are located within the Fourth Gospel itself. Glen Lund, "The Joys and Dangers of Ethics in John's Gospel," in *Rethinking the Ethics of John: "Implicit Ethics" in the Johannine Writings*, ed. Jan G. van der Watt and Ruben Zimmermann, WUNT 291 (Tübingen: Mohr Siebeck, 2012), 264–89. See also Urban C. von Wahlde, *The Johannine Commandments: 1 John and the Struggle for the Johannine Tradition* (New York: Paulist, 1990); Käsemann, *The Testament of Jesus*; Jack T. Sanders, *Ethics in the New Testament: Change and Development* (Philadelphia: Fortress, 1975), 91–100; Jürgen Becker, "Feindesliebe—Nächstenliebe—Bruderliebe: Exegetische Beobachtungen als Anfrage an ein ethisches Problemfeld," *ZEE* 25 (1981): 5–17; Meeks, "The Ethics of the Fourth Evangelist." See Hartwig Thyen, *Studien zum Corpus Iohanneum* (WUNT 214; Tübingen: Mohr Siebeck, 2007), 623–30, and Labahn, "It's Only Love," 22–24, for a survey of this topic. Johannine ethics is often reduced to the "new commandment" and deemed a sectarian and/or docetic restriction of the Synoptic love command. Certain ideological emphases in the Fourth Gospel also appear to stand in tension with the nature of traditional ethical discourse. E.g., the Fourth Gospel's dualism proves resistant to human development, which is vital to ethical formation, and its predeterminative presentation seems to preclude independent agency, a necessity for moral development. These observations are taken largely from Meeks, "The Ethics of the Fourth Evangelist," 318–19.

that the Fourth Gospel is "laden with ethical implications."[73] Together with Ruben Zimmermann, the guild has begun to ask whether "the problem perhaps lies not in the absence of ethical issues but rather in the one-sidedness of the search for a particular form of ethics."[74] Such thinking has resulted in promising new avenues of research such as attending to the Gospel's imagery for ethical content,[75] considering the ethical implications of the Law in the Fourth Gospel,[76] examining the Gospel's "narrative ethics,"[77] approaching ethics via the concept of imitation[78] or as the natural outgrowth of certain

---

[73] Johannes Nissen, "Community and Ethics in the Gospel of John," in *New Readings in John: Literary and Theological Perspectives; Essays from the Scandinavian Conference on the Fourth Gospel in Aarhus 1997*, ed. Johannes Nissen and Sigfred Pedersen, JSNTSup 182 (Sheffield: Sheffield Academic, 1999), 194–212. See also D. Moody Smith, "Ethics and the Interpretation of the Fourth Gospel," in *Word, Theology, and Community in John*, ed. John Painter, R. Alan Culpepper, and Fernando F. Segovia (St. Louis: Chalice, 2002), 109–22.

[74] Zimmermann, "Is There Ethics in the Gospel of John?," 57.

[75] Jan G. van der Watt, "Ethics Alive in Imagery," in *Imagery in the Gospel of John: Terms, Forms, Themes, and Theology of Johannine Figurative Language*, ed. Jörg Frey, Jan G. van der Watt, and Ruben Zimmermann, WUNT 200 (Tübingen: Mohr Siebeck, 2006), 421–48.

[76] Jan G. van der Watt, "Radical Social Redefinition and Radical Love: Ethics and Ethos in the Gospel According to John," in *Identity, Ethics, and Ethos in the New Testament*, ed. Jan G. van der Watt, BZNW 141 (Berlin: Walter de Gruyter, 2006), 107–33; Kanagaraj, "Implied Ethics"; Jan G. van der Watt, "Ethics of/and the Opponents of Jesus in John's Gospel," in *Rethinking the Ethics of John: "Implicit Ethics" in the Johannine Writings*, ed. Jan G. van der Watt and Ruben Zimmermann, WUNT 291 (Tübingen: Mohr Siebeck, 2012), 175–91.

[77] See Zimmermann, "Is There Ethics in the Gospel of John?," 63–69; Michael Labahn, "Der Weg eines Namenlosen—Vom Hilflosen zum Vorbild (Joh 9): Ansätze zu einer narrativen Ethik der sozialen Verantwortung im vierten Evangelium," in *Die bleibende Gegenwart des Evangeliums: Festschrift für Otto Merk*, ed. Roland Gebauer and Martin Meiser (Marburg: Elwert, 2003), 63–80; J. Bolyki, "Ethics in the Gospel of John," CV 45 (2003): 198–208; Udo Schnelle, "Johanneische Ethik," in *Eschatologie und Ethik im frühen Christentum: Festschrift für Günther Haufe zum 75. Geburtstag*, ed. Christfried Böttrich (Frankfurt am Main: Peter Lang, 2006), 309–27.

[78] Richard A. Burridge, *Imitating Jesus: An Inclusive Approach to New Testament Ethics* (Grand Rapids: Eerdmans, 2007). See also his "Imitating Jesus: An Inclusive Approach to the Ethics of the Historical Jesus and John's Gospel," in *John, Jesus, and History*, ed. Paul N. Anderson, Felix Just, and Tom Thatcher, Early Christianity and its Literature (Atlanta: SBL, 2009), 281–90; Christos Karakolis, "Semeia Conveying Ethics in the Gospel according to John," in *Rethinking the Ethics of John: "Implicit Ethics" in the Johannine Writings*, ed. Jan G. van der Watt and Ruben Zimmermann, WUNT 291 (Tübingen: Mohr Siebeck, 2012), 192–212. Rudolf Schnackenburg, *Die sittliche Botschaft des Neuen Testaments: Die urchristlichen Verkündiger*, vol. 2, HTKNTSup 2 (Freiburg et al.: Herder, 1988).

theological topics[79] (like divine love[80] and mission[81]) that are presented in the narrative.[82]

3.2 The Tension between Johannine Christology and Johannine Ethics

"Imitation ethics" recognizes that the source material for ethics need not be limited to Jesus's teachings. Rather, like Graeco-Roman *bioi* written during that time period, the deeds of the story's hero become an ethical example.[83]

---

[79] Rainer Hirsch-Luipold, "Prinzipiell-theologische Ethik in der Johanneischen Literatur," in *Jenseits von Indikativ und Imperative*, ed. Friedrich Wilhelm Horn and Ruben Zimmermann, WUNT 238 (Tübingen: Mohr Siebeck, 2009), 289–307; van der Watt, "Ethics of/and the Opponents of Jesus in John's Gospel"; Zimmermann, "Is There Ethics in the Gospel of John?"; Volker Rabens, "Johannine Perspectives on Ethical Enabling in the Context of Stoic and Philonic Ethics," in *Rethinking the Ethics of John: "Implicit Ethics" in the Johannine Writings*, ed. Jan G. van der Watt and Ruben Zimmermann, WUNT 291 (Tübingen: Mohr Siebeck, 2012), 114–39.

[80] Willard M. Swartley, *Covenant of Peace: The Missing Piece in New Testament Theology and Ethics* (Grand Rapids: Eerdmans, 2006); Stephen C. Barton, "Johannine Dualism and Contemporary Pluralism" (3–18) and Miroslav Volf, "Johannine Dualism and Contemporary Pluralism," in *The Gospel of John and Christian Theology*, ed. Richard Bauckham and Carl Mosser (Grand Rapids: Eerdmans, 2008), 19–50.

[81] Hermut Löhr, "Ἔργον as an Element of Moral Language in John," in *Rethinking the Ethics of John: "Implicit Ethics" in the Johannine Writings*, ed. Jan G. van der Watt and Ruben Zimmermann, WUNT 291 (Tübingen: Mohr Siebeck, 2012), 229–49; Kobus Kok, "As the Father Has Sent Me, I Send You: Towards a Missional-Incarnational Ethos in John 4," in *Moral Language in the New Testament: The Interrelatedness of Language and Ethics in Early Christian Writings*, ed. Ruben Zimmermann and Jan G. van der Watt, WUNT 296 (Tübingen: Mohr Siebeck, 2010), 168–93; Ruben Zimmermann, "Metaphoric Networks as Hermeneutic Keys in the Gospel of John," in *Repetitions and Variations in the Fourth Gospel: Style, Text, Interpretation*, ed. Gilbert van Belle, Michael Labahn, and P. Maritz, BETL 223 (Leuven: Peeters, 2009), 381–402.

[82] These publications represent an exciting new movement in Johannine studies, and they have added immeasurably to an evolving discourse. This project, which brings Johannine Christology into conversation with Johannine ethics, joins this movement and specifically engages the latter two approaches. See also the volume from Sherri Brown and Christopher W. Skinner, eds., *Johannine Ethics* (Minneapolis: Fortress, 2017). *Rethinking the Ethics of John* (full citation given above) is responsible for the most significant advances in the area of Johannine Ethics. The introductory essays by Labahn and Zimmermann (cited above) have greatly influenced my own approach to the issues. The entire volume has influenced this essay, especially those chapters by Glicksman (83–101), Rabens (114–39), Loader (143–58), Weyer-Menkhoff (159–74), van der Watt (175–91), Karakolis (192–212), Stare (213–28), Caragounis (250–63), Lund (264–89), and Anderson (290–318). Where appropriate, I have engaged these more substantively in my discussion below.

[83] Burridge, *Imitating Jesus*, 19–32, 330–46. Jesus is imitable in comparison to other divine figures like Yahweh or Sophia, since he has a body and lives on earth as a human man. William Loader, "The Law and Ethics in John's Gospel," in *Rethinking the Ethics*

In John, Jesus's injunctions to his disciples to do as he does (13:14–15; 15:10) and to love as he loved (15:12) support this idea.[84] However, as Wayne Meeks has described, the lofty Jesus of the Fourth Gospel does not provide a readily accessible example for moral living.[85] It is precisely Johannine Christology, which presents Jesus as exalted above other human beings and as one with the Father, that makes Jesus appear to be inimitable in some respects.[86] Herein lies the tension with John's elevated Christology and ethics.

A helpful example of this tension and the need for clarification can be found in John 6, where Jesus feeds the multitude and offers the Bread of Life discourse. In some ways this episode is an expected target for discussions of ethics in the Fourth Gospel. Miroslav Volf contends, "Jesus embodied God's love for the world by feeding the hungry."[87] Since Jesus cares that people eat, the implication is that believers should take up this ethical principle and imitate his physical work to care for physical needs.[88] But the Johannine version of this miraculous feeding complicates such a reading. Compassion, a significant element in the Markan and Matthean versions of this story (Mark 6:34; Matt 14:14) and elsewhere in Synoptic healing stories (Luke 7:13; 13:34 cf. Matt 23:37–39), is completely absent from the Johannine episode.[89] Rather, this Johannine sign

---

of John: "Implicit Ethics" in the Johannine Writings, ed. Jan G. van der Watt and Ruben Zimmermann, WUNT 291 (Tübingen: Mohr Siebeck, 2012), 101.

[84] Jesus's signs can be seen as concrete examples of his care for the world. Karakolis, "Semeia Conveying Ethics," esp. 212.

[85] Meeks, "The Ethics of the Fourth Evangelist."

[86] The christological purpose of the Fourth Gospel and its "larger than life" characterization makes the Johannine Jesus difficult to imitate. Lund, "Joys and Dangers," 278.

[87] Volf, "Johannine Dualism," 41.

[88] Bruner, The Gospel of John, 366. See also Karakolis, "Semeia," who calls Johannine signs, "concrete examples of Jesus's loving care for the people of the world." While some of Karakolis's macrolevel insights are helpful in understanding Johannine ethics, such an approach does not admit the complications that come along with the striking lack of ordinary compassion shown by the Johannine Jesus. Nowhere does the Fourth Gospel make Jesus's care for physical welfare explicit, though it may appear implicitly in some of his signs. Cf. R. Alan Culpepper, "John 5:1–18: A Sample of Narrative Critical Commentary," in The Gospel of John as Literature: An Anthology of Twentieth-Century Perspectives, ed. Mark W.G. Stibbe, NTTS 18 (Leiden: Brill, 1993), 193–207.

[89] Cf. John 4:35, which closely parallels Matt 9:35–38 but includes no mention of compassion. See Schnackenburg's discussion of how the Fourth Gospel turns even those "human elements" to emphasize another (spiritual) level: "With the synoptists we have the warm, compassionate devotion of Jesus to the people. The characteristic sematic fields of 'mercy' and 'pity' are found in all three synoptists but are missing entirely in John." Schnackenburg, Jesus in the Gospels, 241. Cf. D. Moody Smith, Johannine Christianity: Essays on Its Setting, Sources, and Theology (Columbia, SC: University of South Carolina Press, 1984), 179.

comes with an undertone of rebuke.⁹⁰ Even when the Johannine Jesus is not reluctant with his signs or when they are not coupled with rebuke, his purpose is explicit—to reveal God and to elicit belief, not to show compassion for the needy party (9:3; 11:15). Even Jesus's display of grief in 11:33–35 is accompanied by an explanation in 11:40 that all was done for the glory of God.

This episode comes on the heels of a discourse where Jesus has just outlined his credentials for his opponents, stating that John the Baptist, the Father, and Moses (through the Scriptures) testify on his behalf. Beyond these personal testimonies, Jesus's works also testify to his identity and authority (5:31–46). In fact, each sign works to clarify Jesus's identity, and onlookers respond accordingly (2:11; 4:48, 53–54; 5:18, 36; 6:14, 29, 48–51; 9:3, 33, 35–38; 11:15, 25–27). Here in John 6, Jesus rebukes the crowd for whom he had just miraculously supplied a meal: "You are looking for me, not because you saw signs, but because you ate your fill of the loaves. Do not work for the food that perishes, but for the food that endures for eternal life" (6:26–27). Instead of offering more bread to the hungry people, Jesus declares that he is the Bread of Life and offers himself as food.

Jesus's response seems to argue in favor of those who find the christological focus of the Fourth Gospel to be problematic for what can be considered normal ethical conduct, which demands attention to the basic needs of another (food, clothing, shelter). If Johannine Jesus-followers encountered hungry people, should they be moved to give those people actual bread? Or does the narrative suggest that providing "food that perishes" is unimportant in light of "food that endures for eternal life"?⁹¹ Might the critics be right that the christologically-rich Johannine narrative is ethically bankrupt?

3.3 What Are We Looking for in the Pursuit of "Johannine Ethics"?

3.3.1 The Approach

To respond to the idea that the Fourth Gospel may be ethically bankrupt, we should first briefly clarify what we are looking for in the pursuit of Johannine ethics.⁹² An ethical text is usually defined as a text that offers reflective orientation towards one's way of life, defining how to behave according to a specific

---

90　Stern responses often accompany Johannine signs—"what concern is that to you and me?" in John 2:4, "unless you see signs and wonders you will not believe" in John 4:48, "do not sin anymore so that nothing worse happens to you" in John 5:14.

91　See, for example, Robert H. Gundry, *Jesus the Word according to John the Sectarian* (Grand Rapids: Eerdmans, 2002).

92　Such an extensive question cannot be covered exhaustively here. The brief clarification here will be sufficient for the purposes of this essay.

value system and in relation to a certain social group or society at large.[93] The Fourth Gospel is certainly not a formal ethical treatise, and it contains little by way of traditional ethical content. Adding to this difficulty, the term "ethics" is complex in its own right. Scholarship represents a variety of perspectives on what exactly it means for a text to be "ethical."[94] A search for ethical *content* implies looking for explicit statements—in the form of direct imperatives or intentional reflections on the "rightness" or "wrongness" of specific actions—something the Fourth Gospel has very little of.[95] Rather than seeking the ethical *content* within the narrative, a rhetorical approach[96] asks what influence the story would have had on those who were exposed to it, especially those who considered it an authoritative or foundational document for their religious community.[97] Thus, we are particularly interested in the story's ability to influence an audience-member to think or to act a certain way. Johannine

---

[93] Labahn, "'It's Only Love,'" 7.

[94] At times "ethics" is used broadly (almost synonymously with morality), but at other times it is used quite narrowly to indicate an explicit articulation of a moral system or explicit reflection on the rightness or wrongness of specific practices and thoughts. 19th-century German scholarship restricted ethics to the social sphere, leaving morality to the personal sphere, but this distinction has largely fallen away with time. When I speak of ethics, I use it in its broadest sense, almost synonymous with morality, however, I include the implicit understanding that normal moral or ethical conduct includes a social component.

[95] The Gospel does contain some direct commands including the love command and others. Lund, "Joys and Dangers"; von Wahlde, *Johannine Commandments*.

[96] Since James Muilenburg's famous address ("Form Criticism and Beyond," *JBL* 88 [1969]: 1–18), rhetorical criticism (RC) has experienced a renaissance in biblical studies. See Margaret D. Zulick, "The Recollection of Rhetoric: A Brief History," in *Words Well Spoken: George Kennedy's Rhetoric of the New Testament*, ed. C. Clifton Black and Duane F. Watson, Studies in Rhetoric and Religion 8 (Waco: Baylor University Press, 2008), 7–19. Rhetorical studies in the FG include classical and modern approaches like Margaret Davies, *Rhetoric and Reference in the Fourth Gospel*, JSNTSup 69 (Sheffield: JSOT Press, 1992); William M. Wright, *Rhetoric and Theology: Figural Reading of John 9*, BZNW 165 (Berlin: Walter de Gruyter, 2009); Martin, *Judas and the Rhetoric of Comparison in the Fourth Gospel*; Myers, *Characterizing Jesus*; George L. Parsenios, *Rhetoric and Drama in the Johannine Lawsuit Motif*, WUNT 258 (Tübingen: Mohr Siebeck, 2010).

[97] Some Johannine scholars pursue the implicit ethics within the text of the Fourth Gospel, seeking to identify value systems that undergird the happenings of the narrative. Still others consider the ethos of the narrative—noticing the lived behavior that is reflective of an implicit value-system. These concepts are somewhat ambiguous and often interconnected. A rhetorical approach to ethics is inclusive of both the narrower conception of ethics as a value system and ethos. See Jan G. van der Watt, "Ethics and Ethos in the Gospel according to John," *ZNW* 97 (2006): 147–76.

ethics, then, will be found in the rhetorical communicative exchange between the story and the audience.[98]

3.3.2 The Audience

"The origin of the Johannine Gospel is the greatest riddle presented to us by the earliest history of Christianity."[99] This statement made by Adolf von Harnack may now seem a bit hyperbolic given the surge of interest in the "Johannine Community" and the situation behind the Fourth Gospel in recent decades. In the 1960s and 1970s two innovative theories about the Johannine situation changed the face of Johannine studies. In his *History and Theology in the Fourth Gospel*,[100] J. Louis Martyn presented the concept of the "two-level drama," and Raymond E. Brown's *The Community of the Beloved Disciple*[101] supplied a similar paradigm for the background of the Fourth Gospel. The theory suggests that the Fourth Gospel "tells the story both of Jesus and of the community that believed in him."[102] Brown clarifies, "*Primarily*, the Gospels tell us how an evangelist conceived of and presented Jesus to a Christian community in the last third of the first century, a presentation that indirectly gives us an insight into that

---

[98] Kelly R. Iverson ("Orality and the Gospels: A Survey of Recent Research," *CurBR* 8 [2009]: 71–106; "A Centurion's 'Confession': A Performance-Critical Analysis of Mark 15:39," *JBL* 130 [2011]: 329–50; ed., *From Text to Performance: Narrative and Performance Criticisms in Dialogue and Debate* [Eugene, OR: Wipf & Stock, 2014]), William D. Shiell (*Delivering from Memory: The Effect of Performance on the Early Christian Audience* [Eugene, OR: Wipf & Stock, 2011]), Whitney Shiner (*Proclaiming the Gospel: First-Century Performance of Mark* [Harrisburg, PA: Bloomsbury T&T Clark, 2003]), Michael Whitenton (*Hearing Kyriotic Sonship: A Cognitive and Rhetorical Approach to the Characterization of Mark's Jesus* [Leiden: Brill, 2016]) and others have made a good case for considering the performance of these texts. As performed stories, the communicative exchange includes the lector/performer who mediates the relationship between the story and the audience. We will see below how the performance of the text can influence its rhetorical effect on the audience.

[99] Martyn, *History and Theology*, 28 n2. Martyn is quoting von Harnack's *Lehrbuch der Dogmengeschichte* (1931), 1:108.

[100] Martyn, *History and Theology*.

[101] Brown, *Community*. Brown had given brief attention to a similar understanding of the Johannine community in his Anchor Bible Commentary on the Gospel, which was published just before Martyn's work.

[102] Brown, *Community*, 17. In Bultmannian terms, the Fourth Gospel is primarily about the early church situation within which it was composed, and the story of Jesus is of only secondary focus. Bultmann, *Theology of the New Testament*, 5. Bultmann speaks, of course, more of the earliest church as it had developed at the time of the Johannine writings. Still, he comments that the Fourth Evangelist takes traditional material and gives it allegorical or symbolic meaning. This is likely what Brown means when he says that the story of Jesus is not the primary focus for Bultmann. Brown, *Community*, 6–7.

community's life at the time when the Gospel was written."[103] Martyn notes that the two-level drama becomes apparent through signs of the Evangelist's concern to illustrate the essential unity of the *einmalig*[104] drama (of Jesus's earthly life) and the contemporary drama (the experience of the Johannine community).[105] The former becomes the vehicle for the latter, and the integrated narrative attests to the unity of the two.[106] Martyn's contribution was a "sea change in Johannine Studies," and since the time of its writing, many Johannine scholars have found some form of this basic thesis convincing.[107] The analysis of Wayne Meeks rings true, "Louis Martyn's ingenious 'two-level' reading[108] ... has been widely accepted in its general outline if not in all its

103 Brown, *Community*, 17. Emphasis original. This paper will focus on Martyn's work, which preceded Brown's monograph on the subject. Martyn does not emphasize Johannine Christology to the extent that Brown does. However, since the synagogue-church conflict is seen to center on Jesus's status, the two presentations are not so different.

104 *Einmalig*, meaning "unique" or "first," is often used in reference to an initial read-through. Martyn retains the term in this sense and suggests such glosses as "once upon a time" or "back there" referring to the furthest level back in the narrative past. Martyn, *History and Theology*, 40.

105 Martyn, *History and Theology*, 40. This is not necessarily the case with every Johannine episode. It is important to notice, then, that the "level" of the Johannine community does not compete with the "level" of the *einmalig*. See also D. Moody Smith, "The Problem of History in John," in *What We Have Heard from the Beginning: The Past, Present, and Future of Johannine Studies*, ed. Tom Thatcher (Waco: Baylor University Press, 2007), 312.

106 In Martyn's terms, the Fourth Gospel did not merely repeat past tradition, rather, it connected tradition to contemporary concerns. Thus, modern readers must attend both to the tradition behind the text and to the ways the author has interpreted the tradition in light of his own audience-situation. Martyn, *History and Theology*, 27–32.

107 D. Moody Smith, "The Contribution of J. Louis Martyn to the Understanding of the Gospel of John," in *History and Theology in the Fourth Gospel*, 3rd ed., NTL (Louisville: Westminster John Knox, 2003), 20. The theory does, of course, have its detractors. The fact that the two-level drama theory seems unique to the Fourth Gospel has brought this consensus into question. Tobias Hägerland, "John's Gospel: A Two-Level Drama?" *JSNT* 25 (2003): 309–22. It is not my purpose here to thoroughly outline or defend the two-level drama hypothesis. Rather, with other recent scholars, I see some aspects of the approach as helpful while maintaining a more flexible approach. For example, John Ashton admits that we must infer information about the Johannine community from its writings and that this involves conjecture. However, he affirms the "surprising amount of positive data" in the Gospel and reminds us that without a hypothesis on the Johannine community, the text would be unintelligible. Ashton, *Understanding the Fourth Gospel*, 100. For a fuller discussion, see Martyn, *History and Theology*, 56–66, esp. 61–62 n75 for a less rigid approach taken by Morton Smith. See also Martyn, *History and Theology*, 109.

108 Martyn's claim for the integration of the two narrative levels rests on both literary and historical observations. He matches literary elements, which stand in tension with the *einmalig* of Jesus's life, with historical data from the community's time period. For example, he takes the references to expulsion from the synagogue based on confession of Jesus

details."[109] D. Moody Smith noted, "(this) vehicle may not have been perfect, but it has proven good enough to maintain itself and to stand correction."[110] The general import for understanding the Johannine community is this: as Jews who consider Jesus Messiah, the Johannine community had been shaken by developing tensions that eventually led to the separation from the synagogue and the experience of hostility.[111] Focusing primarily on readership and

as Messiah in 9:22 as a reference to formal separation of the Johannine Jesus-followers from the synagogue. Martyn, *History and Theology*, 46–47. He argues that the phrase συνετέθειντο οἱ Ἰουδαῖοι indicates a formal agreement before the time of John's writing. The anachronistic usage of ἀποσυνάγωγος γένηται in response to a messianic confession of Jesus further supports Martyn's contention that elements of this narrative depict the time of the Johannine community, as neither formal expulsion from the synagogue nor widespread formal messianic claims about Jesus can be appropriately attributed to the time of Jesus's earthly life. This interpretation is reinforced by the reappearance of ἀποσυνάγωγος γένηται (in various forms) in 12:42 (in reference to fear of the Pharisees) and 16:2 (in the context of Jesus comforting his disciples who will face persecution after he is gone). Taking these references together, Martyn sees in the Fourth Gospel's presentation of the man born blind a reflection of the Johannine community's situation. This theory takes into account the *Birkath ha-Minim*, which was circulated near the end of the first or beginning of the second century CE. Martyn's dating of *the Birkat Ha-Minim* at 85 CE has been challenged since his initial publication, and he extended the range to between 85 and 115 CE, though he still thinks an earlier date is more likely. For a defense of Martyn's general reconstruction and a discussion of these dates, see Joel Marcus, "Birkat Ha-Minim Revisited," *NTS* 55 (2009): 523–51.

109   Smith, "Contribution," 7–8; Wayne A. Meeks, "Breaking Away: Three New Testament Pictures of Christianity's Separation from the Jewish Communities," in *"To See Ourselves as Others See Us": Christians, Jews, "Others" in Late Antiquity*, ed. Jacob Neusner, Ernest S. Frerichs, and Caroline McCracken-Flesher, Studies in the Humanities 9 (Chico, CA: Scholars Press, 1985), 95. Numerous scholars adopted the two-level drama approach, although many felt the need to qualify some of the specifics given by Martyn and/or Brown. Wayne Meeks exemplified such an approach when he called the 12th Benediction a "red herring" and questioned Martyn's chronology. He nonetheless considered much of Martyn's theory valid. Scholars who accepted and built upon this approach include Klaus Wengst, Alan Culpepper, Jerome Neyrey, David Rensberger, and John Ashton, to name a few. See Smith, "Contribution," 12–18; Klaus Wengst, *Bedrängte Gemeinde und verherrlichte Christus*, 4th ed., Kaiser Taschenbücher 114 (Munich: Christian-Kaiser, 1992); R. Alan Culpepper, *The Johannine School*, SBLDS 26 (Missoula, MT: Scholars Press, 1975); Culpepper, *Anatomy of the Fourth Gospel: A Study in Literary Design* (Philadelphia: Fortress, 1987); Jerome H. Neyrey, *An Ideology of Revolt: John's Christology in Social-Science Perspective* (Philadelphia: Fortress, 1988); David K. Rensberger, *Johannine Faith and Liberating Community* (Philadelphia: Westminster, 1988); Ashton, *Understanding the Fourth Gospel*.

110   Smith, "Contribution," 6.

111   Martyn's suggestion that John's Gospel—or at least certain conflict stories—should be read on two levels was widely accepted. Key among the theory's adherents were Raymond Brown (mentioned above) and C.K. Barrett, whose revised commentary followed closely

purpose, studies that have come out of the two-level drama theory consider these contemporary events and issues that have shaped the Johannine story.[112] James Dunn strongly emphasizes the vital role particular historical context plays in the interpretive process, "with John in particular," because "only by uncovering its historical context can we hope to hear it as the first readers were intended to hear it."[113] Thus, moving on to examine the exchange between the audience and the text, we will do well to keep in mind that the experience of the audience was fraught with conflict—division and schisms from within, rivalry and hostility from without.[114] The Johannine believers saw themselves as threatened by the world, particularly the Jewish authorities, and ostracized from their religious community.[115]

on the heels of Martyn's *History and Theology*. Smith, "Contribution," 14. Brown and Barrett had mentioned the link between the Fourth Gospel and the *Birkath ha-Minim* independently of Martyn. However, Martyn is credited with this theory because he developed and defended it to an unprecedented extent. Barrett clearly affirmed Martyn's approach, listing it in the forefront of his discussion on recent advances in Johannine research. Barrett, *The Gospel According to St. John*; Smith, "Contribution," 14.

112 Martyn, *History and Theology*, 29. His argument is strongest in John 9, the story of the blind beggar. According to Martyn, the evangelist rehearses a traditional miracle story in John 9:1–7, a story he expands in John 9:8–41. He chooses this passage because its form as a traditional miracle story makes the uniquely Johannine interpretation stand out. Martyn, *History and Theology*, 35. Martyn notes links with Synoptic traditions: Mark 8:22–26; Mark 10:46–52; Matt 9:27–31; Matt 20:29–34; Luke 18:35–43. The first section (vv. 1–7) testifies to a traditional event in the life of Jesus, while the second (vv. 8–41) integrates current events in the Johannine church into the expanded narrative. In general defense of this two-level reading, Martyn presents indications in the text that Jesus's works are continued in the work of the community. For example, he takes 14:12 ("the one who believes in me will also do the works that I do and, in fact, will do greater works than these, because I am going to the Father"), to help explain 9:4 ("We must work the works of Him who sent me while it is day"). Martyn suggests that these references illustrate that Jesus's departure troubled the community, and his absence constituted a significant problem within their group. The Evangelist addresses the problem of Jesus's absence by affirming (14:12) and illustrating (ch. 9, in the two-level reading) that Jesus has an enduring presence with his disciples.

113 Dunn, "Let John Be John," 295. Dunn's summary of the situation behind the Fourth Gospel adopts much of the portrait presented by Martyn's thesis.

114 Charles H. Talbert, *Reading John: A Literary and Theological Commentary on the Fourth Gospel and the Johannine Epistles*, Reading the New Testament Series (Macon, GA: Smyth & Helwys, 2005), 66. Talbert emphasizes exclusion from the synagogue, but also points out that if the Johannine epistles are seen as before or concurrent with the Gospel, struggles within the community over orthodox Christology and correct behavior should also be considered.

115 The following issues concerning the conflict most likely centered on the christological confession of the community which affirmed Jesus's unity with God and its inclusion of questionable people and/or groups. Both Martyn and Brown suggest that the Johannine group may have included some members that the Jewish authorities of the day did not

3.3.3   The Rhetorical Exchange between the Story and the Audience

Considering that the Fourth Gospel was likely written to a community facing opposition and in need of a firm identity, attention to the rhetorical situation could illuminate the Gospel's emphasis on mutual love and its bleak picture of the outside world. Not only does this understanding of the Johannine situation make us as readers more adept interpreters (making sense of the polemical language toward the religious leaders, the emphasis on fostering the internal bond of the community, the sensitivity to resistance from the outside world), it also allows us to see how the story itself pulls its audience into the rhetorical communicative exchange. Because the drama unfolds in two levels, the Gospel has an implicitly *metaleptic* undertone in which the boundary between the narrative world and the world of the audience becomes blurred (or in some cases, explicitly broken). According to David Herman, "metalepsis stems from disrespecting (or actively abolishing) the distinction between a story world and the world(s) from which the addressees or recipients relocate in order to engage a 'fictional pact' vis-à-vis the story-world in question."[116] This dynamic is evinced by various aspects of the Fourth Gospel that overlap with the two-level drama:[117] (1) a self-aware narrator who references himself and the audience as "we" or "us" (1:14, 16; 21:24), (2) hindsight comments that disrupt narrative time (2:22; 12:16) (3) anachronistic language and themes that move the audience's mind to their contemporary time (9:22; 12:42; 16:2),[118] (4) the

---

approve, like Gentiles or Samaritans. Martyn, Brown, and others have offered various schema for series of crises within the community. See, for example, Loader, "Law and Ethics." However, it is enough for us to say here that the situation was one of crisis, suffering, and a sense of social persecution.

116   David Herman, "Toward a Formal Description of Narrative Metalepsis," *Journal of Literary Semantics* 26 (1997): 134. Here I am using the term neither in its limited ancient context (*Inst. Orat.* 8.6.37–38) nor in its most technical usage in contemporary narratalogical studies. Instead, I use the term *metaleptic* generally to refer to any place where the narrative boundary is blurred, at any diegetic level, with varying degrees of subtlety or clarity. Metaleptic boundary crossing can happen at various levels and in various directions. These moments in the Fourth Gospel most closely imitate two types of *metalepsis* described by David Moessner. The first *metaleptic* breach occurs when the narrator shows signs that the narrative world has affected his own world. The second occurs when the narrator directly addresses the audience, thus breaking the boundary between the narrative world and the world of the audience. David P. Moessner, "Diegetic Breach or Metaleptic Interruption? Acts 1:4b–5 as the Collapse Between the Worlds of 'All That Jesus Began to Enact and to Teach' (Acts 1:1) and the 'Acts of the Apostles,'" *BR* 56 (2011): 30–31.

117   As we will see, the first three of these bring the situation of the audience into the narrative world, and the latter two elements facilitate the extension of meaning from the narrative world to the world of the audience.

118   I cannot comprehensively demonstrate or defend the *metaleptic* aspects of the Fourth Gospel here. While I am saving full treatment of the Fourth Gospel's *metaleptic* aspects

character of the Beloved disciple (with whom audiences would identify),[119] and (5) the large amounts of extended discourse material that would be performed as if directed to the audience in first person address.[120] This collection

---

for a separate project, two elements are worthy of mention here. Herman ("Narrative Metalepsis," 139–46) suggests specific textual clues that indicate *metaleptic* breaches, including lexical ambiguation (reiterated verbal items that cue an "expectation of sameness") and register manipulation (using similar language in different contexts to control and challenge meaning). Both of these appear in the Fourth Gospel specifically in the context of suffering. An example of lexical ambiguation is found in the use of the term ἀποσυνάγωγος (to describe the general fate of anyone who would confess Jesus as Messiah [9:22], implied as the punishment for the blind man [9:34], again as the general response for believing in Jesus [12:42], and the expected response to Jesus's disciples). This vocabulary hinges these narrative frames together and links them to the situation in the world of the audience. Further, an example of register manipulation is found as the theme of rejection is presented from various perspectives and in various contexts in the Fourth Gospel. The narrator gnomically speaks of the rejection of the Word in the prologue (1:10–11), the narrative relays the rejection of the character Jesus throughout the story, and Jesus tells his disciples directly that they will be rejected/hated as he was (15:18–21; 16:1–2, 33). The change in register gradually pushes the boundary, closing the distance between the rejection recounted in the text and the experience of the audience outside of the narrative. This accomplishes "de-differentiation" of the narrative frames, which brings the audience to an understanding that together, these episodes carry a collective message about the theme of rejection and their own experience.

119 Ute E. Eisen, "Metalepsis in the Gospel of John—Narration Situation and 'Beloved Disciple' in New Perspective," in *Über die Grenze, Metalepse in Text- und Bildmedien des Altertums*, ed. Ute E. Eisen and Peter von Möllendorff (Berlin: de Gruyter, 2013), 318–45.

120 Shiner, *Proclaiming the Gospel*; Kelly R. Iverson, "Incongruity, Humor, and Mark: Performance and the Use of Laughter in the Second Gospel (Mark 8.14–21)," NTS 59 (2013): 2–19; Thomas E. Boomershine, "The Medium and Message of John: Audience Address and Audience Identity in the Fourth Gospel," in *The Fourth Gospel in First-Century Media Culture*, ed. Anthony Le Donne and Tom Thatcher, LNTS 426 (London: T&T Clark, 2011), 92–120. Boomershine suggests that considering performance should significantly affect how we interpret the Fourth Gospel and how we conceive of the audience. He makes the case that the audience would hear more than half of the story as Jesus speaking. His data concerning Jesus's speeches and their addressees opens up a wealth of opportunities to explore how the audience would have identified with various characters. I am less convinced that the Gospel was geared exclusively toward Jews who were not following Jesus as Messiah. It seems that such a suggestion is just one of the many potential addressees of the text. Characters like Nicodemus or Joseph of Arimathea would invite identification with Jesus-following audience members who were struggling with their allegiance, while characters like the Samaritan woman might indicate an audience that extended beyond the traditional Jewish community. Regardless, his demonstration of how the audience is invited by the story to enter into a relationship with the character Jesus and his demonstration of how that relationship develops until the audience is included in the inner circle of disciples were extremely enlightening. See also Eisen, "Metalepsis in the Gospel of John" on how Jesus's discourses often shift so that the narrator seems to become the

of *metaleptic* elements "dissolves the border not just between diegetic levels, but also between the actual and the non-actual—or rather between the two different systems of actuality."[121]

Because this *metaleptic* dynamic blurs the boundary between the narrative world and the world of the audience, we do well to extend our search for the "content" of Johannine ethics outside of the narrative world. Rather than expecting the Fourth Gospel to offer direct moral teaching within the narrative, we can look for where and how the narrative engages the audience by using the story to create space for ethical deliberation. As Kobus Kok explains,

> Moral language entails a particular ordering of beliefs, norms and behaviour in terms of a particular constructed reality which is related to but in reality removed from actual reality ... In the telling of the story, the ethical basis and motivation of particular behaviour (ethos) becomes clear, against the background of the macro-narrative of the Gospel.[122]

For the Fourth Gospel, the particular constructed reality is the narrative world, which corresponds to the real world and creates a point of entry for the audience. The unique aspects of the narrative then challenge norms (values, identity, implied rules or principles) and direct behavior (*ethos*, practical lifestyle, *Lebensstil*) for the particular socio-historical and cultural context of the Johannine community.[123]

So, the rhetorical dynamic of the Fourth Gospel is one that draws the audience *into* the story rather than simply doling *out* information. As Michael Labahn suggests, the Gospel leaves "gaps" for the audience to fulfill creatively.[124]

---

speaker, and the audience would feel addressed directly. Cf. Culpepper, *Anatomy of the Fourth Gospel*, esp. 31.

121 Herman, "Narrative Metalepsis," 134. While Herman's approach to these elements within postmodern (anti)narrative focuses on *metaleptic* layers within the narrative world, our application of these ideas to the Fourth Gospel extends to the world outside the narrative.

122 Kok, "As the Father Sent Me," 169.

123 Leander E. Keck, "Das Ethos frühen Christen," in *Zur Soziologie des Urchristentums: Ausgew. Beitrage zum frühchristlichen Gemeinschaftsleben in seiner gesellschaftlichen Umwelt*, ed. Wayne A. Meeks (Munich: Kaiser, 1979), 13–36; Kok, "As the Father Sent Me," 169; Jan G. van der Watt, ed., *Identity, Ethics, and Ethos in the New Testament*, trans. F.S. Malan, BZNW 141 (Berlin: Walter de Gruyter, 2006), v–ix.

124 Michael Labahn, "'It's Only Love'—Is That All?," in *Rethinking the Ethics of John: "Implicit Ethics" in the Johannine Writings*, ed. Jan G. van der Watt and Ruben Zimmermann, WUNT 291 (Tübingen: Mohr Siebeck, 2012), 26. He suggests that the audience would draw upon "real knowledge outside the textual world," like other oral or written sources about Jesus, to fill in these gaps.

Jan van der Watt similarly suggests that to understand Johannine ethics, one must first recognize the rhetorical power of the narrative, which he describes in terms of "performative power" that "implies a radical involvement" on the part of the audience and a "radical challenge" offered by the story. As both of these authors point out, the narrative offers clues concerning "the direction the text encourages the reader to take."[125] To see one important example of how this works in the Fourth Gospel, we will consider how use of the encomiastic topics draws the audience in, facilitating identification with Jesus and guiding the audience in their ethical deliberation.

4 The Theme of Unity as the Bridge between Elevated Christology and Elusive Ethics

It is true that the Fourth Gospel rhetorically emphasizes elevated Christology. As we established earlier, the encomiastic topics revealed a consistent foundation for Jesus's exalted status: his unity with the Father. This theme of unity, which grounds Jesus's exalted status, is also explicitly linked to Jesus's actions in the Fourth Gospel. Further, the encomiastic topics are extended to include Jesus's followers in the narrative as well as his followers among the audience of the Fourth Gospel. Drawing the audience into the story, the Fourth Gospel engages the Johannine Jesus-followers in the process of ethical deliberation. This provides an inroad within Johannine Christology for the pursuit of Johannine ethics.

4.1 *Unity with the Father as the Motivation for Jesus's Actions*
Moving beyond simple imitation ethics, Karl Weyer-Menkhoff suggests that "since ethics reflects upon the question of how to act properly, one should search for explicit *evaluation* of Jesus's actions given by the Gospel itself."[126] He analyzes the concepts of the work of God and the work of Jesus in the Gospel, concluding that the two are closely connected. Jesus repeatedly refers to his connection with the Father when he is asked about what he does or why he

---

125 Jan G. van der Watt, "Ethics through the Power of Language: Some Explorations in the Gospel according to John," in *Moral Language in the New Testament: The Interrelatedness of Language and Ethics in Early Christian Writings*, ed. Ruben Zimmermann and Jan G. van der Watt, vol. 2, WUNT 296 (Tübingen: Mohr Siebeck, 2010), 143–48.

126 Karl Weyer-Menkhoff, "The Response of Jesus: Ethics in John by Considering Scripture as Work of God," in *Rethinking the Ethics of John: "Implicit Ethics" in the Johannine Writings*, ed. Jan G. van der Watt and Ruben Zimmermann, WUNT 291 (Tübingen: Mohr Siebeck, 2012), 160, emphasis mine.

does it (5:19, 36; cf. 3:35; 4:34; 10:18, 32, 37–38; 14:10–11; 17:4). Thus, in addition to forming the basis of Jesus's exalted status in the Fourth Gospel, unity with God is also determinative for Jesus's actions and his mission.[127]

4.2 The Extension of Unity in the Encomiastic Topics

Having used the encomiastic topics to present unity with God as the basis for Jesus's status and for his actions, the Fourth Gospel extends these encomiastic topics to include Jesus's followers. The extension of these topics to believers establishes that unity with God can be the determinative factor for their identity and actions as well.[128] Not only do the topics extend to Jesus's followers in the narrative world, these topics extend beyond the narrative into the sphere of the audience. Thus, the topics reach into the arena within which Johannine ethics can be found—the rhetorical exchange that takes place between the story and the audience member. Each of the encomiastic topics will be revisited below with a view to how they are extended to Jesus's followers both within the narrative and among the audience.

4.2.1 Origin

The Johannine prologue, which introduced the unity of Jesus with God also extends this topic to Jesus's followers. The Word who was with God in the beginning gives those who believe in him the power "to become children of God." Though these believers come from different earthly and physical family lines, the Fourth Gospel introduces a new family "not of blood or the will of the flesh or of the will of a man, but of God" (1:13). In his conversation with Nicodemus,

---

127 Zimmermann, "Is There Ethics in the Gospel of John?," 70–74. Zimmermann, "Metaphoric Networks," which makes this argument based on the metaphor complex of mission in the Gospel.

128 Zimmermann makes a similar argument demonstrating that the christological figures and titles in the Fourth Gospel also extend to Jesus's followers. This makes it possible, he says, to extract these "from a position of exclusivity and to turn them into interpretive concepts or life coping mechanisms for the Johannine Christians ... [T]he categorical structure valid for the relationship between Jesus and God is transferred to the relationship between Jesus and his disciples (see 15:9; 17:20–23; 20:21)." Zimmermann ("Is There Ethics in the Gospel of John?," 70–74) discusses numerous places where christological titles and images used to describe Jesus are extended to include his followers. These will be referenced throughout our discussion of the encomiastic topics below. Those lying outside of the scope of the encomiastic topics include the image of the source of living water (4:14; 7:27), the temple, the concept of being "holy" (17:17; 6:69; 10:36), and even the claim "I am" (9:9). Cf. Mary L. Coloe, *God Dwells with Us: Temple Symbolism in the Fourth Gospel* (Collegeville, MN: Liturgical, 2001), 3, 220–21; Klaus Scholtissek, *In ihm sein und bleiben: Die Sprache der Immanenz in den Johanneischen Schriften*, Herders biblische Studien (Freiburg: Herder, 2000), 372.

the Johannine Jesus calls this being born again, from above (3:3, 7), or being born "of the Spirit" (3:5). As the narrative unfolds, Jesus, who is presented as the unique "Son of God" (1:34, 49; 3:18; 11:4, 27; 19:7; 20:31), institutes a new extended family. Those who believe become children of God (1:12), are received into the house of the Father (14:1–2), and call God Father (20:17).

In Jesus's final moments on the cross, a moving scene transpires: "When Jesus saw his mother and the disciple whom he loved standing beside her, he said to his mother, 'Woman, here is your son.' Then he said to the disciple, 'Here is your mother.' And from that hour the disciple took her into his own home" (19:26–27). Though there are many ways to understand the symbolic significance of both figures, the scene seems to introduce a new family that comes through birth from above, not natural relation.[129] This is reinforced by the fact that, while his earthly brothers did not believe in him (7:5), the risen Jesus calls his disciples "my brothers" and refers to God as "my Father and your Father" (20:17). Since the Beloved Disciple is representative of ideal discipleship for the audience, this scene from the cross extends the formation of the new family to the Johannine community.[130] Further, the image would resonate with the audience given their experience of isolation from their current religious community. Jesus's words, "I will not leave you orphaned" (14:8), which make use of this family theme, would be poignant for a group who feels ostracized from its religious and cultural community. Spoken in the context of an extended first-person discourse, the audience would experience these words spoken directly to them as if from Jesus himself. Just as the characters in the story are offered a new family, the audience is assured that they too are a part of this family—the same family to which Jesus himself belongs.

4.2.2 Nurture and Training

The Fourth Gospel also presents Jesus as a teacher with credentialed authority, whose words came from the knowledge received from the Father (3:31–35; 5:19–24; 6:45–46; 7:16–18; 8:26–28; 12:47–50). Jesus extends this credential to his followers, saying that those who have come to him have learned from the Father (6:45). Teaching from the Father will also be facilitated by the Spirit in Jesus's absence (14:25–26). Knowledge from the Father, given to Jesus, is declared again through the Spirit and passed on to his followers (16:13–15). Thus

---

129 Brown, *The Death of the Messiah*, 1023–25; Veronica Koperski, "The Mother of Jesus and Mary Magdelene: Looking Back and Forward from the Foot of the Cross in John 19, 25–27," in *The Death of Jesus in the Fourth Gospel*, ed. Gilbert van Belle, BETL 200 (Leuven: Leuven University Press, 2007), 858; Coloe, *God Dwells with Us*, 185–90.

130 Eisen, "Metalepsis in the Gospel of John," 333–34.

Jesus's followers are credentialed because, like Jesus, their unity with God (facilitated through Jesus and the Spirit) ensures their proper training.

Further, Jesus's words in John 16:7 ("Nevertheless I tell you the truth: it is to your advantage that I go away, for if I do not go away, the Advocate will not come to you; but if I go, I will send him to you") would have significance for the Johannine audience. John Ashton suggests that the profound sense of loss so pervasive in the Farewell Discourse is indicative of the community situation. Though on one level the passage describes the departure of Jesus from his disciples, on another level the passage encourages the Johannine community who had lost their own community leader.[131] He writes, "It is not just Jesus's own disciples who are being assured that he will not leave them bereft; subtly and indirectly the members of the community are being told that the prophetic and teaching functions so vital for its survival will not cease abruptly after the death of its present leader."[132] Through this discourse (again part of an extended first-person address which would have been performed directly to the audience), the Fourth Gospel assures its audience of sustained authority and leadership through the Advocate, the Spirit, whose role is to teach and remind them of Jesus's teaching (14:16, 26). Testifying on Jesus's behalf (15:26), the Advocate ensures the Johannine community's connection to Jesus and to the authority of his Father even in the absence of Jesus and their community leader.

In the prologue Jesus was described as "the one who is in the bosom of the Father" (εἰς τὸν κόλπον τοῦ πατρός, in 1:18). As Alicia Myers points out, this same imagery is used (only one other time in the Gospel) to describe the Beloved Disciple who is "in the bosom of Jesus" (ἐν τῷ κόλπῳ τοῦ Ἰησοῦ, in 13:23). She writes, "The image again stresses the closeness between this particular disciple and Jesus, while also encouraging the audience to recall its parallel from 1:18."[133] The extension of this imagery to the Beloved Disciple affirms his authority as one who has also been taught and nurtured by Jesus. Nurture and training for Jesus's followers similarly flows from their unity with Jesus, mirroring Jesus's unity with God.

---

131 Ashton, *Understanding the Fourth Gospel*, 418–53.
132 Ashton, *Understanding the Fourth Gospel*, 452.
133 Myers, *Characterizing Jesus*, 66–7. Cf. Eisen, "Metalepsis in the Gospel of John," 331–33. See also Alicia D. Myers, "'In the Father's Bosom': Breastfeeding and Identity Formation in John's Gospel," *CBQ* 76 (2014): 481–97 which further considers the ancient Mediterranean milieu of the breastfeeding imagery and its role in forming the identity of the Johannine community.

4.2.3 Pursuits, Deeds, and Other External Goods

While the Fourth Gospel focuses on the "fine actions" of Jesus rather than the deeds of his followers, the Johannine Jesus does predict that his followers will perform comparable and even greater deeds than he performed (14:12). There are several things that believers are told to do in the Fourth Gospel. The love command (13:34 and 15:12) and the instruction to follow Jesus's example in the foot washing (13:14–15) dictate the believers' ethical imperative toward one another; the command to keep Jesus's word (14:23) and his commandments (14:15; 15:10) dictates the believers' ethical imperative toward God, and the commissioning of believers dictates the ethical imperative toward "the world" which is not yet a part of the group (15:27; 17:18; 20:21). The instructions to believe in Jesus (14:11–12, 29), to abide in Him (15:4 and 15:7), and to abide in his love (15:9–10), speak to the means of "bearing fruit" in these other areas.[134]

In John 6 we encounter what may be the most directly ethical question in the Gospel: "What must we do to perform the works of God?" The answer? "This is the work of God, that you believe in him whom he has sent" (6:28–29).[135] We see here that the Johannine conception of ethics includes belief as an ethical action. This makes sense considering what we have seen above—that proper actions in the world are a result of relationship to God. The prologue revealed that Jesus's work in the world was to lead the way to God, to show the world the God they had not been able to see—a mission that was only possible because of Jesus's complex and mystical unity with God (1:18).[136] Since belief is the means by which Jesus's followers are brought into unity with God, belief is the fundamental ethical action.

Karl Weyer-Menkhoff's discussion of this dynamic is helpful: "Not even Jesus accomplishes the works of God autonomously but rather responsively ... Believing could be defined as a mode that enables humans to act in such a way that God becomes co-actor."[137] Believing in Jesus is the gateway for Jesus's

---

134 Lund, "Joys and Dangers." See also von Wahlde, *Johannine Commandments*.
135 On the importance of believing in John, see Brian K. Blount, *Then the Whisper Put on Flesh: New Testament Ethics in an African American Context* (Nashville: Abingdon, 2001), 98–99.
136 Definitions of ἐξηγέομαι in Henry George Liddell and Robert Scott, *A Greek-English Lexicon* include "to lead," "to show the way to," "to expound," "to tell at length, relate in full." Various interpretations have been suggested for the complex phrase, μονογενὴς θεὸς ὁ ὢν εἰς τὸν κόλπον τοῦ πατρός. However it is interpreted (even readings that take υἱός), this description emphasizes Jesus's unity with God as the reason he could be the revealer of God. Bultmann, *John*, 81–83; Bruner, *The Gospel of John*, 40–41.
137 Weyer-Menkhoff, "Response of Jesus," 164.

followers to share in the unity he has with the Father.[138] Thus, the Fourth Gospel focuses not on the specific ethical actions that will result from this proper relationship, but on the *necessary first action* of believing. Though anyone could see and attempt to imitate Jesus's specific actions, it is only those who believe in Jesus who also take part in the unity with God that enables them to act in accordance with their new identity and mission."[139] The simple yet paradoxical requirement of doing the work of God is to believe. The whole goal of the Gospel is that the audience might believe that Jesus is the Christ, the Son of God, and that by believing, they might have life in his name (20:31). The act of believing then establishes the community's identity and verifies the community's authority (the first two encomiastic topics). The support of a new family and the confidence inspired by confirmation of their proper training will result in (the third encomiastic topic) noble deeds.[140] As Frank Matera says, "Faith is an ethical action, then, because it requires those who believe to alter the fundamental way in which they know and understand themselves."[141]

Extension of this topic to the audience is again facilitated in the narrative through the Beloved Disciple. After Jesus's death, the Beloved Disciple (with Peter) reaches the empty tomb. In the simple statement "he saw and believed" (20:8), this disciple is again set apart from the others. While the other disciples do not understand (20:9) or believe, the Beloved Disciple sees and believes. Not only that, but he has passed on his testimony so that the audience may believe: "He who saw this has testified so that you also may believe" (19:35).[142]

Further, the Johannine Jesus prays, "I ask not only on behalf of these, but also on behalf of those who will believe in me through their word" (17:20). His request is that the future believers would be one with each another, one with him, and one with the Father—for the benefit of the world. In the performance of this text, the audience would hear Jesus pray directly for them. Further, the resurrected Jesus also references the audience when he says, "blessed are those who have not seen and yet have come to believe" (20:29). As Brian Blount has pointed out, ethics has not been *reduced* to mere belief; rather, "ethics has been integrally connected with belief ... Johannine belief, by its very nature, must bear behavioral fruit. The new life it conjures will be lived concretely. It will

---

138 Peder Borgen, "God's Agent in the Fourth Gospel," in *The Interpretation of John*, ed. John Ashton (London: SPCK, 1986), 67–78.
139 Rabens, "Ethical Enabling," 122.
140 See the analysis of the Johannine opponents, which demonstrates that response to Jesus (instead of heritage or any other factor) determines ethics in Jan G. van der Watt, "Ethics of/and the Opponents of Jesus in John's Gospel."
141 Matera, *New Testament Ethics*, 103.
142 Eisen, "Metalepsis in the Gospel of John," 334–36.

be lived in love."[143] Thus, the audience is challenged to believe in Jesus and, experiencing the unity brought about by belief, to join God's mission for the world. It is this unity and mission that should drive the audience member's actions in the world.

Twice in the Fourth Gospel, the Johannine Jesus speaks directly in terms of imitating specific actions. The first instance comes in the upper room where Jesus washes his disciples' feet. Jesus says, "you also ought to wash one another's feet ... you also should do as I have done to you" (13:14–15). However, the symbolic act does more than set an example to be imitated.[144] This episode depicts the trajectory of Jesus's disciples being brought into the unity that Jesus shares with the Father. Initially, Peter resists Jesus's act. In response to Peter's resistance, Jesus says, "unless I wash you, you have no share with me" (13:8). These words show that the foot washing had a unifying relational effect, initiating the disciples into the family or "household" of God.[145] The act of foot washing, seen in its ancient context, symbolized not only humility but also hospitality.[146] In this way, the narrative nods to the practical result of the internal unity—that it is opened to the world at large inviting them to share in the unity.[147] Further elaborating, Jesus explains, "Do you know what I have done to you? ... Very truly, I tell you, servants are not greater than their master, nor are messengers greater than the one who sent them.... Very truly, I tell you, whoever receives one whom I send receives me; and whoever receives me receives him who sent me" (13:13, 16, 20).

---

143 Blount, *Then the Whisper Put on Flesh*, 99. See further, Rensberger, *Johannine Faith and Liberating Community*. His closing thoughts, where he explains how 1 John 3:16–17 interprets the love command in terms of meeting concrete physical needs, are especially poignant (128–32).

144 For a thorough treatment of the concept of mimesis in the Fourth Gospel, see Cornelis Bennema, "Mimesis in John 13: Cloning or Creative Articulation?," *NovT* 56 (2014): 261–74. He suggests that mimesis primarily involves, "the creative truthful, bodily articulation of the idea and attitude that lie behind the original act" rather than exact replication. We see here how the idea behind the act of foot washing includes the theme of unity which is meant to empower acts of service.

145 On foot washing as a welcome into God's household see Mary Coloe, "Welcome into the Household of God: The Foot Washing in John 13," *CBQ* 66 (2004): 414. As Jesus welcomed in his followers, followers are to welcome in others.

146 Jo-Ann A. Brant, *John*, Paideia (Grand Rapids: Baker Academic, 2011), 205–6.

147 As Alan Culpepper and others have pointed out, the episode also directs the audience's attention forward to Jesus's death, another example of service to the point of extreme sacrifice. R. Alan Culpepper, "The Johannine Hypodeigma: A Reading of John 13," *Semeia* 53 (1991): 133–52. See also Brown, *The Gospel According to John*, 2:551 on the parallel "taking off" and "taking up" from John 10 that connects the foot washing to Jesus's death.

The sent language here shows that the foot washing also brings the disciples into Jesus's mission. As we saw above, Jesus's deeds always flow out of his understanding of his mission as the "sent one" of the Father. Utilizing harvest imagery, Jesus says that his "food" is to do the will of the one who sent him, and he sends his followers "to reap that for which you did not labor" (4:37–38). Later in the narrative, Jesus says in a prayer to the Father, "As you have sent me into the world, so I have sent them into the world" (17:18). And he tells his followers directly, "As the Father has sent me, so I send you" (20:21). In this way, Jesus's mission to the world becomes the mission of his followers.[148] Thus, shared mission extends the encomiastic topic of pursuits and deeds to include Jesus's followers. Just as Jesus's pursuits and deeds flowed from his connection with the one who sent him, so his followers' pursuits and deeds should flow from their shared unity with God.

The mission is to extend the unity with God to include the world (cf. 17:11b, 20–23).[149] As John 3:16 states plainly, it was God's love for the world (at large) that prompted his sending of Jesus. Throughout the Johannine narrative, the inclusiveness of this mission—for the world—is reiterated.[150] Jesus was sent to enlighten *the world*, to take away the sin of *the world* (1:29), to give life to *the world* (3:16–17; 6:33, 51), to save *the world* (4:42; 12:47) to show *the world* the love

---

148 Zimmermann, "Metaphoric Networks," 70–74; Kok, "As the Father Sent Me."
149 The import is encapsulated in 17:23, "I in them (unity between Jesus and the believers) and you in me (unity between the Father and the Son), that they may become completely one (unity among the believers), so that the world may know that you have sent me and have loved them even as you have loved me (extension of love to the world)." Scholarly opinion (though split) may tip in favor of seeing αὐτούς as referring to believers, and thus the verse only suggests that the world sees that he loves the believers (not that he loves the world at large) (e.g., Brown, *Gospel According to John*, 2:771; Dietzfelbinger, *Abschied*, 321; and Thyen, *Das Johannesevangelium*, 699). Dietzfelbinger admits that there is some support for taking *autous* (them) as the world (e.g., J.H. Bernard, *A Critical and Exegetical Commentary on the Gospel According to St. John*, 2 vols., ICC [Edinburgh: T&T Clark, 1928], 2:578–79), and this should be considered strongly given the other emphases on God's love and mission for the world in the narrative. At the same time, whether κόσμος is taken as a collective noun and the referent of αὐτούς or if αὐτούς refers to the believers, the extension of God's love to the world is a viable reading. In the latter case, the extension of God's love to the world would be indirect. Yes, the world would be seeing that God loves his own, but the sight of the believers who are in unity with Jesus and with one another (in love) would invite those who make up the κόσμος to believe and be transferred into the community of love.
150 Mira Stare, "Ethics of Life in the Gospel of John," in *Rethinking the Ethics of John: "Implicit Ethics" in the Johannine Writings*, ed. Jan G. van der Watt and Ruben Zimmermann, WUNT 291 (Tübingen: Mohr Siebeck, 2012), 213–28.

he shares with the Father (14:31; 17:23).[151] Jesus asks in his last prayer: "I in them and you in me, that they may become completely one, so that *the world* may know that you have sent me and have loved them even as you have loved me" (17:21).[152] Through the disciples, the world has the chance to receive the one who sent them (Jesus), and thus the one who sent him (God).[153] Unity with Jesus not only enlists the disciples in the mission but enables them to complete it. Volker Rabens demonstrates this dynamic in the context of the first love command. Citing John 13:34 ("even as I have loved you, that you also love one another"), he writes, "Jesus's love for them is not only the model but also the enabling force of their love."[154] The enabling effect of unity with Jesus is made

---

[151] Those who protest, citing 1 John 2:15, oversimplify the Johannine use of language. "In reality this text ... is a dualistically coloured warning against toying with the world ... John remains faithful to his single-minded and urgent call to ... love." Schnackenburg, *Moral Teaching*, 322, 327.

[152] John's portrayal of the relation between the Father, the Son, and the believers makes the simultaneous affirmation of God's love for the world and the denial of Jesus's and the believers' love for the world virtually impossible. Volf, "Johannine Dualism," 42–43; Schnackenburg, *Moral Teaching*, 328. "The Father dwells in the Son, and the Son dwells in the believers (17:21) ... (therefore) we cannot plausibly read John as ascribing love of the world to the Father but denying it to the Son and the believers ... Clearly, then, John has expressed the Synoptics' 'love of one's neighbor' as 'love of the brethren,' and hence he cannot be using this in any exclusive sense ... It is self-evident ... that he did not mean to forbid Christians to play the part of the Good Samaritan." For some interpreters, the Gospel's sharp distinction between those who believe and those who do not argues against such an inclusive approach. Gundry, *Jesus the Word*, 56–59; Meeks, "The Ethics of the Fourth Evangelist"; Ntumba V. Kapambu, "L'amour Fraternel: Testament, Don, Statut et Signe D'identité : Une Lecture de Jn 13, 34–35," *Telema* 127 (2006): 53–65. Meeks suggests that even if the Gospel does show that God loves the world, it would be unrealistic that the community, so hated by the world, would be able to maintain this perspective. According to Kapambu, it is precisely this irrational love that is both an identity marker for the believers and a testament to unbelievers. But we must consider, with Richard Burridge, "the paradox that (Jesus) delivers his ethical teaching in the presence of sinners whom he accepts, loves, and heals." Burridge, "Imitating Jesus," 284; Richard B. Hays, *The Moral Vision of the New Testament* (San Francisco: Harper San Francisco, 1996), 140. Volf further argues that while the Fourth Evangelist employs dualistic language, the larger scope of the Fourth Gospel shows that God's mission is to break these dualities down: "[D]uality between God and world is transformed into communion between God and Jesus's disciples. As a consequence, oppositional dualities within the creation are overcome too ... John's accounts of creation and redemption together undercut dualistic modes of thought" (pp. 42–43). D. Moody Smith similarly explains that the internal love is essential to the believers' mission to the outside world. D. Moody Smith, *The Theology of the Gospel of John*, New Testament Theology (Cambridge: Cambridge University Press, 1995), 148.

[153] Smith, *Johannine Christianity*, 216–20.

[154] Rabens, "Ethical Enabling," 120.

explicit in the context of the second love command: "Abide in me as I abide in you. Just as the branch cannot bear fruit by itself unless it abides in the vine, neither can you unless you abide in me. I am the vine, you are the branches. Those who abide in me and I in them bear much fruit, because apart from me you can do nothing" (15:4–5).[155]

Given the socio-religious context of the Fourth Gospel, a life-orientation in which unity with the Father determines action would stand in stark opposition to another determinative moral force: Torah. The Torah was seen as the God-given source for wisdom and salvation.[156] But, as Andrew Glicksman has argued, the Fourth Gospel presents the Word as greater than Sophia, taking the place of Torah as the source for wisdom.[157] Though many of the values of the Torah would by default stay imbedded within the community, the basis for right living becomes unity with God and his mission for the world rather than Torah.[158] As Jesus justified his own actions based not on the Law, but on his union with the Father, the Johannine community is offered an ethic based on their transformed identity in unity with God, the well-being of the community, and the mission for the world.[159] This does not, however, imply that Johannine ethics leaves the sphere of concrete actions in the real world. The examples of love (the foot washing and Jesus's sacrificial death) were concrete, lowly, and gruesome physical acts. John's presentation of a real material incarnation, a physical life, and a visible human death suggests that imitation of Jesus's love

---

[155] This vineyard imagery stands at the center of the Farewell discourse, offering a guide to the disciples for Jesus's impending departure. As Jesus had challenged the institution of Judaism during his time on earth, the disciples were to similarly stay rooted in Jesus, the new vineyard, as the determining factor for "bearing fruit." Chrys C. Caragounis, "'Abide in Me': The New Mode of Relationship between Jesus and His Followers as a Basis for Christian Ethics (John 15)," in *Rethinking the Ethics of John: "Implicit Ethics" in the Johannine Writings*, ed. Jan G. van der Watt and Ruben Zimmermann, WUNT 291 (Tübingen: Mohr Siebeck, 2012), 250–63.

[156] Schnackenburg argues that the Logos concept reflects the Jewish idea of Wisdom, who was the sibling of the Torah (Wis 8:7; *2 Apoc. Bar.* 54.12–14; Ps 119). "The Logos … assumes the salvation-bringing functions that were ascribed to the Torah in Judaism." Schnackenburg, *Jesus in the Gospels*, 285.

[157] Andrew T. Glicksman, "Beyond Sophia: The Sapiential Portrayal of Jesus in the Fourth Gospel and Its Implications for the Johannine Community," in *Rethinking the Ethics of John: "Implicit Ethics" in the Johannine Writings*, ed. Jan G. van der Watt and Ruben Zimmermann, WUNT 291 (Tübingen: Mohr Siebeck, 2012), 83–101.

[158] Loader, "Law and Ethics"; Lund, "Joys and Dangers," 283.

[159] Johannine discipleship (understood in terms of covenant) depicts a transformative identity-shift for a community in a socio- and theological identity crisis. Rekha M. Chennattu, *Johannine Discipleship as a Covenant Relationship* (Peabody: Hendrickson, 2006).

would similarly take place in the material, physical world—in the realm of social ethics.[160]

4.2.4 Suffering and Death

While the Fourth Gospel vividly depicts Jesus's noble death within the narrative, the suffering and death of his followers is not recounted. However, the Fourth Gospel does address this topic in reference to those who follow Jesus. Addressing his disciples, the Johannine Jesus says,

> Very truly, I tell you, unless a grain of wheat falls into the earth and dies, it remains just a single grain; but if it dies, it bears much fruit. Those who love their life lose it, and those who hate their life in this world will keep it for eternal life. Whoever serves me must follow me, and where I am, there will my servant be also. Whoever serves me, the Father will honor (12:24–26).

Using the image of wheat, which must die in order to bear fruit, the Fourth Gospel puts the suffering of Jesus's followers in the same sphere of Jesus's "noble death"—which would benefit others and would have lasting value over and above the cost.[161] Jesus's death functions to open the community to include the world at large, as his earlier words remind us, "I, when I am lifted up ... will draw all people to myself" (12:32). Through his death, Jesus reveals the extreme sacrificial service to be practiced outside of the community in order to fulfill the mission of bringing the world back into unity with God.

The narrative presents the expectation that as Jesus suffered a noble death, his followers will also. Though differing in degree, Jesus tells his followers that their suffering will also benefit the world. As Jesus said, "Very truly, I tell you, you will weep and mourn, but the world will rejoice" (16:20). Jesus specifically

---

160   Blount, *Then the Whisper Put on Flesh*, 101–3. Put another way, "The ethical appeal to love one another has as many expressions as there are needs and challenges in the larger Johannine situation." Paul N. Anderson, "Discernment-Oriented Leadership in the Johannine Situation," in *Rethinking the Ethics of John: "Implicit Ethics" in the Johannine Writings*, ed. Jan G. van der Watt and Ruben Zimmermann, WUNT 291 (Tübingen: Mohr Siebeck, 2012), 304–8. Anderson's examination of the epistles further demonstrates how such a shift would necessitate dialectical engagement on the part of the community (290, 307).

161   Zimmermann, "Is There Ethics in the Gospel of John?," 70–74. On "noble death" see Neyrey, *The Gospel of John*, 282–312. See also Demosthenes (*Epitaph.*), Thucydides (2.42–44), Plato (*Menex.* 237, 240e–249c), the progymnasmata attributed to Hermogenes (16) and Theon (*Prog.* 110), and Aristotle (*Rhet.* 1.9.16–25). Neyrey also locates these themes in 1 Macc 4 and 9, 2 Macc 6–7, 4 Macc 5–11, and Josephus, *Ant.* 17.152–54, 295–300.

links the suffering of his followers to their connection with him: "If the world hates you, be aware that it hated me before it hated you ... If they persecuted me, they will persecute you" (15:18–20).[162] Jesus's followers are thus united with him in suffering and—like Jesus, they are "with God" (16:32b).

Further, the Johannine narrative specifically addresses the deaths of two of its main characters. The risen Jesus describes the death by which Peter "would glorify God" (21:18–20). When Peter asked if the Beloved Disciple would suffer the same fate, Jesus responded with the enigmatic statement, "If it is my will that he remain until I come, what is that to you? Follow me!" (21:22). Though this led to a rumor that this disciple would not die, the narrator clarifies that Jesus did not actually say he would not die. This episode, like Jesus's farewell discourse, is indicative of the sense of loss experienced by the Johannine community. Jesus's words that this disciple might remain seem strange at first, since the community appears to be dealing with the reality that they have lost or will soon lose their leader. However, use of the word "remain" (here the infinitive form of μένω) resonates with other significant uses of this word in the narrative.[163] Forms of μένω are used to describe the relational dynamic between the Spirit, Jesus, and the Father[164] as well as the relational dynamic between Jesus, his followers, and the Sprit.[165] Significantly for the discussion of the topic of death, earlier in the narrative the crowd issued a challenge: "We have heard from the law that the Messiah remains forever. How can you say that the Son of Man must be lifted up?" (12:34).

---

[162] The Johannine Jesus's prediction "they will put you out of the synagogues" (16:2) would have had significance for the situation of the early readers of the Fourth Gospel (as we have discussed above).

[163] Admittedly, recognition of such verbal resonances would vary within a diverse audience. First-time hearers or less attentive listeners would perhaps not immediately make the connections that could be apparent to repeat-listeners, those with keen understanding, or those (like the lector her/himself) who would have occasion for extended reflection on the Gospel. For more on sensitivity to the complexity of performance and diverse audience reception, see Whitenton, *Hearing Kyriotic Sonship* and Kelly R. Iverson, "An Enemy of the Gospel? Anti-Paulinisms and Intertextuality in the Gospel of Matthew," in *Unity and Diversity in the Gospels and Paul: Essays in Honor of Frank J. Matera*, ed. Christopher W. Skinner and Kelly R. Iverson (Atlanta: SBL, 2012), 7–32.

[164] The Spirit remains on Jesus at his baptism (1:32), Jesus claims "the Father remains in me" (14:10) and that he remains in the Father's love (15:9).

[165] Jesus asks or declares that his followers remain in him (6:56) and in his word (8:31), tells his followers that the Spirit remains with them, and says that he has appointed them so that they might go and bear fruit and that their fruit might "remain" (15:16). The key to this is remaining in him as he remains in the Father (15:4–9).

Though it is a difficult concept, according to the Fourth Gospel, "remaining" can include suffering, departure, and even death. Jesus died, yet he remains in the Spirit. The Beloved Disciple presumably died, but lives on in the testimony to the Johannine community. Despite the possibility of suffering, the Beloved Disciple exhibits the behavior of the disciple *par excellence*, following Jesus to the end.[166] The Johannine audience is called to do the same. Struggling to believe in the generations after Jesus's departure, facing the death of their own leader, and battling conflict and hostility in the religious community, they too can bear fruit that remains.

The emphasis on Jesus's noble suffering and death would have been significant to the community, who felt ostracized and persecuted.[167] In the face of crisis, the Johannine community could find solidarity in the noble death of their hero, Jesus, and their community leader. The Gospel narrative ascribes meaning to their suffering, showing how the persecution and suffering of Jesus were a part of bringing about God's mission to the world. Practically speaking, the extension of this topic challenges the Johannine community to resist capitulating or otherwise avoiding suffering. Rather, if they endure as Jesus did, they will fulfill their role in continuing God's mission to reconcile the world to himself. At this juncture the relationship among the encomiastic topics becomes clearer. Given such a challenge, a foundation of identity and community belonging would be essential, lest the community falter in order to regain the comfort from their previous group. Affirmation that they had the proper teaching would give the Johannine Christians confidence in their testimony. The vision of a sharing with Jesus in God's mission would motivate bold and compassionate behavior even in the face of suffering.

4.3   *Summary*

The Fourth Gospel's use of the encomiastic topics demonstrates that those who believe in Jesus (both within the narrative and among the audience) are brought into the unity with God that formed the basis for Jesus's identity and his actions. A new family with a new credential for authoritative training, a new mission to determine deeds and pursuits, and a shared suffering for the benefit of the world—the particular Johannine use of these topics and the *metaleptic*

---

166   Grounded in his unity with Jesus (depicted in his closeness to Jesus at the Last Supper), he persevered even when there could have been dire consequences (following Jesus to the cross). He believed when he saw the empty tomb and was the first to recognize Jesus as the risen Lord (21:17). Eisen, "Metalepsis in the Gospel of John," 336–39.

167   Blount, *Then the Whisper Put on Flesh*, 104–7.

force of narrative reveals a rhetorical trajectory that demonstrates unity with God through belief in Jesus as the basis for both the elevated Christology and the implicit ethics in the Fourth Gospel.[168]

In light of our rhetorical analysis, what *can* we say about Johannine ethics, and what remains unsaid? First, while the Fourth Gospel's elevated Christology appears in tension with the pursuit of Johannine ethics, the theme of unity reveals Jesus's elevated status as a foundational part of John's ethical presentation.[169]

Second, because belief in Jesus brings the disciples into his mission for the world and empowers them to act in such a way as to fulfill that mission, the Fourth Gospel presents belief as an essential ethical action.[170] Rather than dictating the *end* (a system of rules to guide behavior or a list of specific actions), the Fourth Gospel presents the *means*—unity with God. Thus, belief is the foundational ethical action from which other proper actions fitting various contexts will flow.

Third, the imitative element of Johannine ethics is Jesus's unity with God—in identity and mission—and the resulting life orientation that manifests itself in concrete behavior in the world. In the narrative, believers are called to imitate Jesus's acts of service within the community and his extreme sacrifice (to the point of persecution and death). These particular examples[171] point to the larger imitative element of Jesus's life orientation—the unity with God from

---

168   Zimmermann ("Is There Ethics in the Gospel of John?," 80) calls it "responsive, reactive ethics."

169   As the Fourth Gospel's use of the encomiastic topics demonstrated, Jesus's unity with the Father is the basis of his elevated status. While many of Jesus's actions are not intended to be directly imitated, these actions (as well as Jesus's words) demonstrate his oneness with the Father and elicit the response of belief.

170   Believing is seen as an ethical action in the Fourth Gospel since it brings believers into unity with Jesus, allowing them to share in the very element that established Jesus's elevated status—relational unity with God. This relational unity transforms the believer's identity so that they are both brought into God's mission for the world and empowered to act in such a way as to work toward its fulfillment.

171   The foot washing initiates the disciples into the empowering unity of identity and mission and serves as an example for the kinds of actions that make for the kind of community that will empower the shared mission. It is in this context that the disciples are given the new commandment: to love one another as Jesus loved them (13:34). "Love one another" and "wash one another's feet" have implications for actions within the group. Further, the foot washing and Jesus's sacrificial death embody the abstract imperative "love one another" and demonstrate that obedience to this command is carried out in the real world with practical acts of service.

which his actions flow, and they set creative boundaries for what ethical behavior should look like inside the community and in the outside world.[172]

Fourth, although the Fourth Gospel does not present an exhaustive ethical system or provide a comprehensive set of guidelines for ethics, it nonetheless presents a flexible approach to ethics for a struggling community. We must admit that the Fourth Gospel does not address many topics that we might expect to be treated in an ethical text.[173] Rather, the story sets the stage for the community to do this work and establishes the necessary understanding of identity so that they can do it well. Even where the Fourth Gospel gives specific practical ethical instructions (e.g., the foot washing and the love command), the relational unity with Jesus is emphasized. The other imperatives are left open. What is important is unity with Jesus as both the example and the "enabling basis" of the disciple's actions.[174]

Fifth, to articulate Johannine ethics, we must move beyond the narrative world of the Fourth Gospel to explore how the audience might have appropriated the ethical presentation within the story. The narrative shows that unity with Jesus and mutual love within the community empowers the audience to join Jesus in fulfilling God's mission for the world.[175] It is plausible then, that the rhetorical trajectory of the Gospel would move the audience to continue believing, to embrace their identity in unity with Jesus, to act in ways that build a mutually-supportive community, and finally to extend that inner-community love to the world outside in pursuit of God's mission to reconcile the world to himself. Practically, this could mean that the community would collectively engage in discerning ethical parameters guided by this identity and mission.[176] Perhaps the process would begin with the long-held values of the Torah as a foundation; however through the guidance of the Spirit, the community's ethics would likely grow and develop as they considered the corporate memory

---

172 Lund, "Joys and Dangers," 283. Lund also shows how Jesus justifies his own actions based not on the Law, but on his union with the Father. He describes Jesus's ethics as "relational, not informational."

173 Burridge, *Imitating Jesus*, 330–32. This raises important questions about how ethical decision-making worked within the community. Lund, "Joys and Dangers." He helpfully suggests that a number of moral imperatives in the Fourth Gospel itself, paired with corporate memory of Jesus, values from the Torah, community deliberation, and guidance from the Holy Spirit would mitigate the dangers of this unconventional ethic. He offers 1 John as one example of a later community taking up this Fourth Gospel's ethics and amending them to their own situation.

174 Rabens, "Ethical Enabling," 122.

175 Marianne Meye Thompson, *The Incarnate Word: Perspectives on Jesus in the Fourth Gospel* (Peabody: Hendrickson, 1993), 103; Hays, *Moral Vision*, 150–51.

176 Anderson, "Discernment-Oriented Leadership," 307.

of Jesus, the welfare of the community, and the mission to open the community to a diverse world.[177] Rhetorically speaking, the story has an engaging effect for the audience that engenders allegiance and is itself empowering, even when the message would have been a challenging one, given their experience of persecution.[178]

5 Conclusion

As we have seen, the Fourth Gospel incorporates the encomiastic topics to show that Jesus exceeds even the highest expectations for an honorable hero in the ancient world. More importantly we discovered that Jesus's exalted status is grounded in his connection with God, his Father. The encomiastic topics, which established Jesus's exalted identity, are extended to the followers of Jesus in the narrative and to the Johannine audience. Thus, as Jesus's connection with the Father forms the basis of his actions, the believers' connection to God becomes the basis for living properly.[179] Not only do the members of the Johannine community see their own story within the story of Jesus, the Fourth Gospel tells the story of God's mission for the world. In Johannine terms, the key to ethics is understanding one's place within the larger story of God's mission for the world. As Kobus Kok explained, behavior is rooted in "the Universal Godly Narrative" or "a particular understanding of God and his story with the world."[180] Believing in Jesus, Johannine believers can join him, allowing the mission for the world to determine their actions in it. With its elevated Christology, the Fourth Gospel offers an identity-making story for a community in crisis; with its elusive ethics, the Fourth Gospel engages and empowers the struggling audience to join in a mission bigger than their own suffering.

---

177 Lund, "Joys and Dangers," 280–81.
178 See Demetrius, *Eloc.* 222 on the rhetorical strategy of leaving things unmentioned.
179 Van der Watt, "Ethics and Ethos in the Gospel according to John," 148–63. Richard Hays also suggests that the promise and role of the Spirit explains the absence of moral instruction in the text. This amounts to the reality that "the specific behavior that issues from union with God need not be spelled out in detail, for those who abide in Jesus will intuitively know what is right and do it." Hays, *Moral Vision*, 153.
180 Kok, "As the Father Sent Me," 171.

CHAPTER 15

Jesus and the Demonic Powers in the Johannine Tradition

Jin Ki Hwang

1   Introduction

In the Fourth Gospel, John does not report Jesus's performing exorcisms, which is one of the most prominent aspects of Jesus's healing ministry in the Synoptic Gospels (e.g., Mark 1:21–28, 32; 3:11–12). But this should not be interpreted as meaning John has little interest in demon possession or Jesus's victory over the demonic powers. John uses the language of demon possession in the Fourth Gospel (chs. 7, 8, 10). And according to John, Jesus not only knew that Satan, the father of lies, was already working to deceive people (John 8:44; 12:31) and would make Judas of Iscariot, one of his twelve disciples, hand him over to death on the cross (John 6:70–71; 13:27), but he also taught his disciples that his death would bring judgment upon Satan (John 12:31; 16:11; cf. John 16:33). Furthermore, the victory over the demonic powers seems to be a controlling theme even in the Johannine epistles (e.g., 1 John 2:13–14; 3:8; 4:4; 5:5, 18–20). In the present paper, I will examine John's perception of demon possession and his theological emphasis on the victory over the demonic powers laid out in the Johannine literature and their possible influences in other early Christian writings (e.g., Polycarp, Ignatius, Irenaeus).

2   Demon Possession and Exorcism in the Fourth Gospel

2.1   *Demon Possession*

In the Synoptic Gospels, demon possession is often related to physical illnesses. For example, in Matt 9:32 and 12:22, the δαιμονίζομαι verb is used to explain the cause of blindness and muteness, respectively. In the Fourth Gospel, however, the δαιμονίζομαι verb is used only once for Jesus's Judean opponents' accusation of him for demon possession, based on what he did or said (John 10:21).[1]

---

[1]   The term οἱ Ἰουδαῖοι in the Fourth Gospel often points to Jesus's opponents—whether rendered as "the Judeans" or "the Jews." Based on his comparison of the polemic between Jesus

Similarly, the phrase δαιμόνιον ἔχειν (John 7:20, 8:48, 52; 10:20) also points to demon possession and is used exclusively for their accusations of Jesus.[2] It is also interesting to note that the phrase "coming in of Satan" (εἰσέρχεσθαι εἰς … ὁ σατανᾶς) constitutes another reference to demon possession in the Fourth Gospel, which is employed for Judas of Iscariot, one of the Twelve (John 13:27; cf. also Luke 22:3).[3]

In a recently published article on the language of demon possession in the Fourth Gospel, An-Ting Yi suggests an anthropological understanding of it.[4] Yi claims that, by calling Jesus "demon possessed," Jesus's Judean opponents try to "reinforce their established status" (John 7:20; 8:44, 48; 10:19–21). This suggestion has much to commend it for it explicates the language of "demon possession" in close connection with that of "Spirit possession," which is prominent in the Fourth Gospel. For John, both may "define group boundary."[5] However, it is doubtful whether Jesus tries to "reinforce" his "social status," especially when he claims that his Judean opponents are children of the *diabolos* (devil; 8:44). Besides, John's theology cannot be simply reduced to a "dualism."[6] The controversy between Jesus and the Judeans regarding demon possession discloses Jesus's unique identity as the One coming from God the Father—namely, the Son of God.

---

and "the Judeans" in John 8:38–47 with the paradigms of apocalyptic polemic in 1QS and *Testament of Twelve Patriarchs*, two Jewish documents, Urban C. von Wahlde (*Gnosticism, Docetism, and the Judaisms of the First Century: The Search for the Wider Context of the Johannine Literature and Why It Matters*, LNTS 517 [London: Bloomsbury T&T Clark, 2015]), suggests that the polemic in the former itself is "a Jewish convention" and "anti-opposition" "rather than anti-Jewish" (166) and that οἱ Ἰουδαῖοι may well point to "the religious authorities in Jerusalem with whom the Johannine community saw themselves in conflict and who were ultimately responsible for the exclusion of the Johannine community from the synagogue" (169). On the other hand, Stanley E. Porter (*John, His Gospel, and Jesus: In Pursuit of the Johannine Voice* [Grand Rapids: Eerdmans, 2015], 170–73) basically takes οἱ Ἰουδαῖοι in a religious-ethnic sense but at the same time points out that "the author of John's Gospel, rather than having strong anti-Jewish tendencies, merely employed clear terms and used reasonable linguistic means *to depict Jesus's opponents*" (173; emphasis added).

2 Graham H. Twelftree, "*In the Name of Jesus*: A Conversation with Critics," *Journal of Pentecostal Theology* 17 (2008): 163: "Nevertheless, the Fourth Evangelist not only maintains the category of demon possession, but does so through having—at least at first sight—Jesus, and Jesus alone, repeatedly charged with having a demon."
3 Eric Plumer, "The Absence of Exorcisms in the Fourth Gospel," *Bib* 78.3 (1997): 363.
4 An-Ting Yi, "'You Have a Demon!': An Anthropological Reading of the Notion of Possession in the Gospel of John," *BTB* 46.3 (2016): 115–22.
5 Yi, "'You Have a Demon!,'" 121.
6 Yi, "'You Have a Demon!,'" 121.

2.2 Exorcism

In the Synoptic Gospels Jesus himself cast out demons (or unclean spirits) to demonstrate his divine authority and power (Mark 1:21–28). Jesus also expected his disciples to do the same, namely, to cast out demons with his authority and in his name (Mark 6:7–13; cf. Luke 10:17). Interestingly, it was John (who is generally identified as the Fourth Evangelist) who brought up the issue of a certain man who was casting out demons in Jesus's name while not following him along with the Twelve. Yet Jesus told John not to stop that man (Mark 9:38–39/ Luke 9:49–50). What is more, according to the longer ending of Mark (which can still be considered belonging to the Marcan tradition), exorcism is presented as one of the prominent "signs" (σημεῖα) that early Christ-believers are expected to perform in Jesus's name and that is also comparable to spiritual gifts such as speaking in tongues (16:17). In the Fourth Gospel, however, exorcism is not presented as one of the signs Jesus himself performed, and not even mentioned at all (cf. John 12:31). Jesus never asked or expected his disciples to cast out demons in his name or by whatsoever means.

If so, then, how can one explain the huge gap between the Synoptic accounts of Jesus's healing ministry and those in the Fourth Gospel? It should be first mentioned that John himself knew the exorcisms practiced by Jesus and his disciples (cf. Mark 9:38–39). He must have also known the exorcism stories reported in the Synoptic Gospels, although he chose not to explicitly mention them in the Fourth Gospel. Edwin Broadhead finds a clue for this possibility in John 6. Broadhead claims that Jesus's appellation "the Holy One of God" in John 6:69 may be taken as an echo of an exorcism account in Mark 1:24.[7] When Peter confesses that he believes and knows that Jesus is "the Holy One of God," Jesus recognizes that the demonic powers are currently at work and calls one of his twelve disciples "a *diabolos*" (John 6:70; cf. Mark 8:33/Matt 16:23). Similarly, in 1 John, Jesus is also called "the Holy One": "But you have been anointed by the Holy One, and all of you have knowledge" (2:20).[8] But in 1 John, "the Holy One" is related to the anointing or bestowing of the Spirit (cf. also 1 John 2:27) rather than to exorcism. And in 1 John, Jesus is also described as the "Righteous [One]" (2:1). There is no indication of exorcism here either. But even in 1 John, it is the *diabolos* who makes people sin; they are under the power of the *diabolos* to the extent that they continuously sin (3:8, 12; cf. 5:19).

John 8 may be noted as another example that shows John's awareness of the exorcism stories preserved in the Synoptic Gospels. The controversy between

---

[7] Edwin Broadhead, "Echoes of an Exorcism in the Fourth Gospel?" *ZNW* 86 (1995): 118.
[8] All scriptural citations are taken from NRSV unless specified otherwise.

Jesus and the Judean leaders (8:48, 52; cf. also 7:20;[9] 8:44; 10:20–21) seems to parallel the "Beelezebul" controversy in the Synoptic Gospels (Mark 3:22–27 pars.) both in the language of demon possession (δαιμόνιον ἔχειν / Βεελζεβοὺλ ἔχειν) and the narrative structure (a controversy about demon possession being followed by Jesus's Judean opponents' accusation that he is demon possessed). John also highlights that Jesus healed the blind young man by the power of God's Spirit, but not by demonic power (John 9:1–3, 31–33; 10:21; cf. Matt 12:22, 28; Mark 3:22).

Nonetheless, as Broadhead points out, John "emphasizes the cosmic victory over demonic powers" in the Fourth Gospel.[10] John does not present exorcism as one of Jesus's signs probably because they "do not in and of themselves underline Jesus's uniqueness" (Plumer)[11] or because they are not able to "convey the grand cosmic scale and other-worldly-setting of the battle" that he believes is "taking place and was won in the cross event, yet adumbrated throughout the life and ministry of Jesus" (Twelftree).[12]

3 The Theme of the Victory Over the Demonic Powers in the Fourth Gospel

John's emphasis on the cosmic and eschatological victory over the demonic powers in the Gospel indeed constitutes a "theological" framework for the saving works of God the Father and the Son in the world.

3.1 *Jesus's Victory Over the Power of Darkness*

At the beginning of the Fourth Gospel, John recounts the story of creation. It declares:

---

9   Plumer, "The Absence of Exorcisms in the Fourth Gospel," 360, commenting on John 7:20, claims that "the reflections are seen through a glass, darkly; for in John the focus of attention has shifted to the unique Christology."

10 Broadhead, "Echoes of an Exorcism in the Fourth Gospel," 118,

11 Plumer, "The Absence of Exorcisms in the Fourth Gospel," 356.

12 Twelftree, "*In the Name of Jesus*," 163. See also idem, "Exorcisms in the Fourth Gospel and the Synoptics," in *Jesus in Johannine Tradition*, ed. Robert T. Fortna and Tom Thatcher (Louisville: Westminster John Knox, 2001), 141: "The battle with Satan permeates the proleptic ministry of Jesus, reaching its climax and realization in the cross event—the grand cosmic exorcism. In this way FE [Fourth Evangelist] is able to affirm the lie of Satan's control of this world is far more pervasive than the possession of some sick individuals and that the defeat of Satan requires more than isolated exorcisms."

> In the beginning was the Word, and the Word was with God, and the Word was God. He was in the beginning with God. All things came into being through him, and without him not one thing came into being. What has come into being in him was life, and the life was the light of all people.
> JOHN 1:1–4

This retelling of the creation account provides a theological perspective on the works of the Logos, the Son of God, in the world. As an agent of creation,[13] the Logos not only brought the life and existence to the world but also was the light of all people (John 1:3–4). John continues to say that "the light shined and the darkness did not prevail [οὐ κατέλαβεν]" (John 1:5). Here "the darkness" (ἡ σκοτία) may be considered *an oblique reference to demonic powers*. And the καταλαμβάνω verb can mean the overtaking of a hostile divinity, as in Mark 9:18 (BDAG). The shining of the light that the darkness did not prevail against signifies God's victory over the controlling power of darkness and chaos in the first creation. But because of human sin, the world was placed under darkness and its power. This is why the Logos (the Son of God) had to come in flesh as the light of the world and shine his light to all people so that they could be freed from the power of darkness (John 1:9, 14; cf. John 8:12). The world did not readily receive or recognize him (John 1:10). But to those who do receive him and believe in his name, the Logos would give the privilege to become God's children (John 1:12–13; cf. 3:3 [born from above]; 3:8 [born from the Spirit]). In the remainder of chapter 1 and in chapter 3 of the Fourth Gospel, John makes it clear that "Jesus" is the very Logos and light of all people—even the Son of God who came to save the world from darkness and give eternal life to the people in the world (John 1:14, 33–34; 3:16).

3.2   *People Under the Power of the Diabolos*

In the Fourth Gospel, John highlights Jesus's identity as the light of the world. Jesus claims: "I am the light of the world. Whoever follows me will never walk in darkness but will have the light of life" (John 8:12). But not everyone who

---

13   Cf. T.E. Pollard, *Johannine Christology and the Early Church* (London: Cambridge University Press, 1970), 20–22, who considers Jesus's role as the Logos in mediating God's activity in creation one aspect of the "three-fold mediatorship of the Son of God" presented in the Fourth Gospel. John Ronning, *The Jewish Targums and John's Logos Theology* (Peabody: Hendrickson, 2010), 26–27, considers the overcoming of the light over darkness in John 1:5 a reference to the first creation just as "the division of light and darkness at the Red Sea" in the Targum tradition (e.g. *Tg. Neof.* Exod 13.21–22; cf. *CTg. T.* Exod 14.30) may be "part of a reenactment of the first three days of creation (most obviously with the third day corresponding to the drying up of the Red Sea, and dry land appearing)."

hears and sees Jesus physically comes to the light. There are still many others who would love the darkness more than the light, hoping that their evil deeds might not be revealed (John 3:18–20). They would not believe Jesus's testimonies to the truths about his identity and works and to the things from above (John 3:12). In chapter 8, Jesus addresses the unbelieving Judeans in particular: "You are from your father the devil, and you choose to do your father's desires. He was a murderer from the beginning and does not stand in the truth, because there is no truth in him. When he lies, he speaks according to his own nature, for he is a liar and the father of lies" (8:44). Here the unbelieving Judeans are considered to have been born of the *diabolos*, their father. And the *diabolos* is described as "a murderer [ἀνθρωποκτόνος] from the beginning"[14] and "a liar and the father of lies." Judas of Iscariot, the betrayer of Jesus, was also named a *diabolos* (John 6:70–71; 13:27 ["someone into whom ὁ σατανᾶς entered"]). The primary purpose of the signs Jesus performs is to make those who are blinded by the *diabolos* and walk in the darkness believe the truth to which Jesus testifies. But the unbelieving Judeans and Judas of Iscariot are attached to the *diabolos* and end up working for the *diabolos* to kill Jesus on the cross.

3.3 God's Agents vs. Satan's Agents

In three places, the unbelieving Judeans accuse Jesus of being an agent of Satan, based on what he does or says (John 7:20; 8:48, 52). But in chapter 8 Jesus claims that it is not he but they who are agents of the *diabolos* (who is also called *daimonion*) (John 8:44). Their claim is also countered by another group of Judeans (John 10:20–21). What is more, the one who was born blind but is now healed recognizes his recovery of sight as the undeniable evidence of the outworking of God's power in Jesus (John 9:31–33). For him, Jesus cannot be a sinner but must be the one who was sent by God himself (παρὰ θεοῦ), that is, an agent of God (John 9:16; 33; cf. John 6:46).[15] On the other hand, Judas of Iscariot is portrayed as one of the agents of the *diabolos*, concerning whom Plumer well points out:

---

14   Charles K. Barrett, *The Gospel according to St. John*, 2nd ed. (Philadelphia: Westminster, 1978), 349, suggests that the devil is called ἀνθρωποκτόνος because the devil "robbed Adam of immortality" and "destroys the life God creates."

15   Peder Borgen, "God's Agent in the Fourth Gospel," in *The Interpretation of John*, ed. John Ashton (Philadelphia: Fortress, 1986), 67–78, demonstrates that the mission of Jesus, the Logos and the Son as the agent of God, can be understood against the background of the Jewish halakic principles of agency (e.g., *Mek. Ex.* 12.3; 12.6; *m.Ber.* 5.5; *b.B.Metzia* 96a; *b.B.Qam.*113b; *b.Erub.* 31b–32a; cf. John 6:38; 10:38; 12:44, 45; 14:9, 24) and Jewish Merkabah traditions (e.g., Philo, *Conf.* 146; *Leg.* 1.43; cf. John 1:14, 18; 6:46).

> [I]n the Fourth Gospel the place of the demons has been taken by human beings in their subservience to the world. Nevertheless, St. John is emphatic that in the last analysis Jesus is contending not against flesh and blood but against Satan himself. In a sense those at enmity with Jesus are merely instruments by which Satan executes his will (8,44). The supreme illustration of this is Judas, who is said to have been literally possessed by Satan just prior to the betrayal (13,27).[16]

3.4 Jesus and the Judgment Over the Demonic Powers

In the Fourth Gospel, John stresses that "the ruler of this world will be thrown out" (12:31) when Jesus is "lifted up from the earth" to draw all people to him (12:32). The ὑψόω verb is also used in three other places in the Fourth Gospel (3:14; 8:28; 12:34), where it likewise refers to Jesus. And John makes it clear that Jesus's death on the cross indeed points to his exaltation as the Son of Man (3:14; 12:32–34) and to his recognition as the *Ego Eimi* (8:28; cf. Exod 3:14). The coming of the *Parakletos* (the Spirit of Truth) not only serves as the evidence of Jesus's ascension to heaven (returning back to God the Father) (16:8), but it also confirms that "the ruler of this world" has already been condemned (16:11). Jesus won the victory over Satan when he was lifted up on the cross. However, it should be also noted that Jesus claims to have won the victory over the world when he heard people confess their faith (16:30–33). Hence, it is true that his death on the cross is a sign that points to Jesus's decisive victory over Satan and his powers and demonstrates his divine glory as the exalted Son of Man. Yet the theme of victory over Satan was already in place even before his crucifixion.

4 The Theme of the Victory Over the Demonic Powers in the Johannine Epistles

4.1 Jesus's Victory Over the Power of Darkness

In 1 John, Jesus is the Logos of life who was with God in the beginning and appeared to us (1 John 1:1–2). And the light is described as the divine attribute just as in the Fourth Gospel. In 1 John, God is identified as "light" (1 John 1:5), and Jesus is identified as "God's son" (1 John 1:7) and *Parakletos* before God the Father (1 John 2:1; cf. John 14:16 ["another *Parakletos*"]). The light is already shining in the world; some people are already walking in that light, whereas others are still blinded by the darkness and walking in darkness until now (1 John 2:9, 11). Just as in the Fourth Gospel, the darkness in 1 John is also an

---

16 Plumer, "The Absence of Exorcisms in the Fourth Gospel," 363.

oblique reference to the power of the *diabolos*, who is also called "the evil one," an adversary of "the One who is from the beginning" (1 John 2:13–14). First John does not use the καταλαμβάνω verb ("to prevail"), but the παράγω verb ("to pass away"[17]) in 2:8 seems to indicate the present reality of the victory of the light over the darkness: "the darkness is passing away and the true light is already shining" (cf. 1 John 2:17). That Jesus won the victory over the darkness is also indicated by the existence of those who are having fellowship with God and his Son and walk in the truth and light (1 John 1:3, 6–7, 9).

4.2 People Under the Power of the Diabolos

In 1 John, the one who does sin is considered to have been born of the *diabolos* because the *diabolos* sins from the beginning (1 John 3:8). The Son of God appeared in order to destroy the works of the *diabolos*, which obviously includes not loving one's brother (1 John 3:8). Cain was born of the *diabolos*, and he hated his brother and became a murderer (ἀνθρωποκτόνος) like him (1 John 3:12, 15). In 1 John, the *diabolos* is not identified as "a liar and the father or lies." But whoever denies that Jesus is the Christ and the Son of God is now identified as "a liar" and "antichrist" (1 John 2:22). In contrast, whoever believes that Jesus is the Christ and the Son of God is "born of God" and does not sin (1 John 3:9, 10, 23); this person is expected to love both God the Father and his other children, who are also born of him (1 John 5:1).

4.3 God's Agents vs. Satan's Agents

First John considers it important to discern whether or not a spirit is indeed from God (1 John 4:1) and, by implication, whose agent a certain prophet or preacher is. John declares: "Every spirit that confesses Jesus Christ as the one who became flesh has come from God; but every spirit that does not confess him as such is not from God and is the spirit of antichrist" (1 John 4:2–3). The passage highlights as well that the spirit of antichrist is already working in the world (1 John 4:3). In addition, the false prophets who are possessed by that spirit of deceit also deceive the world with their false teachings (1 John 4:1, 5, 6). The false teachers, also called ἀντίχριστοι (agents of Satan) in 1 John, can be compared to Judas of Iscariot in the Fourth Gospel, who was one of Jesus's twelve disciples but betrayed Jesus. It may be inferred from 1 John 2:18–19 in particular that at least some of those agents of Satan were indeed in-group members (cf. 1 John 4:3). In the Fourth Gospel, Judas and the unbelieving Judeans worked for the *diabolos* to kill Jesus on the cross. But in 1 John, the primary role of the agents of Satan are more focused on teaching and spreading their false

---

17 According to BDAG, the verb has an active sense if used in a passive form.

teachings. The same appears in 2 John because there the one who denies that Jesus came in flesh is also presented as ὁ πλάνος (a false prophet) and ὁ ἀντίχριστος (an agent of Satan; 2 John 1:7). In the Johannine literature, Satan's agents can be defeated by the truth, as Twelftree aptly points out: "Demon possession is combatted through knowing the truth: Jesus."[18]

4.4 Jesus and the Judgment Over the Demonic Powers

In the Fourth Gospel, Jesus claimed to have won the victory over the world (John 16:33) and talked about his judgment of the ruler of the world (John 12:31). But in the Johannine Epistles, it is the children of God who win the victory over the world (1 John 5:4,18) or over the evil one (who is an adversary of "the One whose origin is from beginning"; 1 John 2:13–14). And the children of God are none other than those who believe that Jesus is the Son of God (1 John 5:4–5; cf. 1 John 3:23). In 1 John, the *diabolos* is not identified specifically as "the ruler of this world." But the demonic powers working in the world are still recognized as a present reality: "We know that we are God's children, and that the whole world lies under the power of the evil one" (1 John 5:19). But the theme of cosmic, eschatological judgment over Satan itself is not apparent in the Johannine Epistles (cf. 1 John 2:18, 28; 3:2; 4:17).[19]

5 John's Perception of Demon Possession and Theological Emphasis on the Victory Over the Demonic Powers Reflected in the Early Christian Writings

This section examines the possible influences that John's perception of demon possession and his theological emphasis on the victory over the demonic powers may have had in other early Christian writings, particularly in those considered to be in the Johannine tradition (e.g., Polycarp, Ignatius, Irenaeus).

5.1 *Polycarp of Smyrna*

According to Irenaeus, Polycarp was "instructed by apostles" and "conversed with many who had seen Christ" (*Haer.* 3.3.4). He is also known as a disciple of

---

18　Twelftree, "*In the Name of Jesus*," 163 (author's emphasis).
19　In the book of Revelation, the demonic power is still operational, but Jesus is declared "the ruler of the kings of the earth" (1:5) and "the Lion of the tribe of Judah, the Root of David" who has conquered (5:5). Not only that, "our brothers" also did conquer the *diabolos*, the accuser before God, "by the blood of the Lamb and by the word of their testimony" (12:11). God's children will be victorious and inherit the new heaven and new earth and new Jerusalem (21:1–7).

John. We consider Polycarp's *Letter to the Philippians* because it seems to reflect a Johannine influence, although it makes no explicit mention of demon possession or exorcism. In 7:1, Polycarp explicitly quotes 2 John 1:7. The wording is not exactly the same, but he uses most of the key words in it.

> 2 John 1:7 οἱ μὴ ὁμολογοῦντες Ἰησοῦν Χριστὸν ἐρχόμενον ἐν σαρκί· οὗτός ἐστιν ὁ πλάνος καὶ ὁ ἀντίχριστος.
> Pol. *Phil.* 7:1 Πᾶς γὰρ ὃς ἂν μὴ ὁμολογῇ Ἰησοῦν Χριστὸν ἐν σαρκὶ ἐληλυθέναι, ἀντίχριστός ἐστιν

> For anyone who does not confess that Jesus Christ has come in the flesh is antichrist.
> LCL

Polycarp also uses Johannine language when he identifies those who do not confess the gospel of the cross as Satan's agents: "[W]hoever does not confess the witness of the cross is from the devil [ἐκ τοῦ διαβόλου]" (Pol. *Phil.* 7.1; cf. John 8:44; 1 John 3:8). Polycarp also characterizes them as "whosoever distorts the words of the Lord for his own passions, saying that there is neither resurrection nor judgment," and as "the firstborn of Satan [πρωτότοκός ἐστι τοῦ σατανᾶ]."[20] Here "the witness of the cross" and "the words of the Lord" are what the agents of Satan deny in their teaching. Just as in John and 1 John, the primary role of Satan's agents is teaching and spreading the false teachings so that people would walk away from the faith. On the other hand, the theme of the cosmic eschatological victory or judgment over the demonic powers is not obvious in Polycarp's writings.

5.2 *Ignatius of Antioch*

Ignatius is also considered one of the disciples of John (see *Martyrdom of Ignatius* 1). The Johannine perception of demonic powers and of the Holy Spirit as the Spirit of Christ is reflected in two of Ignatius's epistles (e.g., Ign. *Eph.* [long recension[21]] and *Phld.* [long recension]).

---

20 According to Irenaeus, Polycarp indeed called Marcion "the first-born of Satan" when he happened to meet him (*Haer.* 3.3.4; cf. also Mart. Pol. 23:3 [from the Moscow Manuscripts]).

21 The additional elements in the long recensions may be attributed to fourth-century interpolator(s) (see Ehrman's notes in *Apostolic Fathers*, 1:210). However, whoever was responsible for those elements, there are some obvious clues to the Johannine influences in them. The English texts of the short recensions are taken from *Letter of Ignatius* in LCL, while those of the long recensions, from *Epistle of Ignatius* in ANF 1:45–126.

Ignatius's *Epistle to the Ephesians* can be first mentioned. In Ign. *Eph.* 9:1 (long recension), the demonic powers are presented as "the spirit of deceit." The language of demon possession is not used here. Instead, demon possession is perceived as something like receiving "the wicked doctrine of the strange and evil spirit" or being under the power of "the spirit of deceit." Quite contrary to the Holy Spirit (the Spirit of Christ),[22] this spirit of deceit "deceives the people," "does not speak the things of Christ, but his own," and "is lying, fraudulent, soothing, flattering, treacherous etc." The agents of the spirit of deceit, namely, the agents of Satan, made some efforts to deceive the recipients of the letter. But the recipients are commended for "not allowing their entrance." It is also stated that Jesus, who was crucified and is exalted, will deliver them from the power of the deceitful spirit. The theme of the victory over the demonic powers appears in Ign. *Eph.* 13:1 (short recension), according to which "the powers of Satan are destroyed" when the recipients of the letter "come together more frequently to give thanks and glory [Or: *to celebrate the eucharist and give glory*] to God" and "his destructive force is vanquished" by their faith (LCL).

Ignatius's *Epistle to the Philadelphians* may also be considered:

> If any one preaches the one God of the Law and the prophets, but denies Christ to be the Son of God, he is a liar, even as also is his father the devil, and is a Jew falsely so called, being possessed of mere carnal circumcision. If anyone confesses Christ Jesus the Lord, but denies the God of the law and of the prophets, saying that the Father of Christ is not the Maker of heaven and earth, he has not continued in the truth any more than his father the devil, and is a disciple of Simon Magus, not of the Holy Spirit. If any one says there is one God, and also confesses Christ Jesus, but thinks the Lord to be a mere man, and not the only-begotten God, and Wisdom, and the Word of God, and deems Him to consist merely of a soul and body, such one is a serpent, that preaches deceit and error for the destruction of men.
>
> Ign. *Phld.* 6:1 [long recension]

Here christological titles such as "the Son of God," "the only-begotten God," "the Word of God [Logos]" reflect the Johannine Christology.[23] Deception is what

---

22 For the Johannine concept of the Spirit as "the Comforter" and of Satan as "the wicked, deceitful, and seducing spirit," see Ign. *Phld.* 5:2 (long recension).

23 The Johannine Christology is also reflected in Ign. *Magn.* 8.2: "For the most divine prophets lived according to Jesus Christ. For this reason, also, they were persecuted. But they were inspired by his gracious gifts, so that the disobedient became fully convinced that there is one God who manifested himself through Jesus Christ his Son [τοῦ υἱοῦ αὐτοῦ],

characterizes the devil, "the father" of lies (cf. John 8:44). Whoever denies that Jesus is "the Son of God" is "a liar" like the devil (cf. John 1:1, 14, 18; 1 John 2:22). As an agent of Satan, such a person can also be considered "a disciple of Simon Magus, not of the Holy Spirit" and even "a serpent" (cf. John 6:70–71; 13:27; Irenaeus, *Haer*. 1.27.4). The Johannine language of demonic powers is pretty much obvious in this passage. But the theme of the cosmic, eschatological victory or judgment over the demonic powers is not so apparent in this letter.

5.3   *Irenaeus of Lyons*

Irenaeus himself confesses that when he was young he learned from Polycarp, a disciple of John (*Haer*. 3.3.4; cf. also Eusebius, *Hist. eccl.* 5.20.4–6). His *Against Heresies* is replete with ample evidence of the Johannine influence. In book 5, Irenaeus relies primarily on the book of Revelation to explain about the demonic powers and present the theme of the cosmic, eschatological victory over the demonic powers (e.g., *Haer*. 5.28.2; 5.35.2). However, there are also some clues pointing to the influences from the Fourth Gospel or the Johannine epistles. For example, in book 5 Irenaeus cites John 8:44 (*Haer*. 5.22.2; 5.23.2) and calls the devil "a murderer from the beginning" and "the serpent" who is "a liar" (*Haer*. 5.23.1; 5.24.1). Deception is presented as what the devil has been doing from the beginning (*Haer*. 5.23–24). And Jesus is described as God's son, who was sent to "destroy our adversary" (which is the devil) and "perfect man after the image and likeness of God" (*Haer*. 5.21.2). Irenaeus also cites John 5:43 and explains that those who did not believe in Jesus because he came in the Father's name are none other than followers of Antichrist, who came in his own name (*Haer*. 5.25.4).

In book 1, Irenaeus refutes one of the heretics, Marcus, who claims to have the "greatest knowledge" and is "perfect adept in magical impostures," for being demon-possessed and "the precursor of Antichrist" (*Haer*. 1.13.1). Marcus is the one who deceptively makes people receive the spirits that "are earthly and weak, audacious and impudent, sent forth by Satan for the seduction and perdition of those who do not hold fast that well-compacted faith which they received at first through the Church" (*Haer*. 1.13.4).[24] Then, Irenaeus presents what an unknown divine elder and preacher of the truth spoke against Marcus to reveal the problems of his false teaching:

---

who is his Word that came forth from silence [αὐτοῦ λόγος ἀπὸ σιγῆς], who was pleasing in every way to the one who sent him." Pollard points out that "the Word of God issuing from silence" refers to "the incarnation," which is "the focal point of Ignatius' theology" (*Johannine Christology and the Early Church*, 31, 33).

24   The English texts of Irenaeus's *Against Heresies* are taken from ANF 1:315–578 unless specified otherwise.

> "Marcus, thou former of idols, inspector of portents, Skilled in consulting the stars, and deep in the black arts of magic, Ever by tricks such as these confirming the doctrines of error, Furnishing signs unto those involved by thee in deception, Wonders of power that is utterly severed from God and apostate, Which Satan, thy true father, enables thee still to accomplish, By means of Azazel, that fallen and yet mighty angel,—Thus making thee the precursor of his own impious actions." Such are the words of the saintly elder.
>
> Haer. 1.15.6

Here the Johannine language of demonic powers seems to be in use when Satan is described as Marcus's "true father" and Marcus is presented as an agent of Satan ("By means of Azazel, that fallen and yet mighty angel"). Similarly, in book 5, Irenaeus depicts the Marcionites, the Valentinians, and all the Gnostics as the "agents of Satan" (*organa Satanae*; *Haer.* 5.26.2). And in book 3, Irenaeus widens the scope even further and calls whoever spreads false doctrines the "agents of Satan, sent forth for the purpose of overturning the faith of some, and drawing them away from life" (*Haer.* 3.16.1). Although neither the Fourth Gospel nor any of the Johannine epistles are explicitly cited in any of these places, Irenaeus's identification of the false teachers with the children of Satan or agents of Satan likely points to Johannine influence (cf. John 8:44; 1 John 2:18–19; 2 John 1:7).

Lastly, it will be necessary to consider how Irenaeus intentionally uses the Fourth Gospel to refute the heretics. For example, in book 1, Irenaeus summarizes how the Valentinians make use of the Fourth Gospel (particularly ch. 1) to justify their doctrines (*Haer.* 1.8.5; cf. 3.11.1) and then refutes them by using the very same Gospel material (*Haer.* 1.9.1–3; cf. also 3.11.7; 3.16.2[25]). Irenaeus concludes:

> Jesus who suffered for us, and who dwelt among us, is Himself the Word of God. For if any other of the Aeons had become flesh for our salvation, it would have been probable that the apostle spoke of another. But if the Word of the Father who descended is the same also that ascended, He, namely, the Only-begotten Son of the only God, who, according to the good pleasure of the Father, became flesh for the sake of men, the apostle

---

25 Pollard (*Johannine Christology and the Early Church*, 42) aptly points out: "If the Western Church treated St. John's Gospel with suspicion because of its popularity with the gnostics, then it was probably due to Irenaeus' masterly use of it in the task of refuting Gnosticism that this suspicion was dispelled and the gospel accepted."

certainly does not speak regarding any other, or concerning any Ogdoad, but respecting our Lord Jesus Christ.

Haer. 1.9.3

In book 2, Irenaeus continues to refute the Valentinian teaching of thirty Aeons based on Jesus's age, by making an appeal to the fact that Jesus began his ministry at the age of thirty and celebrated at least three Passovers since then (John 2, 6, 12–13, 18; *Haer.* 2.22.3).[26]

Irenaeus also summarizes the "possession Christology" of Cerinthus and the Ebionites in book 1, as M.D. Goulder identifies it (*Haer.* 1.26.1–2).[27] According to Cerinthus, Jesus is not the incarnate Son of God but a son of Joseph and Mary. Jesus performed miracles while he was possessed by Christ who is spirit. In book 3, Irenaeus reports that when John once met him in Ephesus, he called him "the enemy of the truth" (*Haer.* 3.3.4) and then refutes Cerinthus's false teaching on God and Jesus again by appealing to the logos Christology in John 1 (*Haer.* 3.11.1–6).

In book 3, Irenaeus even goes further to state that John composed the Fourth Gospel and his letters because he "foresaw" the arising of the false doctrines (*Haer.* 3.16.5 [citing John 20:31; 1 John 2:18–22]) and because he wanted to "remove" or "put an end to" all the false doctrines presented by such heretics as Cerinthus, the Nicolaitans, and Marcion, and "to establish the rule of truth in the Church, that there is one Almighty God, who made all things by His Word, both visible and invisible; showing at the same time, that by the Word, through whom God made the creation, He also bestowed salvation on the men included in the creation" (*Haer.* 3.11.1).[28]

26　Cf. *Haer.* 2.22.6, where Irenaeus claims, based on John 8:57, that the Pharisees believed Jesus to be nearing 50.

27　M.D. Goulder, "John 1,1–2,12 and the Synoptics," in *John and the Synoptics*, ed. Adelbert Denaux, BETL 101 (Leuven: Leuven University Press, 1992), 204.

28　The *Acts of John*, a second-century Christian writing, may be compared with the documents of three apostolic fathers. This work reflects a perspective of "a Christian group which feels itself bound to the apostle John as the guarantor of a tradition of 'Johannine' theology"—if "transmuted into gnostic terms" (Kurt Schäferdiek, "The Acts of John," in *New Testament Apocrypha*, vol. 2, *Writings Relating to the Apostles: Apocalypses and Related Subjects*, ed. Wilhelm Schneemelcher, English translation ed. R. McL. Wilson [Louisville: Westminster John Knox, 1992], 166–67). Unlike the Fourth Gospel or the Johannine Epistles, John's practice of casting out demons is mentioned and recognized in it. John is reported to ask the Lord to drive out the demon: "Thou who dost ever comfort the humble and art called to aid, who dost never need to be summoned, for you yourself present before we begin, let the unclean spirits be driven out from the sons of Antipatros!" (*Acts of John* 57).

6 A Summary and Conclusion

Thus far, I have articulated John's perception of demon possession and his theological emphasis on the victory over the demonic powers laid out in the Forth Gospel and the Johannine epistles. The Johannine epistles (especially 1 John) largely share John's language of demonic powers and theological emphasis on the victory over the demonic powers. In 1 John, for example, Jesus's identity and work are presented within the theological framework of the victory over the demonic powers. And the Christ-believers engage a war against the agents of Satan (antichrists) as Satan is still operational through his deceptive power. The theme of the cosmic, eschatological judgment over the demonic powers is not so apparent in the Johannine epistles. Yet the Christ-believers are expected to entertain the victory over the demonic powers not by exorcism but by knowing and believing the truth, the gospel of Jesus Christ the Son of God who came in flesh and died on the cross to save us from our sins. The Johannine language of demonic powers and theological framework of the victory over the demonic powers also find their expressions in some of the early Christian writings attributed to Polycarp, Ignatius, and Irenaeus. Standing in the Johannine tradition themselves, these writers characteristically utilize the Johannine material in their battling against the agents of Satan and their false teachings.

Brief Concluding Observations on This Volume on Johannine Christology

Stanley E. Porter

This volume on Johannine Christology presents itself as a singular volume on a prescribed topic, Johannine Christology. In one sense, it is just such a volume. However, it is much more than that, in that it explores a variety of topics within the broad scope of Johannine Christology, sometimes within traditional boundaries and sometimes by moving beyond those boundaries into new and often less well-explored areas. By way of conclusion, let me draw a few observations regarding these essays that might help to frame a suitable response to them.

The first and most obvious conclusion to draw is that this collection of essays does not contain the final word on Johannine Christology. This may appear to be a self-evident statement. However, it bears repeating. If nothing else, the essays within this volume bear witness to the fact that the topic of Johannine Christology is not a stale or stagnant one, and certainly not one that has exhausted all of its possibilities. Quite to the contrary. There are still areas meriting further exploration and development, as a number of the chapters in this volume well attest. There are admittedly a number of topics that address some of the well-known areas within Johannine Christology. For example, there are several essays that accept or even argue in more detail for some of the traditional categories within Johannine Christology, such as its high Christology, its development of messianic language, its promotion of christological motifs previously identified, and the importance of the concept of the "word." Perhaps others could be mentioned as well. Nevertheless, even in these essays, I believe that there are regularly presented new insights that cause us to revisit even traditional topics and pose renewed questions about what we might assume are assured results of scholarship as we delve further into the field. A volume such as this is not designed—nor should it seek—to overthrow or, worse yet, neglect previous scholarship and findings in Johannine Christology in a misguided quest for the novel or new that does not connect with the tradition of Johannine scholarship. A volume such as this is warranted if for no other reason than it maintains lines of connection between traditional scholarship and new thought regarding the Johannine literature, in this case Johannine Christology.

A second observation concerns methodology. Questions of method should be and in fact are being increasingly recognized as essential to doing biblical studies. In previous days and forms of scholarship, an exegete or scholar was able simply to claim to represent the text, as if all interpreters agreed upon the evidence and the best means for weighing it and presenting what was often seen as self-evident results. Those days are long gone (or at least should be), and we should not be disappointed that they are. This methodological age in which current scholarship exists has made us aware that scholars approach texts, including the Johannine literature, with not just interpretive questions in mind but theoretical approaches and orientations to how they best think to arrive at the answers to these questions. For some, such times have become unsettling and disturbing, as these methodologically-aware explorations have sometimes called many of the previously agreed scholarly results into question and have thrown exegetical method into disarray. This volume is not focused upon method, but there is plenty of variety in the methods used within to explore questions of Johannine Christology, and these are found not just in the section on Johannine literary features but in the other parts as well. Some of the proposals are positive and some of them are negative. For example, some of the essays calls into question previous methodological orientations within scholarship, such as the developmental hypothesis or the means of identifying and comparing various motifs. Others take a more positive approach by invoking new and varied methods that are not as well-tried in Johannine studies. Some of these examples include use of Michael Riffaterre's model of intertextuality, theories of tragedy, the use of linguistic frames or scenarios, specific linguistic models, elements of French narratology, and narrative criticism more broadly defined. The days of a more narrowly confined historical-critical exegesis seem to be long behind us in Johannine studies, and the essays in this volume provide support for attempts to introduce and develop new methods that may have new potential for exploring Johannine Christology. Such interest will no doubt continue to grow within scholarship in the years ahead, as scholars realize that some of the tools that have traditionally been used are yielding less and less that is significant and that new tools are needed to mine more deeply into the New Testament texts.

One of the major advances in Johannine studies over the last major period of time, and a third observation about the essays in this volume, is appreciation for a variety of literary features of the text. This is not a new movement, as literary criticism of the New Testament, including the Johannine literature, began to be seriously undertaken nearly forty years ago with work by Alan Culpepper and others. However, this volume shows that there are still new areas of exploration, even within what is recognized as a major area of Johannine studies, where new insights may be gained, not just for literary appreciation of the Johannine Gospel but for christological purposes. Earlier studies of the literary character of John's Gospel explored a range of substantial topics, such as plot, setting, point of view, and the like. Only more recently has the topic of character and its development come to the fore as an area of active interest. In some ways, this is surprising, since character has always been an important literary feature of narrative texts, even such texts as the Gospels. Nevertheless, recent literary criticism under the influence of a variety of literary, narratological, and linguistic factors has delved more deeply into what constitutes character and what the implications of character depiction are for the meaning of a narrative. The results of such exploration are found, sometimes implicitly and sometimes explicitly, within a number of the essays in this volume. For example, several of the essays depict Jesus as an active participant within the narrative, embodying and exemplifying meaningful characteristics that reveal his persona as a character and, with it, the Christology of the text, its author(s), and possibly even his own. One could argue that character studies should always have been at the heart of New Testament studies, as the New Testament is in many respects an assemblage of accounts of various characters, whether depicted directly or indirectly, by means of Gospels or the book of Acts, or even by means of letters to a variety of churches and individuals. Such an approach is bound to bring new insights to Christology when one appreciates that theological conclusions must be embodied and are reflections of the actions and depictions of characters as they present themselves and are responded to in the text.

A fourth major observation concerns the importance of narrative, a feature that is also important for the fifth and final feature noted below. One of the major characteristics of many if not most of the essays in this volume is the treatment of the text, in this case in most instances the Johannine Gospel, as a narrative. Some treatments of Johannine Christology in the past have tended to characterize the Christology as "high" (however this is defined), but more than that have tended to view it statically. In such a conception, John's Gospel is then often seen as a later synthesis of a developing Christian community that embeds within its account a set of developed theological ideas, especially some concerning Jesus as the Christ and being at one with the Father, with a variety of further implications. A healthy corrective to this systematic way of describing Johannine Christology has been the recognition of narrative theology within the Gospel accounts themselves, and in particular within the Johannine Gospel. In other words, rather than being a static depiction of the Johannine Christology, the Gospel presents a narrative unfolding of Johannine

Christology, one that emerges over the course of the text from its beginning in the prologue and its culmination in the resurrection and/or final appearances of Jesus. A number of the essays in this volume are concerned to ensure that their christological conclusions are reflective of a respectable appreciation of the unfolding of the Johannine narrative. As examples, there are several essays that are concerned with seeing how the prologue of the Gospel connects with the rest of the Gospel, not just in terms of word frequencies or sources, but in terms of progressive revealing of the Johannine Jesus and hence the Gospel's Christology. One of the authors even speaks of how the Gospel narrative is a "quest for the Messiah," beginning in the prologue with the witness of John the Baptist, and then develops further into Jesus as the one who reveals the Father and does his work. Another along a similar vein sees the prologue as introducing a process that results in the revelation of the identity of Jesus, thus providing a context for perspectives on the Johannine Jesus. Other essays are concerned with other narrative features, such as particular scenes that reveal character and Christology. One of these is the recognition scene, in which some characters recognize and others do not recognize Jesus as the "word," thus creating dramatic irony within the narrative itself. Even essays that are not as explicit in their use of narrative do not hesitate to make observations about how Jesus is presented in different ways within the narrative according to the circumstances of the plot of the Gospel as it unfolds. I suspect that this kind of narrative theology will continue to be important in Johannine studies and move further beyond simply literary and presentational issues to more substantive theological issues such as seen here in Christology.

I conclude with a fifth observation on the essays within this volume by noting that many of them are concerned with various dimensions of what is often called context in biblical studies. The term "context" is a difficult word, as it can encompass anything from the immediate environment of a particular text, such as the few words on either side of a given word, all the way up to a broad historical or cultural context. I prefer to think of context in relation to several different layers. These include the textual context, that is, the environment of any wording as it occurs within the text. This textual context is very important, as it is the immediate context in which we encounter the text itself. There are a number of essays within this volume that focus upon various dimensions of the textual context. That is, they are concerned to identify and then scrutinize wordings both large and small that appear within the Johannine literature, in particular the Johannine Gospel, but also sometimes in relationship to other wordings found in other texts, such as Revelation or even the Pauline letters. Some of the essays in this volume identify particular blocks of such wordings, such as the Book of Signs, or temple language, or Passover passages, while others are concerned with very specific wordings found within the Johannine literature, such as language regarding "word," Messiah, or the like. There is also a second layer of context that must be recognized and that is the context in which a text is created and received, meaning not just the authorial context of creation but the audience context of reception and reading. This situational context has long been appreciated within Johannine studies, especially when scholars of the past have been concerned to examine various language and source issues regarding the Johannine literature, but also theories regarding layers of developments of the Johannine community and hypotheses regarding its reading and response of the Johannine material. A number of essays within this volume are concerned with the situational context. These include essays that attempt to decipher particular wordings on the basis of whether they resonate better with one situation or another, such as that of Qumran or Hellenistic Judaism, or the nature of zealotry, or the political climate of the Gospel's reception, or even the literary atmosphere in which the text would have been read. There is a third context that must be taken into account as well and that is the cultural context. Whereas the situational context is the context that reflects the situation in which such a text as the Johannine Gospel or Revelation or another text might have been written and then read, the cultural context concerns the larger cultural conventions of language, social relations, textual conventions, genre, and ideas and concepts that come to characterize and direct the literary production within a culture. All of the essays in this volume, one might well posit, are concerned in varying ways with the cultural context of the Johannine literature and its formulation of Johannine Christology, even if some are more explicitly aware of this context than are others. An explicit example is the essay on crucifixion in the Roman empire and how that relates to the presentation of the Christology of John's Gospel. More implicit are essays that treat a variety of literary motifs or concepts and assess the relationship between the Johannine literature and its Christology with how these concepts are used within the wider cultural context. The differentiation of context and its implications for the study of the Johannine literature, and in particular its Christology, is an area that awaits further exploration, and the essays in this volume only offer a sample of some of the possibilities.

There is much more that one might say about Johannine Christology than has been stated within this volume, and that is how it should be. This is not a volume designed to raise and much less to answer all pertinent questions regarding Johannine Christology. This is a volume that is designed to present a range of essays by an equally wide range of scholars, in both interests and career progress, and that raises some important questions and suggests some possible answers in the hope that they help to generate further thought regarding the important topic of Johannine Christology.

Modern Authors Index

Agnew, V. 95
Akala, A.J. 25
Aland, K. 171
Alexander, T.D. 208
Allen, G. 95
Anders, M. 207
Anderson, G. 178
Anderson, P.N. 255, 261, 278–80, 301, 305
Anderson, R.D. 264
Ashton, J. 25, 56, 57, 60, 62, 65, 67, 68, 70, 246, 260, 285, 286, 294, 296
Aune, D.E. 264, 267

Backus, J.M. 157
Baek, K.S. 121
Bal, M. 173
Bammel, E. 247
Barrett, C.K. 27, 33–35, 90, 140, 163, 203, 204, 216–18, 235, 245, 250, 261, 262, 286, 287
Barton, S.C. 280
Bauckham, R. 4, 75, 76, 88, 206, 209, 280
Baur, F.C. 2, 11, 13
Beale, G.K. 170, 178–80, 216
Beasley-Murray, G.R. 172, 176, 182, 183, 204, 232, 233, 250, 261
Berger, P.L. 95
Berkhof, L. 175
Bernard, J.H. 203, 298
Betz, O. 56, 57, 267
Bickerman, E.J. 97, 107
Biddle, M. 171
Bienaime, G. 241, 242
Bieringer, R. 38
Black, C.C. 103, 262, 283
Bliss, M.T. 264
Blount, B.K. 295, 297, 301, 303
Boda, M.J. 212
Bolognesi, G. 264
Bolt, J. 175
Boomershine, T.E. 289
Borgen, P. 261, 296
Boring, M. 277
Bottrich, C. 279
Bousset, W. 261

Bowden, J. 171
Boxall, I. 228
Brant, J.A. 90, 249, 253, 254, 297
Brawley, R.L. 107
Bretschneider, K.G. 263
Broadhead, E. 309, 310
Brodie, T.L. 94, 203, 204
Brooke, G.J. 100
Brown, G. 170
Brown, R.E. 4, 63, 75, 76, 88, 123, 128, 129, 133, 135, 138, 143, 148, 150, 158, 184, 201, 203, 204, 211, 216, 220, 229, 239, 260–62, 274
Brown, S. 7, 239, 240, 245, 250, 252, 253, 257, 265, 280, 284–88, 293, 297, 298
Brown, T.G. 27
Browning, D.C. 221
Bruce, F.F. 150, 187, 190
Brueggemann, D.A. 103
Bruner, F.D. 272, 273, 281
Bryan, S.M. 93, 105
Bultmann, R.K. 53, 75, 112, 113, 137, 172, 183, 201, 203, 215, 250, 261, 269, 284
Burer, M.H. 48
Burkett, D.R. 267
Burney, C.F. 27
Burridge, R.A. 279, 280, 299, 305

Caquot, A. 177
Caragounis, C.C. 280, 300
Carnazzo, S.A. 204
Carson, D.A. 138, 143, 170, 172, 175, 180, 182, 184, 203, 213, 216, 218, 273, 278
Catchpole, D.R. 31
Chanikuzhy, J. 176
Charlesworth, J.H. 60, 234
Chester, A. 175
Chilton, B. 104, 175
Cirafesi, W.V. 170, 175, 180, 181, 183
Clark-Soles, J. 255
Clarke, K.M. 26
Coakley, J.F. 13
Cohen, S.J.D. 91
Cole, R.D. 212
Collins, J.J. 101, 113, 119

Coloe, M.L.   205, 214, 292, 293, 297
Conrad, E.W.   212, 213
Cory, C.   245
Court, J.M.   98, 187
Courtes, J.   6, 187, 188, 191
Coutsoumpos, P.   2, 3
Craigie, P.C.   206
Cross, A.R.   208
Cross, F.L.   170
Crossan, J.D.   130, 145, 148
Cullmann, O.   55, 58, 60–63, 65, 66, 69
Culpepper, R.A.   90, 103, 104, 131, 155, 187, 204, 251, 262, 279, 281, 286, 290, 297, 323

Dabrowa, E.   125
Dahl, N.A.   67
Dahlen, K.   207
Daly-Denton, M.   100, 103, 105, 106, 108
Danby, H.   241, 244
Davies, J.A.   177–79
Davies, M.   283
Davies, W.D.   205
Davis, M.   188
De Boer, M.C.   157, 165
De Vaux, R.   140
Delcor, M.   177
Denaux, A.   41
Desmond, A.T.   176
Dietzfelbinger, H.   278
Dillard, R.B.   207
Dillon, J.   194
Dodd, C.H.   32, 38, 75, 104, 162, 204, 216, 272
Domeris, W.   176
Dreyer, Y.   267
Duhaime, J.   121
Duke, P.D.   103, 131, 136
Dunn, J.D.G.   13, 16, 91, 261, 287

Eckhardt, B.   101
Edwards, R.B.   166, 187
Eisen, U.E.   289, 293, 294, 296, 303
Ellens, J.H.   267
Ellis, P.F.   203
Emadi, M.H.   178
Erho, T.M.   121
Evans, C.A.   58, 61, 75, 90, 170, 175, 183, 184, 210

Fay, R.C.   13
Fee, G.D.   17, 18
Feuillet, A.   262
Firth, D.G.   103
Flesher, C.M.   286
Fletcher-Louis, C.   176, 178, 180
Flint, P.W.   100, 115, 121
Fortier, T.   95–97
Fortna, R.T.   168, 310
Fowler, J.W.   261
Freed, E.D.   211, 218, 253
Frerichs, E.S.   286
Frey, J.   229
Funk, R.W.   170, 203

Gallarte, I.M.   12
Gathercole, S.J.   11, 174, 176, 208
Gaventa, B.R.   168
Gebauer, R.   279
Gillingham, S.E.   100
Girard, M.   155
Glenny, W.E.   170
Glicksman, A.   280, 300
Goldstein, J.A.   97, 101
Goodman, P.   241
Goppelt, L.   170
Goulder, M.D.   320
Greimas, A.J.   6, 187, 188, 191
Grigsby, B.H.   215
Groenewald, A.   99
Gundry, R.H.   282

Haenchen, E.   171, 181, 184, 203
Hagerland, T.   285
Hagner, D.A.   111
Hahn, F.   267
Halliday, M.A.K.   170
Hambly, W.F.   170, 171
Hamilton, N.Q.   176, 181
Hanson, A.T.   227
Harnack, A.   284
Harris, E.   90, 162
Harris, M.J.   16, 19
Harris, J.R.   38
Hastings, C.   171
Havea, J.   38
Hays, R.B.   277, 299, 305, 306

MODERN AUTHORS INDEX

Hayward, C.T.R.   177, 179
Heil, J.P.   180
Hengel, M.   64, 91, 97, 128, 148, 171, 268
Hengstenberg, E.W.   171
Herman, A.   193, 194
Herman, D.   288–90
Herzog, W.R.   175
Hess, R.S.   177
Hiebert, R.J.V.   99
Hinchman, L.P.   96
Hinchman, S.   96
Hinrichs, B.   260
Hirsch-Luipold, R.   280
Hirsch, E.D.   263
Hoare, R.W.N.   183
Holtzmann, H.J.   35, 36
Hooker, M.D.   172
Horbury, W.   59, 97, 101
Horn, F.W.   277, 280
Horrell, D.G.   31
Hoskins, P.M.   205, 206, 211, 215
Hoskyns, E.C.   203, 204
Hossfeld, F.-L.   98, 99, 107
Houlden, J.L.   277
Howard-Brook, W.   135, 141, 142, 144
Howard, W.F.   27
Hua, A.   95
Hugenberger, G.P.   170
Hurtado, L.   69
Hwang, J.K.   8
Hylen, S.   90

Iverson, K.R.   284, 302

Jansen, A.   264
Japhet, S.   207
Jarvis, C.A.   156
Jaubert, A.   273
Jenkins, R.   95
Johnson, E.E.   156
Johnston, P.S.   103
Jones, L.P.   218
Just, F.   255, 279

Käsemann, E.   90, 261, 262, 278
Kanagaraj, J.J.   278, 279
Kapambu, N.V.   299

Karakolis, C.   279–81
Karrer, M.   267
Keck, L.E.   134, 290
Kee, H.C.   267
Keener, C.S.   26, 33, 56, 58, 61, 63, 65–67, 91, 92, 171, 204, 214, 278
Keith, C.   69
Kennedy, G.A.   263
Kerr, A.R.   91, 171, 181, 205
Kierkegaard, S.   277
Kinlaw, P.E.   262
Kirk, A.   130
Kirk, J.R.D.   11, 175
Kittel, R.   99
Klawans, J.   104
Kline, M.G.   172, 177–81
Köstenberger, A.J.   27, 55, 56, 58, 60, 63–65, 67, 91, 97, 204, 216, 217, 278
Koester, C.R.   135, 152, 204, 213, 215, 218, 220, 247, 248, 256
Kohanski, A.   194
Kok, K.   280, 290, 298, 306
Koperski, V.   293
Kraus, H-J.   99
Kristeva, J.   94
Kysar, R.   261

Labahn, M.   38, 279, 280, 283, 290
Ladd, G.E.   55, 56, 62, 63, 68–70, 75
Lagrange, M-J.   149
Lam, T.Y.   6
Lapsley, J.E.   140
Larsen, K.B.   199, 201
Larson, K.   207
Lausberg, H.   264
Le Donne, A.   156, 289
Lee, D.   248, 249
Leivestad, R.   267
Levine, B.A.   207, 212
Liddell, G.   295
Lieu, J.   106
Lightfoot, R.H.   203
Lincoln, A.T.   201, 241, 242, 244, 245, 248, 251, 253
Lindars, B.   187, 261
Loader, W.   262, 280, 288, 300
Loder, J.E.   261

Lohr, H.   280
Lohse, E.   277
Lund, G.   278, 280, 281, 283, 295, 300, 305, 306
Luttwak, E.N.   113

MacDonald, D.R.   94
MacRae, G.W.   241
Magness, J.   118
Malan, F.S.   290
Malatesta, E.   204, 250
Malina, B.J.   175, 192
Maloney, L.M.   36, 98
Manns, F.   243
Marcus, J.   174, 286
Maritz, P.   280
Marshall, I.H.   55, 57, 59, 62, 70, 229
Martín-Asensio, G.   170
Martin, M.W.   264, 265, 283
Martin, J.R.   176
Martyn, J.L.   35, 62, 66, 256, 260, 284-88
Marxsen, W.   277
Mastin, B.A.   203
Matera, F.J.   277, 296
Matthiessen, C.M.I.M.   170
McCaffrey, J.   206
McDermott, J.M.   267
McDonagh, F.   171
McDonald L.M.   26
McGrath, J.F.   260
McHugh, J.   140
Meeks, W.A.   25, 131, 262, 278, 281, 286, 290, 299
Meiser, M.   279
Menken, M.J.J.   100
Merz, A.   68, 69
Metzger, B.M.   246
Meyers, C.L.   212
Meyers, E.M.   212
Michaels, J.R.   136, 138, 146, 204, 208
Milgrom, J.   207, 208, 212
Miller, E.L.   165, 166
Modrzejewski, J.M.   91
Moehring, H.R.   97
Moessner, D.P.   288
Moloney, F.J.   23, 25, 91, 104, 143, 145, 203, 214, 229, 239-46, 250, 252, 254, 257, 258, 267, 278

Moo, D.J.   138
Morgan, M.L.   208
Morris, L.L.   65, 68, 184, 213, 216
Mosser, C.   280
Motti, I.   208
Motyer, S.   91
Moule, C.F.D.   141
Moyise, S.   100, 106
Müller, M.   171
Muilenburg, J.   283
Murray, G.   270
Myers, A.D.   92, 260, 265-67, 283, 294

Nagy, G.   188
Neusner, J.   42, 97, 207, 216, 217, 286
Neville, D.J.   38
Newsom, C.   120, 140
Neyrey, J.H.   248, 260, 264, 267-70, 272, 273, 275, 286, 301
Ng, W.-Y.   221, 222
Nicholson, G.C.   25, 90
Niebuhr, R.   277
Nielsen, J.T.   273, 274, 279
Numada, J.   4
Nygren, A.   277

O'Day, G.R.   103, 134, 135, 138, 140, 143, 145, 146, 149, 156
Oesterly, W.O.E.   99
Ong, H.T.   2
Orton, D.E.   264
Oyen G.V.   38

Painter, J.   31, 33-36, 38, 41, 42, 46, 48-50, 51, 53, 55, 57, 60, 66, 279
Pancaro, S.   105
Parsenios, G.L.   90, 283
Pate, C.M.   64, 69
Patillon, M.   264
Pedersen, S.   279
Peláez, J.   12
Perkins, L.   90
Petersen, D.L.   208, 212
Phillips, P.M.   90, 155, 162
Phillips, T.E.   170
Pickering, S.R.   245
Pietersma, A.   100, 102
Pitts, A.W.   3, 4

MODERN AUTHORS INDEX

Plumer, E.   308, 310, 313
Pokorny, P.   277
Pollard, T.E.   55, 261, 311, 318, 319
Pomykala, K.E.   115
Porter, S.E.   11–17, 19–21, 23, 24, 26, 27, 58, 69, 75, 86, 90, 94, 98, 103, 107, 170, 171, 182–84, 208, 210, 211, 215, 216, 222, 308
Potterie, I. de la   244, 270
Pregeant, R.   277
Prigent, P.   231, 232

Rainbow, P.A.   19–22, 24–27
Rabens, V.   280, 296, 299, 305
Ramaroson, L.   155
Rebell, W.   277
Rensberger, D.K.   286, 297
Retief, C.I.   128
Riches, J.K.   183
Ridderbos, H.   203, 204, 210, 217
Riffaterre, M.   4, 93–96, 98, 104, 105, 108, 323
Ringe, S.H.   140
Ripley, J.J.   92
Rius-Camps, J.   246
Robinson, A.T.   12, 13, 18, 19
Rochais, G.   165
Rodriguez, J.   95–97
Rohrbaugh, R.L.   175, 192
Ronning, J.   311
Rose, D.   176
Rowland, C.   227, 229
Runge, S.E.   158–60

Sanders, E.P.   104, 171, 176, 203, 278
Schachter, L.   177, 178
Schaferdiek, K.   320
Schenke, L.   244
Schiffman, L.H.   121
Schnackenburg, R.   171, 184, 204, 261, 263, 277, 279, 281, 299, 300
Schneemelcher, W.   320
Schneider, J.   247
Schnelle, U.   35, 36, 278, 279
Scholtissek, K.   38, 278, 292
Schrage, W.   277
Schreiner, T.R.   58–62, 64, 69
Schuchard, B.G.   104, 106, 107, 181
Schüssler Fiorenza, E.   131
Schultz, B.   119

Scott, J.C.   130
Scott, R.   295
Segovia, F.F.   279
Senior, D.   133
Shiell, W.D.   284
Shimoff, S.R.   177
Shiner, W.   284
Shore, V.   267
Silva, M.   21, 58, 59, 67
Simmons, B.E.   196
Sizer, S.   208
Skinner, C.W.   155, 255, 265, 280, 302
Sloyan, G.S.   64
Smalley, S.S.   6, 223–27, 231, 233, 234
Smith, D.   91, 171
Smith, D.M.   56, 59, 60, 63–65, 68, 70, 71, 91, 203, 272, 273, 278, 279, 281, 285–87, 299
Smith, M.   91
Smith, R.L.   212
Springer, D.W.   26
Stare, M.   280, 298
Stegner, R.   210
Stevens, C.S.   5
Stevens, G.B.   27
Stibbe, M.W.G.   281
Stovell, B.M.   90
Strauss, D.F.   2, 11
Strecker, G.   35, 36, 277
Strikovsky, A.   221
Strotmann, A.   38
Stuhlmacher, P.   91, 261
Swain, S.R.   27
Swartley, W.M.   280

Talbert, C.H.   287
Thatcher, T.   33, 69, 129, 130, 139, 142, 143, 156, 255, 279, 285, 289, 310
Theissen, G.   68, 69
Theobald, T.   278
Thompson, M.M.   90, 91, 260, 305
Thyen, H.   272, 273, 278
Tigay, J.   179
Tillmann, N.   99
Tov, E.   120
Tovey, D.M.H.   5, 157, 162, 163
Trost, T.D.   4, 117
Trozzo, L.   7, 8
Tsumura, D.T.   177

Tuckett, C.M.   31, 64, 65, 68, 70
Turnage, M.   115
Twelftree, G.H.   308, 310, 315

Um, S.   205

van Belle, G.   31, 274, 278, 280, 293
van der Kooij, A.   99, 101
VanderKam, J.   115
van der Watt, J.G.   277–81, 283, 290, 291, 296, 298, 300, 301, 306
van Ruiten, J.   178
van Tilborg, S.   27
Verheyden, J.   38
Vermes, G.   62, 221, 243
Vernant, J.-P.   200
Vielhauer, P.   67
Volf, M.   281
von Möllendorff, P.   289
von Wahlde, U.C.   204, 255, 278, 283, 295, 308

Wainwright, E.M.   38
Wallace, D.B.   252
Walton, J.H.   178
Watson, D.F.   283
Weinfeld, M.   177, 178
Weitzman, S.   208
Wendland, H.-D.   277
Wengst, K.   57, 58, 278, 286
Wenham, G.J.   177, 178, 180

Westcott, B.F.   171, 203
Westfall, C.L.   15, 69, 90, 170
Wetter, G.P.   263
Weyer-Menkhoff, K.   280, 291, 295
Whitacre, R.A.   201
Whitenton, M.   284, 302
Wiesen, D.S.   268
Williams, C.H.   33, 227, 229
Williams, J.J.   102
Wilson, R.McL.   320
Witherington, B.   55, 58, 61, 63, 66
Wolfsdorf, D.   136
Wright, A.M., Jr.   4, 117
Wright, A.Z.   6
Wright, B.G.   102
Wright, C.H.   212
Wright, W.M.   283

Yadin, Y.   120
Yee, G.A.   206, 240, 241, 243, 244
Yi, A.-T.   308
Yule, G.   170

Zager, W.   277
Zangenberg, J.   274, 275
Zenger, E.   98, 99, 107
Zervos, G.   101, 102
Zimmerman, R.   277–81, 290–92, 298, 300, 301, 304
Zugibe, F.T.   128
Zulick, M.D.   283

Ancient Sources Index

Old Testament

Gen 1–9	76, 82, 85, 88
Gen 1–4	174
Gen 1–3	5, 18, 79, 88 169, 170, 172, 175, 176, 178, 180–84
Gen 1:1–2	83, 170–72
Gen 1:1	37, 172
Gen 1:2–3	37, 76–80, 84, 87
Gen 1:2	77, 79, 82, 171
Gen 1:3	37, 195
Gen 1:6–7	84
Gen 1:6	37
Gen 1:9	37
Gen 1:11–31	84
Gen 1:11	37
Gen 1:14–18	173
Gen 1:14	37, 173
Gen 1:20	37
Gen 1:24	37
Gen 1:26–27	173
Gen 1:26	37, 173, 180
Gen 1:27	173
Gen 1:28–30	173
Gen 1:28	180
Gen 1:29	173
Gen 1:38	173
Gen 2:15–19	173
Gen 2:15	178
Gen 2:19	173
Gen 2:20	173
Gen 2:21	171
Gen 2:22–23	173
Gen 2:23–24	171
Gen 3	176
Gen 3:1	181
Gen 3:7	171
Gen 3:8	177
Gen 4:1–16	34
Gen 4:2	197
Gen 6–9	79
Gen 9:14–17	78
Gen 12–22	251
Gen 21–22	80
Gen 47:3	197
Gen 49:9	100
Gen 49:11	217
Exod 3	116, 117
Exod 3:1	80
Exod 3:12	239
Exod 3:13	77
Exod 3:14	22, 313, 195
Exod 4:8–9	239
Exod 4:9	206
Exod 4:17	239
Exod 4:28	239
Exod 4:30	239
Exod 7:3	239
Exod 7:9	239
Exod 7:15–21	204
Exod 8:23	239
Exod 10:1–2	239
Exod 11:1–12:33	142
Exod 11:9–10	239
Exod 12	142
Exod 12:1–36	206
Exod 12:1–2	206
Exod 12:10	146, 147, 215
Exod 12:13	239, 206
Exod 12:21–22	142
Exod 12:22	107, 211
Exod 12:25	211
Exod 12:26	212
Exod 12:46	146, 205, 210, 215, 272
Exod 13:5	212
Exod 13:9	239
Exod 13:21–22	196
Exod 13:21	244
Exod 14:27–28	207
Exod 15:11–18	232
Exod 16:3	195
Exod 17	204
Exod 17:1–7	243, 247
Exod 19	206
Exod 19:10–11	207
Exod 19:10	209
Exod 19:15	207
Exod 19:16	214
Exod 23:16	241
Exod 24	206
Exod 25–40	178

Exod 28:17–20	178
Exod 29:10–21	206
Exod 29:35–37	206
Exod 31:14–17	92
Exod 31:13	239
Exod 31:37	239
Exod 32:25–29	92
Exod 33:7–11	232
Exod 34:6	233
Exod 34:22	241
Exod 35:2	92
Exod 39	178
Lev 1–7	206
Lev 1:2	211
Lev 4:22–35	208
Lev 8:14–30	206
Lev 14:4	211
Lev 14:6	211
Lev 14:49	211
Lev 14:51	211
Lev 14:52	211
Lev 16:1–28	206
Lev 23	241
Lev 23:34	241
Lev 23:39–43	242
Lev 23:39	241
Lev 24:16	254
Lev 26:11–12	230
Lev 26:12	177
Lev 69	211
Num 3:7–8	178
Num 6:3	209
Num 8:7	207, 212
Num 8:8–13	206
Num 8:21	209
Num 8:26	178
Num 9:6–12	206
Num 9:6–7	207
Num 9:7–10	208
Num 9:12	146, 205, 210, 215
Num 9:13	206
Num 11:18	209
Num 15:32–36	92
Num 18:5–6	178
Num 19	207, 218
Num 19:1–31	212
Num 19:1–22	208
Num 19:5–6	208
Num 19:6	211, 220
Num 19:10	208
Num 19:12	209
Num 19:18	211
Num 20:1–13	247
Num 20:8–13	243
Num 21:9	115
Num 24:17	61
Num 25:1–13	92
Num 27:16–17	272
Num 27:17	272
Num 29:12	241
Num 31	211
Num 31:19	209
Num 31:23	209, 212
Num 33:51–53	115
Deut 6–9	255
Deut 6:22	239
Deut 7:19	239
Deut 11:3	239
Deut 11:26–28	255
Deut 11:28	255
Deut 13:1–5	92
Deut 13:2–3	239
Deut 13:28	239
Deut 13:46	239
Deut 16:1–8	206
Deut 16:13	241
Deut 16:16	241
Deut 17:6–7	180
Deut 18	114
Deut 18:15–18	248
Deut 18:15	61
Deut 18:20	92
Deut 21:22–23	144
Deut 23:14	179
Deut 29:2	239
Deut 32:34	22
1 Sam 1–19	241
1 Sam 1:1	165
1 Sam 2:10	58
1 Sam 20–26	100
1 Sam 21:6	209
1 Sam 24:6	58
1 Sam 26:16	58

ANCIENT SOURCES INDEX

2 Sam 1:14	58	Neh 8:14	241
2 Sam 1:16	58	Neh 8:15	242
2 Sam 5:2	197	Neh 8:16–18	242
2 Sam 7	65		
2 Sam 7:2–3	100	Ps 22	137–39
2 Sam 7:2	59	Ps 22:1	209
2 Sam 7:5	215	Ps 22:6–7	137
2 Sam 7:11–29	59	Ps 22:18	137, 138
2 Sam 7:11	215	Ps 22:21	138
2 Sam 14:28–18:33	100	Ps 22:24	137, 138
2 Sam 23:1–7	100	Ps 27	249
2 Sam 23:2	58	Ps 27:1	196
		Ps 31:5	209
1 Kgs 8:2	241	Ps 33:6	37
2 Kgs 16:10–18	207	Ps 34:19–20	147
2 Kgs 21:18	149	Ps 34:20	146, 147, 205, 210
2 Kgs 21:26	149	Ps 34:21	146
		Ps 36:9	249
1 Chr 15:12	209	Ps 42:1–2	247
1 Chr 15:14	209	Ps 43:3	249
1 Chr 17:10–17	59	Ps 50:9	211
1 Chr 23	100	Ps 63:1	247
1 Chr 23:32	178	Ps 65:5	98, 106
1 Chr 25:1–8	100	Ps 68	92, 93, 98, 99, 102–104, 108, 109
1 Chr 29:5	209		
1 Chr 29:15	209	Ps 68:2–5	98
1 Chr 29:16	209	Ps 68:5–13	99
1 Chr 29:17	209	Ps 68:5	108
1 Chr 29:18	209	Ps 68:6–14	98
1 Chr 29:19	209	Ps 68:9	103
1 Chr 29:34	209	Ps 68:10	98, 99, 104–108
1 Chr 30:3	209	Ps 68:14–20	98
1 Chr 30:15	209	Ps 68:21–22	98, 99
1 Chr 30:17	209	Ps 68:22–23	107
1 Chr 30:18	209	Ps 68:22	98, 105, 107, 108
1 Chr 31:18	209	Ps 68:23–29	98
		Ps 68:23–24	98, 99
2 Chr 16:14	149	Ps 68:26	98
2 Chr 29–31	209	Ps 68:30–34	98
2 Chr 29–30	207	Ps 68:35–36	98–100
2 Chr 30:1–4	207	Ps 68:36–37	102
2 Chr 30:16	207	Ps 69	4, 93, 141, 144
2 Chr 35:11	207	Ps 69:4	98
		Ps 69:9	93, 98, 214–16
Ezra 6:19–22	207	Ps 69:13–14	142
		Ps 69:17	142
Neh 3:16	149	Ps 69:21	98, 142, 218
Neh 8	242	Ps 69:22–23	98
Neh 8:13–14	242	Ps 69:25	98

ANCIENT SOURCES INDEX

Ps 69:30–36	142	Isa 52:1b	230
Ps 69:35–36	216	Isa 52:6	22
Ps 77:21	197	Isa 53	68
Ps 78:14	196	Isa 55:1–11	141
Ps 78:70–72	272	Isa 55:1	248, 210
Ps 78:70–71	197	Isa 60:1	249
Ps 79:13	273	Isa 60:19–20	249
Ps 80:2	273	Isa 61:10	230
Ps 80:8–18	198	Isa 63:1–6	232
Ps 89:2–4	60	Isa 63:11	197
Ps 95:7	273	Isa 66:17	209
Ps 100:3	273		
Ps 110	178	Jer 2:21	198
Ps 113–118	243	Jer 7:1–11	99
Ps 118:27	242	Jer 12:3	209
Ps 119	300	Jer 12:6	99
Ps 119:105	249, 196	Jer 12:10–11	198
Ps 120–134	243	Jer 15:15	99
Ps 132:11	60	Jer 23:4–6	272
Ps 132:12	60	Jer 26:1–19	99
		Jer 31:10	197
Prov 3	38	Jer 31:12–14	217
Prov 6:28	249		
Prov 8:1–9:6	230	Ezek 1:28	270
Prov 8:21–36	83	Ezek 8:16	244
Prov 8:22	196	Ezek 15:1–5	198
Prov 13:14	247	Ezek 17:1–6	198
		Ezek 19:10–14	198
Eccl 24:23	187	Ezek 28:13	178
		Ezek 28:14	179
Isa 4:5	244	Ezek 34	272
Isa 5:1–7	198	Ezek 34:1–6	272
Isa 6:1	20	Ezek 34:13–14	272
Isa 6:9	210	Ezek 34:15–31	257
Isa 7:1	77	Ezek 34:23	272
Isa 12:46	196	Ezek 34:30	230
Isa 16:5	252	Ezek 34:31	273
Isa 25:6	217	Ezek 36:25	212
Isa 25:8	230	Ezek 37:27	230
Isa 40–55	22	Ezek 40–48	207
Isa 40:3	42, 43	Ezek 44:4	270
Isa 40:13	15	Ezek 44:14	178
Isa 41:4	22	Ezek 45:25	241
Isa 43:10	22	Ezek 47:1–5	243
Isa 43:13	22		
Isa 43:25	22	Dan 2:46	270
Isa 44:6–8	253	Dan 7	22, 174
Isa 46:4	22		
Isa 48:12	22	Hos 10:1–2	198
Isa 51:12	22		

ANCIENT SOURCES INDEX

Joel 3:18	143, 217	Matt 3:3	41, 42
Joel 4:18	243	Matt 3:11–12	41
		Matt 3:11	161, 167
Amos 9:13	143	Matt 3:16–17	46
Amos 9:13–14	217	Matt 3:17	46
		Matt 5:21–22	174
Mic 5:2–4	272	Matt 5:27–28	174
Mic 5:8	100	Matt 5:33–34	174
		Matt 5:38–39	174
Hag 1:4–8	99	Matt 5:43–44	174
		Matt 9:27–31	286
Zech 1:16	208	Matt 9:32	307
Zech 2:4–5	208	Matt 12:22	307, 310
Zech 2:10	208	Matt 12:28	310
Zech 2:14–15	230	Matt 14:14	281
Zech 3:7	208	Matt 15:21	218
Zech 6:12–15	208	Matt 16:16	69, 174
Zech 7:3	99	Matt 20:29–34	286
Zech 8:9	208	Matt 21:12–13	214
Zech 10:6	208	Matt 21:12	213
Zech 11:12–13	209	Matt 22:43	100
Zech 12:7	208, 212	Matt 23:37–39	281
Zech 12:8	212	Matt 26:36–46	269
Zech 12:10–14	213, 221	Matt 26:61–65	271
Zech 12:10	205, 212, 213	Matt 26:61	214
Zech 12:12	212	Matt 27:9–10	209
Zech 13:1	205, 212, 216, 218, 221, 247	Matt 27:31	218
Zech 14	242, 247	Matt 27:32	132, 218
Zech 14:1–21	232	Matt 27:34	106
Zech 14:6–9	242	Matt 27:35	137
Zech 14:8	146, 216, 243	Matt 27:37	134
Zech 14:11	232	Matt 27:38	133
Zech 14:17–21	216	Matt 27:39–42	137
Zech 14:20–21	208, 216	Matt 27:45	146
Zech 14:20	243	Matt 27:46	137, 140
Zech 14:37–38	247	Matt 27:48	98, 106, 211
Zech 14:38	247	Matt 27:50	143, 144, 272
Zech 14:21	93, 214, 216	Matt 27:51	146
		Matt 27:52–53	146
Mal 3:1	216	Matt 27:55	139
Mal 3:3	61, 216	Matt 27:57–60	148
		Mark 1:1	62
New Testament		Mark 1:3	41, 42
		Mark 1:7–8	41
Matt 1:1	62	Mark 1:7	161, 167
Matt 1:6–17	63	Mark 1:10–11	46
Matt 2:7b	229	Mark 1:10	44
		Mark 1:11	44, 46

Mark 1:21–28	307, 309	Luke 6:14	174
Mark 1:24	309	Luke 6:37–38	229
Mark 1:32	307	Luke 7:13	281
Mark 3:11–12	307	Luke 9:49–50	309
Mark 3:16	174	Luke 10:17	309
Mark 3:22–27	310	Luke 13:34	281
Mark 3:22	310	Luke 18:35–43	286
Mark 4:24b	229	Luke 19:45–48	214
Mark 6:7–13	309	Luke 19:45	213
Mark 6:34	281	Luke 20:42	100
Mark 7:1–4	216	Luke 22:3	308
Mark 8:14–21	289	Luke 22:39–46	269
Mark 8:22–26	286	Luke 22:66–71	271
Mark 8:29	69	Luke 22:70	270
Mark 8:33	309	Luke 23:11	218
Mark 9:5	230	Luke 23:26	132, 218
Mark 9:38–39	309	Luke 23:27	132
Mark 9:41	63	Luke 23:33	133
Mark 10:46–52	286	Luke 23:34	137
Mark 11:15–19	214	Luke 23:35–39	137
Mark 11:15	213	Luke 23:36	106
Mark 12:36	100	Luke 23:38	134
Mark 14:32–42	269	Luke 23:39–43	133
Mark 14:58–63	271	Luke 23:39	133
Mark 14:58	214	Luke 23:44–45	146
Mark 14:62	270	Luke 23:45	146
Mark 15:20	218	Luke 23:46	144, 209, 272
Mark 15:21	132, 133	Luke 23:49	139
Mark 15:24	137	Luke 23:50–53	148
Mark 15:26	134		
Mark 15:27	133	John 1–12	83
Mark 15:29–31	137	John 1–2	5, 161, 165, 169, 175, 183–85, 266
Mark 15:33	146		
Mark 15:34	137, 140, 209	John 1:1–2:25	182
Mark 15:36	98, 106, 211	John 1:1–2:12	320
Mark 15:37	143, 144, 272	John 1	114, 122
Mark 15:38	146	John 1:1–18	155, 165, 233
Mark 15:40	139	John 1:1–14	231
Mark 15:43–46	148	John 1:1–13	39
Mark 16:9	230	John 1:1–9	156
Mark 16:23	309	John 1:1–5	40, 165, 233
		John 1:1–4	81, 311
Luke 1:27	63	John 1:1–3	83
Luke 3:4	41, 42	John 1:1–2	231
Luke 3:15–17	41	John 1:1	19, 38, 40, 46, 48, 49, 62, 265, 266
Luke 3:16	161, 167		
Luke 3:21–22	46	John 1:1b	39
Luke 3:22	46	John 1:3–4	311

ns INDEX

ANCIENT SOURCES INDEX

John 1:3	47, 49, 51, 172, 194	John 1:25	42, 43
John 1:4–9	83	John 1:26–27	41, 42
John 1:4–5	38, 39, 172, 234	John 1:26	145, 167
John 1:4	84, 166	John 1:27	38, 40, 41, 43, 44
John 1:5	84, 87, 311	John 1:28	43
John 1:6–18	165	John 1:29–36	210
John 1:6–9	38	John 1:29–34	41, 171
John 1:6–8	38, 47	John 1:29	142, 147, 204, 206, 215, 232, 273, 298
John 1:6	40, 165		
John 1:7–8	159	John 1:30–34	47
John 1:7	38, 84, 85	John 1:30–33	41, 43, 44
John 1:7b	47	John 1:30	40, 41, 43, 44, 46, 161, 167
John 1:8	85	John 1:31	47, 145, 204
John 1:9–13	233	John 1:31–34	43, 46
John 1:9	26, 38, 85, 166, 171, 311	John 1:31–33	46
John 1:10–13	246	John 1:31–32	44
John 1:10–11	266	John 1:32–34	267, 272
John 1:10	46, 171, 172	John 1:32	171, 302
John 1:11–13	246	John 1:33–34	40
John 1:11	26, 111, 163	John 1:33	40, 145, 204
John 1:12–13	265, 311	John 1:34	23, 44, 46, 54, 265–67, 293
John 1:12	251, 293	John 1:35–42	41, 44
John 1:13–14	171	John 1:35–37	44
John 1:13	292	John 1:35–36	43
John 1:14–2:25	6	John 1:36	215, 232
John 1:14–18	37, 166, 227	John 1:38	44, 267
John 1:14	26, 38–40, 46, 47, 49, 85, 182, 184, 205, 225, 229, 230, 232, 233, 234, 265 288, 311, 312, 318	John 1:39	45
		John 1:40–41	45
		John 1:41	41, 45, 46, 67, 114, 267
		John 1:42	173
John 1:15	3, 38, 40, 41, 43, 44, 47, 161, 167	John 1:43–51	41, 44, 45
		John 1:43	45
John 1:16–18	38, 39, 167	John 1:45	114, 136, 140
John 1:16	233, 288	John 1:46	192
John 1:17–18	46, 85	John 1:48	171, 260
John 1:17	39, 86, 162–64, 233	John 1:49–51	46
John 1:18	19, 24, 38–40, 45–47, 85, 86, 163, 164, 168, 226, 265, 294, 295, 312, 318	John 1:49	46, 70, 265–67, 293
		John 1:50	71
		John 1:51	45, 46, 171, 174, 225, 234
John 1:19–12:50	64	John 2:1–4:54	214
John 1:19–51	41	John 2	114, 142, 180, 217, 320
John 1:19–42	41, 47	John 2:1–25	6, 205, 213
John 1:19–28	38, 41, 43	John 2:1–11	149, 214, 216, 218, 219
John 1:19–20	64	John 2:1	213, 218, 219
John 1:19	41, 42	John 2:3	218
John 1:20	42	John 2:4	214, 218, 219, 282
John 1:23	41, 42, 114	John 2:5	218
John 1:24	41, 64	John 2:6	204, 208, 214, 216, 218, 219

John 2:7	219	John 3:16	46, 47, 49–51, 298, 311
John 2:8–9	216	John 3:17	26, 50, 51, 84
John 2:8	314, 219	John 3:18–21	85
John 2:9–10	219	John 3:18–20	312
John 2:9	145	John 3:18	46, 266, 293
John 2:10–11	142	John 3:19–21	35, 39, 84
John 2:11	213, 216, 219, 220, 232, 239, 282	John 3:19	26, 48, 85
John 2:12–25	214	John 3:22–36	39
John 2:12–22	205	John 3:22–30	47
John 2:12	140, 180, 218	John 3:25	208
John 2:13–25	169, 175, 180, 210	John 3:29–34	44
John 2:13	206, 214	John 3:31–36	47
John 2:14–17	214	John 3:31–35	266, 293
John 2:14–16	214, 215	John 3:31–34	37, 47
John 2:16–17	215	John 3:31	26, 39
John 2:16	93, 214	John 3:34–35	37, 51
John 2:17	4, 92, 93, 98, 103, 104, 108, 136, 142, 210, 214, 215	John 3:34	50, 51, 267
		John 3:35	46–49, 51, 270, 292
John 2:18–22	114, 214	John 4	117, 205
John 2:18–19	214	John 4:5–42	145
John 2:18	213, 239	John 4:7	145, 216
John 2:19–25	182	John 4:10–15	143
John 2:19–22	147	John 4:10–14	146
John 2:19–21	139, 215	John 4:10	143, 145
John 2:19	105, 213, 215, 275	John 4:12	253
John 2:20	309	John 4:14	145, 204, 292
John 2:21–22	39	John 4:15	216
John 2:21	6, 182, 205	John 4:19	267
John 2:22	39, 214, 275, 288	John 4:21–24	205
John 2:23	214, 239	John 4:25	45, 67
John 3	114, 115	John 4:26	23
John 3:1–21	39	John 4:34	47, 50, 93, 141, 226, 267, 292
John 3:1	149		
John 3:2	26, 239, 267	John 4:35	281
John 3:3–7	265	John 4:37–38	298
John 3:3	26, 293, 311	John 4:42	135, 151, 267, 298
John 3:5	204, 293	John 4:45	214
John 3:7	293	John 4:46	214
John 3:8	265, 309, 311	John 4:48	239, 282
John 3:11	229	John 4:53–54	282
John 3:12	34, 39, 309, 312	John 4:54	239
John 3:13–21	39	John 5–12	205
John 3:13	25	John 5–10	240
John 3:14	115, 135, 271, 313	John 5	115, 117, 228, 256
John 3:15	135	John 5:2–9	145
John 3:16–20	88	John 5:2	204, 209
John 3:16–17	85, 298	John 5:9	205
		John 5:10	104

ANCIENT SOURCES INDEX

John 5:14	282	John 6:32	116
John 5:17–23	37	John 6:33	25, 298
John 5:17–18	48	John 6:35	24, 195
John 5:17	37, 47, 49, 51, 206, 227	John 6:36	195
John 5:18	20, 44, 261, 271, 282	John 6:38–40	195
John 5:19–30	47, 48	John 6:38	25, 26, 50, 93, 267, 312
John 5:19–24	266, 267, 293	John 6:39	50, 267
John 5:19–20	37, 47–49, 51	John 6:41–42	26
John 5:19	49	John 6:41	24, 25
John 5:20	47–49, 51	John 6:42	25, 140, 195, 265
John 5:23	50, 267	John 6:44	50
John 5:24	50, 267	John 6:45–46	266, 293
John 5:25–29	86	John 6:45	136, 293
John 5:30–47	86	John 6:46	26, 312
John 5:30	37, 50	John 6:48–51	282
John 5:35	79, 86	John 6:48	24
John 5:36	37, 50, 141, 226, 267, 282, 292	John 6:50–51	26
		John 6:50	25
John 5:37–38	267	John 6:51	24, 25, 298
John 5:37	50, 86, 267	John 6:53–58	195
John 5:38–39	86	John 6:53–56	204
John 5:38	50, 267	John 6:56	302
John 5:39	267	John 6:57	50
John 5:41–44	86	John 6:58	25, 26
John 5:43	26, 318	John 6:60	163
John 5:45–47	86	John 6:62	25
John 5:45	115, 116	John 6:67–71	69
John 5:46–47	267	John 6:69	292, 208
John 5:46	115, 116, 136	John 6:70–71	307, 312, 318
John 6	281, 320	John 7–10	243, 258
John 6:1–14	210	John 7:1–10:21	7, 240, 244–46
John 6:2–13	149	John 7–8	240, 241, 246
John 6:2	239	John 7:1-8:59	245
John 6:4	206	John 7	244, 307
John 6:14–15	62	John 7:1-13	244–46
John 6:14	26, 205, 239, 267, 282	John 7:1–2	246
John 6:15	122	John 7:1	241
John 6:16–21	145	John 7:2–10	103
John 6:20	23	John 7:2	244
John 6:22–71	210	John 7:3–13	46
John 6:26–27	282	John 7:3–9	246
John 6:26	239	John 7:3	140
John 6:28–29	295	John 7:5	140, 246, 293
John 6:28	196	John 7:10	140
John 6:29	50, 267, 282	John 7:12	246
John 6:30	239	John 7:13	25, 246
John 6:31–33	26	John 7:14–8:59	244–46, 206
John 6:31	136	John 7:14–52	256, 258

342 ANCIENT SOURCES INDEX

John 7:14–36	244–46	John 8:14	26
John 7:14–24	246	John 8:16	50, 267
John 7:16–18	266, 293	John 8:17	136
John 7:16	50, 247, 267	John 8:18	24, 267
John 7:17	267	John 8:21–30	249
John 7:19–24	247	John 8:21–29	196
John 7:19–23	117	John 8:21	26
John 7:19	241	John 8:22	26
John 7:20	308, 310, 312	John 8:23	21, 26
John 7:22–24	247, 206	John 8:24	21–23
John 7:25–31	46, 247	John 8:25	22
John 7:25	241	John 8:26–29	37
John 7:27	26, 292	John 8:26–28	266, 293
John 7:28	26, 50, 247, 267	John 8:26	26, 50, 267
John 7:29	50, 267	John 8:28	21–23, 135, 271, 313
John 7:30	241	John 8:29	23, 50, 267
John 7:31	239	John 8:30	249, 250
John 7:32–36	246	John 8:31–59	249, 250
John 7:32	241, 247	John 8:31–58	250
John 7:33	26, 50, 247, 267	John 8:31–47	211
John 7:34	26	John 8:31–38	251
John 7:35	26	John 8:31–32	251
John 7:36	26	John 8:31	21, 250, 252, 302
John 7:37–8:59	245	John 8:32	250
John 7:37–52	245, 247	John 8:33	92, 250
John 7:37–39	204, 247, 248	John 8:37	163, 241
John 7:37–38	145	John 8:38–47	308
John 7:37	248	John 8:38	37
John 7:38	145	John 8:39–44	34
John 7:39	131	John 8:39–40	251
John 7:40–44	248	John 8:39	21
John 7:40	267	John 8:40	21, 37, 241
John 7:41–42	70	John 8:42	26, 50, 251, 267
John 7:41	267	John 8:44	229, 307, 308, 310, 312, 316, 318, 319
John 7:44	141		
John 7:45–46	248	John 8:47	26, 37, 252
John 7:47–49	248	John 8:48	252, 308, 310, 312
John 7:50–52	149, 248	John 8:49–50	252
John 7:52	192	John 8:49	252
John 7:53–8:11	136	John 8:52	308, 310, 312
John 8	23, 114, 116, 163, 249, 307, 309	John 8:50–51	252
		John 8:50	252
John 8:8	136	John 8:51	252
John 8:12–59	245, 248, 256, 258	John 8:52–59	44
John 8:12–30	248	John 8:52	252, 253
John 8:12–20	249	John 8:53	252, 253
John 8:12	4, 21, 24, 39, 85, 116, 161, 195, 249, 311	John 8:54–55	252
		John 8:54	232, 253, 267

ANCIENT SOURCES INDEX 343

John 8:56	252	John 10	307
John 8:57	252, 320	John 10:1–21	245, 254, 257, 258
John 8:58–59	37	John 10:1–5	257
John 8:58	20–23, 167, 196, 252, 253	John 10:7	24, 197, 254
John 8:59	241, 252, 254	John 10:8	197
John 9–10	241, 246	John 10:9–10	197, 272
John 9:1–10:21	245, 254	John 10:9	24, 254
John 9	114, 256, 257, 286	John 10:10	26
John 9:1–41	245, 254–56	John 10:11	24, 117, 254, 269
John 9:1–7	35, 286	John 10:14	24
John 9:1–5	255, 258	John 10:15–18	93
John 9:1–3	310	John 10:16	117
John 9:2	255	John 10:17–18	92, 275
John 9:3	281, 282	John 10:17	138
John 9:4	50, 267, 287	John 10:18	144, 269, 272, 292
John 9:5	39, 85, 161, 254, 255	John 10:18a	133
John 9:6–7	255	John 10:19–21	308
John 9:7–15	257	John 10:20–21	310, 312
John 9:7	204, 209	John 10:20	308
John 9:8–41	286, 287	John 10:21	307, 310
John 9:8–34	35	John 10:22–39	206
John 9:8–12	255	John 10:22	103, 209
John 9:9–13	256	John 10:23	205
John 9:11	209	John 10:28–33	37
John 9:13–17	255	John 10:30–36	20
John 9:14	205, 256	John 10:30–33	44
John 9:15–34	256	John 10:30	167, 225, 261, 273
John 9:15	209	John 10:32	292
John 9:16	239, 256, 258, 312	John 10:33	37, 271
John 9:17	256, 267	John 10:34	136
John 9:18–23	255	John 10:36–38	265, 267
John 9:19	258	John 10:36	26, 50, 267, 292, 206, 209
John 9:20	258	John 10:37–38	292
John 9:21	256, 258	John 10:38	24, 261, 312
John 9:22	240, 256, 286, 288, 289	John 10:40–41	44
John 9:24–34	255	John 10:41–42	43
John 9:28–29	114	John 10:41	239
John 9:31–33	256, 267, 310, 312	John 11:4	232 266, 293
John 9:33	282, 312	John 11:9–11	98
John 9:34	256, 289	John 11:9–10	85
John 9:35–41	35, 258	John 11:15	282
John 9:35–38	35, 255, 257, 281, 282	John 11:25–27	282
John 9:38–39	309	John 11:25	24, 116, 197
John 9:38	257	John 11:27	26, 266, 267, 293
John 9:39–41	35, 39, 255	John 11:28	267
John 9:39	26, 229, 257	John 11:33–35	282
John 9:40–41	257	John 11:40	232, 282
John 9:41	257	John 11:42	50, 267

John 11:45	198	John 13:5	145, 204, 209
John 11:47–12:8	210	John 13:6	209
John 11:47	239	John 13:8	209, 297
John 11:48–50	108	John 13:10	209
John 11:48	122	John 13:13	267, 297
John 11:52	135	John 13:14–15	281, 295, 297
John 11:55	206, 209, 220	John 13:14	209
John 12–13	320	John 13:16	297
John 12	122	John 13:18	138, 141
John 12:1–8	149	John 13:20	50, 261, 267, 297
John 12:12	209	John 13:23	294
John 12:13	26, 267	John 13:27	307, 308, 312, 318
John 12:14	136	John 13:33–34	26
John 12:16	39, 136, 288	John 13:34–35	50
John 12:18	239	John 13:34	295, 299, 304
John 12:20	86	John 14–17	229
John 12:23	131	John 14–16	53
John 12:24–26	300	John 14:1–2	293
John 12:27	26, 269, 270	John 14:2	26
John 12:31	307, 309, 313, 315	John 14:3	26
John 12:32–34	271, 300, 313	John 14:4	26
John 12:32	135, 149–51, 313	John 14:5	26
John 12:34	106, 135, 302, 313	John 14:6	24, 117, 163, 197
John 12:35–36	85, 87	John 14:8	168, 293
John 12:35	86, 87, 162	John 14:9	312
John 12:36–46	87	John 14:9a	168
John 12:36–37	201	John 14:10–11	292
John 12:36	87, 162	John 14:10	25, 302
John 12:37–41	87, 88	John 14:11–12	295
John 12:37	239	John 14:11	25
John 12:38–40	210	John 14:12	26, 131, 287, 295
John 12:38	138, 141, 210	John 14:15	295
John 12:41	20	John 14:16	27, 294, 313
John 12:42–43	87, 148	John 14:17	27
John 12:42	124, 240, 286, 288, 289	John 14:18	26
John 12:43	232	John 14:20	25
John 12:44–45	87	John 14:23	295
John 12:44	50, 267, 312	John 14:24	50, 197, 267, 312
John 12:45	50, 87, 261, 267, 312	John 14:25–26	293
John 12:46	26, 39, 85, 88	John 14:25	197
John 12:47–50	266, 293	John 14:26	27, 50, 208, 294
John 12:47	26, 88, 298	John 14:27	26
John 12:49	50, 267	John 14:28	26, 227
John 13–21	206	John 14:29	295
John 13:1–17:26	211	John 14:31	92, 298
John 13	206, 297	John 15	206, 300
John 13:1	26, 131, 206, 269	John 15:1	24, 117, 198
John 13:3	26, 131, 270	John 15:2	198

ANCIENT SOURCES INDEX 345

John 15:3	209	John 17:1–3	52
John 15:4–9	302	John 17:1	52
John 15:4–5	300	John 17:3	39, 50, 52, 267
John 15:4	295	John 17:4	141, 226, 292
John 15:5	24	John 17:5	52, 226, 232
John 15:6	198	John 17:6–19	52
John 15:7	198, 295	John 17:6	52, 53
John 15:8	232	John 17:8	26, 50, 52, 267
John 15:9–10	295	John 17:11	26, 40, 52, 131, 208, 298
John 15:9	292, 302	John 17:12	23, 141, 138
John 15:10	281, 295	John 17:14	26, 52
John 15:12	281, 295	John 17:16–19	52
John 15:15	37	John 17:16	26
John 15:16	198, 302	John 17:17–18	53
John 15:18–27	105	John 17:17	52, 163, 206, 209, 292
John 15:18–25	198	John 17:18	26, 40, 50, 53, 267, 295, 298
John 15:18–21	289		
John 15:18–20	302	John 17:19–23	117
John 15:20	212	John 17:19	138, 206, 209
John 15:21	50, 267	John 17:20–26	52, 53, 229
John 15:22	26	John 17:20–23	292, 298
John 15:23–25	105	John 17:20	296
John 15:23	105, 108	John 17:21–23	52, 53, 267
John 15:25	98, 105, 108, 136, 138, 141, 142	John 17:21	25, 50, 52, 299
		John 17:23	50, 267, 299
John 15:26	27, 294	John 17:24–25	53
John 15:27	295	John 17:24	23, 52
John 16:1–2	289	John 17:25	50, 52, 267
John 16:2	92, 126, 211, 240, 288, 302	John 17:28	138
John 16:4	212	John 17:36	138
John 16:5	26, 50, 267	John 18	19, 320
John 16:7	26, 294	John 18:1	232
John 16:8	313	John 18:2	143
John 16:10	26, 131	John 18:4–5a	270
John 16:11	307, 313	John 18:4	23, 269, 270
John 16:13–15	293	John 18:5	143
John 16:13	27	John 18:6	23
John 16:17	26, 309	John 18:8	23, 269, 270
John 16:20	300	John 18:9	141
John 16:27	26	John 18:10–11	270
John 16:28	26, 131	John 18:11	269
John 16:30–33	313	John 18:19	270
John 16:30	26	John 18:20	271
John 16:32	139	John 18:23	271
John 16:32b	302	John 18:28–19:16a	134
John 16:33	289, 307, 315	John 18:28	142, 273, 209
John 17	53	John 18:30	143, 271
John 17:1–5	52	John 18:33	133, 136

John 18:34–37	271
John 18:35	143
John 18:36–37	133
John 18:36	143
John 18:37	26, 123, 195
John 18:38	267, 271
John 18:39	136, 142, 267
John 19	142
John 19:1	134
John 19:2–3	133
John 19:2	220
John 19:3	136
John 19:4	267, 271
John 19:5	136
John 19:6	271
John 19:6a	132
John 19:7	261, 266, 271, 293
John 19:11–12	271
John 19:11	143
John 19:12–16	271
John 19:12	123, 133
John 19:13–42	211
John 19:14–15	133
John 19:14	136, 142, 147, 206, 273
John 19:15	136
John 19:16b–42	127
John 19:16b–18	132
John 19:17	132, 220, 269, 271
John 19:18	127, 133
John 19:19–22	134
John 19:19	136, 267, 271
John 19:20	134–36, 220, 266
John 19:21–22	271
John 19:21	135
John 19:22	136, 267
John 19:23–37	205, 213
John 19:23	138
John 19:23a–25a	137
John 19:24	138, 141
John 19:25–37	219
John 19:25–27	218
John 19:25–26	219
John 19:25	139, 218
John 19:25b–27	139
John 19:26–27	140, 293
John 19:26	219
John 19:27	140, 219
John 19:28–30	141
John 19:28–29	98 107, 108
John 19:28	108, 138, 141, 218, 219
John 19:29	107, 211, 218–21, 273
John 19:30	141, 143, 145, 219
John 19:31–37	144
John 19:31	205, 206, 220, 266
John 19:33	142
John 19:34–35	6
John 19:34	145, 146, 203, 204, 209, 219
John 19:35	203, 219, 220, 232, 296
John 19:36–37	146, 205, 209, 210, 217, 222
John 19:36	6, 138, 141, 142, 146, 206, 210, 215, 273
John 19:37	210, 212, 218, 221
John 19:38–42	147
John 19:38–41	267
John 19:38	148, 149, 205
John 19:39–41	275
John 19:39–40	149
John 19:39	149
John 19:40	205, 275
John 20:6	267
John 20:8	296
John 20:9	296
John 20:12	205
John 20:14	200
John 20:17	25, 293
John 20:18	275
John 20:19	275
John 20:20	200
John 20:21–23	275
John 20:21	40, 50, 267, 292, 295, 298
John 20:22	143, 208
John 20:24–29	199, 233
John 20:26	275, 200
John 20:27–28	200
John 20:28	19, 226, 262
John 20:29	53, 296
John 20:30–31	64, 267
John 20:30	136, 239
John 20:31	136, 201, 267, 293, 296, 320
John 21:4–8	275
John 21:6	149
John 21:9	275
John 21:10–11	275
John 21:11	149 , 232
John 21:12–14	275
John 21:15–17	49

ANCIENT SOURCES INDEX

John 21:17	303		Gal 1:1	17
John 21:18–20	302		Gal 2:20	17
John 21:22	302		Gal 3:13	130
John 21:23	232		Gal 4:4	6, 17
John 21:24	136, 288			
John 21:25	136, 275		Eph 4:13	17
			Eph 5:19	18
Acts 1:4b–5	288			
Acts 1:6	59		Phil 2:6–11	13, 16
Acts 1:20	98			
Acts 7:44	230		Col 1:13	17
Acts 13:25	41		Col 1:15–20	13, 16
Acts 14	200		Col 1:15	227
Acts 14:11–12	200		Col 3:16	18
Acts 15:16	230			
Acts 21:24	209		1 Thess 1:10	17
Acts 21:26	209			
Acts 24:18	209		2 Thess 2:13–14	18
Rom 1:1–4	17, 18		Titus 2:13	16
Rom 1:3	63			
Rom 1:9	17		Heb 1:2	227
Rom 3:19	106		Heb 9:13	221
Rom 5:1–8	18		Heb 9:19	211
Rom 5:10	17		Heb 12:2	131
Rom 8:3	17			
Rom 8:9–11	18		Jas 4:8	209
Rom 8:9	17			
Rom 8:11	17		1 Pet 1:22	209
Rom 8:29	17			
Rom 8:32	17		1 John 1:1–3	233
Rom 9:5	15		1 John 1:1–2	313
Rom 10:9	15		1 John 1:3	314
Rom 15:3	98		1 John 1:5	313
			1 John 1:6–7	314
1 Cor 1:9	17		1 John 1:7	313
1 Cor 1:18	131, 268		1 John 1:9	314
1 Cor 1:23	131		1 John 2:1	309, 313
1 Cor 2:16	15		1 John 2:9	313
1 Cor 8:6	17		1 John 2:11	313
1 Cor 12:3	15		1 John 2:13–14	307, 314, 315
1 Cor 12:4–6	18		1 John 2:15	299
1 Cor 14:21	106		1 John 2:17	314
1 Cor 15:28	17		1 John 2:18–22	320
			1 John 2:18–19	314, 319
2 Cor 1:19	17		1 John 2:18	315
2 Cor 12:9	230		1 John 2:22	314, 318
2 Cor 13:14	18		1 John 2:27	309

1 John 2:28	315	Rev 3:20	229
1 John 3:2	315	Rev 5:5–14	226
1 John 3:3	209	Rev 5:5–6	226
1 John 3:8	307, 314, 316	Rev 5:5	315
1 John 3:9–10	314	Rev 5:9	232
1 John 3:12	34, 314	Rev 5:12	231
1 John 3:15	314	Rev 5:25–29	228
1 John 3:23	314, 315	Rev 6:9	231
1 John 4:1	314	Rev 7:14	232
1 John 4:2–3	314	Rev 7:15	230
1 John 4:3	314	Rev 10:1–3	234
1 John 4:4	307	Rev 11:15	226
1 John 4:5	314	Rev 12:9–10	26
1 John 4:6	314	Rev 12:11	232, 315
1 John 4:17	315	Rev 12:12	230
1 John 5:1	314	Rev 13:6	230
1 John 5:4–5	315	Rev 14:1	224
1 John 5:4	315	Rev 15:5	230
1 John 5:5	307	Rev 17–18	224
1 John 5:6–8	204	Rev 17:17	231
1 John 5:13	201	Rev 19:9–10	232
1 John 5:18–20	307	Rev 19:11–16	226, 228, 233
1 John 5:18	315	Rev 19:11–12	231
1 John 5:19	315	Rev 19:13	231, 232
1 John 5:20	226	Rev 19:15	231
		Rev 19:16	231
2 John 1:7	314, 316, 319	Rev 19:19	231
		Rev 20:4	231
Rev 1:1–16	228	Rev 21:1–8	230
Rev 1:1	32, 223	Rev 21:1–7	315
Rev 1:2	231	Rev 21:3	229, 230, 233
Rev 1:4	32	Rev 21:5–8	230
Rev 1:5	232, 315	Rev 21:5	231
Rev 1:8	226	Rev 21:9–27	230
Rev 1:9	32, 231	Rev 22:1–2	231
Rev 1:12–20	226	Rev 22:3	226
Rev 1:12–18	234	Rev 22:5	201
Rev 1:12	231, 233, 234	Rev 22:6	231
Rev 1:13	226, 233	Rev 22:7	228, 229
Rev 1:17–18	226	Rev 22:8	32
Rev 1:17	226, 270	Rev 22:11	228
Rev 1:18	226	Rev 22:12	228
Rev 2–3	223	Rev 22:13	226
Rev 2:1–7	226	Rev 22:16	226
Rev 2:13–22	228	Rev 22:20	228
Rev 2:16	226	Rev 22:21	229
Rev 3:11	226		
Rev 3:14	226		

ANCIENT SOURCES INDEX

Old Testament Apocrypha

1 Esdras
1 Esd 7:10   209
1 Esd 7:11   209

1 Maccabees
1 Macc 1:11   102
1 Macc 1:21   101
1 Macc 1:22   101
1 Macc 1:34   102
1 Macc 1:36   101
1 Macc 1:37   101
1 Macc 1:39   101
1 Macc 1:43   102
1 Macc 1:45   101
1 Macc 1:46   101
1 Macc 1:47   101
1 Macc 1:48–53   102
1 Macc 2   92
1 Macc 2:8   101
1 Macc 2:23–26   102
1 Macc 2:26   101
1 Macc 2:27–38   101
1 Macc 2:27   101
1 Macc 2:29–41   101
1 Macc 2:32–41   118
1 Macc 2:38   101
1 Macc 2:42–43   101
1 Macc 2:44–48   101
1 Macc 2:44   102
1 Macc 2:50   101
1 Macc 2:58   101
1 Macc 3:4–5   101
1 Macc 3:5   102
1 Macc 3:6   102
1 Macc 3:8   102
1 Macc 3:15   102
1 Macc 3:20   102
1 Macc 4   102, 268, 300
1 Macc 4:11   102
1 Macc 4:30   101, 102
1 Macc 4:49   101
1 Macc 4:50   101
1 Macc 4:56   102
1 Macc 4:57   101
1 Macc 5:9–23   102
1 Macc 5:43   101
1 Macc 5:44   101
1 Macc 6:21   102
1 Macc 7:5   102
1 Macc 7:36   101
1 Macc 9   102, 268, 300
1 Macc 9:23   102
1 Macc 9:25   102
1 Macc 9:43–49   102
1 Macc 9:69   102
1 Macc 9:73   102
1 Macc 10:43   101
1 Macc 10:61   102
1 Macc 10:83   101
1 Macc 10:84   101
1 Macc 11:4   101
1 Macc 11:21   102
1 Macc 11:25   102
1 Macc 13:49–53   101, 102
1 Macc 13:52   101
1 Macc 14:4–15   102
1 Macc 14:14   102
1 Macc 15:9   101
1 Macc 16:20   101

2 Maccabees
2 Macc 1:33   209
2 Macc 6–7   268, 300
2 Macc 6:30–31   102
2 Macc 10:6–8   242
2 Macc 12:38   209

4 Maccabees
4 Macc 5–11   268
4 Macc 17:20–22   102

Bar
5:8–9   244

Sirach
Sir 15:3   247
Sir 24   230
Sir 24:3   37, 38
Sir 24:7   230
Sir 24:11   230
Sir 24:21–26   247
Sir 49:16   179

Wisdom of Solomon
Wis 7–8	38
Wis 7:7	37
Wis 8.7	300
Wis 9:17	37
Wis 18:14–16	2

Old Testament Pseudepigrapha

1 Enoch (1 En.)
1 En 142	38
1 En 47.3	100
1 En 108.3	100

2 Enoch (2 En.)
2 En 24.1–5	78

3 Enoch (3 En.)
3 En 23–24	79
3 En 23.1–2	76
3 En 23.1	76
3 En 23.9	77
3 En 23.15–17	77
3 En 24.3–4	78
3 En 24.4	77
3 En 24.23	77, 78

3 Baruch (2 Apoc. Bar.)
2 Apoc Bar 54.12–14	300

4 Ezra (4 Ezra)
4 Ezra 6.38–40	78
4 Ezra 7.28–29	61

Joseph and Aseneth (Jos. Asen.)
Jos. Asen. 12.1–3	78

Jubilees (Jub.)
Jub 3:1–31	178
Jub 3:26–27	178
Jub 49:13–14	146

Psalms of Solomon (Pss. Sol.)
Pss. Sol. 17.22	59

Testament of Adam (T. Adam)
T. Adam 2.10	78

Testament of Judah (T. Jud.)
T. Jud. 24	61

Apocalypse of Moses (Apoc. Mos.)
Apoc. Mos. 29:3–6	178

Aristobulus Fragment
5.9–10	79

Josephus

Jewish War (J.W.)
J.W. 1.7.3	118
J.W. 1.673	149
J.W. 2.8.2–13	119
J.W. 4.7.2	120
J.W. 5.451	128
J.W. 7.203	269

Antiquities of the Jews (Ant.)
Ant. 8.101	241
Ant. 13.5–9	67
Ant. 14.9	134
Ant. 15.409	134
Ant. 17.152–54	300
Ant. 17.271–285	62
Ant. 17.295–300	300
Ant. 18.1.5	119
Ant. 19.162	66
Ant. 20.167–172	66
Ant. 20.188	66

Early Christian Authors

Augustine

City of God (Civ.)
Civ. 22.17	145, 268

Eusebius

Historia ecclesiastica (Hist. eccl.)
Hist. eccl. 3.23	32
Hist. eccl. 3.24.2	32
Hist. eccl. 3.24.6–7	32
Hist. eccl. 3.24.17–25.7	33
Hist. eccl. 3.39.1–7	33
Hist. eccl. 3.39.4	36

Hist. eccl. 5.8.2–4	32
Hist. eccl. 5.20.4–6	318
Hist. eccl. 6.14.4b–7	32
Hist. eccl. 6.14.7	11
Hist. eccl. 13.12.9–16	79

Ignatius
To the Ephesians
Ign. Eph. 9:1	317
Ign. Eph. 13:1	317

To the Philadelphians
Ign. Phld. 5:2	317
Ign. Phld. 6:1	317

To the Magnesians
Ign. Magn. 8:2	317

Irenaeus
Adversus haereses (Haer.)
Haer. 1.8.5	319
Haer. 1.9.1–3	319
Haer. 1.9.3	320
Haer. 1.13.4	318
Haer. 1.15.6	319
Haer. 1.16.3	34
Haer. 1.24.4	150
Haer. 1.31.1	318
Haer. 2.22.3	320
Haer. 2.22.6	320
Haer. 3.1.1–2	32
Haer. 3.3.4	315, 316, 318, 320
Haer. 3.11.1–6	320
Haer. 3.11.1	319, 320
Haer. 3.11.7	319
Haer. 3.16.1	319
Haer. 3.16.2	319
Haer. 3.16.5	34, 320
Haer. 3.16.8	34
Haer. 3.21.10	173
Haer. 3.39.1	32
Haer. 5.4.1	318
Haer. 5.21.2	318
Haer. 5.22.2	318
Haer. 5.23–24	318
Haer. 5.23.1	318
Haer. 5.23.2	318
Haer. 5.25.4	318
Haer. 5.26.2	319
Haer. 5.28.2	318
Haer. 5.33.4	32
Haer. 5.35.2	318

Justin Martyr
Apology 1
13.4	268

Martyrdom of Polycarp (Mart. Pol.)
23:3	316

Polycarp
To the Philippians (Pol. *Phil.*)
Pol. *Phil.* 6.3	34
Pol. *Phil.* 7.1–2	34
Pol. *Phil.* 7.1	316

Other Ancient/Classical Writings

Aeschylus
Prometheus vinctus (Prom.)
Prom. 480	58

Aphthonius the Sophist
38	276

Aristotle
Poetics (Poet.)
Poet. 1382a 21–25	188
Poet. 1385b 12–16	188
Poet. 1454b 23–24	199

Demetrius
De elocutione (Eloc.)
Eloc 222	306

Euripides
Hippolytus (Hipp.)
Hipp. 516	58

Homer
Odyssey (Od.)
Od. 16.182	200
Od. 19.528–538	192, 200

Horace
Epistles (Epis.)
Epis 1.16.48   148

Isocrates
Demonicus (Dem.)
43   268

Philo
De confusion linguarum (Conf.)
Conf. 146   312

De Gigantibus (Gig.)
Gig. 22   79

Legum allegoriae (Leg.)
Leg. 1.43   312

De vita Mosis (Mos.)
Mos. 1.18–23   266
Mos. 1.32–50   266

De Opificio (Opif.)
Opif. 7   80
Opif. 22   80
Opif. 26   80
Opif. 27–28   80
Opif. 29   80
Opif. 30   81
Opif. 31–32   81
Opif. 31   81, 83
Opif. 32–33   81
Opif. 34–36   82
Opif. 55–61   82
Opif. 168   82
Opif. 168–72   82, 83
Opif. 168–69   82
Opif. 169–70   82
Opif. 170–71   79

Plato
Menexenus (Menex.)   268

Pliny the Elder
Naturalis historia (Nat.)
Nat. 5.73   119

Plutarch
Brutus (Brut.)
Brut 36   274
Brut 52   274

Caesar (Caes.)
Caes 66.4–7   269
Caes 68.1   274
Caes 69.1–2   274
Caes 69.3   274
Caes 69.5–8   274

Cicero (Cic.)
Cic 49.3–4   274

Demosthenes (Dem.)
Dem 30.4–5   274

Timoleon (Tim.)
Tim 39   274

Ps.-Hermogenes (Ps.-Herm)
Ps.-Herm 16–17   274
Ps.-Herm 16   268

Pseudo-Manetho
Apotelesmatica
4.198–200   148

Quintilian
Declamationes (Decl.)
Decl. 274   128

Seneca
Ad Marciam de consolation (Marc.)
Marc. 20.3   128

Suetonius
Vespasianus (Vesp.)
Vesp. 4.5   113

Tacitus
Historiae (Hist.)
Hist. 2.72   269
Hist. 4.11   269
Hist. 5.13   113

ANCIENT SOURCES INDEX

Thucydides
History (*Hist.*)
Hist 2.42–44   268, 300

Dead Sea Scrolls

1Q34   117

1QH^a 10:13   115

1QM   121

1QS 8.13   42
1QS 9.9–11   42
1QS 9.11   61

1QSa = 1Q28 2.11–17   61
1QSa = 1Q28 2.12   60

1QSaII 12–21   61

1QSb V 20–29   61

3Q15   221

4Q174 3.11–12   61

4Q175   42

4Q266   60

4Q276–7 (4QTohorot B^a)   221

4Q276   221

4Q285   119

4Q394 3–7i   221

4Q504   117

4QFlor I 11   61

4QpIsa III 23–25   61

4QMMT   115, 116, 121

4QSM 5   61

4QTest 1–8   61

11Q14   119

Rabbinic and Jewish Literature

m. Ber.
5.5   312

m. Mid.
2.6   243

m. Sheq.
6.3   243

m. Suk.
3.3–9   243
4.5   243
4.9–10   243
4.9   244
5.1–4   243
5.2–4   244
5.4   244

b. Abod Zar
8a   179

b. B.Metzia
96a   312

b. B.Qam.
113b   312

b. Erub.
31b–32a   312

t. Suk.
3.2   243
3.11–12   24

Tg. Neofiti (*Tg. Neof.*)
Exod 13.21–22   311

Tg. T.
Exod 14.30   312

Tg. Pseudo-Jonathan (*Tg. Ps.-J.*)
2.15   178

8.20	178

Gen. Rab.
28.18	243
34.9	179

Eccl. Rab.
1.8	243

Song Rab.
1.7	244

Mek. Ex.
12.3	312
12.6	312

Printed in the United States
By Bookmasters